Jerry Engle
7718 u. Monroe
Niles, Ill.

AN ILLUSTRATED BOOK OF KNOW-HOW
FOR THE CAMP WORKER

# Camp Counseling

by

## A. VIOLA MITCHELL, A.B., M.A.

ASSISTANT PROFESSOR OF HEALTH AND PHYSICAL EDUCATION
BUENA VISTA COLLEGE, STORM LAKE, IOWA

and

## IDA B. CRAWFORD, A.B., M.A.

FORMER ART SUPERVISOR, WINTHROP COLLEGE
ROCK HILL, SOUTH CAROLINA

SECOND EDITION

ILLUSTRATED BY IDA B. CRAWFORD

# W. B. SAUNDERS COMPANY

Philadelphia and London · 1955

TO

**The Camping Movement**

*May It Have a Long and Glorious Future*

# TO AN OLD CAMPER

You may think, my dear, when you grow quite old
  You have left camp days behind,
But I know the scent of wood smoke
  Will always call to mind
    Little fires at twilight
  And trails, you used to find.

You may think some day you have quite grown up,
  And feel so worldly wise,
But suddenly from out of the past
  A vision will arise,
    Of merry folk with brown, bare knees
  And laughter in their eyes.

You may live in a house built to your taste
  In the nicest part of town,
But some day for your old camp togs
  You'd change your latest gown,
    And trade it all for a balsam bed
  Where the stars all night look down.

You may find yourself grown wealthy,—
  Have all that gold can buy,
But you'd toss aside a fortune
  For days 'neath an open sky,
    With sunlight on blue water
  And white clouds sailing high.

For once you have been a camper
  Then something has come to stay
Deep in your heart forever
  Which nothing can take away,
    And heaven can only be heaven
  With a camp in which to play.

—MARY S. EDGAR

From *Wood-Fire and Candle-Light*
Published by The Macmillan Co.

# Preface to the Second Edition

IN REVISING "Camp Counseling," the aim throughout has been to make the book more usable for camp workers. To this end, many users have been consulted by both the publishers and the author and deep appreciation is expressed to them for their thoughtful and helpful comments, many of which have been incorporated in the present edition.

Whereas the general make-up of the book remains the same, countless changes have been made to bring the materials up to date and in line with current developments and thinking. Various sections have been completely rewritten, notably those dealing with understanding campers, program planning, spiritual life in camp, school camping, aluminum foil cookery, and camp pests.

In many cases, it has been found possible to shorten and clarify directions for performing various skills. An annotated listing of available Audio-Visual Aids in the field has been included and many new drawings, both those of an incidental nature and those illustrating new camping techniques, have been added. The bibliographies for supplementary reading have been completely revised and brought up to date.

The index is complete and includes cross-indexes; it is hoped that users will familiarize themselves with it and find it helpful in their use of the book. A selected bibliography and a listing of publishers and organizations associated with camping has been included.

As in the first edition, the content and presentation of the material have been kept close to the recommendations for courses in camp counseling as set up by the American Camping Association.*

VIOLA MITCHELL

*Storm Lake, Iowa*
January, 1955

---

* "Camp Leadership Courses for Colleges and Universities," Chicago, American Camping Association, 1949.

# References for the Instructor in Counseling

Allen, Hugh D.: Here's a Way to Better Counselor Training. C.M., Feb. 1950

Bassett, Jeanne: A College Trains Counselors. C.M., Feb., 1944.

Camp Counselor Training. Girl Scouts (#19–136), 1947.

Camp Leadership Courses for Colleges and Universities. A.C.A., 1949.

Charting Outdoor Education. C.M., May, 1946.

Guide for Trainers of Day Camp Directors. Girl Scouts.

Hammett, Catherine T.: A Camp Director Trains His Own Staff. A.C.A., 1948.

Hartwig, Marie, and Peterson, Florence: Camp Counselor Training Wookbook. Burgess, 1950, 104 pp.

Joy, Barbara Ellen: Methods and Practical Procedures for Conducting Camp Leadership Training Courses in College, Camp, and Institute. Camp Publications, no. 40.

Joy, Barbara Ellen: Outline of Course in Camp Administration and Organization. Camp Publications, no. 37.

Joy, Barbara Ellen: Value and Use of Bulletin Boards in Camp. Camp Publications, no. 12.

Mortensen, Martin: Training Leaders in Camping and Outdoor Education. Jr. H. and P.E., June, 1952.

Roloff, Louise L.: A Course in Outing and Mountaineering. Jr. H. and P.E., Nov., 1951.

Stultz, Richard E.: Good Training Means Good Counseling. C.M., Jan., 1951.

Training for Outdoor Leadership. Girl Scouts (#19–436), 1950.

## Counselor-in-Training (C.I.T.) Programs

Clark, Leslie S.: Teen-age Camp Counselor Trainees. Jr. H. and P.E., June, 1954.

Hower, Marjorie A.: How One Camp Organized a Successful Program for Counselors in Training. C.M., March, 1953.

Report Made on C.I.T. Survey. C.M., Feb., 1954.

Sinn, Mrs. B. A., and Pels, Mrs. Herbert: Good Counselors Are Made in Camp. C.M., Feb., 1950.

Welch, Emily H.: Counselor Training Can be Professional. C.M., Jan., 1951.

# Preface and Suggestions for Use

IT IS HOPED that this camping manual will prove useful as a basic source book for both experienced and inexperienced camp counselors. It is obviously impossible to include in one volume all the materials camp workers need to fit them for carrying on the broad and varied program of a modern summer camp, but as much material as seems practicable has been treated in some detail. Since some important aspects have only been touched upon, extensive bibliographies have been included at the end of each chapter to supplement the materials of the text.

This book is designed to meet the needs of at least five classes of persons: (1) college students taking courses in camp leadership or camp counseling; (2) prospective camp counselors enrolled in the between-season training courses given by various organizations; (3) counselors participating in pre-camp training courses at camp; (4) counselors on the job in camp; and (5) camp directors who are conducting precamp or in-training programs.

The Counselor, since he occupies such an influential position with youngsters, needs to be a well-rounded and well-adjusted person. He must have as a working background some knowledge of the history, philosophy and objectives of camping. He must understand people and be able to appreciate their varying personalities and characteristics—both the older ones who will be his staff associates and the youngsters who will be his campers. He needs to have personal skill in one or more camp activities and must have the "know how" of teaching others. Above all, since camping is carried on mainly in an outdoor environment, he must have the camping and wood-craft knowledge and skills necessary to live comfortably, happily and safely in the out-of-doors.

The ideal counselor training course would have an enrollment of around sixteen and would be carried on in a camping situation, with children of camp age in attendance. In such a laboratory, prospective counselors could see the things discussed put into practice under actual camp conditions. Unfortunately, such a Utopian set-up is rarely possible, and the majority of courses must be carried on under classroom limitations. A resourceful instructor, however, will make opportunities for at least a few excursions out-of-doors on cook-outs, overnight sleep-outs, weekend camping trips, and perhaps a four-to-ten-day camping trip to climax the end of the course. Diverse teaching

vii

methods keep interests alert and make for thorough learning as they appeal to the visual-minded, the auditory-minded, and those who learn best by "doing" or actually experiencing a thing. The following techniques are suggested:

1. Study of the text, amplifying it by demonstrations, experimentation, discussion, testing, and so forth.
2. Supplementary reading—no course can be adequate which does not acquaint the student with the wealth of materials available on various phases of camping:
   (*a*) Certain readings specified for the entire group.
   (*b*) Special reading for those interested in some particular phase, such as nature study, dramatics, waterfront, or arts and crafts.
3. Round table, panel or class discussions growing out of talks, outside readings, or topics assigned for special study.
4. Special reports made by groups or individuals.
5. Teacher, group or individual demonstrations.
6. Special projects, such as collecting camp poetry or songs, making articles of camp equipment, waterproofing matches, making spatter prints, and so on.
7. Bringing in visiting consultants such as camp directors, Boy or Girl Scout leaders, Red Cross waterfront or first aid workers, and school personnel in such related fields as sociology, nature study and home economics.
8. Bulletin board displays, changed frequently and on schedule by members of the group. Attention drawn through the use of colored mounting paper, colored thumb tacks, printed topical headings, and other means.
9. Use of the many good slides and movies now available. (See pp. 383–388.)
10. Check lists used to record the specific achievements of class members.
11. Exhibits of camp bulletins, pamphlets, books, model campsites, arts and crafts projects, naturelore, camping and woodcraft skills, tools, and the like.
12. Scheduled laboratory periods for practicing campcraft skills. Field trips, overnight or weekend trips. Sponsoring such trips for neighborhood children.
13. Preparing annotated bibliographies. One important phase of a training course is browsing through the literature of camping and allied fields to acquaint the student with sources so that he can quickly find what he wants when he wants it.
14. Writing term papers on chosen topics or those pertaining to the job the student expects to have in camp next season.
15. Planning and participating in cook-outs, overnight trips and weekend trips. This affords opportunity for democratic practice in planning

program, food, equipment, duty charts, menus, food lists, and so on, as well as gives actual practice in camping techniques.

16. Making a loose leaf camping notebook or scrapbook.

Though there is a continuing and rapid growth in the quality and quantity of training in camping colleges are giving, it continues to lag far behind what is needed for approximately 400,000 camp staff members who are hired every year. Approximately 50 colleges own or have access to camp facilities and 280 give courses in camping, some of them on "campsites."*

Obviously no practical course in camping can be carried on without a minimum of camping equipment such as knives, hatchets, files, cooking utensils, blanket pins, tents, and so on. Students may be asked to buy their own, or equipment may be loaned or rented to them by the sponsoring agency.

Most groups will find the list of additional readings at the end of each chapter too extensive for the time available. These lists are purposely left so that the instructor can go through them, eliminating any books or pamphlets unavailable in his particular situation and selecting according to the particular needs and interests of his group. To avoid repetition, only skeletal information is given at the ends of chapters for sources referred to in several chapters; complete data are in the Bibliography given on pages 389 and 390.

VIOLA MITCHELL
IDA BARKSDALE CRAWFORD

* McBride, Robert E.: Camping at the Mid-Century, p. 4.

# Acknowledgments

THE AUTHORS wish to express their sincere appreciation to Misses Barbara Ellen Joy and Marjorie Camp of the Joy Camps, Hazelhurst, Wisconsin, and to Mr. Frank Bell and Miss Hannah Bell of Camps Mondamin and Green Cove, Tuxedo, N. C. Their careful reading of the manuscript and their constructive criticism have been most helpful.

Grateful acknowledgment is also made to the following publishers who have generously given their permission for the use of quotations. To Bobbs-Merrill for use of the work of James Whitcomb Riley; to Coronet Magazine for the quotation of Carl Schurz; to Agathe Deming Arnn; to Mrs. Elizabeth Cumming, Davidson College, N. C., for help in obtaining the poem by Charles Mitchell; to Houghton Mifflin for use of the works of Longellow and Thoreau; to Doubleday-Doran for the poem of Walt Whitman; to The Chilton Greetings Co. for use of the poem from The Friendship Book; to Scribners for the use of the work of Robert Louis Stevenson; to The House of Hubbard for Elbert Hubbard's Epigram; to the Indianapolis News for "Yours"; to the Macmillan Company for Mary S. Edgar's poems; to the Open Road Publishing Company for the poems of Deep River Jim; to Reilly & Lee Company for permission to use the poem of Edgar A. Guest; and to H. Armstrong Roberts for permission to use the photograph on the front cover.

To the countless publications from all fields of camping we express our indebtedness for help they have given us in suggesting ideas and furnishing information. To the many individuals whose helpful suggestions and constructive criticism have, we hope, helped us to improve and make more functional this new edition.

To Doris Poeckes, Carolyn Claussen, and Mary Ann Wixon for their painstaking care and loyal devotion to the preparation of the manuscript for the second edition.

We wish also to express our regret at not being able to give recognition for the use of some of the material. In spite of diligent search and the writing of many letters, it has been impossible to trace some of the quotations and ideas for camp "fixings" to their original sources.

# Contents

# PART IV.  CAMPCRAFT AND WOODCRAFT

**PART I**

# Growth and Objectives of the Camping Movement

Who can measure all the good
Born within a tangled wood?
There the boy in dreams can see
Just the man he hopes to be
And in silent hours can plan
His conception of a man;
Here beneath the friendly leaves
Find the standards that he weaves.
EDGAR A. GUEST*

## Chapter 1

# THE CAMPING MOVEMENT

### NATIVE HERE AND TO THE MANNER BORN

THE NICE thing about this reasonable old world is that it has a past and a present as well as a future; and so it is with camping. It has a good record, a better present, and an almost unlimited future—in fact, just as fine a future as we of the present care to make it.

To understand why the oak tree bears acorns we must recall that it originally came from an acorn, and to understand our friends we must know something of their backgrounds, for only then can we perceive those little things which explain "why and how they tick." So it is with camping. Camping is a native of the United States, for, like many of America's progressive ideas, it was "born and reared" in solid, austere New England, and the majority of the camps are still located in that region. It was a "Yankee notion" which, in the approximately ninety-five years since its birth in 1861, has resulted in the establishment of an estimated 12,000 camps of many different kinds serving about 4,000,000† boys and girls each summer. Well may we ask what has caused this mushrooming growth now so widespread throughout the United States and Canada. The answer is not a simple one,

* Copyrighted and reproduced by permission of Mr. Guest's publishers, The Reilly & Lee Company.
† McBride, Robert E.: Camping at the Mid-Century. ACA, p. 11.

for each camp may answer truly urgent needs unique to the particular community it serves.

## Why the Summer Camp?

Each summer, as the last ties of school are broken, youth equips itself with a heterogeneous assortment of duffel and hies itself off to summer camp. Collectively, it is the annual exodus from the hot, stuffy, smelly, noisy city and away to the open spaces of good old Camp Wahoo, but, individually, it is infinitely more. Each camper has some secret and deep-seated longings which he hopes camp will satisfy for him; each parent has visions of the return of a better adjusted, healthier and happier child, made so by his summer's experiences.

Yes, this is *Camp*, the great melting pot of childhood, where youth has a chance to live in a youth's world populated with persons from diverse regions, creeds and sometimes even nationalities and races. What an opportunity for the development of true democracy and the real understanding which alone can lead to the establishment of "One World"! As Mr. Watson B. Miller has stated, "Camping, at its best really practices what we preach about democracy."*

A wise person once said, "There is nothing new under the sun" and camping is certainly no exception. Only the concept of it has changed, but it will continue to vary as it keeps pace with the changing needs and desires of society.

## Early Campers

Early peoples needed no wooden houses, for they were nomadic by nature and traveled about according to the seasonal movements of game and other sources of food and clothing. They actually "camped" 365 days of the year. The Indians were the first great American campers, and experts they were at it, for they have left us vast stores of wood lore and camping "know how," developed by their understanding hearts, their seeing eyes, and their sensitive, intelligent hands.

The moment the Pilgrim Fathers landed on American shores they, too, became campers in every sense of the word, for their very existence depended upon their ability to wrest a living from the elements. The history of America is rich in the lore of its early explorers and frontiersmen who matched wits with Nature in a constant struggle for clothing, food and shelter. Their deeds of valor and courage play an important part in our development, and our hearts beat high with excitement and pride as we read of the prowess of such American campers as Kit Carson, Daniel Boone, Theodore Roosevelt, Daniel Beard and Ernest Thompson Seton. Early

* From Proceedings, 1947, of the Southeastern American Camping Association.

pioneers had to be self-reliant and ingenious, for there was no supermarket where "Junior" could pick up a pound of hamburger, no department store to supply a pair of jeans, and no hardware store to furnish a ten-penny nail. Almost every growing thing had value as a source of food, medicine, clothing or shelter. The pioneers *had* to know and understand nature, for there was no time for mistakes when selecting proper wood for an axe handle or the best herb to use for sickness and pain. Hunting and trapping animals to supply furs, food and clothing necessitated an intimate knowledge of animal ways of life.

It is human nature to forget the disagreeable and recall only the pleasant; thus the glamorous, exciting exploits of our forefathers have largely blinded us to the privations, dangers and hardships which were the very core of their daily lives.

## Life Was Mainly Rural

At the time of the signing of the Constitution our national population was 98 per cent rural, but with the coming of the machine age and the increasing tendency to cluster about concentrated areas of employment, this percentage has decreased until now only about 45 per cent of our people live in what could be classed as small town or rural areas. This trend toward city life has had a marked influence upon American lives, particularly on the lives of American youth.

Let us, like Alice, step through the looking glass into a typical farm scene of several generations ago. There we find boys and girls whose knowledge of nature seems almost innate, for, as with the pioneers, each plant, animal and tree had some utilitarian value. Theirs was a manner of life in which manual training, arts and crafts, and home economics, though not known as such, were simply accepted as an essential part of everyday living, "learned by doing" under the personal tutoring of parents and other adults. Formal school training in readin', writin' and 'rithmetic was confined to the few winter months when the services of the children could best be spared from the many farm duties.

Chores about the farm furnished vigorous exercise, and the whole country-side provided ample room in which to run and jump and shout during leisure time. Nor was there a lack of social contacts, for families were large and close-knit, and members enjoyed the companionship of brothers and sisters of approximately the same age as they worked and played together. Visitors, even though strangers, provided welcome diversion and were urged to make extended visits, for distances were too great and traveling too hazardous and uncomfortable to warrant brief overnight visits or a casual evening of bridge. For close neighbors, there were numerous social affairs such as corn huskings, bellings, house and barn warmings, taffy pulls, spelling bees, and singing schools.

## Modern Urban Life

Now let us move forward to take a look at the modern urban child. He spends a long nine or ten months in an overcrowded school geared to meet college entrance requirements and sometimes seemingly oblivious of his real needs and wishes. His life is regulated by schedules and bells, and he is subjected to the formal teaching methods made necessary when large numbers of students must meet course and credit standards.

Camping has no quarrel with formal education, for it is undoubtedly striving valiantly to do its best under the handicap of the difficulties to which it is subjected. But camping can and does supplement formal school education by supplying a type of education best carried on in the informal atmosphere of the summer camp where youngsters sleep, work, eat and play with counselors and fellow-campers in an atmosphere of friendly rapport and cameraderie. Here the child can know nature, including human nature, at its best—an opportunity too often denied under the public school regime.

The present economy does not encourage large families, and the child often lives entirely with adults in a small cottage or apartment where there is no room to run, jump, climb and throw. When he indulges his perfectly normal craving for action, his antics are likely to end unhappily as his ball crashes through the Kwality Grocery plate glass window, he tramples in Mrs. Jones' prize petunia bed, or his noise drives old Grandma Finkelstein to bellicose retribution. For engaging in what should be the birthright of every child, he is likely to receive a good "bawling out," physical punishment, or even disciplinary measures as a juvenile delinquent. Can we wonder that he is puzzled and sometimes rebellious? Our modern knowledge of childhood shows us how irritating and warping it can be to live amidst the constant "do's" and "don'ts" of people crowded in on all sides like sardines.

Both parents are often employed outside the home, and their free time is spent in pursuits which continue to segregate them from their offspring. There is little time for recreation or even for being together. Instead of giving themselves in companionship, understanding and sympathy, parents try to substitute with liberal allowances for movies, funny books and other items which are supposed to buy happiness. The child has large quantities of leisure time, since his existence in the modern push-the-button age of labor-saving devices makes chores practically nonexistent.

Children quickly fall into the pattern set by their parents and become victims of the "spectatoritis" developed by depending on commercial organizations for ready-made entertainment and recreation which are all too often merely time-consuming busywork. It is easy to understand the elation such a child derives from struggling and sweating to build a bean-hole or a lean-to, for this activity fulfills the universal desire to do something constructive and useful; to display something *he* has made with *his* own hands. Children work like little beavers on camp projects and do not consider it work at all, for, as Sir James Barrie said, "Work is only work when you would rather be doing something else."

Many parents realize the shortcomings of city life, and nostalgic memories of their own rural upbringing make them determined to give their children a taste of it through summer camping even though it means sacrificing and scrimping through all the other months of the year.

## SOME PIONEERS IN THE CAMPING MOVEMENT

### The First School Camp (1861)

Frederick William Gunn, who is generally accorded to be the *Father of Organized Camping,* was the founder and head of the Gunnery School for Boys in Washington, Connecticut. With the coming of the Civil War, his students, boylike, wanted to live like soldiers and were sometimes permitted to march, roll up in their blankets and sleep outdoors. The Gunnery School continued to run throughout a part of the summer, and in 1861, yielding to the wishes of the boys, Mr. and Mrs. Gunn packed the entire student body up for a gypsy trip to Milford on the Sound, four miles away, where they spent two weeks in boating, sailing, tramping and fishing. The experiment proved so successful that it was repeated at two-year intervals with some of the former students returning to join in the excursion.

A new site was later selected at Point Beautiful on Lake Waramauge, seven miles from the school, and the name was changed from Camp Comfort to Gunnery Camp. Mr. Gunn's camp was definitely a school camp, for he simply moved his already organized school outdoors for a brief session, a custom which he continued until 1879. However, the objectives of school camping as we know it today are very different.

### The First Private Camp (1876)

Dr. Joseph Trimble Rothrock, a practicing physician of Wilkes-Barre, Pennsylvania, combined his interests in forestry and conservation with his desire to do something for frail boys by establishing a "School of Physical Culture" where these children could improve their health by living out-of-doors in tents while continuing their education. The school, which was located on North Mountain in Luzerne County, Pennsylvania, lasted from June 15 to October 15 and had twenty pupils and five teachers. The student paid $200 tuition for the four months, but the income failed to meet expenses, and Dr. Rothrock abandoned the idea in favor of spending the next year on an Alaskan expedition. Various attempts to revive the school under different leadership were likewise financially unprofitable, and it was permanently closed within a few years.

## The First Church Camp (1880)

The Reverend George W. Hinckley, of West Hartford, Connecticut, saw in camping an opportunity to know his boys more intimately and so have a more lasting influence upon them. In 1880 he took seven members of his church on a camping trip to Gardners Island, Wakefield, Rhode Island. The results must have been gratifying, for he later founded The Good Will Farm for Boys, at Hinckley, Maine. His schedule called for a "sane and sensible" religious and educational morning program with afternoons spent in such activities as swimming, baseball and tennis, and evenings devoted to singing, talks and various other forms of entertainment.

## The First Private Camp Organized to Meet Specific Educational Needs (1890)

In 1880, while traveling on Asquam Lake near Holderness, New Hampshire, Ernest Berkely Balch chanced upon Burnt Island, which apparently was unowned. It seemed a perfect spot for carrying out his plan to provide a place where boys from well-to-do families could come to avoid idling away the summer at resort hotels. A year later he returned with five boys and erected a small frame shanty which they christened "Old '81." The group was somewhat surprised, no doubt, by the arrival of a man who claimed to be the owner, but they were certainly not outdone, for they purchased the entire island for the sum of $40. They called their island retreat Camp Chocorua because of its superb view of Chocorua Mountain, thirty miles away, and it continued to exist until 1889.

From the first, the boys had a camp uniform of gray flannel shorts and shirts with scarlet belt, cap, and shirt lacing. All camp work was done by the boys, who were divided into four crews, each with a leader, called the "stroke." One crew was off duty each day while the other three spent about five hours as kitchen, dish or police crews. Spiritual life was carefully planned, and the services must have been quite impressive as the boys came singing through the woods, dressed in cotta and cassock, to the altar of their chapel, which was set deep in a grove of silver maples.

The camp had an average of five staff members and twenty-five boys who competed in tennis, sailing, swimming, diving and baseball. Winners were awarded ribbons bearing their names, the event and the date. Definite objectives for Camp Chocorua were the development in the boy of (1) a sense of responsibility, both for himself and for others, and (2) an appreciation of the worthwhileness of work. The Camp Chocorua silver pin was given annually to the two or three campers best incorporating qualities of "manliness, justice, truth, and conscientiousness." It was intended as a symbol of recognition for innate qualities and not as a reward to be worked for; in fact, those who consciously set out to win it were said to stand little chance of doing so, and no award at all was made in the years when none were judged worthy.

## The First Y.M.C.A. Camp (1885)

Summer F. Dudley, a young resident of Brooklyn, was associated with his father and brother in the manufacture of surgical instruments. His first venture in camping was to take seven members of the Newburgh, New York, Y.M.C.A. on an eight-day fishing, swimming and boating trip to Pine Point on Orange Lake, six miles away. Since the boys had had their heads shaved close in what they deemed proper preparation for the trip, their camp was appropriately dubbed Camp Bald Head.

Dudley spent the next several years in conducting other camping trips for boys and entered the Y.M.C.A. as a full-time worker in 1887. He died in 1897 at the untimely age of forty-three. His last camp on Lake Champlain near Westport, New York, was renamed Camp Dudley in his honor, and is the oldest organized camp still in existence.

## Camping for Girls (1892 and 1902)

In 1891 Professor Arey of Rochester, New York, established Camp Arey as a Natural Science Camp, and a year later he lent it for a month's use by girls. Mr. and Mrs. Andre C. Fontaine took over the camp in 1912 and from that time on conducted it as a camp exclusively for girls. The first camp founded expressly for girls was Camp Kehonka for Girls at Wolfeboro, New Hampshire, which was established by Laura Mattoon in 1902.

## THE PERIODS OF CAMPING

Organized camping, during its comparatively brief life cycle, has been classified by Dimock* as passing through three stages of development as to its main emphasis. These are (1) the recreational stage, (2) the educational stage, and (3) the stage of social orientation and responsibility. As with any movement, no sharp line of demarcation can be drawn between these periods, for the changes were gradual and overlapping, and at no time was there perfect unanimity of opinion among leaders or uniformity as to the programs and practices of the various camps.

### The Recreational Stage (1861–1920)

Early experiments in camping were fostered by public-spirited men who saw in them an opportunity to provide a better way for boys to spend the summer than in loafing about in idleness or harmful pursuit in the city. The main idea was to provide wholesome, healthful fun while "roughing it" in

* Dimock, Hedley S.: Administration of the Modern Camp, p. 24.

the out-of-doors. High moral and spiritual values were ever held in high esteem, but were supposed to be "caught" like mumps or measles from mere association with fine, upright leaders. There was no thought of financial gain from the project, and this very lack of adequate financial backing caused the early demise of many camps.

It was common for one or two adults to start out on a trip with as many as forty or fifty boys and a meager supply of equipment. The expeditions were, almost without exception, built around the strong personality of a man who kept the respect and admiration of the boys by his unselfish motives, sympathetic understanding, tactful leadership, and sound principles of the intermixture of work and play. Ralph Waldo Emerson's statement that "Every institution is but the lengthened shadow of a man" certainly applies to these early camps.

The movement was slow to "catch on," for there were probably no more than twenty-five to sixty camps in existence in 1900.

## The Educational Stage (1920–1930)

History has repeatedly demonstrated that bursts of energetic change and development inevitably follow wars, and one example in the years following World War I was a decided increase in the number of organized camps and a corresponding alteration in their methods and program. Progressive education, with its foundation of psychology and mental hygiene, was stressing the individual needs of the child, and camps responded by adding a variety of activities such as dramatics, arts and crafts, dancing and music to their repertoire. Thus it became an objective of camping to supplement the enlarged school curriculum. New testing methods had demonstrated that personality, character and spiritual growth were not inevitably "caught," but must be "taught" and planned for if optimum results were to be obtained.

## The Stage of Social Orientation and Responsibility (1930———)

Continued research in testing methods and evaluation showed that camps were not always measuring up to the high aspirations held for them, but, again, ever-resourceful camp directors proved equal to the occasion and progress continues to be made.

Proponents of camping were shocked by a 1930 study of over a hundred camps which revealed that instead of inevitably producing the good health everyone had assumed, camping was sometimes actually detrimental to health and that the longer a child stayed in camp the more likely his health was to suffer. Camps sought to remedy the situation by adding physicians, nurses and trained dietitians to their staffs and by engaging in more healthful practices including cutting down on the general tempo of camp life.

We know that a society is only as strong as its individual citizens and that only by grounding each in the principles of democracy can we guard our

American people against the infiltration of communism. Camping, which deals with individual campers during their most formative years, accepts its share of this responsibility as it provides an opportunity for each person to live democratically in a democracy. Ideally, camping is an experience in group living at its best where the individual camper can develop independence, self-control and self-reliance as he helps to plan and accept responsibility for his own way of life throughout the day. Camps are trying to adapt themselves to the needs of the child instead of remolding the child to fit into the ways of the camp.

This period has also seen a phenomenal growth in the amount of camp literature published.

## THE ORGANIZATION OF THE CAMPING PROFESSION

In the early days of camping, camps varied greatly with each setting its own standards and solving its own problems as it best saw fit. Realizing the mutual values of associating and discussing with others of like interests and problems, camp directors and other interested parties began to meet and plan cooperatively. The first such formal meeting was held in Boston in 1903 and was attended by about a hundred men and a sprinkling of women.

The Camp Directors' Association of America was founded in 1910 with Charles R. Scott as its first president, and the National Association of Directors of Girls Camps began in 1916 with Mrs. Charlotte V. (Mrs. Luther Halsey) Gulick as president. The Mid-West Camp Directors' Association was founded in 1921. The three organizations joined forces as the Camp Directors' Association, with George L. Meylan as president, in 1924.

### The American Camping Association

The name of the above organization was changed to the American Camping Association in 1935 and the group has grown remarkably, having a membership of over 5000 in 1953.* It represents camping of all types and through its affiliation with the Canadian Camping Association includes in its membership camp directors and camp staff, educators and others interested in camping in the United States and Canada. Many members are from such related fields as sociology, psychology and education.

*What It Does.*      Some of the purposes of the American Camping Association as stated in its Constitution† are:

1. To advance camping in all its branches so as to reach a constantly growing number of young people and adults.
2. To serve as the voice of camping people, nationally and locally.
3. To act as a channel through which new trends in camping can be disseminated.
4. To assume leadership in developing camping in new areas.

* American Camping Magazine, April, 1954, p. 38.
† File Folder of the American Camping Association Convention, 1952.

5. To develop standards and operating codes for the improvement of camp practices.

6. To provide fellowship for camping people and those in allied fields who are interested in the progress of camping.

7. To interpret camping to related fields and to the general public.

8. To serve as the organization through which trained and practicing camp directors endeavor to express the views of the profession and strive to lead in shaping policies and techniques of camping in the United States.

In its 1948 and 1950 national conventions, the American Camping Association adopted standards for camps covering personnel, program, camp-site facilities and equipment, administration, health, sanitation and safety. All camps which wanted to be certified as members of the American Camping Association were to present evidence of their compliance with the standards by December 31, 1954. The object is, of course, to raise the quality of all organized camps in the United States. The Association sponsors conferences, workshops, and the writing and publishing of books and pamphlets pertaining to the many areas in the camping field.

*The Organization.* The American Camping Association is divided into forty-four sections which hold annual meetings. The sections are, in turn, divided into seven regional groups which meet biannually. The national meetings of the whole association are held in the alternate years.

*Membership.* Several types of memberships are open to organized camps, depending upon their size. Individual memberships for a year cost five dollars, and a student membership may be secured for three dollars. Each type of membership includes a subscription to the publication of the organization, the *Camping Magazine*, which is published monthly except during July, August, September and October.

## The Association of Private Camps

This organization was founded in the northeastern and New England states in 1940 and is a strong organization with a membership representing about 250 private camps. Its headquarters is at 55 West 42nd Street, New York City and annual meetings are held in that city. It issues a newsletter, sponsors research and study groups, maintains a counselor placement service, aids in educating the public about camping, and serves as a clearing house for matters pertaining particularly to private camps.

## THE VARIETIES OF CAMPS

Many organizations have recognized the opportunity to further their objectives which are inherent in camping, and the result has been the establishment of a multitude of camps, each modeled after the ideas of the group sponsoring it. It would be virtually impossible to list all the types of camps found in the shifting panorama of camping, but they fall roughly into three groups according to their sponsorship: (1) private, (2) agency, and (3) municipal.

## Private Camps

Private camps are sponsored by persons who, while usually quite mindful of the best interests and welfare of their campers and of the importance of their work as a service to humanity, still must look upon camper fees as the direct means of earning a living for themselves.

In general they must charge a somewhat higher fee, which ordinarily limits their patronage to the children of the upper middle class or well-to-do, and their greater finances sometimes enable them to provide somewhat more in the way of equipment and facilities than do the other sponsors.

Much pioneering in camping has taken place in the private camps, where the long term of eight or ten weeks affords enough time for the camper to make real progress toward realizing definite camping objectives. Most private camps draw their clientele from various areas, thus providing a change of environment and the broadening influence of association with campers from other regions. There are about 2500 private resident camps in the United States.*

## Agency Camps

Agency camps are largely nonprofit-making and are supported by the public, largely through the Community Chest, public tax or private subscription. The small fee charged makes camping possible for children from even low-income families and camperships are often available for those who cannot pay even this small fee. The large number of campers handled during a season necessitates a rapid turnover, so that the average child can be accommodated for only a week or two. Although this is undoubtedly a handicap in achieving camping objectives, it is not so great as it would seem, for the camping period is often but a continuation of the regular yearly program carried on by the organization in the city and is conducted by its year-round employees.

Agency camps are usually located near the homes of the campers whom they serve, so that transportation costs are cut to a minimum. They are the largest group in camping and are doing some excellent work in the field.

1. *Boy Scouts.* The Boy Scouts were organized in England by Lord Robert Baden-Powell and imported to the United States by Daniel Beard and Ernest Thompson Seton. Their first camping here was carried on at Camp Becket in 1909, and camping has occupied an important place in their program ever since. In 1949, they operated 831 resident camps in addition to much day and troop camping.† They now carry on camping activities on a larger scale than does any other organization in the United States. They have contributed much to the development of new camping techniques and their low-priced literature is outstanding in the field.

* File folder of the American Camping Association Convention, 1952.
† Benson and Goldberg: The Camp Counselor, p. 5.

2. *Girl Scouts*.     The Girl Scouts were chartered in 1912, and this same year, their founder, Juliette Lowe, established Camp Lowland. Camping has always been a vital part of their program and their inexpensive and very worthwhile literature has made an invaluable contribution to the field. Their standards as set up for various phases of Girl Scout camping have many times led the way for all. This organization has been active in furthering unit rather than mass camping and in stressing the pioneering type of activity. It had 678 resident camps in operation in 1949.*

3. *Camp Fire Girls*.     Mr. and Mrs. Luther Halsey Gulick organized and established the Camp Fire Girls in 1912, largely to meet the needs of their own seven daughters. The organization's first camp was at Lake Sebago, Maine. It was called Wohelo, a word formed from the first two letters of Work, Health and Love, and since adopted as the watchword of the Camp Fire Girls. The group's symbol is "fire" around which the first homes were built, and the effectiveness of its program is heightened by the ceremony, legends, Indian lore, poetry and music upon which the program is based. The organization now sponsors more than 165 camps.*

4. *The 4-H Clubs*.     4-H Club Camps are promoted for rural boys and girls who have been selected to receive extra training to better fit them for leadership in their own home communities.

5. *Welfare Agencies and Social Settlements*.     These pioneers in the camping movement directed their efforts primarily toward supplying camping opportunities for those financially unable to pay any or more than a small part of their own expenses. Some of their early ventures were known as Fresh Air Farms or Fresh Air Camps, since many of their protégés came from crowded tenement districts where grass and trees are novelties and the sun's rays shine between the tall buildings only for a short time each day when the sun is directly overhead. Many suffer from malnutrition, so that good nourishing food and other health measures occupy a prominent place in the program.

Mothers and babies as well as older children are sometimes included in the program, which supplies a much needed and worthwhile service.

6. *Y.M.C.A. and Y.W.C.A.*     Both these organizations early recognized the possibilities in camping as a new approach to character-building and both promote it as an important part of their all-year program. They have made valuable contributions to camping. The Y.M.C.A. now operates

* Benson and Goldberg: The Camp Counselor, p. 6.

about 641 camps in the United States and the Y.W.C.A. about 200.* The Y.M.C.A. often holds camping periods for girls when the area is not served by the Y.W.C.A.

7. *Other Groups.* Among other groups which sponsor camping are Pioneer Youth, Boys' Clubs of America, Girls' Clubs, Salvation Army, Jewish Community centers, and various churches, labor unions and other organizations, and various business and industrial concerns.

## Public Camps

Public camps are generally free or inexpensive to their users, since they are supported by taxes or other fees assessed from the general public.

1. *Municipal.* The growth of municipal camping progressed slowly at first, since most cities were concentrating on equipping and maintaining the playgrounds they had already started. The public is notoriously loathe to give financial support to recreation, taking the short-sighted stand of preferring to spend money on jails and other correctional institutions which might largely be dispensed with were a good program of character training and recreation provided for youth. The greatest growth of municipal camping has been in the field of day camping and it will no doubt continue to stride rapidly forward in the future.

2. *The United States Forest Service and the National Park Service.* These encourage family camping by offering sites and facilities in government-owned areas. They also often have areas and facilities available for rent to organizations not having their own campsites.

## Day Camps

A resident camp is one in which campers remain for at least a week, while a day camp is ordinarily located near the homes of its campers so that the children can sleep and eat their morning and evening meals at home. The patrons of day camps arrive by bus or private car at about 9:30 A.M. and spend the day in camping activities, going home again about 4:30 P.M. They often bring the ingredients for a noon cook-out with them. Day camps usually operate from one to five days a week and their convenience and low cost bring camping to many who are too young or financially unable to participate in resident camping. Day camping was originated by the Girl Scouts in 1922 and is now sponsored by such other organizations as Boy Scouts, Y.W.C.A., Y.M.C.A., Camp Fire Girls and the like, as well as by cities and private individuals. There are about 1000 privately sponsored day camps in the United States and 3000 sponsored by groups.†

## Schools Camps

School camping, or "outdoor education," has seen a phenomenal growth within the past twenty years or so. The greatest development has been in

* Benson and Goldberg: The Camp Counselor, p. 4.
† File folder of the ACA Convention, 1952.

Michigan which now has over seventy-five school districts incorporating it as a part of the regular school curriculum. Many other states are experimenting in this field; among them are California, Florida, Illinois, Indiana, Missouri, New York, North Carolina, Ohio, Texas and Washington. One of the big drawbacks is, of course, the increased cost which is sometimes as much as two or three times that of regular school.

*Objectives.*    The objectives of school camping are very much the same as those of camping in general and the idea of having school sponsorship is to bring the benefits of outdoor living to all or nearly all children of school age, instead of to only about 12 per cent who now enjoy them. The main aim is to leave to the classroom those subjects which can best be taught there and take to the campsite other subjects which can better be demonstrated in the outdoor environment. It is often possible to elaborate on and make more meaningful to the child, subject matter he has already studied in the classroom. Learning starts from the time the child begins to pore over a map to trace the route of the school bus to camp and to work harmoniously with his group to plan equipment lists, procedures and program. As in any camping, the whole experience is one of democratic living where the child learns self-reliance and develops his own ingenuity in adapting himself to a comfortable, yet simple, life. Often he learns for the first time to be on his own, as he accepts responsibility for dressing himself, caring for his living quarters, and sharing in the planning of his own program. He finds ample opportunities to put into practice things he has learned in theory and he will be motivated to investigate and learn still more in order to fulfill his felt needs. Many areas of learning are naturals for camp living; among these are homemaking, woodworking, nature study, arithmetic, health education, arts and crafts, conservation, social science, dramatics, music, moral and spiritual values, physical education, worthy use of leisure time, and the social graces and amenities of living happily and cooperatively with others. What the child doesn't already know, he avidly seeks to learn as his interests are aroused and he sees how helpful and satisfying such information or skills really can be.

*Organization and Administration.*    Schools acquire facilities for school camping in many and varied ways. In some cases, grounds and buildings are donated or loaned by service organizations and public-spirited individuals. In others, properties are rented from public or private owners and in a few instances schools purchase land and construct their own camp buildings. Some schools utilize the opportunities offered by local, state or national parks. Some colleges arrange to rent or borrow a campsite as a training ground for prospective teachers and invite the school campers in to provide a realistic situation.

In most instances a school starts its program on a modest basis with one or two grades day-camping for from one to several days or sometimes staying only overnight. The next year, the same grades may do resident camping for a week or two in the fall or spring. As rapidly as possible the experience is extended to more and more grades each camping for one or two weeks, so that several schools now keep their camps open for the entire school year. Some substitute or supplement school year camping with summer camping.

Usually the money for group equipment and the general running of the camp comes out of regular school funds, as for any other school activity, with the participants paying for various personal items such as their own food. Campers are often encouraged to earn or save out of their allowances for their expenses. The cost is cut to a minimum by having the pupils help plan, cook and serve their food, wash dishes and engage in general camp tasks. Participation in camping is usually optional.

Most often it is members of the fifth and sixth grades who engage in this new method of education (40 per cent), with those of the seventh and eighth grades next (26 per cent), while an appreciable number of communities sponsor school camping for both younger and secondary school pupils. A few communities conduct camp for atypical groups, such as the handicapped and those who have dropped out of school.

In order to best integrate school with camp life, the regular teachers accompany their students and help carry on what they have jointly planned back in the classroom. When the camp is only conducted for a few months out of the year, the camp director and other staff personnel are often employed in other capacities about the school for the rest of the year. Communities holding camp for several months usually hire a full-time camp director and a few counselors who remain on the campsite to supplement the regular classroom teachers. Personnel from the State Department of Conservation and from the Audubon Society, other consultants and local volunteers often help out. In some cases, State Departments of Instruction and Conservation share the problem of providing leadership.

Classroom teachers are trained by a variety of techniques to play their strategic role in the whole process. Some take summer or winter school courses as a part of their teacher training program. Often, the school camping experience is conducted as laboratory or field training, or as an extension or in-service course. National School near Sussex, New Jersey, under the leadership of L. B. Sharp, is a pioneer in the training of leaders for school camping.

*Planning.* The worth of the whole experience depends largely upon skillful and thorough planning with both parents and children actively participating. The first step is often to call a mass meeting of all interested parties followed by a general discussion and the appointment of committees to begin the consideration of various phases of the plan. It is necessary to interpret carefully the proposed program to parents and community and to show them that it is not just another frill but an investment of tax money which can and should pay big dividends. By their enthusiastic understanding and support, parents and community workers can aid in many ways such as securing facilities, supplies, finances, needed work at the campsite, transportation, and proper physical and psychological preparation of the youngsters. In addition, teacher-student planning and evaluation before, during, and after the excursion are likewise important.

## Special Types of Camps

Besides general camps which usually feature such activities as woodcraft and campcraft, naturelore, trips, arts, crafts, aquatics, and sports and games there are a number of special camps for those with special interests or needs. Some, such as salt-water camps, ranch camps, mountain-climbing camps, and pioneer or trip camps, capitalize upon their particular environments. Others, such as hockey, tennis, aquatic, horseback-riding, dramatic, music, dance, religious education, tutoring, language, nature, and research camps, appeal to specialized interests. Still others minister to the needs of such handicapped persons as cardiac, diabetic, epileptic, crippled or "problem" children. Still others are coed, family, adult or golden age (for those over sixty) camps.

## MODERN CAMPING TRENDS

### Decentralization

As camping grew in popularity, the attendance at individual camps increased from the original seven to ten campers to an average of 100 to 200 or even more. To meet the demands of such numbers, camps adopted what might be called a *centralized plan* with buildings arranged Army-style in formal, straight lines on either side of a central street or in a hollow square or circle with such buildings as the mess hall and main lodge in the center. Sleeping quarters, like Army barracks, had long rows of cots for campers and counselors. More and more activities were added to the program, each under the direction of a specialist or head. However, experience convinced many camps that a child subjected to this mass type of camping was sometimes lost in the shuffle, for the methods used were often the very ones he had left the city to escape.

Many camps now follow the system of *unit* or *decentralized camping*, which has been spark plugged by the Girl Scouts. Here the large group is broken up into smaller units of twelve to twenty-four campers who live more or less independently and carry on their own activities just as though they constituted a small camp of their own. The unit is sometimes called a section, division or village. The members of the unit are homogeneous, grouped according to similarities in age, camping experience and general development. Each unit has its own buildings, close enough to the main dining room and lodge for convenience, yet sufficiently secluded to permit carrying on most of its existence independently.

Each unit has a unit house for group meetings, a latrine and bath house, and an outdoor kitchen. Sleeping tents or cabins for campers under ten to twelve years of age usually accommodate six to eight campers with one or more counselors. Four to six older campers occupy a cabin with their counselors lodged separately but nearby. There is a difference of opinion as to the advisability of having counselors sleep in the same cabin with campers. Those in favor of separate sleeping quarters advance the thought that parents do not feel it necessary to sleep in the same room with their children and that the privacy afforded is welcomed by both campers and counselors.

The decentralized plan of camping is particularly popular in the short-term camps such as those sponsored by agencies and schools. Private camps which usually have the campers for from four to ten weeks, often prefer a system in which campers choose their own activity groups on the basis of mutual interests, skills and physical ability.

### Program

The early centralized program was rigidly scheduled with activities arranged like school classes and each camper required to participate in those selected as "good for him." He was supposed to come "bug-eyed" with curiosity to nature study at 9 o'clock and maintain this state of blissful attention for exactly an hour, then magically change into an equally enthusiastic tennis student. The program was planned by the camp or program director, sometimes with the assistance of a few chosen counselors, and was intended to absorb every waking moment of the day. Often tutoring in school subjects or special instruction in music, dramatics or dancing was included at the request of parents.

Program is no longer considered a schedule of activities offered each day or week, but rather the sum total of every experience the child has from the time he enters camp until his final "goodbye." Campers and staff are assuming increasing responsibility in helping to plan the camp program.

### Motivation

To motivate the old program, elaborate systems of achievement charts and awards were set up, and competition was sometimes sadly overstressed. Some camps have reacted so violently to this practice that they now refuse to use anything resembling a check list or awards of any type. They give various reasons for their aversions: (1) Campers become so intent on working for awards that they miss the real values inherent in the activities themselves. (2) Regardless of the care taken in planning any system of awards, some campers or groups seldom win and thus acquire a hopeless "what's the use of trying" attitude. Others win too frequently and become insufferably "cocky." (3) The extreme competitive spirit engendered leads to petty bickerings and jealousies which are entirely contrary to the atmosphere camp is trying to create. The desire to win sometimes becomes so keen as to lead to such examples of poor sportsmanship as sprinkling sand on another cabin's floor to keep it from winning a neatness award. (4) The motivating power of the awards is so great that lazy counselors can lie down on the job and exert themselves no more than if they were watching dogs chase a mechanical rabbit at a dog race.

Modern camps tend to minimize awards and make them a result of what is done rather than a definite goal to be worked for and obtained. High camp morale, tradition, a word of commendation from sincere and enthusiastic counselors, and the impetus of group approval and self-satisfaction should furnish enough reward to carry along activities which have natural appeal and worth for youngsters. Campers are encouraged to compete against their own records rather than against the records of others.

## Planning for Individual Differences

The modern camp tries to learn the wishes and needs of each camper and set up a wide range of possibilities for meeting them. Units in a decentralized system usually plan their activities around their own living needs. The unit is small enough to permit the close knit atmosphere of family life, with each camper recognized as a personality whose opinions are respected and needs considered by understanding fellow-campers and counselors.

At one time it was customary to assign campers to their cabins without making any effort to determine how they would "fit." In fact, a deliberate attempt was often made to separate friends and break up cliques so that campers would be forced to form new friendships. We now know that a child benefits from camp in direct proportion to his happiness in it, and every effort is made to fill cabins and units with persons who are already congenial or who can learn to adjust themselves to a happy life together.

## Leadership

The first camp counselors were often college athletes, selected because of their reputations in sports with their primary appeal coming from their prowess on field or gridiron. They often knew little and cared less about the needs, desires and natures of children.

With the change in camp philosophy and program has come a demand for counselors who love children and are interested in them and whose sympathy with child nature enables counselor and camper to live together in mutual confidence and friendly rapport. Program specialists are still often employed for such activities as campcraft, swimming, crafts and dramatics, but the trend today is largely to hire general counselors of good character, with wide interests and skills and, most important of all, a deep understanding of children.

The ratio of counselors to campers has changed from the one counselor to sixteen campers of the early days to one counselor for each six to eight campers today.

## Healthful Practices

Health has always been claimed as a main objective of camping, but early camps deluded themselves that good nourishing food plus living in the out-of-doors would add up to good health as inevitably as night follows day. After the 1930 study had exploded this theory, great changes came about in camp health practices and program. One innovation has been the requiring of a complete health examination for every camper and staff member (1) to prevent the importing and spreading of contagious diseases and (2) to learn of individual weaknesses which need to be corrected or at least protected by a modified program. Trained nurses, doctors and dietitians are a part of the regular camp staff.

Camp personnel now realize the serious error of scheduling every moment so that campers engage in a feverish round of overstrenuous activities from reveille to taps. Serenity and calm are at last winning due recognition, and campers, with careful guidance, are being more often left to follow their own interests even though it occasionally be no more strenuous than sitting under a tree day-dreaming or watching a colony of ants as they carry on their particular form of social living. The rest hour following lunch is inviolate, and campers are encouraged at all times to strike a sane balance between active and inactive pursuits, making sure there is enough vigorous exercise to keep them strong and produce a pleasant, healthful tiredness by nightfall.

## Indiginous Program and Facilities

The literature of a camp once flamboyantly proclaimed its broad and beautiful acreage, its elaborate equipment and its mammoth main lodge. The wide array of town sports provided required an elaborate outlay of balls, bats, headgear, masks, uniforms, and so forth, together with a collection of level playing fields, swings, slides and teeters. Camps now largely omit town sports, concentrating instead on those activities which are natural to the camp environment and can be done better in camp than in town. Campcraft and woodcraft skills, trips and outpost camping have largely crowded out city and school activities in the better camps.

Camp acreage is still broad and lovely, but it is largely the beauty with which nature has endowed it rather than man-made additions dictated by artificial city standards. Buildings are adequate but not overelaborate, and campers are urged to carry on simple construction to fulfill their own needs for living simply and comfortably. They are encouraged to use native materials for the construction of their temporary or semipermanent improvements.

## The Back-to-Nature Movement (INDIGINOUS)

Teaching campers to know and love nature has been another constant aim of camping, but efforts often produced lip service with little real feeling and appreciation back of it. Nature study was likely to consist of a casual stroll by disinterested campers to pluck an occasional flower or cage an unlucky bug which happened to flit across the path, then a saunter back to camp to kill and mount the "haul" and carefully label it with a botonical jawbreaker. The amount of true nature appreciation thus developed is certainly open to question.

In a present-day set up it is hard for a camper to escape nature, for he lives right in the midst of it as members of his group carry on a large share of their activities in the out-of-doors. It is almost impossible for him to spend so many hours smelling, hearing, touching, tasting and seeing the wonders of nature without becoming a saner, finer, and stronger self, and developing a deep and abiding love for all nature. How can he help knowing nature after selecting native wood for a sundial, shelter, bridge or dam and locating and preparing barks, roots and berries for dyeing what he has made?

## Camping for Everyone

Younger and older campers are attending camps now, and persons of all ages are being urged to stay for a longer season to provide more time for being integrated into the environment and for reaping richer benefits. The rapid growth of low-cost agency camping has brought the experience within the realm of possibility of nearly all, but the percentage of children participating in organized camping is still small. Ninety-seven per cent of camping is done by school-age children, with the ages of nine to fourteen years being the most common in organized camps.

There has also been a great development in such phases as work camps, golden age camps (for those over sixty), adult camps, day camps, school camps, year-round camps, brother-sister camps and coed camps.

## Discipline

The word "discipline" comes from disciple and originally meant "to develop by instruction and exercise," but usage has made such a horrible thing of it that its sound strikes fear to the hearts of campers, counselors and camp directors alike. This misapprehension is largely unfounded, for a good camp is a happy place where good will and consideration for others are the order of the day and where the spirit of good rapport makes serious problems largely disappear.

Our increased knowledge of problem children reveals that they are often reacting to "problem" situations and that shortcomings cease to rear their ugly heads when environments are improved. We know, too, that it is seldom safe to judge people by what they "appear" to be, for their overt acts are often mere pretense used to cover up their true feelings. We now realize what a personal tragedy it is for the cocky camper when we take him "down a peg" by making him run the gauntlet or by letting a bigger boy "knock some sense into his head," for his braggadocio is really only a disguise for an underlying inferiority complex and such treatment but further irritates his sore spots. Much better results follow when we learn to search for and eradicate causes instead of launching a direct attack upon symptoms.

We must not get the idea from this discussion that camp is a thoroughly unbridled place where each person does exactly as he pleases. On the contrary, when skillfully conducted, it is a place of superior discipline, for it brings about the best control of all, the kind which comes from within the person and makes him *want* to do what is right because his better nature demands it. A minimum of camp rules are necessary and agreed upon by all as we look on them as "ways we have found to work best."

## The Promotion of One World

Someone has said that "We must remember that it takes both the black and the white keys on the piano to play *The Star Spangled Banner*," and many camps, realizing the importance of furthering better relationships between races, nationalities and creeds, have made a definite effort to provide broadening contacts for campers.

## ADDITIONAL READINGS

### GENERAL

#### BOOKS AND PAMPHLETS

A.C.A., The.—What Is It? ACA.

Benson and Goldberg: Camp Counseling McGraw-Hill, 1951, chap. 1.

Burns, Gerald: Program of the Modern Camp. Prentice-Hall, 1954, chaps. 1 and 2.

Dimock, Henley S.: Administration of the Modern Camp. Ass'n Press, chap. 1.

Dimock, Henley S., and Statten, Taylor: Talks to Counselors. Ass'n Press, chap. 1.

Established Camp, The—Girl Scouts, chap. 1.

Geist: Hiking, Camping and Mountaineering. Harper, chaps. 5 and 6.

Jacobs, Eveline E.: A Guide to Standards for Resident Camps for Crippled Children. National Society for Crippled Children and Adults, 1954.

Laws and Regulations Relating to Organized Camping. Publication of the State of California Recreation Commission, Jan., 1951, 187 pp.

Ledlie, John A. (Ed.): Young Adult and Family Camping. Ass'n Press.

McBride, Robert E.: Camping at the Mid-Century. ACA, 1953, 41 pp.

Osborne: Camping and Guidance. Ass'n Press, Preface and chap. 1.

Resident Camp Standards. Camp Fire Girls, 36 pp.

Sharp, L. B., and Partridge, De Alton: Some Historical Backgrounds of Camping. Bull. National Association of Secondary School Principals, vol. 31, no. 147, May, 1947.

#### MAGAZINE ARTICLES*

Burns, Gerald: A Short History of Camping. C.M., Feb., March, April, 1949.

Burns, Gerald: Trends in Camping. C.M., Nov., 1950.

Carlson, Reynold E.: Camping and Municipal Agencies. C.M., April, 1945.

Co-Ed Camping. C.M., May, 1950.

Dimock, Hedley G.: Coeducational Program in Brother-Sister Camps. C.M., Feb., 1953.

Freeberg, W., and Heffington, C.: State Laws and Regulations Affecting Camps. C.M., March, 1951.

* In this and in all other lists in this book, C.M. means *Camping Magazine*.

Gibson, H. W.: History of the Organized Camp. C.M., Jan., Feb., March, April, 1936.

Isserman, Ruth: Careful Pre-Grouping Leads to Happy Cabin Mates. C.M., Dec., 1952.

Joy, Barbara Ellen: The Role of *Real* Camping. C.M., May, 1947.

Joy, Barbara Ellen: Getting More Real Camping into Camps. Jr. H. and P.E., Jan., 1948.

Klusmann, Wes: And So to Camp. C.M., June, 1953. (Stresses real camping rather than city recreation.)

McClusky, Howard Y.: Camping Comes of Age. C.M., May, 1947.

McQuarrie, Agnes M.: A Camp of Firsts. Jr. H. and P.E., May, 1953. (Handicapped children.)

Ransom, John E.: Church Camp Aims and Objectives. C.M., May, 1950.

Sharp, L. B.: Give Camping Back to the Campers. C.M., March, 1940.

Smith, Leon H.: Family Camping—20 Year Success Story. C.M., March, 1952.

## DAY CAMPING

Camp Fire Girls: Guide for Day Camping. Camp Fire Girls, Inc.

Day Camp Book, The—Girl Scouts, 1942, #19–605.

Hutler, Albert A.: Day Camping Has A Mission. C.M., March, 1953.

obe, Mabel: The Handbook of Day Camping. Ass'n Press, 1949, 189 pp.

Proposed Standards for Day Camping. C.M., Jan., 1954.

## SCHOOL CAMPING

Baer, J. S.: They Go to School Outdoors. Parent's Magazine, Nov., 1947.

Clarke, James Mitchell: Public School Camping. Stanford U. Press, 1951, 184 pp.

Cleveland Heights Schools: Camping Education: Handbook for Teachers. Cleveland, Ohio, Cleveland Heights Public Schools, 1950.

De Witt, R. T., and Wilson, G. M. (Ed.): School Camping at Peabody. Peabody, 1953, 71 pp.

Donaldson, George W.: School Camping. Ass'n Press, 1952, 140 pp.

Extending Education through Camping, Board of Education. Life Camps, 1948, 127 pp.

Freeberg, William H.: Outdoor Education in Southern Illinois. Jr. H. and P.E., April, 1953.

Gilliland, John W.: School Camping. Association for Supervision and Curriculum Development, 1954, 64 pp.

Goodhue, Sarah E.: Camping—Introduction to School. Jr. H. and P.E., Jan., 1954.

Harrison, Paul E.: Education Goes Outdoors! Jr. H. and P.E., Dec., 1953.

Hoskin, Dale: Outdoor Education, A Handbook for School Districts. Los Angeles, Office of the County Superintendent of Schools, 1952, 82 pp.

MacMillan, Dorothy Lou: Outdoor Education. Laramie, Wyoming, Bureau of Education Research and Service, 1952, 25 pp.

Manley, Helen, and Drury, M. F.: Education through School Camping. Mosby, 1952, 348 pp.

Masters, Hugh B.: Values of School Camping. Jr. H. and P.E., Jan., 1951.

Michigan Department of Public Instruction, Lansing, Mich.: Youth Love Thy Woods and Templed Hills, 1949.

Place of Camping in Education, The—Report of Committee on Camping in Education. Jr. H. and P.E., Jan., 1950.

Raab, George E., and Shotts, J. Kenneth: A Close-Up of School Camping. Jr. H. and P.E., May, 1952.

Sharp, L. B., and Partridge, E. De Alton: Camping, and Outdoor Education. National Association of Secondary School Principals.

Smith, Julian W.: Community School Camping. Jr. H. and P.E., June, 1951.

Smith, Julian W.: By 1960 Every Boy and Girl A Camper. C.M., Nov. and Dec., 1951.

Smith, Julian W.: Status of School Camping. C.M., June, 1952.

Studebaker, John W.: The Role of the School in Camping. C.M., May, 1948.

Studebaker, John W.: Camping in Education and Education in Camping. School Life, July, 1948.

Thurston, Lee M.: Community School

Camping. Superintendant of Public Instruction, Lansing, Michigan, 1951, 39 pp.

University City Public Schools: Sixth Grade School Camping. University City, Mo., 1949.

University City Schools: School and Camping Curriculum. University City, Mo., 1951.

Vannier, Maryhelen, and Foster, Mildred: Teaching Physical Education in Elementary Schools. Saunders, 1954, chap. 14.

Vinal, William G.: The Outdoor Schoolroom for Outdoor Living. Vinal, 1952, 70 pp.

Weil, Truda T.: The School Camp-Out Outdoor Classroom. Jr. H. and P.E., May, 1950.

Willis, Margaret, and Alton, Mary J., Adult Study Camps. Franklin Press, 1951, 85 pp.

Every little boy has inside of him an aching void which demands interesting and exciting play. And if you don't fill it with something that is interesting and exciting and good for him, he is going to fill it with something that is interesting and exciting and isn't good for him.

THEODORE ROOSEVELT, JR.

## Chapter 2

# THE OBJECTIVES OF CAMPING

WHAT FACTORS have caused the phenomenal growth of camping within less than a century? What makes camping so attractive to youngsters that they eagerly look forward to it throughout the long months of winter? What does it offer to parents that they are eager to finance a share in it for their children? Why are camp directors, counselors and other staff members willing to devote their summer months to it? The answer cannot be summed up in one terse, clear-cut sentence, for camping has many facets to account for its popular appeal.

### Camp Provides an Ideal Learning Climate

Someone has said that "boys and girls do not go to camp to be educated but that they cannot camp without being so." Though this may not be literally true in the mental gymnastics sense of education, it is true in the broader sense, for the better camp offers the ultimate in opportunity to develop the mind, heart, eyes, ears, coordinations, appreciations, and even the soul of youth. Montaigne has said, "It is not a soul, it is not a body we are training up; it is a man, and we ought not to divide him into two parts."

If the above claims seem impossible to achieve in a brief period of two months at the most, let us consider life in a summer camp a bit more closely. Camp possesses a camper entirely. Here he eats, sleeps, works, talks and plays twenty-four hours a day, seven days a week with scarcely any outside influences to distract him. Camp is home, school, gang, church and playground to him in contrast to his city "assembly line" existence, where he passes along as on a conveyor belt to have spiritual development screwed on at one spot, a few nuts and bolts in his mind adjusted at another, then home for refueling and repairs, and off with the gang for some rounding out as to the "facts of life." Counting hours, two months spent in camp are the equivalent of a whole year in school.

In camp, the child lives in a realm of youth, in a true laboratory where he actually practices helping to plan by democratic processes for his own health, work and recreation. Camp program is not bound by tradition, a necessity to meet course and graduation requirements, but can be altered freely to satisfy the inner drives and needs of the participant. His attendance is voluntary, and this very lack of compulsion puts him in the mood to enter wholeheartedly into what he is doing, for he himself has helped to select it. Staff personnel are sympathetic and understanding, and the camper learns to appreciate them as real people who can laugh and play and enjoy carrying on camp activities just as he does. The informal, good-natured, mutually helpful atmosphere is a true revelation to the unfortunate camper who comes from a home full of tension and petty bickering. Contrary to those who feel that the efficacy of a medicine can be measured only by its bitterness, camp "climate" proves to be just right for nurturing unhampered growth and development.

A camper learns because he is dealing with things which have real meaning and interest for him. We all know how easy it is to emerge entirely unscathed from a boresome lecture, for we have a neat little trick of closing our eyes to unwelcome sights and our ears to information which has no meaning for us. But what camper can fortify any of his senses against the instruction he needs for next week's canoe trip or the wood lore which will enable him to select good firewood or berries and bark to stain the belt he has just knotted?

## Camp Is Chuck Full of Fun

To the camper, the main reason for coming to camp is to have fun, the fun which comes from adventure, learning new things, being with old friends and acquiring new ones, and cramming time with a glorious assortment of new accomplishments, friendships, and memories to last his life through.

Fun is the cornerstone for building children's ideals, as is so beautifully expressed in:

### THE BIRTHRIGHT OF CHILDREN*

All children should know the joy of playing in healthful mud, of paddling in clean water, of hearing birds sing praises to God for the new day.

They should have the vision of pure skies enriched at dawn and sunset with unspeakable glory; of dew-drenched mornings flashing with priceless gems; of the vast night sky all throbbing and panting with stars.

They should live with the flowers and butterflies, with the wild things that have made possible the world of fables.

They should experience the thrill of going barefoot, of being out in the rain; of riding a white birch, of sliding down pine boughs, of climbing ledges and tall trees, of diving head-first into a transparent pool.

They ought to know the smell of wet earth, of new mown hay, of sweet fern, mint, and fir; of the breath of cattle and of fog blown inland from the sea.

They should hear the answer the trees make to the rain and the wind; the sound of rippling and falling water; the muffled roar of the sea in storm.

They should have the chance to catch fish, to ride on a load of hay, to camp out, to cook over an open fire, tramp through a new country, and sleep under the open sky.

They should have the fun of driving a horse, paddling a canoe; sailing a boat. . . .

One cannot appreciate and enjoy to the full extent of nature, books, novels, histories, poems, pictures, or even musical compositions, who has not in his youth enjoyed the blessed contact with the world of nature.

HENRY TURNER BAILEY

## Camp Teaches Us New Skills and Ways of Spending Leisure Time

Wouldn't it be wonderful to receive the keys to a pastry shop and be told, "Help yourself—it's all yours"? Can you imagine the delight of punching a finger through a crusty cherry pie, pinching off the corner of a chocolate fudge cake or plunging both hands deep into the cookie jar and stuffing your mouth with the goodies? Camp gives such an opportunity, figuratively speaking, through its chance for exploration and experimentation in the social, manual, aesthetic and spiritual fields. It affords the time and tools to acquaint a person with varied interests, to contribute vocationally and avocationally to his present and future happiness.

He learns the self-respect and pride which come from doing a job well. Terminology changes from a dictatorial "do" to a suggestive "let's," and emphasis is placed on self-reliance, "stick-to-it-iveness" and thoroughness. Cleaning the unit house, slicing onions, or repainting the canoe become

* From Proceedings for 1946 of the National Education Association of the United States; reproduced by permission.

minor obstacles to be hurdled for the satisfaction of living in an orderly place, eating a delicious stew, or going on that canoe trip which is just around the last slap of the brush. No amount of salary or blue ribbons can compensate either camper or counselor for a lack of real purpose in what he is doing. Proudly he displays his badge of accomplishment won by hard work done with a will and with heroic good humor.

The courage to think, the daring to create, and the heroism to be original have marked explorers, scientists and thinkers from the beginning of time. So, with definite intent, camps instill in the camper a belief in himself and a desire to express himself creatively, for no one laughs at him or thinks him queer if he dares to be different and to stand for what he really thinks and feels.

Camp teaches that time is not so many suitcases to be stuffed full to overflowing with carelessly chosen this and that all rolled together in a jumble. Instead, it is a continuous interlude in which the thoughtful camper can find time and space for everything really worth while from his early morning dip to a stroll to the ridge to watch the sunset. Camp experiences afford him the resourcefulness to use leisure time beneficially and not regard it as a period to be dreaded because "I've nothing to do." The happiest people are those whose lives and minds are so crammed with projects and things that they are waiting to do that the day never holds enough hours. It is trite but true that there is really nothing boring—only bored people.

## Camp Adjusts Us Socially

The universe is balanced and adjusted so that each part works in harmony with all the others. The earth is held in its orbit by its relationship to other planets, and moon, sun and tides all behave as they do because of their pull and push on each other. We take their orderly synchronization for granted, but we can imagine the chaos that would result should one part decide to act up a bit. Camp, like the universe, is a cooperative community where people react on each other and where the actions of one have an effect upon all the others. Each person is accepted as an individual with powers as well as responsibilities equal in importance to everyone else's. The ideal in camp education is to give campers an approach to life which is individual and creative, yet also cooperative; to make people independent and self-reliant, yet harmonious and disciplined.

A camper learns that he may have a voice in making decisions, but not always his own way; that he has a right to his views, but that he must concede that same privilege to others.

When we place a number of jagged rocks in a smooth spherical container and shake them continuously for a time, they eventually become smooth and fit together compatibly. So it is with human relationships. Maladjusted, selfish and conceited campers, when put in a wholesome environment and guided by the loving hands of understanding adults, usually lose their rough edges and become socially adjusted, well-behaved youngsters with that inner sense of security and acceptance they have been so ardently seeking in their misguided ways.

## Camp Develops Good Habits and Good Character

In introducing herself, Maggie Owen, twelve-year-old autobiographer, writes, "I resolve to be a noble woman but 'tis hard to be noble in a house along with people not noble."* This offers a potent argument for placing children in an environment of high traditions and ideals.

Camp is a place where neatness of person, belongings, cabin and grounds is the expected thing and is brought about by the camper's own efforts as he wields a broom, plies a needle, or uses enough determination to wash— even behind his ears.

Camp is a place where the camper shoulders responsibility for his own welfare and happiness as well as that of his comrades. One taste of having the boat drift away because *he* failed to tie it properly or of having the whole group go to bed hungry because *he* forgot the food he had volunteered to bring, will cure him permanently of such misguided notions as "what I do is my own business."

Camp is a place where a camper must learn to stand on his own two feet, for counselors, although fond of him and anxious to help, are impartial and will not intercede for him as his parents may have done each time he got into difficulties.

Living with nature and being guided by nature's rules teaches him resourcefulness, originality and self-reliance. He learns to consider well before starting a project, but, having once started, to pursue it zealously to the end instead of leaving a clutter of half-finished undertakings about him, discarded like hot potatoes at the first waning of enthusiasm. He has a chance to develop qualities of leadership as well as followership; to be modest in winning, as well as courageous in defeat. He learns that many of the richest values in life have no monetary value at all. In fact, in a *good* camp he will be exposed to stimuli and opportunities for the development of almost every trait exemplified in the great.

## Camp Keeps Us Safe and Healthy

The instinct to protect its young is a characteristic of every animal, and the bear, the fox or the deer is willing to give its very life for that purpose. Parents, likewise, want the security and peace of mind which come from confidence that their children are well and happy and in trustworthy hands. This desire figures prominently in the mind of the camp administrator as he

* From *The Book of Maggie Owen*, by Maggie-Owen Wadelton, copyright 1941. Used by special permission of the publishers, The Bobbs-Merrill Company.

carefully plans safety precautions and time for eating, sleeping, resting, working and playing. These elaborate safeguards, together with vigorous physical life and a serene, yet exciting, daily existence, can do much to bring about glowing mental and physical health.

### Camp Develops an Interest in and Love for the Out-of-Doors

One can scarcely realize the lack of interest in and love for the out-of-doors many city children have until one sees a group of them turned loose with nature. Incredible though it may seem, even college students who aspired to be counselors have shown so little vision and curiosity about anything beyond their city experiences that the mere thought of existing through a weekend camping trip without benefit of radio or a game of bridge was enough to produce visions of dullest boredom. Appreciations come from the heart more than the mind; correspondingly, an appreciation of nature comes about only through living with it and making its intimate acquaintance.

### Camp Has Great Spiritual Values

In addition to formal and informal worship services, camp provides the experience of Christian living in a group. Camp is a suspended bit of time where one can *live* the experiences of nature, may listen to the wisdom of the elements, and hear God speak; a place where one may feel His touch in the soft breeze and see His handiwork in the intricasies of a spider web bejeweled with dew.

## ADDITIONAL READINGS

American Camping Association Standards. ACA, 1953, 8 pp.

Benson and Goldberg: The Camp Counselor. McGraw-Hill, chap. 2.

Bentley, Bradford M.: What Parents Expect from Camp. C.M., April, 1948.

Dimock: Administration of the Modern Camp. Ass'n Press, chap. 1.

Dimock and Statten: Talks to Counselors. Ass'n Press, chaps. 2, 5, 8 and 13.

Graham: The Girls' Camp. Woman's Press, chap. 2.

Ledlie and Holbein: The Camp Counselor's Manual. Ass'n Press, chaps. 1 and 2.

Marks of Good Camping: A Synthesis of Current Standards. New York, Ass'n Press, 1941.

# PART II

# The Camp Counselor

ENTHUSIASM
PERSONALITY
CHARACTER
INITIATIVE
SINCERITY
CHEERFULNESS
LOVE OF NATURE
SENSE OF HUMOR
SYMPATHY
IMPARTIALITY
LOVE OF CHILDREN
HEALTH
TACT

Ideals are like the stars; you will not succeed in touching them with your hands, but like the sea-faring man on the desert of waters, you choose them as your guides, and, following them, you reach your destiny.

CARL SCHURZ*

## Chapter 3

# THE COUNSELOR'S JOB

BEFORE DECIDING to become a camp counselor, you should size up the job from all angles, for only then can you be sure of that compatibility which makes work so fascinating that it scarcely seems work at all. Not everyone would be happy or successful as a counselor, and, for his own sake as well as that of the camp and campers, it is best to find it out as early as possible.

## CHARACTERISTICS OF A GOOD COUNSELOR

### Love of Children

A counselor is, as the name implies, one who counsels; you are parent, teacher, friend, companion and guide to your charges—the campers—and must have vision enough to see their possibilities and wisdom enough to anticipate and accept their limitations. You must be patient with and appreciative of the ungifted, handicapped or maladjusted child as well as the talented, amiable one, and you must have no illusions, realizing that both will turn up in the assortment of personalities with which you deal.

* Reproduced by permission of Coronet Magazine.

## A Leader and Model

You must be a leader who sets standards and goals and who, by your own example of honest, clean, straightforward living, inspire your group to emulate you. The ability to attract youngsters will be one of your most price-less assets, but woe be unto you if your underlying character be base and un-principled, for your very attractiveness will then but make your influence the more sinister. Campers pick up your bad habits and become boisterous, slangy, vulgar, complaining or boastful, as you set the pattern.

Pretense and sham are soon spotted in the intimacy of camp life. You might as well face it; everything you are and say and do will be carefully observed by your bright-eyed youngsters who will be quick to detect and equally quick to dislike hypocrisy. They will soon see through an attempt to cover up sloppiness by an "Oh, I just never could keep my room straight and my desk in order." Such a weak-kneed excuse as "I can't ever find time" is similarly revealing.

Youth is the period of hero worship, and a child's heart is full of faith and love. There is nothing in the world more painful or demoralizing to him than to discover that his beloved idol has feet of common clay and that his seeming virtues are but a thin veneer. Every prospective counselor must ask himself if he is willing to live like an inspiring rather than a disillusioning model.

## Youthful in Spirit yet Mature in Judgment

Camp directors demand counselors with mature judgment. This is not always a matter of chronological age, for some attain it early, while others live to be ninety-seven without ever having demonstrated a particle of it. Campers are too precious to entrust to those whose actions are determined by capriciousness and whim. Yet, with good judgment, you must retain that youthfulness of spirit which keeps you perennially curious and craving the new, so that, regardless of passing birthdays, you can still enjoy wading in a babbling brook, hunting the hiding place of a frog, or digging for pirates' gold with your campers.

## Skills

You must also take stock of your skills. What can you do? Is there any skill in which you excel? Is your tennis, camp cookery, swimming or wood-craft of such quality that you could teach it to someone else? Can you step into a group which is unduly alarmed over a snake and, by looking at it, give reassurance as to its harmlessness? Can you start a fire in a steady downpour to dry out sopping campers? Can you oversee packing a canoe so that it rides properly in the water? Can you tell poison ivy from Virginia creeper?

Even a program specialist needs a general backlog of wood lore and camping skills, for camping is essentially an outdoor process and a modern camp coordinates the many facets of program into one grand experience in out-of-door living. It isn't enough to "just love" nature; you must also know something about it. Can you imagine a doctor saying, "Nurse, look on page 199 in 'Surgery' by Dr. Cutsomemore and see if I'm to tie this thing to that"? An admittedly absurd example; but, if you think you can get away with anchoring a canoe with a French love knot, you are being equally impractical.

You may get along beautifully with children and your personality may just burst through at all points, but, unless you can *do* something, your charming smile will soon wear thin. You need not despair if you do not already know these things, for the main requirement is a willingness to learn, and there are numerous organizations and books to teach you, if, like the Dickens character, "Barkis is willin'." Many an excellent counselor acquires much of his skill and knowledge while on the job in camp.

## Fortitude

You must be able to find happiness in doing a job well and in serving others without thought of personal gain or self-aggrandizement. You must like hard work and plenty of it, for, except for brief periods of "time off," you will be on duty twenty-four hours a day. You must have enough persistence and will power to replace your wishbone with a backbone and must realize that genius is but 1 per cent inspiration and 99 per cent perspiration. If you are still convinced that you want to spend a summer where you can do something and be something worth while, then blessings on you, for in you and those like you lie the hope and future of the summer camp movement. A director knows that the success of his camp stands or falls by the quality of his counselors, and may all praise and honor go to him who attains the height of achievement in this chosen field.

## HOW DO YOU RATE?

If you would like to know your possibilities for success and enjoyment as a counselor, you may get some idea by rating yourself on the tests given here. Remember there is no use in cheating, for no one else will be so tolerant with you when you actually have to face the music. Check each trait in the proper column.

## *Health*

1. Stamina enough to last through a strenuous day

2. Regular, well-balanced meals

3. Regular sleep in sufficient quantity

4. Smoking not at all or moderately and in an appropriate place

5. Abstinence from intoxicating liquors (can't be tolerated at camp)

6. Sufficient vigorous exercise each day

*Acceptability to Others*

|     | Almost Never | Seldom | Half the Time | Usually | Always |
| --- | --- | --- | --- | --- | --- |
|     | 1 | 2 | 3 | 4 | 5 |

7. Pleasing and neat appearance

8. Cleanliness of person and clothing

9. Graciousness and mannerliness

10. Tact (ability to speak truthfully, but without offending or hurting others)

11. Cooperativeness (even when carrying out the plans of others)

12. Cheerfulness (without sulkiness and grouches)

13. Sense of humor (even when the joke's on you)

14. Good English (without excess slang or profanity)

15. Warmth (a friendly personality that attracts—not an iceberg)

16. Poise (even in emergencies or embarrassing situations)

17. Appreciation of the beautiful in deed, music, nature and literature

| | Almost Never | Seldom | Half the Time | Usually | Always |
|---|---|---|---|---|---|
| *Adaptability to Camp Life* | 1 | 2 | 3 | 4 | 5 |

18. Love of children (even the less attractive and "naughty" ones)
19. Enjoyment of hard work (even when it means soiling person and clothing)

20. Skills and knowledge of outdoor living (in rain, as well as sunshine)
21. Adaptability (can happily change plans to fit in with others or the weather)

22. Can "take" as well as "give" orders
23. Love of fun (can see possibilities for enjoyment in almost any situation)

24. Interest in a wide variety of fields

25. Specialization (ability to "do" at least one camp activity well)

26. Initiative (ability to get started without outside prodding)

27. Promptness at all appointments and in all tasks

28. Dependability (do *what* you say you will *when* you say you will)

29. Industry (want to be constantly up and doing)

30. Persistence (finish what you start with dispatch and thoroughness)
31. Curiosity (want to know about many things just for the sake of knowing)

32. Neatness (keep own living quarters neat and clean)

## EMOTIONAL MATURITY

"When I was a child, I spake as a child, . . . but when I became a man, I put away childish things" is not necessarily true of adults, who sometimes unconsciously cling to childish ways of thinking and acting. A person who harbors such childish traits is said to be emotionally immature, and, though frequently at a loss to understand why, he is often unhappy, for his behavior keeps him at constant odds with himself and his associates. He often feels mistreated and deprived of his just dues. Camp directors look upon a counselor's degree of emotional maturity as one of the surest indices of his probable success.

Your physical and mental maturity tell nothing of your emotional maturity, for the fact that you are strong as an ox or fleet as a deer does not indicate that you have learned to face up to life squarely and solve your problems in an adult way. Indeed, you may be a straight "A" student at school and still be unable to apply any of your intelligence to solve your own problems and help you deal more effectively with people. Here is a self-rating chart to help you estimate your emotional maturity.

| | Almost Never | Seldom | Half the Time | Usually | Always |
|---|---|---|---|---|---|
| | 1 | 2 | 3 | 4 | 5 |
| 1. Can you accept criticism without undue anger or hurt, analyzing it objectively and acting upon it if justified; disregarding it, if not? | | | | | |
| 2. Do you avoid being overcritical of others, denouncing them for each small fault, instead of judging them on the basis of over-all merit? | | | | | |
| 3. Are you genuinely pleased at the successes of your family and friends? Can you sincerely and wholeheartedly compliment them when deserved? | | | | | |
| 4. Do you refrain from listening to and repeating little items of gossip about others? | | | | | |
| 5. Watch your conversation for a few days. Do you talk largely about other people and things rather than about yourself? | | | | | |
| 6. Are you altruistic, often putting the welfare and happiness of others above your own? | | | | | |
| 7. Are you free from emotional outbursts of anger, tears, etc.? | | | | | |
| 8. Do you face disagreeable duties promptly and without trying to escape by playing sick or making excuses? | | | | | |
| 9. Can you stay away from home a month or more without undue homesickness? | | | | | |
| 10. Can you weigh facts and make decisions promptly, then abide by your decisions? | | | | | |
| 11. Do you postpone things you want to do now in favor of greater benefits or pleasure later? | | | | | |

| | Almost Never | Seldom | Half the Time | Usually | Always |
|---|---|---|---|---|---|
| | 1 | 2 | 3 | 4 | 5 |

12. Are you usually on good terms with your family and associates?

13. When things go wrong, can you objectively determine the cause and remedy it without alibiing for yourself and blaming it on other people or things?

14. When disagreeing with another, can you usually work out a mutually satisfactory agreement which leaves no hard feelings?

15. Can you enjoy informal social events without a "wallflower" feeling?

16. Do you get real enjoyment out of doing little things for others, even though you know they will likely remain unknown and unappreciated?

17. Do you wear neat but modest clothes with no tendency to gaudiness or overdress?

18. Are you ordinarily free from worry and remorse over past sins and mistakes that can't be remedied now?

19. When dealing with others, can you make decisions fairly, regardless of personal dislike or resentment?

20. When you are the leader of a group, do you use democratic methods and avoid dictating or forcing your will upon others?

21. Are you loyal to your friends, minimizing or not mentioning their faults to others?

22. Are you free from "touchiness," so that others do not have to handle you with kid gloves?

23. Do you act according to your honest convictions regardless of what others may think or say about it?

24. Do you have a kindly feeling toward most people, a deep friendship for some, and no unhealthy attachments to any?

25. Do you feel that you usually get about what you deserve? Are you free from a feeling that others "have it in for" you?

In order to make a rough estimate of your over-all emotional maturity, total all scores and divide by 25 (the number of items rated). If you have proceeded honestly and objectively, an average of 4 or 5 means that you are quite acceptable, a rating of 3 indicates you are about average, and an average of 1 or 2 shows that you are below average and should take drastic measures to bring your emotional development up to a par with your physical and mental maturity. Here are some suggestions to help you attain emotional maturity:

1. Face your deficiencies frankly and resolve to eradicate them just as quickly and completely as possible.

2. Set out to acquire definite skills and interests which have social rather than selfish or personal values.

3. Make it a point to associate with a number of emotionally mature people. Observe them and try to determine why they are so.

4. If you feel a need for help, seek someone qualified and discuss the problem frankly and openly with him. Be willing to act on any recommendations he may make.

5. Get wrapped up in causes so big and worthwhile that they completely absorb you, making you forget about yourself and your troubles.

## WHAT REWARD FOR THE COUNSELOR?

The foregoing traits characterize an ideal counselor and have no doubt convinced you by now that no camp director need waste his time looking for such a paragon of virtue on earth. Certainly no one but an angel with a halo perched over one ear and strumming on a harp of gold could qualify! Do not despair, however, for there is hope for anyone who scores fairly high on the tests and sincerely wants to score higher. Let us see what rewards you may expect for your summer's work. If you have had no experience and little special training, your monetary reward may be meager, but your board and room and the privilege of being in an environment for which campers pay several hundred dollars should not be passed over lightly. Camps sometimes pay a part or all of your transportation expenses, and some provide for having a part or all of your laundry done. There are few needs and little temptation to spend money in camp, so that whatever cash you receive is largely clear.

As a leader, you will have all the opportunity and stimuli you could ask to achieve the objectives of camping for yourself, for you will be spending your time in the same out-of-doors, under the same sun, and in the same friendly, cooperative atmosphere as do the campers.

You will gain close friends of all ages and will have an unparalleled opportunity to acquire the techniques of happy group living and develop into an emotionally mature person. You will have a chance to improve your own skills in camp activities and to secure practice in leadership and group work which may later prove a decided professional advantage to you. You will also derive the satisfaction that comes to all good teachers—the knowledge that you have made a real contribution to the growth and development of the youth of America.

# GETTING A JOB

## Making Application

When aspiring to be a counselor, you should investigate a number of camps, diligently reading their booklets and talking with former counselors and other interested persons about them. Select three to five of them which especially appeal to you because of their location (a different section of the country will broaden your horizons), length and dates of season, general policies, program, objectives, and types and ages of children served. Write a letter of inquiry to each, using a good quality stationery and your best handwriting or typing. Camp directors receive hundreds of applications each season, and those which are messy, incomplete or not clearly expressed land in the wastebasket where they rightfully belong. You must remember that you are trying to sell yourself and that merchandise always sells better when attractively packaged.

Make your letter sincere and human, rating yourself honestly and claiming only what you can live up to, for you must remember that, if selected, you will be called upon to give "proof of the pudding." Make the letter brief (not more than one single-spaced typewritten page) and supplement it with a data sheet including such information as your name, address, date of birth, education, present occupation, work experience, exact dates available, special camp training (courses in sociology, psychology, education, physical education, mental hygiene, first aid, aquatics, art, music, journalism, creative writing, geology, astronomy, dramatics, nature study, and so on). Many camps prefer to have this information on their own uniform blank forms, and if interested in your application will send back an application blank for you to fill out. Give names of three persons (teachers, ministers, employers and the like) who know you well and can speak knowingly of your qualifications; be sure to ask their permission before using their names. If the distance is not too great, indicate a willingness to go for an interview, for a face-to-face talk greatly helps both the prospective counselor and director decide how well you would fit into the particular situation. Include a stamped self-addressed envelope for convenience of reply.

If an interview is granted, you must make your appearance neat and well groomed, and on time to the minute. Enter in a poised, friendly manner, wearing your most sincere smile. Noisiness, overfamiliarity and boisterousness are most objectionable. Answer questions frankly and sincerely, and feel free to ask what information you wish about the camp and its policies. When the interviewer signifies that the interview is over, leave at once.

## Accepting a Position

You should not accept a position until you feel reasonably sure that it suits you well enough to command your utmost loyalty and devotion. Make sure you have a definite understanding as to remuneration, the exact dates you are expected to serve, your responsibilities and duties, rules regarding smoking, time off, and so forth. This is the time to clear up all questions and doubts, for after you have once accepted a job you must not quibble or "weasel" out of obligations. Answer all correspondence promptly, and do not leave your acceptance or rejection of an offer dangling unduly, for the director may lose other desirable applicants while you are trying to make up your indecisive mind. A signed contract is your word of honor that you can be depended upon to arrive on schedule, prepared to carry out all responsibilities agreed upon to the best of your ability.

## THE COUNSELOR'S DUFFEL

After you have accepted a job, you will in all probability receive various pieces of literature from the camp which you should read carefully to fix all pertinent details firmly in your mind.

When you have learned your duties, start intensive preparations to assume them. If possible, take, or at least audit, helpful school courses. You may find general camping books or books on special fields available in your school or public libraries, and you can purchase many worthwhile books at small cost as a beginning for your own personal library. One of the most helpful things a prospective counselor can do is to start a camping notebook in which to jot down every bit of useful information and every helpful idea that comes his way. A loose-leaf cover holding sheets $3\frac{3}{4}$ by $6\frac{3}{4}$ inches is suggested, for you can take it right to camp and carry it in your pocket or duffel. Get as much experience as possible in working with groups of children.

Whispering wind in the tree tops,
Shimmering sun on the lake,
From all of the world's occupations
A life in the open I'd take.*

* From *Deep-River Jim's Wilderness Trail Book*.
Permission by The Open-Road Publishing Co.

## ADDITIONAL READINGS

### BOOKS AND PAMPHLETS

Allen, Hazel K.: Camps and Their Modern Administration. Woman's Press, 1930.

Cheley, Frank H.: After All It's up to You. Wilde, 1935.

Graham: The Girls' Camp, chaps. 1 and 3.

Joy, Barbara Ellen: Professional Relationships in Camp. Camp Publications, no. 6.

Ledlie and Holbein: The Camp Counselor's Manual, chaps. 5 and 6.

Northway: Charting the Counselor's Course, chaps. 1 and 11.

Ott: So You Want to Be a Camp Counselor, chap. 2.

### MAGAZINE ARTICLES

Doherty, J. Kenneth: Counselor Rating Scale. C.M., Feb., 1950.

Graham, Abbie: The Pleasures of Being a Counselor. C.M., Jan., 1944.

Link, Robert E.: What Makes a Counselor. C.M., Jan., 1951.

MacPeek, Walter: The Counselor I Want for My Son. C.M., Feb., 1953.

Ransom, John E.: A Good Basis for Counselor Evaluation. C.M., Jan., 1952.

Trevethan, Percy J.: Guideposts to Sound Leadership. C.M., Dec., 1946.

Unkefer, Dudley: A Yardstick for Staff Members. C.M., Nov., 1946.

What Campers Want in a Counselor. C.M., June, 1953.

A great deal of the joy of life consists in doing perfectly, or at least to the best of one's ability, everything which he attempts to do. There is a sense of satisfaction, a pride in surveying such a work—a work which is rounded, full, exact, complete in all its parts—which the superficial man, who leaves his work in a slovenly, slipshod, half-finished condition, can never know. It is this conscientious completeness which turns work into art. The smallest thing, well done, becomes artistic.

WILLIAM MATHEWS

## Chapter 4

# THE COUNSELOR ON THE JOB

NOW THAT you have battled the currents, shot the rapids and come gliding into dock as a counselor, let us glance at the inside workings of a camp. The many varieties make it hard to generalize, but the following chart shows a typical organization for a medium-sized camp:

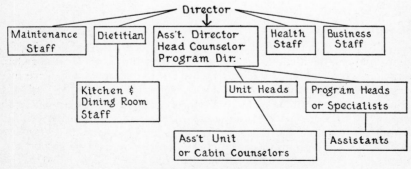

A sample camp organization.

## Camp Director

The highest authority is the Camp Director, who, in the final analysis, is responsible for everything that goes on in camp. Each member of the staff is accountable to him, even though working directly under another person to whom he has delegated responsibility, and no great decision involving the camp as a whole or the welfare of any person in it may be made without his knowledge and consent.

## Assistant Camp Director

The person second in command may be called the Assistant Director, the Head Counselor, or the Program Director, but, no matter what his title, he is the mainspring of the entire camp. He is accountable to the Camp Director and works directly with Program Specialists, Unit Heads, and often their assistants. The whole camp morale, as evidenced by both campers and staff, is largely dependent upon him. His specific duties vary according to the size and general set-up of the camp.

## Program Specialists or Department Heads

Program Specialists or Department Heads are usually found in larger numbers in long-term camps using a centralized system. They head such phases of the camp program as tennis, campcraft, arts and crafts, nature, sailing, trip camping, music or dramatics. Each may have assistants to help him promote and carry on his particular activity and to aid him in securing equipment and keeping it in good repair. He may schedule definite instructional periods for campers or may keep a schedule on which counselors and campers can sign up for his services as they want them. Sometimes he merely keeps himself available at certain hours on stage, tennis courts, archery range, or shop where counselors and campers can come for help or work on these activities. He sometimes has cabin duties or other responsibilities if the demands in his given field are not too time-consuming. Nearly all camps have at least a few specialists such as the waterfront staff, the nurse, and the dietition.

## Unit Heads and Assistants

A Unit Head is in charge of four to six cabins or tents, each housing four to nine campers. Each cabin has one or more Assistant Unit Heads or Cabin Counselors who live and work intimately with the campers and serve more or less as "camp parents." A Unit Head works closely with his assistants, helping them plan with the campers a unit program suited to their needs and interests. He arranges with his assistants such matters as division of duties and time off and serves as liaison with the Head Counselor. He must make sure that his Unit program coordinates with the over-all program of the entire camp. He may be known by another name as Village Head, Section Head, or the like, depending on the terminology used in his particular camp.

## THE DAILY SCHEDULE

Camp schedules are variable. Here is a sample one:

| | |
|---|---|
| 7:00 | Reveille |
| 7:30 | Breakfast |
| 8:00 | Clean up cabins and camp grounds |
| 9:00 | Activities |
| 11:15 | Recreational swimming |
| 12:00 | Dinner |
| 1:15 | Rest Hour |
| 2:15 | Activities |
| 4:15 | Recreational swimming |
| 5:45 | Supper |
| 6:45 | Evening activities (all-camp, unit, or cabin) |
| 8:45 | Cabin call. Get ready for bed |
| 9:00 | Taps (may be later for older campers) |

## A BIRD'S EYE-VIEW OF A COUNSELOR'S JOB

Once you have accepted a job, your responsibility, both to yourself and to those who have hired you, is to make good.

### Precamp Training

Most camps conduct a precamp training period of from three to ten days which gives the counselor a golden opportunity to get acquainted with the camp director and other staff members, the campsite, and the various but important camp customs and traditions. He will learn in detail what his duties are, and, though he will not yet know all the answers, he will have absorbed enough to face the arrival of the campers with confidence and ease. It is during this important period that the staff lay skeleton plans for the entire season.

### Personal Adjustment

You should try to adjust quickly and happily to camp ways, for you are to be a camper for some little time and have voluntarily closed the door on such pastimes as formal dances and afternoons at the corner drug store. You are on the threshold of a new and thrilling way of life and should determine to have a glorious summer ending with the sense of a job well done and the knowledge that you have won the genuine love and respect of a group of "small fry."

You must remember that you are a model now and should make sure that you are a good one. The double moral standard which makes it all right for counselors to do things that campers may not just won't work, for there is much truth in the old saying, "Your actions speak so loudly that I can't hear what you say."

You must be punctual and thorough in everything you do. If reports are due, you must faithfully keep data for them and turn them in on time.

In camp it's "One for all, and all for one," and the combined efforts of the entire staff must be directed toward just one thing—the greatest possible good for each and every camper. If you are a program specialist, you must make your activity an important and enjoyable one, but must beware of any exaggerated view of its role, for specialists can make themselves mighty obnoxious by attaching undue importance to themselves and their particular activity. Overzealous ones sometimes even vie with each other in a race for camper patronage. Each activity is important or it would not be included in the program, but not so much because of its intrinsic value as through the contribution it makes to the development of finer, more worthwhile campers.

### Personal Habits

Most camps request that counselors who smoke do so at designated times and in designated places and never in front of campers. Such requests are largely irrespective of moral issues and are mainly based upon the fire hazard produced by indiscriminate smoking in rural areas with only simple fire-fighting equipment. The use of intoxicants is prohibited on the campsite and often on time off, for even parents who themselves indulge are likely to object to placing their children in charge of counselors who do.

### The Counselor as a Self-Starter

Those ranking above you in the camp organization are responsible for everything that goes on and may be called to account for any blunders or errors in judgment you make. For this reason, you are urged to assert your initiative and be a self-starter, but you must also remember that it is your obligation to ask for help when faced by a "bigger than thou" problem or one which concerns camp reputation or the safety and health of personnel. Superiors are glad to help, and often their greater training and experience will immediately suggest a solution for your quandary. You should, however, beware of making a nuisance of yourself by being too dependent or by bothering others with little petty problems you can solve for yourself.

### Loyalty

You owe loyalty first, last and always to your camp and camp director. You have chosen this camp above all others because it seems most nearly to fit your objectives and ideals, but as in any situation, you will find things unpleasant to you in it. You should report situations which need correcting to those who can do something about them. If the situation is not corrected or if your dissatisfaction is so great that you cannot adjust yourself happily, you should consider asking for a release, for both you and the camp will be better off if you part company. You should never under any circumstances criticize to outsiders or other counselors and, of course, never before campers. Even when started as good-natured banter, griping will sooner or later prove ruinous to camp morale and also reflect personally on you, the griper. You should bear in mind the story of the man who was entrusted with a secret and, thinking to burst wide open if he did not tell it, dug a hole in the ground and whispered the secret into it. When the grass grew on the spot, the wind blowing through it broadcast his secret abroad. So it is with gossip and criticism.

### Note-Taking

Carry your camp notebook and pencil as regularly as you wear your shoes, for the worst lead pencil in the world is better than a good memory and many a conscientious, well-meaning counselor has failed because he "forgot." Add to your notebook constantly, jotting down games, program material, that new recipe for crab chowder, the sure way to keep Jackie's shoestrings from coming undone, and refresher notes about the needs, interests, accomplishments and signs of improvement on the part of your campers. You should drop in at the camp library now and then for new ideas or ways of doing things.

## THE CABIN COUNSELOR

As a Cabin Counselor you will be responsible for the health, happiness and welfare of your little cabin group and must be on the job twenty-four hours a day, except for the time you are definitely "off duty." During pre-camp training, go to the camp office and write down everything you can learn about the background of each of your campers.

### Your Campers' First Day

When the big DAY arrives, you must scrub yourself to a shiny glow, don your neatest outfit, steady your knees and sally forth with a smile to greet your campers. Refresh your memory as to their names and a few facts about each and try to associate a camper's name with his face quickly for nothing is more flattering to a person than to be called by name. Bid him a hearty welcome into your cabin, tell him your camp name and find out by what name he wants to be known. Help him locate his baggage, usher him into his cabin and help him select a bunk. Indicate the location of the washroom and lavatory, suggest that he change to camp clothes and introduce him to any of his cabin mates who have already arrived. Show him how to unpack and stow his belongings and make up his bed with approved square corners. If he has a list of his belongings pasted inside his trunk, as many camps recommend, ask him to check off the articles as he unpacks; report any discrepancies to the camp office immediately. If any of his gear has not been legibly and indelibly marked, lay it carefully aside for him to mark as soon as there is a brief gap in the program. Campers usually feel more at home when they are all neatly tucked into their new quarters.

In most camps all campers' medicines and first aid equipment are collected and turned over to the nurse or doctor for it is preferred that anyone needing attention, no matter how minor, be referred to the professional person in charge of the campers' health. Even counselors do not render any sort of treatment except in case of emergency. Collect return trip tickets, money, and other valuables and make proper disposal of them at the camp office.

Many camps have all campers check in with the doctor or nurse and meet with the waterfront staff for classification and preliminary instruction in waterfront procedures. Be sure that your group fits in with the established routine in a way most helpful to these busy staff members.

Think of ways to break the ice and start your campers off on friendly chatter; see that all are drawn into the conversation, giving a little extra encouragement to any who seem shy. Request a timid camper to do some little task for you to make him feel needed or ask an old camper to take him to see the council ring, the waterfront, the nature house or to feed the pet rabbits or fasten up the cabin sign which has loosened since last year. As soon as most of your group have arrived, start to weave the members into group unity by playing a get-acquainted game, having a marshmallow roast, selecting a cabin name and yell, or going on a tour of the campsite. Gather them around for a brief discussion of possibilities for program during their stay in camp and find out what different ones of them would like to do. Plan something specific and mutually exciting to look forward to the next day or that afternoon if there is still time.

Before the first meal, go over dining room procedures with them and hold a little forum on good table manners and proper dining-room conduct. Children may come from homes where they have not learned these things and are easily embarrassed if they make a mistake. Stress the importance of cleanliness and neatness at all times, especially when in the dining room. Assign old campers to wait on tables and carry on other duties until newcomers have a chance to get into the swing of things.

A child whose parents have not brought him to camp should write a card home telling of his safe arrival before the first mail goes out. In some camps cabin counselors write a friendly little card or note to the parents too. Parents are naturally lonely and a little fearful as their youngsters launch themselves into a new life, often away from home for the first time, and it is very reassuring to them to know your name and feel that you are sincerely interested in their child's happiness and welfare.

Arrange bed time early the first night for youngsters will be more tired than they realize from the excitement and trip. Keep them happily occupied with quiet games, a good bed-time story, a short discussion of such items of mutual interest as mail call, the main camp rules and why rules are necessary for the general welfare of the camp family. The whole solution to the "rules" situation is to let the campers help make those within their authority. There will be some rules which have been set up and are not subject to alteration, but the right approach usually secures camper support as you show them why they are necessary and really for the benefit of everyone. It isn't hard for Tommy to see that if he doesn't wash his share of the dishes, someone else will have to work overtime; if he doesn't bring his canoe back on time, someone else who is waiting will be cheated; or that he will be too tired to enjoy the cook-out he's planned for tomorrow if he doesn't go to sleep on time tonight. Wedge in several short discussions during the first few days concerning such topics as camp kapers (duties), cooperation in keeping living quarters and grounds spick and span, traditions and special events in the camp program, the camp council and how it works, waterfront procedures, fire drill, safety at all times, sick call, and so forth.

Keep your campers active and busy during the first two or three days for that is the peak of the danger period from homesickness.

Watch your campers carefully for signs of contagious disease, especially during their first few days in camp, for it is easy to see what a catastrophe for the whole camp an epidemic would be.

Try especially hard to get off to a good start with your cabin group in that all-important first week, for it may well determine the tenor of the whole summer. Make opportunities for informal chats and spend as much time with your campers as possible, giving special attention to those who fail to fit in readily. The lonely camper may need help in finding a camp pal or in adjusting himself in other ways to his new mode of life. Your own happiness and sense of well-being depend on a feeling of comradeship with your group, so work hard to get it.

## Cabin Morale

As the days go by, try to weld your cabin into an intimate little family group which fits harmoniously into the bigger family, the unit, or camp proper. All counselors should share enthusiastically in the planning and activities of their campers.

You must be quick to seize opportunities to help your campers grow in character, appreciations and insights; but you must, at the same time, exercise patience, for long-established traits do not miraculously change overnight.

## Camp Housekeeping

Since one of camping's principal objectives is to teach a camper self-reliance, he must learn to keep his own personal belongings in trim. "A place for everything and everything in its place" must be the order of each and every day; since many campers have learned virtually nothing of house-keeping practices at home, you will need to demonstrate and give specific help with correct techniques and will have to supervise closely to see that they are carried out.

Right after breakfast is a good time for members of the entire cabin to straighten possessions and help tidy the abode and adjacent grounds, singing, bantering and enjoying themselves the while. Your attitude here is important, for if you enjoy work and show it by pitching in with a will, your campers will follow suit and all will soon learn how nice it is to live in a clean, orderly cabin. Try to be especially happy and cheerful as you go about your tasks.

On rainy mornings, make up beds right away to keep out dampness. On sunny days, turn back or hang out sheets and blankets to air, bringing them in before five o'clock to avoid evening dampness. Air and turn mattresses and put on fresh linen each week, making up beds with square, hospital-style corners.

Each person should hang or fold his clothing neatly away, tidy his personal effects, and collect his soiled clothing in a bag, ready to send to the laundry. Plying a needle prevents a rip from becoming a tear, and a button sewed on now may prevent later embarrassment or inconvenience. Most camps have tent or cabin inspection one or more times a day, usually unannounced, to encourage continued orderliness. Campers try harder if some little symbol of merit for neatness such as a cardboard broom or a special banner is hung above their cabin door. Then watch them use group pressure to bring an untidy cabin mate into line!

Teach your charges never to borrow toilet articles and towels and to cut other borrowing to a bare minimum, and never to borrow without the express permission of the owner as "borrowing" isn't the correct name for such a practice.

Campers who do their own laundry may need a few helpful hints on how to prevent tattle-tale gray.

In many camps, campers help with various chores, sometimes in an effort to cut down expense and always to create in them an appreciation of the dignity and respectability of work. Such duties may include keeping unit showers, latrines, cabins, unit houses, and main lodge in order, collecting and disposing of trash, helping prepare vegetables and fruit, setting tables, waiting on tables, and washing dishes. They will need counselor help to see that this work is done thoroughly. Try to help them to devise ways to do it more quickly and efficiently.

Stress the importance of placing all waste in conveniently located recep-tacles and point out how ludicrous it is to throw trash on the ground today, for them or a fellow camper who is serving as grounds keeper to pick up tomorrow.

Let campers help you work out a rotating kapers (duties) chart, using some such scheme as this:

|  | Mary | Helen | Jean | Sarah | Peggy | Joan | Mary |
|---|---|---|---|---|---|---|---|
| Clean-up squad—sweep cabin floor.................... | SU | M | TU | W | TH | F | S |
| Woodsmen—clean out ashes in fireplace, bring in wood.... | M | T | W | TH | F | S | SU |
| Table setters—set tables and help prepare vegetables.... | TU | W | TH | F | S | SU | M |
| Hoppers—wait on and clear tables.................. | W | TH | F | S | SU | M | TU |
| Ground keepers — clean up campsite................. | TH | F | S | SU | M | TU | W |
| Kitchen police—help do dishes | F | S | SU | M | TU | W | TH |
| Unit duty—help at the Unit house................... | S | SU | M | TU | W | TH | F |

There are other ways to decide who will do kapers such as drawing "out of a hat," or having campers names listed on a wheel, then spinning another superimposed wheel with the jobs listed on it (campers do the jobs which stop opposite their names). A little thought will help you find some interesting way to make these exciting adventures instead of dreaded chores.

The most careful plan for sanitizing dishes can be totally lost by improper table setting. See that hands are washed clean with soap and water (have the children stop to wash their hands on their way up to set tables) and that they do not touch parts of the dishes that will have contact with food or a camper's mouth (edges of glasses and cups, "business ends" of forks, spoons, knives, and the like).

*Dish Washing.*    When campers wash their own dishes, they can make a game of it and, with plenty of lively singing and joking, make it fun instead of a nuisance. Since there are several duties involved, rotate them as in a kapers' chart, or let them draw lots each time.

Detail one counselor to see that water is heating, ready for use as soon as the meal is over, for dishes wash much more easily when there is no time for food to dry on them. A counselor should handle all hot water, for campers are too likely to scald themselves or someone near. Here is a suggested list of assignments:

1. First scraper—uses rubber scraper to remove food from dishes.
2. Polisher—supplements efforts of first scraper, using paper napkins. Stacks dishes into piles of plates, cups, etc., for washing.
3. Dish washer—washes dishes and wipes off tables.
4. Rinser—arranges dishes in long-handled, wire dish-drains with trays to catch excess water and carries them to the sterilizer.
5. Sterilizer (a counselor)—lowers dishes, still in dish-drain, into boiling water (170° to 180° F.) for one to two minutes or into warm water with sanitizing agent added.
6. Sweeper—cleans around tables after dishes are covered or put away.

Sand (used dry) or wood ashes (with quite hot water) make good substitutes for scouring powder on a trip, and silverware can be thrust up and down in the ground a few times to give it a preliminary cleaning. Since water is often scarce around an outdoor campsite, it is well to wipe the food out of the dishes as much as possible before immersing them in the dishwater.

Hot, soapy water is best for the washing, which should take place in the following order: glassware, silver, dishes and, finally, pots and pans. Have enough hot water available to replace the dishwater as it becomes greasy or cold. It is more sanitary to immerse dishes in scalding water and let them air-dry as they stand in the racks, than to use dish cloths to dry them, except for silverware and pots and pans which might rust. When sanitizers are used on dishes, any taste left may be rinsed off with boiling water.

Wash towels and dishcloths used on dishes after each use and boil them as least once a day.

### Cleanliness

Camp is no excuse for disregarding personal cleanliness, for dirt is the common outlaw of camp life and the sun should never set on a dirty camper. Of course, digging a bean hole or clearing a new trail will make a camper look bedraggled, but it isn't anything a little soap and water won't cure. A swim does not substitute for the daily warm soap bath, which can be had even on the trail, for a pan bath will do when nothing better is available. Washing with soap also has value as a good general preventative against infection. Counselors should make a daily inspection of their campers for cleanliness, scanning particulary the ears, elbows and neck.

One of civilization's unwritten laws is that hands must be washed before

meals and after going to the toilet. See that teeth are brushed in the morning and again before retiring, and toothbrushes hung in an airy place to dry.

Urge girls with long, "stylish", fingernails or toenails to clip them right away, for they are inappropriate for camp life, catch on everything, collect dirt, often scratch the wearer or others, and eventually get jaggedly broken off anyway. Everyone's fingernails should be inspected for proper trimming and cleanliness.

Cabins, units or whole camps often enjoy a special clean-up day when everyone washes his clothes, helps to clean up the cabin and grounds, and then finishes off with a shampoo and hot bath for himself.

## Clothing

Campers should wear clothing appropriate to the weather and the activity. Since mornings and evenings are usually cool, extra clothing is needed then. Shoes should be worn at all times, and campers should be completely "waterproofed" when venturing out on rainy days.

Trading or selling personal possessions is banned, for parents often fail to share in the enthusiasm of the campers for the "bargains" they have made.

## Health and Safety

Since the health of the camper is of the greatest importance, it behooves each member of the staff to appoint himself a committee of one to see that camp facilities for safeguarding health are used—not misused. The close contact of the cabin counselor with his little group puts him in a particularly advantageous position to help in this respect.

A set of scales was once considered the best yardstick for measuring the benefits of camping, for a gain in weight was assumed to represent a corresponding gain in health. We now know this to be in error, for any gain beyond normal for a growing child would benefit only the underweight. For the average child it indicates merely a superabundance of sweets and starches, adding healthful weight to none and burdening the already overweight with additional pounds.

Another far too prevalent idea was that, in order to be and look like a real camper, one must get as sunburned and weather beaten as possible and prove his toughness by scorning attention to such minor (?) details as scratches blisters and mosquito bites. Early campers displayed their scratched, flea-bitten appearance with pride, for, to their warped reasoning, these scars of battle were evidence that they had been "roughing it" and could take it.

*Before Camp Opens.*    During pre-camp training you will have learned much of the health set-up of your camp. Most camps have one or two nurses on duty and a physician in residence or on call. The headquarters of the health department is in the infirmary or health lodge, where there is space to take care of campers needing extra food, rest or special treatment.

You should study the health records of your campers. If a youngster has been at camp before, there will be reports from other summers; for all, there will be a health questionnaire filled out by the parents before camp opened which includes a record of past illnesses, operations, food allergies, colds, sleep-walking tendencies, enuresis (bed wetting), and so forth. The child, in common with all campers and staff, will have been required to be ex-amined by his physician within a few days of the opening of the camp. One of the most important things to notice about him is whether or not his ac-tivities are to be restricted, such as no swimming, no strenuous sports, or no long trips. It is your responsibility to aid in seeing that these instructions are carried out.

*Each Day.*    Each morning, while campers are dressing, eating breakfast or doing cabin clean-up, you should scan them for signs of ailment or injury. Note such symptoms as headache, sore throat, indigestion, sneezing, cough, fever (as indicated by a hot, flushed skin), pimples, skin rashes, swellings, cuts or other irritations, as well as such signs of fatigue as listlessness, irritability, excitable talking, undue noisiness, loss of weight, or paleness. Refer a suspect to the nurse immediately, escorting him there if necessary, for campers sometimes shy away from trips to the infirmary lest they be banned from swimming or some other favorite activity. Show him the wisdom of taking a few moments now to forestall what might develop into an illness of days or even weeks if neglected. Some camps require counselors to turn in accident-health reports each morning so that the nurse can note and call in any campers needing further attention.

When signs of fatigue are rather widespread in a group, it indicates an overstrenuousness of the whole tempo of life, and a light schedule is ad-visable for a few days with extra time provided for rest and sleep.

Sunburn can be a serious as well as painful thing. Teach campers to ac-quire their deep chocolate-brown gradually, exposing themselves only a few moments the first day with a few moments added each succeeding day. Set a good example by not going out to fry yourself once-over lightly in one con-centrated dose. Sun bathers should wear sun glasses or cover their eyes with a towel.

*Friends in the Infirmary.*    It is the custom in most camps to send a camper home or to the hospital if his illness is likely to last more than a few days or if it is of a serious nature at all. However, minor illnesses may often keep him in the infirmary for what may seem like wearisome hours. Thoughtful friends can make the time pass faster by such little remembrances as a round-robin letter, a diary or account of what they are doing, a home-grown poem, a handmade gift from the arts and crafts shop (particularly one with his name on it), or a serenade. A visit during visiting hours is welcome if the nurse permits it; if not, just waving to him through the window helps. With the approval of the nurse, keep him supplied with puzzles, a radio, light reading matter or come in and tell or read him a story. If he's able, he'll enjoy working on a crafts project, his scrapbook, making favors for a group party, or labels for the nature trail. Keep him reminded that all of you miss him and are anxious to have him back again.

## In the Dining Room

Counselors and campers must arrive spic and span and on time for meals. Counselors usually act as hosts, serving the plates family style. Some camps favor having campers sit with their own counselors, while others rotate them so that each acquires a larger circle of acquaintances. Singing or another form of grace helps quiet campers down and puts them in the mood for proper dining-room decorum.

Camps pride themselves on their carefully planned and well-cooked menus, but it is of little avail if campers are permitted to pick and choose what they eat. Food allergies must be allowed for, but you should ascertain from the health staff that they are genuine and not just a way to avoid eating foods for which the camper has a real or imagined dislike. Nearly everyone can and should eat at least a small portion of whatever is on the menu. For this purpose, such devices as forming a "Jack Sprat Club," open only to those who clean their plates, are useful. This practice is not an undue hardship if only small portions are placed on the first serving. Seconds and even thirds are available for those who wish them, but portions should be saved back for the slower eaters so as to provide no incentive to gulp down the first serving as rapidly as possible. Seconds must be asked for politely.

A crowd of girls usually includes a few "reducers," for as Mr. Franklin P. Jones has said, "Women are never satisfied. They are trying either to put on weight, take it off, or rearrange it." Overweight campers may be encouraged to cut down *sensibly* on their intake of carbohydrates and fats; the majority of reducers, however, should be discouraged in their attempts, for camp life is so strenuous that large quantities of energy-yielding foods are needed. The problem may sometimes best be handled by a group study of dietetics including the values of a varied and well-balanced diet. When youngsters understand the importance of each item, they usually become quite cooperative about their eating. Some camps maintain special diet tables for those with idiosyncrosies or those who need to gain or lose weight.

Keep conversation sprightly and cheerful, yet genteel and conducted in low tones. Interesting (but not overexciting) table talk keeps minds busy and, since most of us are limited to doing but one thing at a time, minimizes hurrying and bolting food. Conversation should be general so that all may participate, and none should be allowed to monopolize it; buddies must be separated if they persist in misbehaving. Talking to those at another table is always in poor taste, and no one except hoppers or those whose duties demand it may leave the table until all have finished. Obviously, nothing should be scheduled immediately after the meal, lest it cause campers to race to get through in time for it.

Observe all the precepts of good table manners, such as not talking with the mouth full, breaking bread into quarters and buttering only one portion at a time, cutting meat a piece at a time, proper handling of knife and fork, and the like. Comments about the food and griping or bickering of any sort are not conducive to good digestion and are strictly off limits. Do not embarrass a camper who has violated a rule of etiquette by reproaching him in front of others; it is better to take it up with him privately for his misdemeanor is more likely to be due to lack of ease, desire for attention, or just not realizing the implications rather than a desire to misbehave.

Singing (especially of songs requiring movements) distracts the slower eaters and retards clearing tables, washing dishes, and putting the food away. Many camps follow the practice of having the singing led by a stipulated song leader after everyone has finished eating.

*Eating between Meals.*    Camp meals are planned to include enough sweets to satisfy normal needs, and campers are therefore not encouraged to supplement them with soft drinks, candy and other goodies which may greatly counteract the good effects of the carefully planned diet. If permitted at all, a limit should be put on the daily amount of such items and should be rigidly enforced.

Despite requests to the contrary, many parents seemingly must demonstrate their love by sending their children "gooey" knick knacks from home. Camps sometimes solve the problem by warning the parents in information sent them before camp that such food will be returned unless they care to send enough for the whole cabin group to substitute for a regular dessert. Others simply save the individual packages until enough have accumulated to make a treat for all. Parents may be appeased by suggesting that they send their child fruit, a piece of camp equipment, or things other than food as a token of their affection.

## Rest and Sleep

*Rest Hour.*    As Sancho Panza said, "God bless the man who first invented sleep," and busy camp life makes campers and counselors breathe a sigh of thankfulness for the rest hour which usually comes right after lunch to rejuvenate them for the remainder of the day. It is a siesta when everyone engages in sleeping, reading, story telling, playing quiet games, writing letters or just "settin' and dreamin'." There is no reason for either campers or counselors to dislike it, for the main idea is to rest and relax and allow others to do the same. There are many interesting things to do that provide relaxation without creating a disturbance if one doesn't want to sleep. Absolute quiet must prevail so that those who want to sleep may do so. You as a counselor will need to rest, too, so stay with your campers to set an example of how to use this valuable period wisely. Your camp may call the rest hour by some other name, such as Siesta or FOB (Feet On Bed and Flat On Back).*

*Sleep.*    Camp life is so strenuous that only those who get plenty of sleep can keep up and enjoy it to the fullest. Administering to this need constitutes one of your main responsibilities. The following amounts of sleep (in addition to the one-hour rest period are recommended:

| Ages | Hours of Sleep |
|------|----------------|
| 6– 7 | 11 |
| 9–11 | 10½ |
| 12–14 | 10 |
| 15–17 | 9 |
| Staff | 8 |

* Smith, Billie F.: How 40 Camps Handle Rest Hour. C.M., Dec., 1952.

Children, like adults, differ in their reactions to the excitement and "busy-ness" of camp life, so some may need rest over and above this amount.

As previously mentioned, a common mistake has been to try to crowd too many activities and periods of excitement into the camp day. This is especially true as the last weeks of camp draw near and each counselor grows intent on squeezing some highlight of his particular activity into a last "round-up" of water carnivals, arts and crafts exhibits, horse shows, and what not. The wise camp tries to adopt the saner practice of spreading these special events throughout the entire summer so that campers can leave camp rested and healthy instead of completely frazzled out.

Children sleep better when healthily fatigued, but moderation is ad-visable in all things, and too much excitement and tiredness make sleep fitful and restless.

*Taps.*     The time just before taps affords further opportunity to draw your little cabin group into a compact unit. Everyone should be washed and have his teeth brushed and latrine trip completed in time for a few moments of group planning, evening devotions, discussion, inactive games, or a peaceful, tranquil bedtime story before "lights out." Since it isn't fair to expect campers to change from one mood to another too suddenly, no roughhouse, horseplay or exciting adventure or ghost stories are permissible; only calm, soothing activities which lure the sandman are in order.

As with all rules, you must be firm about enforcing the time for lights out and quiet. Set the standard from the first night in camp. You must not dash out of the cabin at breakneck speed the instant the last camper hits the bed, but should wander leisurely about with a special "goodnight" for each, seeing that he is tucked in and using blanket pins for very small tots who tend to squirm about and expose various odds and ends of their anatomy to the weather. If you are on duty in the cabin or unit, you must stay until the time designated, for if you make a practice of leaving as soon as you think the campers are asleep, they'll play possum until you are gone and then pan-demonium will break loose. Your campers need to feel sure that you are near, ready to help if they become frightened or need you. Night raids on other cabins and impromptu moonlight excursions are definitely out, and night trips to the latrine should be quick and quiet, for there is to be no dis-turbance of any kind until reveille.

## Reveille

When the rising signal sounds, you should be the first out of bed. All should get up immediately to allow ample time to arrange beds and get properly washed and dressed and be on time for breakfast. This will be no trick at all during the first few days campers are in camp for they'll be so excited they'll wake at the crack of dawn and will need to be restrained so others can sleep. If you're going out extra early for a bird walk, don't wake the whole camp as you go by.

You may need to help younger campers manipulate buttons and hair-brushes, but should encourage them to do it themselves as soon as they can. A morning dip may be permitted, but it should certainly not be required for many people react unfavorably to cold water and exercise so soon after rising. For the same reason, a compulsory "daily dozen" before breakfast is frowned upon.

## Visitors' Day

Visitors are a more or less disturbing factor to the smooth-running routine of camp, so that there are usually specified hours and days for them to come. You must be sure to let your own prospective guests know just when to arrive and exactly what time you will have available to spend with them.

Too frequent visits from a camper's parents are prone to take his attention from camp activities and often have a tendency to make him homesick; they also defeat the important objective of emancipating him from his possibly too doting or domineering parents. Therefore, most camps encourage only a minimum of them.

When visiting day arrives, everything from the camp grounds down to Joe's elbows must be looking their best. Campers must be neat and clean and on hand to greet their parents and show off the camp. You, yourself, are a host and must be cordial, friendly and helpful to all and available for a few moments' conversation with the parents of each of your particular campers. Put your best foot forward, for parents will be much happier if they are favorably impressed by their child's counselor. When talking to them, remember that you have one thing in common—the welfare of the camper. Avoid gushing and insincere praise, for parents are fully aware that their children fall far short of being angels. You may comment casually on good points or signs of improvement you have noticed, but must never let yourself be drawn into severe unfavorable comment. If parents persist in trying to engage you in such a discussion, refer them to the camp director or head counselor.

This is a time for campers, too, to learn to be good hosts or hostesses. Encourage them to spare a few moments to be gracious to the parents and guests of other campers as well as to their own.

Avoid showing favoritism and share your time with all the parents. If offered money or expensive presents, tactfully but firmly refuse, explaining that it is against camp policy.

## Time Off

All camps give counselors some time off—usually an hour or two each day, and a longer period each week or two weeks. You probably learned the particulars of this when you signed your contract. This interlude can and should be of great benefit to both you and the camp. Dealing in such intimacy with many personalities exacts a severe toll in nervous and emotional energy and causes patience to grow short, emotions to boil over at trifles, and the sense of humor to forsake its owner completely. Counselors are sometimes unaware of this gradual accumulation of emotional and nervous fatigue and become so attached to their jobs as to be loathe to leave them, even when given time off. Such zealous overdevotion to duty is a sad mistake and sooner or later will produce a dull, cross, bearish person who cannot possibly do his job effectively.

It is important for you to get your mind off camp and everything pertaining to it. You may write letters, make fudge, do your laundry or mending, or go off with a companion or two to roller skate, dance or attend the movies, or you may engage in any other favorite pastime which will temporarily erase camp from your mind. When out in public you must remember that you represent your camp and must conduct yourself so that your actions reflect creditably upon it.

Many small towns do not regard shorts favorably and so it is better to wear ordinary street clothes, although slacks are usually acceptable for women counselors. Drinking in public, driving recklessly and any sort of boisterous or socially unacceptable conduct are in very poor taste. Treat the citizens of the town courteously and fairly, in fact, the same way you expect them to treat you.

Permission to use camp equipment may be arranged for and a good workout on the tennis courts or a boat trip will relax those kinks in your brain and emotions. Use all the time you have, but do not sneak off early or return late, and, of course, you are not priviledged to spend the day before your departure in preparing to leave or the day after your return in recuperating and talking about the big time you had.

## RELATIONSHIPS IN CAMP

### With the Director

The average director is a public-spirited person motivated by a desire to aid constructively in the development of the youth of America. He is sincerely interested in having his camp do a fine job and is vitally concerned with the welfare and happiness of every person in camp, including that of his staff. He is as genuinely interested in each counselor's personal happiness and success as he is in that of the campers, for he knows that it will be reflected in the counselor's relationships with his campers.

Establish and maintain friendly relationships with him, consulting him about problems, but not making yourself a leech, and remembering that there are many important matters demanding his time and attention. Give him complete loyalty at all times. Straighten out any misapprehension you may have by seeking a frank and friendly talk with him. You should try to look at things through the director's eyes and you will often thus gain an entirely different slant which will satisfactorily explain whatever is troubling you.

## With Staff

The esprit de corps of the staff group largely determines camp morale, for counselors cannot do their work well when laboring under tension and vague feelings of insecurity and frustration. Campers are quick to perceive lack of unity in the staff, and it is likely to become a source of comment and disharmony among them as they side with one or another. It therefore behooves each counselor to exert himself to fit in with the group and do his part to keep it harmonious and cooperative.

A morsel of petty gossip or a careless comment can cause the first break in staff morale, for, after the malignant seed has been planted, the cancerous words soon work up to a first-class "feud." Avoid making disparaging remarks about the eccentricities of others, for, unless you are indeed a rare person, it will not be hard for the maligned one to retaliate by finding a vulnerable spot. Before we can develop tolerance in campers, we must first master it ourselves. We must learn to focus on the good things in people and screen out imperfections.

> Do not look for wrong and evil—
> You will find them if you do;
> As you measure for your neighbor
> He will measure back to you.
> Look for goodness, look for gladness—
> You will meet them all the while;
> If you bring a smiling visage
> To the glass, you meet a smile.
>
> AUTHOR UNKNOWN

Strive to get a complete picture of camp and try to fit yourself and your activity into its proper niche. (Notice that the word is "niche," not "pedestal.") Cultivate a sincere interest in the work of other counselors and avoid such boorishness as sneering at the handiwork of the arts and crafts counselor or the perfect chops and lobs of the tennis counselor. Lack of appreciation usually comes from ignorance and is pardonable only if you are willing to learn. Asking another counselor for coaching and help is a sincere compliment to him and will help to brighten his day and establish good relationships.

Every counselor must be modest about his own accomplishments, for conceit is never an endearing trait. Do not presume or ask special favors from staff members or the camp management. Be punctual, pull your share on the oar, and consider nothing too menial for your lily-white hands even though it be as distasteful as cleaning the latrine. It is said that when moving a piano, a certain number get behind and push while one invariably picks up the stool to carry. A good staff member is a pusher, not a stool carrier.

Make friends with many of your fellow staff members, and avoid cliques and special pals, for such relationships are narrowing and likely to cause unfavorable comment and jealousies. Counselors should do things together in varying groups—picnicking, canoeing, reading, singing or chatting.

Be a trustworthy, unbiased friend to your campers, ever willing to help, patient and kind, yet firm. Campers may try you out at first, and your goose is cooked if you fail in the test. Avoid "pets" and show your interest in each by appreciating each constructive thing he does, even though you sometimes have to look for it with a microscope. Don't expect too much of youngsters, for you cannot judge them by adult standards.

Take your job (but not yourself) seriously and keep the objectives of camping ever before you. All want popularity, but you will definitely not arrive at it by sacrificing your principles in order to be a "good sport"; popularity built on such a foundation will not survive. A job poorly done will follow you and be as annoying as a tin can tied on a dog's tail.

## ADDITIONAL READINGS

Benson and Goldberg: The Camp Counselor. McGraw-Hill, 1951, chap. 4.

Bentley, Walter H.: Brass Tacks for Councillors. Boston, 14 Beacon St., 1940.

Burns, Gerald P.: The Program of the Modern Camp. Prentice-Hall, 1954, chap. 17 (representative camp schedules).

Dimock and Statten: Talks to Counselors. Ass'n Press, chaps. 4 and 14.

Hammett and Musselman: The Camp Program Book. Chaps. 5 and 6.

Joy, Barbara Ellen: It's Fair to Expect—C.M., Feb., 1949.

Joy, Barbara Ellen: Suggestions for Good Table Practice and Dining-Porch Procedures. Camp Publications, no. 8.

Joy, Barbara Ellen: Suggestion for Responsibilities of Counselors for Care of Campers. Camp Publications, no. 9.

Ledlie and Holbein: The Camp Counselor's Manual. Ass'n Press, chaps. 7, 9, 16 and 18.

Ott: So You Want to Be a Camp Counselor. Ass'n Press, chaps. 8 and 10.

Rubin: The Book of Camping. Ass'n Press, pp. 9–24.

Smith, Billie F.: How 40 Camps Handle Rest Hour. C.M., Dec., 1952.

Yawger, Richard: What Makes Good Camp Staff Morale. C.M., May, 1953.

## HEALTH, SAFETY AND SANITATION

American National Red Cross: First Aid Instruction Charts. (Order through local chapter.)

Benson and Goldberg: The Camp Counselor. McGraw-Hill, 1951, chaps. 6–8.

Camp Reference and Buying Guide (ACA). (Issued annually.)

Carlson, Agnes M.: Your Dishes—Are They Washed Really Clean? C.M., Nov., 1950.

Dimock: Administration of the Modern Camp. Ass'n Press., chap. 8.

Dirks, Ruth Upton, R.N.: Your Camp Nurse 'On Duty.' C.M., Feb., 1953.

First Aid. Boy Scouts (#3238), 1945.

Fisher, Aileen: Health and Safety Plays and Programs. Plays, Inc., 1953.

Hammett and Musselman: The Camp Program Book. Ass'n Press, pp. 259–60 and chap. 29.

Hudson, Henry W., Jr.: Plan for a Healthy Camp. C.M., Dec., 1951.

Joy, Barbara Ellen: Some Thoughts on Camp Health. C.M., Nov., 1951.

Ledlie and Holbein: The Camp Counselor's Manual. Ass'n Press, chap. 8.

Lorber, Max J., and Frieman, Ray: We Organize a Fire Department. C.M., May, 1942.

Newcomb, Kate Pelham, M.D.: Preventive Medicine in Camp. C.M., Nov., 1945.

Nurse in the Camp Program. Nat'l Org. for Pub. Health Nursing, 1951, 38 pp.

Payne, Elizabeth C., R.N.: The Important Role of the Camp Nurse. C.M., Jan., 1952.

Safety. Boy Scouts (#3347), 1945.

Safety Wise. Girl Scouts (#19–502), 1950.

Scott, Ruth Boyer, R.N.: What Your Camp Nurse Will Want to Know, C.M., Dec., 1953.

Selverstone, Arthur W.: Camp Sanitation Guide. Bead, 1953, 24 pp.

Without halting, without rest,
Lifting better up to best;
Planting seeds of knowledge pure,
Through earth to ripen, through
heaven endure.

EMERSON

## Chapter 5

# THE COUNSELOR MUST MASTER THE TECHNIQUE OF GROUP LIVING

CAMP living, in which you are almost continuously rubbing elbows at close quarters with others, makes it essential that you yourself be able to establish comfortable and satisfactory relationships with your associates. Even our dearest friends and members of our family do things which irritate us at times and sometimes we may be puzzled as they act in ways seemingly foreign to their usual line of conduct. We can be sure, likewise, that our own antics often affect others in the same way. Since nowhere are contacts so constant and possibilities of friction so intense as in camp, you must possess the ability to adapt yourself to others and also to accept and genuinely like many varied types of personalities, finding something interesting and worthy of appreciation in each individual.

You have no doubt pondered at one time or another upon the seeming miracle that out of all the hundreds of people whom you know, no two of them, not even identical twins, look exactly alike. Likewise, no two of the persons you ever know are exactly alike in personality; individuals will, in fact, differ from each other in far more ways than they resemble one another. This is not difficult to understand when you stop to realize that each is the

63

result not only of his particular heredity but of the effect of all persons with whom he has had contact and each and every experience which he has encountered. Even campers of tender years are already becoming as individual and divergent in ways of acting and reacting as a similar group of their elders.

Like any specialist, you must come to your job with a well-equipped bag of tools including those of working with people and with adeptness at choosing the right ones and manipulating them with skill and finesse to do the particular job needed. You must realize that each person acts as he does in an attempt to achieve just one thing—a satisfactory life for himself and an inner sense of peace with himself and with those about him. Often his efforts may seem poorly directed and ill-chosen, for most of us at times display an amazing crudeness and poor judgment in our techniques of daily living. Though we may hate to admit it, every normal individual is selfish and interested primarily in himself. Yet the person who has learned to live "the good life" has learned that he must curb his selfish egocentric tendencies for they are not compatible with his own self-respect and the affection and high regard of others which are so essential to his own sense of well-being.

A young baby expresses responses to such stimuli as pain, discomfort, hunger and thirst; if his needs and wishes are not met, he cries and shows evidences of anger and resentment. His early responses give little or no evidence of such positive reactions as definite pleasure and it is only as he grows older that he begins to show pleasure, affection, consideration for the rights and feelings of companions, and other evidences of becoming a normal, well-adjusted adult. The process of change is very gradual in all, but it progresses much more surely, rapidly and completely in some than in others. Campers are in their formative years during which practices and experiences under skilled leadership can do much to hasten and ensure the full development of a growing ability to fit into society and eventually assume a worthy place in the world of adults.

Everything that happens to a child in camp from the time he neatly makes his bed with square corners in the morning until he lies quietly awaiting sleep, making no sound after taps have been blown, is a means for learning. Your skill in arranging and guiding the events of your camper's day largely determine what the results of his camp experiences will be and whether these experiences will encourage him to evade life by rationalizing, lying and boasting, or to face up to it with unflinching courage and honesty. You must, therefore, understand children and be able to interpret their gropings as they search for satisfactory solutions to their developing problems of living with others.

## CHARACTERISTICS OF CHILDHOOD

As previously pointed out, individuals cannot be classified and fitted into pigeonholes with the proper recipe for understanding and handling of each neatly catalogued in some nearby file. Each has a unique personality brought about by his own heredity and all the bits of learning he has absorbed like a sponge from his particular background and environment. We cannot truthfully say that there is such a thing as an average child but only averages of children. Nevertheless, it will prove helpful to understand these averages since they represent a basic structure upon which each child's own individual characteristics are superimposed.

## The Camper of 6–8

This period might be termed the *individualistic period,* since, although not as completely egocentric as he was, the child's thoughts are still largely centered upon himself and his interest in others is mostly superficial and transitory. A friend of the hour may be an outsider or even the object of quarreling or dislike a short time later. In fact, a child of this age shows more interest in pleasing adults than his contemporaries and can often be motivated to desirable conduct by a bit of praise or other sign of approval from you.

He tends to be incessantly active and cannot be kept still or concentrating on the same thing for long at a time. His interests are keen but fleeting and you may experience a sense of failure if you do not bear in mind that it is perfectly natural for him to suddenly drop a project or game in which he has been absorbed and clamor for something entirely new and different. He is often impulsive and highly unpredictable.

His imagination knows no bounds and he goes into a whirlpool of activity as he clears his cabin dooryard and lines a path with rocks to the door of the "White House" or pioneer's cabin where he and his campmates bunk. He loves to try to creep silently through the woods, stalking in the best manner of Daniel Boone, and only a few rough touches of costume transform him into a handsome Fairy Prince holding sway over his subjects.

It is very important at this time to encourage him to try out his skills along various lines such as music, simple handicrafts, dramatics and sports. However, his coordination is not dependable and his control over his finer muscles is so poor that he finds concentration on painstaking, exacting techniques wearisome and nerve-racking. Simple, large-muscle activities are best. He needs to be protected against overexcitement and fatigue which tend to interfere with his getting sufficient rest and sleep.

## The Camper of 9–11

A camper of this age is beginning to value the approval of those of his own age group and you can utilize this trait as a potent force to steer him in ways which meet the approval of his peers. He can and should be encouraged in his awakening consciousness of the joys and benefits of working with a group in such projects as planning a campfire skit or program, a simple gypsy trip, outdoor meal, or a clean-up project for unit or cabin. His imagination still runs rampant and activities are much more fun when he imagines himself in the role of an Indian brave, a historical figure, or a character from a well-loved story.

He needs to be helped to develop a sense of self-reliance, industry, regularity and dependability. He is supersensitive to ridicule or failure, so use the light touch here. His increasing muscular control calls for further experimentation and skill development in varied crafts and other activities. His confidence in himself and his ability to do simple things in keeping with his capacity needs to be built up, for even when he seems boastful and assertive, it is often really a mask for his underlying sense of insecurity.

He tires easily when activities involve long-continued efforts and his tendency to overdo makes mandatory rigid observance of the rest period and getting adequate sleep at night. He must still be protected against over-fatigue and overexcitement.

## The Camper of 12–15

This age is referred to as the *gang age*, wherein interests in self are shared with a deep loyalty to the group or gang, often to the extent that the camper is willing to sacrifice his own interests for the greater benefit of his group. Desire for the approval of the group is becoming so strong that to be different or stand out from the rest is a major catastrophe. All must act and dress as nearly alike one another as possible even though it involves cutting off and fringing their jeans, engaging in minor acts of vandalism and disobedience, or wearing long fingernails or a crew haircut. Woe be to you as counselor if you try to forcibly buck this current and great will be your rewards if you can create group acceptance and approval of desirable group mores, for the problem of individual misbehaviors will largely disappear under the overpowering force of group pressure. The sense of gang loyalty is not usually quite as strong in girls as in boys.

Loyalty to and enthusiasm for working as a group plus a growing power to discuss and see several sides of a question offer a wonderland of possibilities for learning to plan program and work out common problems by group techniques. Use camper leadership, falling into your role of leader, big brother and counselor to suggest and steer the course inconspicuously. Encourage individuals and committees to assume responsibilities and strive to develop a social consciousness wherein each camper realizes his own responsibility for and obligations to others.

This is the age of acute hero worship and the choice of the right heroes can be a most potent force for good. Campers are thrilled by examples of thoughtfulness, self-sacrifice, valor and honesty in their models and they themselves, even though loudly protesting, appreciate being held to high standards, with regulations being consistently and fairly but not over-rigidly enforced. Above all avoid the fatal error of striving for personal popularity by overleniency or trying to be "just one of the boys."

It is difficult to tell whether this period, with its rapid turnover of moods, interests and general reactions to life, is harder on the individual or on those who associate with him. Rapid physical changes bring profound unrest, making the girl extremely self-conscious about her changing physical appearance and keeping the boy in constant anguish as his voice ranges without warning from treble to bass. Arms and legs are lengthening and hands and feet increasing rapidly in size during growth spurts so that they seem to the owner to stick out like sore thumbs and cannot be kept inconspicuous and controllable by dint of any amount of effort. Puzzled by the rapid physical, emotional and social changes taking place in him, the youngster often covers up his lack of ease by loud talk and laughter and general boistrousness.

## The Camper of 15–20

This may be a period of continued embarrassment due to rapid growth changes still taking place. There is still a struggle to achieve a place of status and acceptance within the group. In fact, acceptance by one's peers and a growing need to become independent of older people and be recognized as a thinking, self-reliant "adult" has become so great that the adolescent is inclined to resent and question critically the motives and wisdom of all those who are older or occupy a place of authority such as parents, teachers, counselors and camp administrators. For this reason, if for no others, it is extremely important to provide practice in budding powers of self-direction by letting campers share in as much planning of their own program and camp government as possible. Wise guidance is still necessary since our untried "adult" is inclined to fluctuate between flashes of new-found maturity and returns to his former immaturity.

This is a period of idealism and of increasing interest in and curiosity about a wide variety of topics, sometimes even ranging to the national and international. Group discussions and informal "bull sessions" are very popular and the participation of older persons who have been places and done things is often welcome. Youth's sense of values and standards is rapidly taking form now.

Camps should provide a progressive program for campers who return year after year so that they do not have to keep "doing the same old things" and what they consider "kid stuff." Camper participation in planning longer and more rugged trips, more elaborate unit improvements and outpost activities, occasional co-ed activities and opportunities to explore and satisfy individual interests and increasing skill will help to keep camp life challenging to growing mental and physical abilities.

## Individual Differences

No two children develop in the same way and a birthday does not miraculously transform a typical twelve-year old into a typical thirteen-year old;

changes are so gradual that they are scarcely discernible to one's everyday associates and they vary in speed and the exact path they follow with each individual. Campers are most commonly divided into living groups according to age, sometimes combined with other factors, but you can be sure that within your own particular group you will find a few unusually mature individuals with the large majority grouped about what might be termed average, and a few trailing behind at the maturity level of those in a younger living unit. In the same way, you may be sure that some will rate high on one scale such as intellectual attainment yet be only average or below it in others such as physical development or social adaptability. Again, you will find that a given individual can reason almost on an adult level in solving some of his emotional problems yet be quite infantile and self-centered about others.

We may well ask ourselves whether or not this spottiness of maturity is desirable and whether we should try to curb it so that emotional, physical and mental development keep pace with each other. Should we try to cast all children in the same mould so that all will be "average?" The answer is "no," for such a result would be both impossible and undesirable to attain. Although, improvement is often pleasing and sometimes even phenominal, we cannot expect marked changes in a child during his brief stay in camp; after all a child is what he is because of *years* of previous experiences and influences. Instead of striving for an average, we should help each camper to become *his* best even though it is not necessarily like anyone else's best. The world needs all types of people to make up a well-rounded society and the butcher, the baker and the candlestick maker all fill their useful places. The introvert with his quiet retiring ways is often through his unassuming devotion and helpfulness the salt of the earth which forms the backdrop for the noisy, happy-go-lucky, self-appointed extrovert leader. You, as counselor, should be like the wise dressmaker who fashions the garment to fit the model, yet allows ample seams and hems for growth and freedom of action. You need only concern yourself with those who are going off on wrong tacks and developing undesirable tendencies, and you must become adept at curbing with one hand while pushing with the other.

Camp can do nothing more important than help campers develop the skills, habits and attitudes essential for fitting comfortably into society, for only those who can establish pleasant relationships with their associates can have good mental health.

You as a counselor must keep a cool head and a steady hand at the helm. Your prayer might well be, "Dear God, give me the strength to accept with serenity the things that cannot be changed. Give me courage to change the things that can and should be changed and wisdom to distinguish one from the other." *

* George Sessions Perry and Isabel Leighton, *Where Away*, Whittlesey House.

## LEARNING IN CAMP

Too often we are inclined to associate the term "learning" exclusively with the formal schoolroom type of information acquired from a book or learned lecture. However, if we take the trouble to cultivate acquaintance, we will often find that a person whose days in school have been most limited possesses a depth of practical lore and ways of living which those with advanced degrees might well envy. Any individual who has been fortunate enough to sample the deep naturelore of the seasoned hunter and trapper or the general know-how of a good camp handy man is aware of how true this is. Everyone is constantly learning, for everything, good or bad, worthwhile or worthless, beneficial or detrimental, is a force for some change in attitudes, knowledge or skills. We can learn to gossip, lie or think low thoughts just as readily as we can learn good ways of spending our time.

### The Kinds of Learning

Owing perhaps to the absence of radio and television, a well-stocked library is often well patronized in camp. Though there are ample occasions for reading and being read aloud to, for round-table discussions and such, by and large, most of a camper's activities are built about learning, practicing and perfecting skills concerned with camp life. He learns how to make his bed and stow his personal possessions neatly, how to set the table properly, and that washing his hands first and handling the tableware carefully will prevent

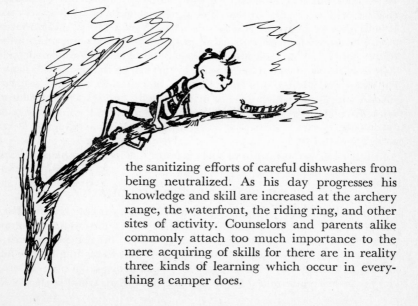

the sanitizing efforts of careful dishwashers from being neutralized. As his day progresses his knowledge and skill are increased at the archery range, the waterfront, the riding ring, and other sites of activity. Counselors and parents alike commonly attach too much importance to the mere acquiring of skills for there are in reality three kinds of learning which occur in everything a camper does.

1. *Primary learnings* are those concerned directly with performing skills. For instance, in planning and going on a cook-out, Diane may learn how to figure menus for a given number; how to select, pack and carry the ingredients; how to prepare the fire and cook the food; how to wash dishes under primitive conditions, and how to put out the fire, bury the garbage and leave a neat campsite for the next passersby. Most of these learnings have little application except when Diane camps now or in later years.

2. *Associated learnings* are directly related to the activity at hand but they also carry over into other related situations. For instance, in the above, Diane has learned principles of arranging a well-balanced menu and some techniques of food preparation which will surely carry over into home situations. Such learnings broaden her horizons and whet her appetite for learning more and more. These learnings are usually of more lasting and practical value than the primary ones.

3. *Concomitant learnings* are the habits and attitudes a camper develops through participating in an activity and they are often the most worthwhile of all. For instance, Diane has learned the value of group planning and giving equal consideration to the wishes of all through helping to plan the cook-out. She has no doubt learned how harmony and good fellowship abound when each assumes responsibility for contributing his share of the work whether it be in helping to gather and pack the food, or select and place wood for the fire. She observes how quickly the miles fly by on a hike and how the work of the cook-out is genuine fun when accompanied by friendly banter and the singing of a merry lilt. She will likely never again be a party to racial discrimination as she works side by side with cheerful Marie, a colored girl, and pretty Marita whose parents came from Mexico, and observes how happily and capably they do more than their share of the work. Perhaps Diane herself will learn to acquiesce more readily to the will of the majority as she shares the disapproval of the others for Kathy who grumbles and throws cold water on any suggestion which did not originate with her. Any fellow camper who tries the technique of crying, stamping her foot, and going into a general tantrum to get what she wants—a technique which may have been successful with her overindulgent parents—soon becomes an object lesson to herself and others as to the futility of such measures in securing the social approval of one's own group.

## THE WELL-ADJUSTED PERSONALITY

The wish for good mental health is universal for, although most of us would fail miserably if asked to tell just what the term means, we all recognize that it involves a general sense of well-being and of living at peace with oneself and the world. A well-adjusted person has stopped reaching for the moon by attempting things beyond his capabilities, yet, at the same time he has picked out his strong points and developed them to a high point of efficiency. He has learned to expect and take the bitter with the sweet in the events of life and has kept his sense of humor strong so that he can laugh at himself when he stumbles yet pick himself up and try once or many times again. He likes people and has learned how much more important it is to dwell upon their good traits rather than pick out their faults and magnify them out of all proportion. He is friendly and outgoing yet not a back-slapper or hail-fellow-well-met whose shallowness soon shows through. He is cheerful and optimistic, yet recognizes and meets problems and takes constructive steps to solve them to the best of his ability instead of dashing hither and yon in ineffective worry and indecision. Perhaps, most of all, his distinguishing mark is that he has largely supplemented juvenile interests in self alone with thoughts of others and of how he may best use his time and talents to serve them and so make the world a better place in which to live.

## THE FUNDAMENTAL WISHES

Five fundamental desires or wishes are present in all of us and the secret of mental health lies in their satisfactory fulfillment. Unsatisfactory achievement of one or more results in a maladjusted misfit who gropes about in impotent ways looking for satisfaction. From the latter group in its extreme form come the "problem child," the juvenile delinquent, the mentally deranged and the hardened criminal. One of the finest things counselors and other leaders of youth can do is to steer the maladjusted into correct paths to achieve their fundamental desires in socially approved ways and thus stave off frustration and disappointment, for the neophyte is often completely at sea as to why he is so often at odds with himself and others.

### The Wish for Recognition

Each camper has a deep-seated desire to stand out as an individual and do something or several things better than the others in his group. He will consequently work like a beaver to run faster, swim better, swear more fluently, make higher school marks, sing louder or recognize more birds than his cabin mates. From his early days, this deep urge drives him from one field of endeavor to another in a search for things which hold his interest and show promise of allowing him to achieve distinction. Often a boy or girl's reluctance to engage in a suggested activity is based on an inner fear that he does not or cannot do it well; John may find many excuses for not going in the water during his swimming period because he feels poorly skilled in swimming or a swimming counselor or fellow camper has made sarcastic remarks about his technique. His attitude often changes to one of tolerance or even enthusiasm when a wise counselor searches out a good point to compliment him on and shows a willingness to help him improve. To work successfully with youngsters, or in fact persons of any age, you need to remember how much better results come from praise than from criticism. There is much truth in the old saying that you catch more flies with honey than with vinegar. Use a word of praise frequently, but avoid overdoing it or giving it when it is not deserved for others are quick to detect the insincerity and will consequently lose faith in and respect for you.

Fat Sue's disinclination to join the group in hiking may be based on her inability to "keep up" and the consequent cruel comments on her physical stature from other hikers. If her problem is ignored, she may learn to snap back and make herself disagreeable just as a tethered dog does when teased by mischievous children or she may fall back on a headache or other excuse for not going. A tactful talk with her may incite her interest in bringing her weight down to normal. In the meantime, she can be encouraged to earn an acceptable place for herself by capitalizing on her strong points such as her ability to see the funny side of things and turn potential catastrophies into occasions for mirth or at least cheerful acceptance.

Bill, who rows poorly and knows it, may be so overwhelmed by the thoughtless taunts and jeers of others that he loses what little coordination he has and flails the water in a truly ludicrous way. You may help him most by unobtrusively suggesting a little private coaching in a remote spot where he can concentrate on mastering his technique without worry about what others are saying or thinking.

A youngster's eagerness to stand well with his peers demands that he receive recognition from them for something he does wells. Oftentimes you may even want to steer the program around a little bit to make room for his scarce talents. Quiet, socially inept Jean may really shine as her ability to draw well and make attractive posters fills an urgent need to advertise the all-camp fair. We are reminded of a story, whose source is now forgotten, of a certain camper whose most outstanding trait seemed to be an ability to make more noise than anyone else. Her counselor, realizing that her frequently annoying breaches of good conduct were in reality an unrecognized and perfectly unconscious attempt to get the personal attention she could obtain in no other way, decided to stage a contest to see who could yell the loudest. Of course Jean won as was anticipated and thus achieved her place in the limelight. Needless to say, adroit handling of the situation was needed to quickly substitute other attainments for Jean so that her continued happiness did not demand frequent repetitions of a display of lung power.

A camper would prefer to have *approved* distinction rather than unfavorable attention, scorn or open ridicule. However, his desire for recognition is so strong that he will go to almost any length to get it, even compromising for unfavorable attention if necessary. The constant trouble-maker or the camp mimic may zealously maintain his title which has brought him the distinction he failed to achieve in more socially approved ways and he would rather be known as bad than be consigned to nonentity.

Nevertheless, he has a gnawing sense of inadequacy and unhappiness and will eventually be glad to exchange his distinction for an approved one if someone will but exercise the tact and patience to steer him into paths where he can succeed. No quick cure can be expected, however, and there will be gradually decreasing periods of backsliding along the way.

Be especially alert to help the shy, retiring camper find successful achievements. "The child who feels inferior can usually be helped to develop abilities which will in time make him truly superior along certain lines. All genuine superiority grows out of a sense of inferiority which has served as a spur to unusual effort."*

## The Wish for Affection

A second fundamental wish is to be accepted by and regarded affectionately by the group. The sense of inner content a camper feels when comrades select him for a tent mate or greet him with a friendly word and smile when he enters the cabin door and the thrill he gets when his cabin mates choose him to represent them on the Camp Council all stem from the fulfillment of this basic desire. The longing to be loved, appreciated, needed and missed when absent is universal. When fulfilled, it produces a feeling of well-being and contentment; when unfulfilled, it brings unconsolable loneliness and unhappiness. A couple of grains of salt should be taken with the camper who says, "I would rather be alone for I find my cabin mates dull and boresome " as he goes off to read a book or stroll through the woods in solitude; the chances are he is really painfully unhappy and in desperate need of some real pals. You may need the utmost tact and persistence to penetrate the wall he has built around himself but the resulting happier, better-adjusted camper will amply reward you.

Your efforts from the first day to build cabin morale and a feeling of group unity and friendly camaraderie are aimed at helping each newcomer feel wanted and accepted. Special pains must be taken with newcomers to camp and with those by nature particularly shy and retiring. Pairing them up or assigning old campers to act as hosts will help. The naturally unattractive camper will challenge you especially to search for his good points and help him fit in. A father, consoling his befreckled little daughter, said, "I love every one of your freckles because they are you." Find out why a camper is disliked or ignored, then set out diligently to remedy the situation.

See that your program is broad and varied enough to provide for the varying interests and abilities of any youngsters. Show the one who is slow to make a place for himself some slight kindnesses but avoid giving him undue attention lest you queer him with the others and stamp him as "counselor's pet." The indirect, well-concealed approach is usually best but it is sometimes more desirable to have a man-to-man talk with him, laying your cards on the

* Fr. Henry C. Link, *The Rediscovery of Man*, 1938 by The Macmillan Company and used with their permission.

table and leading him by his own discussion to discover how his own selfishness and lack of consideration for others, his boasting, his shirking of responsibility, or his crude manners and general boorishness are at fault. It is sometimes wise to choose a time when he is absent and discuss the situation with his mates, for they are often only demonstrating thoughtlessness in their seemingly cruel treatment. Most children are at heart sympathetic and warm-hearted and, when brought to consider the situation in another light, will often lend enthusiastic support to help the offender turn over a new leaf. Tolerance and forgiveness for the shortcomings of others are certainly desirable traits to cultivate and any improvement in the fellow camper will be a cause for rejoicing as his comrades claim their rightful share of the credit. Helping others is one of the most satisfying ways to fulfill one's wishes for recognition and power.

A serious case of maladjustment or continued failure to fit in may call for referral to the camp director or head counselor for more harm than good often follows tampering by those with insufficient training and experience to handle the situation. Sometimes it is best to transfer the camper to another cabin but this step should be a last resort for it tends to leave him with a sense of defeat in the old situation.

"It is a wonderful thing to have somebody believe in you. This is one great benefit of love. Love idealizes its object and exaggerates little tendencies into great virtues and possibilities into genius. Love is action and reaction. Where much is expected of an individual, he may rise to the level of events and make the dream come true." * Campers who try too hard for popularity may defeat their own purpose as they grovel in an all-out effort to win favor. Respect is a very necessary ingredient to true affection.

## The Wish for Power

The desire to control or show power over oneself or other persons or things is also universal. A camper knows the satisfaction of controlling himself when he succeeds in earning a "well done" for his performance of the crawl or lashing an outdoor cabinet or table at the outpost camp. He also demonstrates power over himself when he cures a habit such as procrastination or keeping an untidy room, or when he disciplines himself to finish thoroughly some task such as cleaning up a section of the waterfront or constructing a new foot bridge across a stream. He shows power over others when he assumes the chairmanship of a committee and steers it to a successful completion of its duties, when he can present his beliefs so effectively as to sway the group to accept his viewpoint, or when he can talk his pal, Joe, out of some proposed misdeed.

A camper should be spared the frustration and disappointment which comes from trying to compete with those of superior age, experience or

* *Friendship Book*, published in 1934, Chilton Greeting Card Company, Boston.

ability; for this reason, it is often more desirable to let him compete against his own previous record rather than that of someone else. Again a broad and varied program will provide something in which each camper can experience a satisfactory degree of success.

A misdirected sense of power may partially explain the bully, the strong personality who dominates and does the thinking for one or more weak followers, the individual who enjoys capturing and torturing helpless animals, or the addict to speed boat showing off or fast automobile driving. The leader or brains of the derelict gang is also showing a poorly used natural ability for leadership.

## The Wish for Security

Every person wants to feel safe and secure in his surroundings and with his associates. Campers, particularly when away from home for the first time, miss their familiar routines and ways of life. Camp ways are new and living with a number of other children of the same sex seems very odd especially to an only child. A camper can predict with some certainty how his parents and home playmates will react to what he does. Often he has become quite adept at "getting around" or wheedling what he wants out of one or both parents. Now he is associated with several entirely strange adults as well as his fellow campers. A cross remark, an outburst of temper in his direction or a biting comment from his new associates may rouse resentment or a retreat into his shell. A bad siege of homesickness may be on its way if nothing is done to prevent it.

There are several things you can do to make a camper feel secure or "at home" more quickly. Having a welcoming committee when he arrives to conduct him to his cabin is important; campers should be assigned to their cabins before they come even though changes may be in order within a few days, for keeping them in line a long time while housing decisions are made is very boresome and gives a feeling of insecurity which may overpower the already confused youngster. Give the camper a name tag, including the nickname by which he wants to be known. Use discretion about nicknames, for an undesirable one such as "Fatso" or "Limpy" which is based on a physical defect or undesirable personality trait can be very irritating to him; if he doesn't have a nickname, help him find one lest a bad one later attach itself out of some embarrassing incident. A name tag on the camper's bed and storage compartments also helps. Take the newcomer on a tour of the camp so that he will know how to find his way about and pair him off with a buddy so that he need not wander around alone. Play get-acquainted and funful games in the cabin group and hold an early discussion on camp rules, policies and routines. Explain the dining room procedures before the first meal and eat with your group if camp policy permits it; this will give you a chance to discuss proper table manners as the meal proceeds. Camper misdeeds and breaches of etiquette often stem from not knowing the proper thing to do and may later cause chagrin when the camper discovers his error. Prevent it by anticipating and explaining proper procedures before the need for them arises.

Your own friendly role and warm interest in the welfare and happiness of each camper and quick perception of little things you can do to bring each one into your cabin circle are of paramount importance. Be friendly, yet firm if the need arises, and be consistent in what you do for being able to count on your responses is essential to a camper's sense of security. Keep camper confidences and never let yourself be overheard discussing camper personalities with others. You must make yourself a bulwark to which your charges feel they can come with their problems and misgivings.

A camper's sense of security must include freedom from fear of harm—both physical and social. Fear of being hurt or ridiculed interferes with physical coordination; this explains the superior results obtained by the modern swimming counselor who works his swimmers hard but gives praise and encouragement when it is due rather than the old method of throwing a nonswimmer into deep water and letting him swim or get badly drenched and frightened. Children who are anxious and afraid of being ridiculed may react by stuttering, bed-wetting, retiring into a shell, fighting back, criticizing others, or engaging in malicious gossip.

### The Wish for New Experiences

To do something different and try one's wings in unconquered fields is the reverse of the desire for security and denying it too long results in boredom, bad temper, and misbehavior just to create a little excitement. Varying camp routines and work, with the group evaluating each day's experiences and planning what they want to do next will help avoid this.

Keeping campers busy at something which gives them a feeling of accomplishment is one of the secrets of camp happiness. Trips, cook-outs, "special days," work projects as in camp construction or on a neighboring farm or truck patch, a hobby display, camp play, building a tree house or nature trail, folk dancing, a camp neighbor or foreign visitor who has interesting experiences to relate, all help to meet the demand for new experiences.

### What Happens When the Drives Are Thwarted?

Children are a combination of a lot of good spiced by a bit of bad, and those who long for the perfectly behaved child should remember this little poem:

> Tommy does as he is told!
> No one ever has to scold!
> Quick! Drag him by the wrist
> To see the psychoanalyst!
>                    AUTHOR UNKNOWN

When a child is "bad," it is usually because he has not found a satisfying way to fulfill one or more of his basic needs. Therefore, when trouble arises seek and eliminate the causes. Basic wishes are strong and will be fulfilled by fair means or foul, but children are loathe to sacrifice social approval if they can avoid it and still satisfy their desires.

## KINDS OF LEADERS
### LEADERSHIP

The boss drives his men; the leader coaches them.
The boss depends upon authority; the leader on good will.
The boss inspires fear; the leader inspires enthusiasm.
The boss says, "I"; the leader says, "We."
The boss assigns the tasks; the leader sets the pace.
The boss says, "Get here on time"; the leader gets there ahead of time.
The boss fixes the blame for the breakdown; the leader fixes the breakdown.
The boss knows how it is done; the leader shows how.
The boss makes work a drudgery; the leader makes it a game.
The boss says, "Go," the leader says, "Let's go."
The world needs leaders; but nobody wants a boss.*

There are three kinds of leaders: (1) the autocratic leader, who rules by force and fear of consequences; (2) the laissez faire leader, who operates on the theory that campers must be let do as they please without adult inter- ference; (3) the democratic leader, who can use discipline when necessary, but who customarily leads the group through his ability to command their respect and work and plan cooperatively with them.

### The Autocratic Leader

The autocratic leader considers his own opinions so superior that he is justified in forcing them willy nilly on his charges. His "big stick" methods of control brook no lapse of discipline or questioning of his authority, and he threatens drastic and certain punishment for all dissenters and noncon- formists. Unfortunately, his high-handed tactics accomplish little permanent good, for the exemplary conduct evoked by fear lasts only while he is present —then the lid blows off like Pandora's box of troubles. Some succumb to him and render cringing, boot-licking subservience, becoming so dependent that they are totally incapable of making any decisions for themselves. Others rebel against him and acquire an unreasonable distaste for discipline and authority of any sort or from any source.

The autocrat often demonstrates his own emotional immaturity by meeting misdemeanors and resistance with loss of temper, violent tongue lashings or acts of retribution. Bossing others seems to compensate him in some measure for his own deep-seated feelings of inadequacy.

* Dora, E. Dodge: *Thirty Years of Girls Club Experience*. Worcester Girls Club, 67 Lincoln Street, Worcester 5, Mass.

## The Laissez Faire Leader

He is the opposite of the autocratic leader and asserts no authority at all in a mistaken belief that the group can develop independence and self-reliance only by practicing *complete* self-direction. He realizes that campers should be happy, but is laboring under the delusion that his easy-going, wishy-washy methods of control will bring them true happiness. He tries to play the good sport and always falls in line with whatever his group suggests, but they soon become bored with his lack of force and the resultant pointless program and either sink into complete lassitude or engage in heated arguments among themselves which may almost rival gang warfare. The leader even fails to achieve the popularity he craves, for campers soon lose all respect for a spineless person who lacks the courage of his convictions.

## The Democratic Leader

He is a combination of the other two, for he is a "good sport" and a champion of fun and good times, but he can also administer swift and just discipline when necessary.

He can relax and have a good time with his group, yet steer them away from dangerous or harmful trends. He encourages them to express their views and to participate in self-government and program planning insofar as their ages and abilities permit. He knows that a group which has been working under an autocrat may kick up its heels and be as undisciplined as a spring colt at first and that he can gradually turn the reins over to them only as they prove their capability. The democratic process is slow, for explanations, discussions and group action take time—but the results are worth it.

In the best sense of the word a democratic group is one which has learned to live together in comparative harmony while initiating, conducting and judging its own program; it is willing to abide by the results of its own decisions.

Citizens in a democracy must learn to be good "choosers," and each must be willing to abide by the group choice and pitch in and do his share toward carrying it out. The leader acts as a friendly counsel and guide, helping where he is most needed and seeing that responsibilities and privileges are distributed equitably.

1. A good leader leads by example.

2. He has a good sense of humor and exercises it to avert crises and keep molehills from becoming mountains.

3. His thoughts are not inverted toward himself and how he will be affected by each situation, but rather outward toward the greater "we."

4. He capitalizes on the power of suggestion and subtly plants ideas to sprout and be returned with many variations by the group as their own.

5. He avoids serious misunderstandings and feuds with others by tact and a sincere attempt to see their side of the question as well as his own.

6. When there is work to be done, he is in the midst of it, sleeves rolled up and hands just as dirty as anybody's.

7. He understands and uses the force of group pressure and group opinion. He realizes, too, that there is danger in letting campers entirely rule themselves, for they can be cruel and go to extremes of retribution when judging each other. Hurting people is sometimes necessary, but it is a two-edged sword and must be used only as a last resort.

8. He is ever-mindful of the necessity for "fun," for happy campers seldom become problems. If he is teaching a new skill, he is thorough, but uses an informal, friendly manner rather than a dry, bookish one. He knows the value of a laugh and always has time for a good joke.

9. He knows that campers do not really enjoy slovenly, careless standards of conduct and that they will soon lose respect for a leader who tolerates such laxness. He recognizes that a request gets better response than an order but that, when orders have been found necessary, they must be enforced.

10. He gives praise freely when deserved, but he knows that, if used too often or for mediocre performance, it loses all value. He avoids nagging and excessive fussiness about detail, for he knows that such tactics are inclined to take the heart right out of people and make them stop trying. He never resorts to sarcasm.

11. He foresees an impending crisis and tries to avert it if he can. If Johnny is chanting the disagreeableness of spinach, he does not wait until the whole table is lamenting their pet dislikes, but quietly reminds Johnny, "We talk only about pleasant things, at the table."

12. He shuns public scenes whenever possible. A "bawling out" before others hurts a camper's pride and makes him react by (1) giving up and crawling off to stop trying, or (2) growing resentful and intent on revenge. He gives the erring camper a chance to "save face" by seemingly ignoring his misdemeanor in public. He may later talk to him privately in a frank but friendly manner to show him wherein he was wrong, for "badness" often results from embarrassment or from not knowing just what the right course is. He seldom tells a camper what to do, but helps him to face his problems squarely and work out his own solution through an understanding of underlying causes. He never sends a camper away dejected and hopeless, but shows him that he still has faith in him and is confident that he can and will do a better job in the future. Campers respond magically to adult challenge and trust.

13. He never uses physical punishment, for it seldom brings about the desired result, is usually against camp rules, and might involve him or the camp in legal difficulties for any physical damage that ensues.

14. He uses disciplinary measures sparingly and only when he is convinced that it is in the best interests of the culprit and not out of spite or in an effort to save his own pride. Punishment is so easy to administer and gets

such quick and sure results (outwardly, at least) that it is often misused or overused. The superior counselor handles his group so skillfully that disciplinary problems seldom occur, but, even so, sooner or later the day will come when action can no longer be postponed. He will find that children are usually good sports about accepting punishment which is deserved and not based upon partiality or injustice. When discipline is necessary, it should follow as closely as possible on the heels of the misdemeanor and should bear some relationship to it if possible; for instance, depriving a camper of his dessert would be appropriate only for a dining-room misdeed. Using work as a punitive measure belittles it and drags it down from the place of honor it ought to hold, though it may be fitting when used to impress the camper with the extra labor his thoughtlessness or misdeed has caused someone else.

The democratic counselor could well use the characteristics of the successful teacher as given by H. Q. Cooper:

> The education of a college president.
> The executive ability of a financier.
> The craftiness of a politician.
> The humility of a deacon.
> The discipline of a demon.
> The adaptability of a chameleon.
> The hope of an optimist.
> The courage of a hero.
> The wisdom of a serpent.
> The gentleness of a dove.
> The patience of a Job.
> The grace of God—And
> The persistence of the devil.*

* H. Q. Cooper, quoted by Jackson R. Sharman in *Introduction to Physical Education*, copyright 1934 by A. S. Barnes and Company, Incorporated.

## ADDITIONAL READINGS

### BOOKS AND PAMPHLETS

Baruch, Dorothy: New Ways in Discipline. McGraw-Hill.

Benson and Goldberg: The Camp Counselor. McGraw-Hill, 1951, 337 pp.

Busch: Leadership in Group Work, chaps. 2–6, 9 and 10.

Camping and the Older Boy. Ass'n Press, 1940.

Coyle, Grace Longwell: Group Work with American Youth. Harper, 1948, 270 pp.

Crawford, John and Dorathea: Teens—How to Meet Your Problems. Woman's Press, 1951, 162 pp.

Dimock: Administration of the Modern Camp, Ass'n Press, chaps. 5 and 6.

Dimock and Statten: Talks to Counselors. Ass'n Press, chaps. 6, 7 and 9–12.

Established Camp, The, Girl Scouts, chap. 4.

Fedder, Ruth: A Girl Grows Up, 2nd ed. McGraw-Hill, 1948.

Gallagher, J. Roswell, M.D.: Understanding Your Son's Adolescence. Little.

Langdon, Grace, and Stout, Irving W.: The Discipline of Well-Adjusted Children. Day.

Ledlie and Holbein: The Camp Counselor's Manual. Ass'n Press, chaps. 10 and 12–16.

McKown, Harry C.: A Boy Grows Up. McGraw-Hill, 1949, 333 pp.

Morris, C. Eugene: Counseling with Young People. Ass'n Press, 1954.

Moser, Clarence G.: Understanding Boys through Infancy, Childhood, and Adolescence. Ass'n Press.

Murray, Janet P., and Clyde E.: Guide Lines for Group Leaders. Morrow, 1954.

Ott: So You Want to Be a Camp Counselor. Ass'n Press, chaps. 4 and 5.

Redl, Fritz, and Wineman, David: Controls from Within. Free Press.

Roberts, Dorothy M.: Leadership of Teen-Age Groups. Ass'n Press.

Shacter, Helen: Understanding Ourselves (rev.). McKnight, 1952, 128 pp.

Slavson: Recreation and Total Personality. Ass'n Press, chap. 8.

Soloman, Ben: Leadership of Youth. Youth Service, 1950, 164 pp.

Strain, Frances Bruce: Teen Days. Appleton.

Symonds, Percival M.: Adolescent Fantasy. Columbia U., 1949, 397 pp.

Teicher, Joseph D.: Your Child and His Problems. Little.

Trecker, Harleigh B., and Trecker, Audrey R.: How to Work with Groups. Morrow, 1952, 167 pp.

Ure: Fifty Cases for Camp Counselors. Ass'n Press.

Wittenberg, Rudolph M.: How to Help People. Ass'n Press.

Wittenberg, Rudolph M.: So You Want to Help People. Ass'n Press, chap. 4.

Wolf, Catherine M.: The Controversial Problem of Discipline. Child Study Ass'n of America.

Zerfoss, Karl (Ed.): Readings in Counseling. Ass'n Press, 1952, 639 pp.

### MAGAZINE ARTICLES

Friedrich, John A.: Sociograms Provide Graphic Picture of Camper Group Relations. C.M., Jan., 1953.

Friedrich, John A.: Understanding the Camp Group. C.M., April, 1952.

Ivan, John J.: Rating Camper Behavior. C.M., Feb., 1951.

Rehwinkel, Jeanne: Hearing What Campers Say. C.M., Jan., 1952.

Roth, Dr. Charles: How Bend the Twig. C.M., Feb., 1954.

Vannais, William: We're Recapturing Our Older Boys. C.M., Jan., 1950.

He drew a circle that shut me out—
Heretic, rebel, a thing to flout.
But Love and I had the wit to win,
We drew a circle that took him in.
                    EDWIN MARKHAM*

## Chapter 6

# THE COUNSELOR TRIES TO HELP PROBLEM CAMPERS

ALL OF US are occasionally "problem children," for few of us are sufficiently wise and disciplined to consistently meet thwarted desires with controlled emotional reactions.

### Mental Health

Good mental health gives us the ability to act in a way satisfactory to ourselves and to our associates so that we have a sense of inner calmness and well-being (euphoria). However, such a state is hard to maintain constantly, for the world is full of people, each striving to satisfy his own personal desires, and conflict between individuals is almost inevitable. One's reactions and adaptability to conflict and the onslaughts of nature and circumstance largely determine his degree of mental health.

### Counselors Must Develop Insight

Campers meet with such conflicts and problems, too, and sometimes get off on a wrong tack in socially unapproved conduct which, if unchecked, will sooner or later cause them to be dubbed "problem children." Their efforts to satisfy inner urges are often so devious that they fool themselves as well as

* Used by permission of Virgil Markham.

the counselor as to their real underlying needs and dissatisfactions; for instance, a bullying, loud braggart may be unconsciously trying to hide from himself and others an ingrown sense of insecurity and inadequacy. His obnoxious conduct suggests that he needs a good "bawling out" or a "sound thrashing," but an understanding of his real difficulty shows how harmful to him such treatment would be.

Undesirable behavior is only a symptom and is rarely overcome by direct treatment, for repressing it in one place makes it break out with greater force in another. A camper is not likely to understand why he is "bad," for self-diagnosis is notoriously fallible, and we might as well tell him to stop his tooth from aching as to order him to quit being homesick or noisy. His behavior difficulties are based upon a cause as genuine as is his toothache, and willpower avails but little in either case. Everything he does is for the purpose of meeting some need, even though he himself may be completely unaware of what it is. If his method is objectionable to others, the solution is not to condemn him, but to help him find an acceptable substitute. A counselor must learn to look beyond conduct to its underlying causes; this presents a real challenge, for emotional pains are always more difficult to diagnose than are physical ones. Incidentally, practice in understanding others should help a counselor to understand and better direct himself.

Problems campers are usually the products of problem environments or associates and many arrive in camp with cases already full blown. Conscientious but overdoting parents may have spoiled the child so that he expects the same undue attention in camp where he is surrounded by others, each entitled to his own share of recognition. A child used to living in a household of adults who center all their attention and affection on him, is at a loss when placed with others of his own age. Some children demonstrate an abnormal desire for the love which is denied them at home. Camper difficulties sometimes arise for the first time or, if already present, may get worse when subjected to unwise camp procedures which inadequately meet normal camper needs and desires.

Emotionally stable persons meet problems and frustrations honestly. Those who are emotionally unstable meet them by (1) evasion or withdrawing or by (2) aggression. The strategy and cunning exhibited by the subconscious mind in trying to cover up the real trouble makes an understanding of the problem and its solution difficult, and counselors with little training and experience may grievously aggravate the situation. Serious problems or those which show symptoms of getting out of hand should be taken at once to the Camp Director, Head Counselor or Counseling Expert. There is no such thing as a never-failing remedy or magic recipe, for techniques which will work with one person may be totally unsuccessful with another and the trouble may be "mistreated" instead of treated at the hands of an unskilled counselor.

## THE CAMPER WHO WITHDRAWS OR EVADES

The timid, apologetic camper often goes unrecognized as a problem, but psychologists realize that his very failure to demand attention and his seeming happiness in pursuing his solitary way often indicate a serious trend. On the other hand, the aggressive person makes himself so obnoxious that he is likely to call down upon his head the very attention he needs to help him conquer his difficulties while they are still in the incipient stages.

The evading camper's actions, like the aggressor's, are based upon an inner feeling of dissatisfaction, insecurity or inadequacy, and his behavior may take one of many forms.

*Daydreamers* who keep their reveries within limits often find wholesome relaxation in them; in fact, when kept under control, day dreaming is beneficial. A great doer is always a great dreamer, but only when his dreams prove so stimulating as to make him get up and start changing them into reality. When daydreaming becomes an end in itself and furnishes complete satisfaction for the dreamer, it is harmful, for no one can be kept warm and well fed in an air castle. *Wishful thinkers* persist in believing what they want to believe despite all evidence to the contrary.

*Sorry-for-themselves* retreat into an inner sanctum where they dwell moodily upon how misunderstood and mistreated they are until they become literally obsessed with the idea. They may love to picture themselves as cold and silent in death while those who have wronged them stand by in sorrow and contrition. They may even morbidly play with the idea of suicide to hasten the processes of nature. When faced with the cold fact that the old world will but give them their just dues without humoring or pampering, some want to *run home to mother* to have their aches and bruises kissed away. Others develop a convenient *illness* when faced with unpleasant tasks, while still others become *selfworshipers* to compensate for their lack of status in the eyes of others. Some youngsters who have failed to secure affection and recognition from those of their own age seek the exclusive companionship of more "understanding" (or tolerant) adults and claim to be bored by the juvenile deeds and conversations of their peers.

Failing in attempts at group acceptance, some crowd out unpleasant realization by losing themselves in strictly solitary pursuits such as reading, drawing or canoeing, and so avoid the effort of trying to tailor themselves to fit into group life.

Those who have had their suggestions and remarks jeered at or ignored may try to avoid the possibility of further jolts by degenerating into *"yes" men*, showing little initiative and trying to shrink into the background, where they will attract just as little attention as possible.

Some, especially if besieged by their own consciences or the accusations of others, try to evade blame and responsibility for their acts by *rationalizing*. Forms of rationalization are found in those who assume the *"sour grapes"* attitude of not caring or not really trying. They disdain as "high brow" those who like good music or literature; those good in sports are "brainless wonders"; good students are "greasy grinds," and those with ambition and initiative are "eager beavers." Some *alibi* or *project* the blame onto outside persons or things. They explain their failures by saying that people have it in for them and go out of their way to keep them from achieving success. The umpire cheats them out of winning, or the teacher fails to pass them because he has "pets." They are afraid to face the facts and admit that they, like all humans, have faults and weaknesses.

*Pollyannas* close their eyes to all unpleasantness and difficulty, refusing to worry about anything at all, expressing confidence that everything is pre-destined to turn out for the best. This frees them from any feeling of re-sponsibility for doing necessary work, or recognizing and correcting their own faults. Though sometimes happy and carefree themselves, their un-willingness to pull their share on the oars leaves a disproportionate amount for their companions.

Some, failing to achieve success in a coveted field, "forget it" by *overcom-pensating* in another. Thus the girl who is not blessed with physical beauty may become an outstanding student, seamstress or tennis player. The boy without the coordination and physical stamina to gain athletic prowess may become a skilled violinist, a great scientist or a splendid writer. Thus we see that *substitution* or *compensation* at its best can be a great force for good by leading to the heights of achievement. But when it causes distortion of personality and retirement from human companionship, substitution be-comes a possible evil, bringing great unhappiness to the person and his associates because of his inability to live happily with them.

## THE CAMPER WHO RESPONDS WITH AGGRESSION

The *braggart*, the *bully*, the *smarty*, and the *tough guy* who swaggers about in an attitude of pretended fearlessness and assurance are, in reality, covering up their failure to attract attention by legitimate means. The youngster who *smokes* or *drinks* to excess or who uses *foul language* or *swears* is but indulging in a misguided effort to gain status as an individual. *Bossy, domineering* people exercise power in the only way they can—by making themselves so un-pleasant that others would rather give in than resist.

The *boisterous*, the *show-off*, and the girl who goes to *extremes in dress and make-up*, would prefer to find their niche by other means if they but knew how and had the confidence to try. The antics of the *mimic*, the *cut-up* and the *practical joker* have at one time brought the attention desired and so have been adopted as standard conduct.

The *constant babbler* who monopolizes the conversation subconsciously envies his quieter, more socially acceptable companion who can feel secure of his place without constantly having to occupy the limelight. People *who eat the fastest, most or least,* and those with numerous *food dislikes* or *idiosyncrasies,* are sometimes in the same category with those who bask in the "individuality" of *poor health,* an *unusual ailment* or an *artistic temperament.*

The person who *cries* at the drop of a hat or becomes *hysterical* and throws a *temper tantrum* has probably found these methods effective in getting his own way in the past and so continues his tactics.

The *quarrelsome, stubborn or rebellious* person is so unsure of himself that he uses loud words and violent action to drown out his own misgivings and discourage others from questioning him.

The *intolerant* person who "knows all the answers" is, in spite of his dogmatic statements, really distrustful of his own beliefs and is loathe to listen to others lest they show up his inferior reasoning. The *overcritical* person calls attention to numerous little flaws in others to make himself seem superior by comparison.

Campers who form little *cliques* of two or more persons are demonstrating their inability to make a place for themselves in the larger group. Forcibly breaking up the alliance may drive them into wells of loneliness; a better solution is to lead them gradually into general group participation where appreciation and acceptance by the many supersede devotion from the few.

### Strong Friendships

> I do not love thee, Dr. Fell.
> The reason why I cannot tell;
> But this I know, and know full well
> I do not love thee, Dr. Fell.
> THOMAS BROWN (1663–1704)

For reasons that we often cannot explain, all of us are attracted to some people and repelled by others, but the truly well-integrated person finds it possible to carry on necessary associations with almost everyone in a pleasant manner. Nevertheless, all of us are privileged to find a few harmonious persons who seem to strike us just right and with whom doing almost anything at any time is fun. Such mutual attractions should be encouraged, for they offer life's best experiences and do no harm as long as they permit wholehearted participation in group activities.

Many perfectly wholesome friendships have been condemned as *crushes* by an ill-advised counselor or older person. Most so-called crushes of a camper on a counselor are but a normal attempt on the part of an adolescent to find an object for his ardent admiration and hero worship. Often, he has failed to receive the affection every child needs from parents and friends of his own age and so turns his emotional hunger toward some counselor who has been kind to him. This sometimes creates a delicate situation, for irreparable harm can result from wrong handling and it is easy to obliterate what little confidence the camper has by pointedly ignoring or "squelching" him.

The emotionally mature counselor welcomes this sincere esteem as a rare opportunity to help an adolescent grow and fulfill his personal needs in a wholesome manner. Youth should idealize, and being the object of such admiration should be a challenge to any good counselor to try to prove himself worthy of it. The camper should be treated with impersonal but cordial friendliness, and with careful avoidance of any show of favoritism or partiality. Perseverance will usually turn the situation into a perfectly healthy and worthwhile friendship.

Sometimes an emotionally immature counselor seeks to take advantage of this hero worship, diverting it to fulfill his own need for recognition and affection; he may then do much harm to the camper. As previously mentioned, it is humanly impossible to avoid being more attracted to some campers than to others, but a good counselor keeps such preferences a deep, dark secret. He tries to remain objective at all times and keeps himself above the influence of petty dislikes and differences of opinion. He must remember that the child who is not attractive to him probably affects many others in the same way and so is likely to be most lonesome and in need of affection of all.

When the attachment between two persons is so strong and exclusive as to shut out normal associations with others and make the two jealous and unhappy when apart for even short intervals, steps may be necessary to change the situation. Adults should be positive of a real need before interfering, and then must temper what they do with a light touch and vast quantities of good sense. The situation often requires the aid and advice of a person older and wiser than the counselor.

## THE GOOD COUNSELOR WORKS SLOWLY AND CAREFULLY

1. Snap judgments must be avoided, for human behavior is too complex to solve by a single formula or rule of thumb. The counselor studies all available records concerning the camper and then proceeds to add to this information by his own first-hand observation. He realizes that a change in environment often produces a change in behavior and that the child who has been labeled "bad" at home may completely reverse his conduct when subjected to the new faces, new influences, and new activities of camp.

2. He tries to provide ample opportunity for each camper to satisfy his fundamental desires and to attain the feeling of security which comes from being wanted and needed in his little cabin family. He tries to vary the program so that each child's interests and abilities can find recognition in some part of it.

3. He realizes that misbehavior may be a bid for attention, an expression of insecurity, or a feeling of being unloved and unwanted, and that public reprimand or punishment sometimes only aggravates the situation. No one is really more miserable, no matter how skillfully he hides it, than the "bad" or "problem" child and our happiness at helping him "fit in the groove" is but a drop compared to what he will experience.

4. The counselor tries surreptitiously to draw aggressive or retiring campers into activities which afford them a true feeling of success and achievement. Their distress automatically disappears when they find the path to socially approved answers for their needs and wishes. It is hard to conceive of any youngster who would willingly continue to "get in peoples' hair" if he could otherwise get the attention, affection and recognition he craves.

5. The counselor makes a particular effort to get better acquainted with the camper who seems to be creating a problem for himself or others. This may be a tedious process, for those most needing help are often too timid or proud to ask for or even accept it when offered. This makes the casual approach through a seemingly accidental canoe ride or hike better than the formal conference by appointment. The counselor cultivates the ability to be a good listener, for the problem camper's veneer of bravado usually covers an aching hunger for a trusted older person in whom he can confide, and skillful handling soon finds him chatting busily about all his secret hopes and aspirations.

6. The good counselor seldom gives advice, realizing that discreet questioning and suggestion secure better results by helping the camper work out his own solution.

7. He does not heap coals of fire on a camper's head for his misdeeds. This only produces rebellion or causes the camper to rationalize or project the blame on others and so further blind himself to any real understanding of his problem. It also kills any possibility of building up the desired status of friendship and trust between counselor and camper.

8. The counselor occasionally finds it necessary to hurt a camper who persistently refuses to recognize and accept his share in the responsibility for his difficulties. He uses it only when all kindlier treatment has failed and never because of sadism.

9. Enuresis (bed wetting) may be due to some psychological cause, such as worry and unhappiness, or to some physical basis. The doctor or nurse should be consulted, but in the meantime the camper may be provided with rubber sheets, his liquid intake from 5 o'clock on limited, and he should be urged to visit the latrine before retiring and three or four hours thereafter. For campers who are afraid to wander out alone to a dark latrine, a flashlight and companion should be made available.

## CAMPERS WHO ARE HOMESICK

Campers who give up and want to go home are true problems, for their nostalgia may prove contagious and, if they are allowed to succumb to it and leave camp, it becomes increasingly hard for them ever to sever family ties. Homesickness may be furthered by too many telephone calls or by letters of the wrong sort from "child sick" parents. For this reason, camps frequently send out precamp instructions about the number and types of communications desirable.

The child who has never been away from home may be overwhelmed by the sea of strange faces and unfamiliar surroundings. He may be so painfully shy that it is hard for him to meet or even keep from repelling overtures of friendship, and having to wash and dress before others may be excruciatingly embarrassing to him. He may be afraid of the quiet strangeness of the woods, particularly at night when the rustlings of animal life are magnified a hundredfold by his unaccustomed ears.

Spells of homesickness reach their peak about the third or fourth day of camp and are strongest at mealtime or in the evening. All have their basis in fear, such as fear of strangers, of surroundings, or of not being accepted, and are best treated by trying to make the camper feel desired and at home in the group. The counselor should help him negotiate a camp pal and go out of his way to show him little considerations and signs of affection. Special chores or responsibilities make him feel useful, and activities he especially likes take his mind off himself. It may help to let him "talk it out," assuring him that such feelings are not at all unusual, but are experienced by nearly every one when he first stays away from home. It may help to challenge him to stick it out for a certain number of days with the promise that he may go home at the end of that time if he still wants to. A counselor must realize that he is fighting for more than just another camper on the camp roster; he is, in reality, making an important contribution to speed a youngster on his way toward emotional maturity.

## ADDITIONAL READINGS*

### BOOKS AND PAMPHLETS

Benson and Goldberg: The Camp Counselor. McGraw-Hill, 1951.

Dimock and Statten: Talks to Counselors. Ass'n Press, chap. 11.

Doherty, J. Kenneth: Solving Camp Behavior Problems. Ass'n Press, 1944.

Ledlie and Holbein: The Camp Counselor's Manual. Ass'n Press, chap. 11.

Osborne: Camping and Guidance. Ass'n Press, chaps. 4–6.

Ott: So You Want to Be a Camp Counselor. Ass'n Press, chap. 3.

Redl, Fritz, and Wineman, David: Children Who Hate. Free Press.

Slavson: Recreation and the Total Personality. Ass'n Press.

Ure: Fifty Cases for Camp Counselors. Ass'n Press.

Wittenberg: So You Want to Help People. Ass'n Press.

### MAGAZINE ARTICLES

Handling Discipline Problems. C.M., Nov., 1949.

Josselyn, Dr. Irene: Psychological Needs of the Overprivileged Child. C.M., June, 1952.

* See also listing on page 81.

# PART III

# Camp Activities

Planning is forethought. It pervades the realms of all human action. Whether a man plans a business, a career, a house, or a fishing trip, he is looking into the future in order to arrange his affairs so that they will work out the to best advantage. Applied to our everyday world, planning is nothing but common sense.

C. EARL MORROW*

## Chapter 7

## PLANNING THE PROGRAM

### WHY PROGRAMS DIFFER

IT IS VERY hard to summarize programs for there are as many different sorts of them as there are camps. This is not difficult to understand when we realize how many variable factors enter into determining them. The following are prominent among them.

1. *The objectives of the camp or of the sponsoring organization.* Naturally the activities chosen for the program will be those which best carry out the objectives of the particular camp. We would expect a church camp to lean heavily toward activities of a spiritual nature, a school camp to emphasize particularly the acquiring of school information, and an agency camp to work toward its stated objectives. Special camps such as those featuring dance, music or activities for the physically handicapped will obviously have their programs largely circumscribed.

2. *The philosophy and abilities of the camp director and program director.* Those responsible for setting up the program will almost unconsciously sway it in the direction of the activities which interest them most or in which they feel most competent. An avid fisherman will likely see that poles and tackle and time on the program are adequate for his beloved recreation, a person with a

*From *Planning Your Community*. Reproduced by permission of Regional Plan Association, Inc.

love of music will set the stage for his interest, while a person who likes the sedentary, country-club type of activity will not be likely to promote a strong campcraft and trips program. The better leaders, however, try not to ride their hobbies too hard, and so end up with well-rounded, versatile programs.

3. *The abilities of the staff and resource personnel.* Staff members are usually hand picked by the person responsible for hiring them to head the activities he wants to sponsor; thus they may really reflect the wishes of the director or program director. Other executives hire only a minimum of specialists with most of the staff designated as general counselors, but they, in turn, bring with them an assortment of their own particular skills and interests which contribute to a broad and well-balanced program. The danger in having too many specialists is that, at their worst, they may go all-out in efforts to outdo each other in the promotion of their own particular parts of the program instead of cooperating as a team to produce a unified whole. This is the exception, rather than the rule, however, and may be due to a feeling that rehiring and good recommendations depend on their ability to secure camper patronage. A well-rounded specialist with diverse interests or a general counselor who is skillful, for example, with his knife may bring samples of his work and so inspire others to copy his craft. Another counselor soon has the whole camp singing as he accompanies his work with a merry lilt, while still another seems to have a gift for locating some of nature's creatures up to queer and fascinating antics and he soon transmits his ability to see fascinating things in nature to many others.

4. *The nature of the campsite.* Obviously, mountain-climbing will be supplanted by arts and crafts or waterfront or some other activities if the camp is built on a plateau, and no one will be weaving with honeysuckle if it does not grow in the environment. A widely separated unit in a decentralized camp can build its outdoor kitchen right near its own backyard whereas a centralized unit will have to explore the wild woods to locate a private nook for its members, but that may be a blessing in disguise as it gets the group out into previously unexplored acres.

5. *The equipment and facilities.* A camp with an elaborate outlay of waterfront equipment may produce excellent boat-handling skills and fancy regattas while the camp without enough equipment to go around may find campers and staff busily learning how to use tools and build rafts in order to supply the deficiency. Swimming is almost synonymous with camping to many, yet camps without facilities for it have put on wonderful programs of all too frequently neglected items of program to the benefit and satisfaction of all concerned. Imagination and an outgoing approach can turn a lack of archery equipment into a challenge for Robin Hood and his Merry Men to make their own, again necessitating skill with tools and a knowledge of methods and materials before practice in the skills of the particular sport can be pursued.

6. *The climate*. Camps in hot areas will have their campfire programs without benefit of fire and may schedule an extra long siesta and quiet activities during the heat of the day. Camps with cool mornings and evenings will lean more toward vigorous activities, scheduling swimming toward the middle of the day, and making other appropriate adjustments.

7. *Location and terrain.* When interesting historical sites abound in the vicinity, a camp will wisely capitalize on them and plan several trips to visit them. Paul Bunyan Country will be filled with story-telling and special events built around this favorite character. A seaside camp will plan visits to fish-processing plants and fishing vessels. In one camp with a fairly steep hillside, enthusiasm over skiing and tobogganing on pine needles reigned, spurred on by a local resident who had enjoyed these activities as a boy. In another there was a meandering, babbling brook where campers loved to wade and ferret out the secrets of animal and plant life within and around it.

8. *The campers.* The ages, previous experiences, skills, financial status and social backgrounds of the campers are very influential in determining programs. A camper who has seen his grandparents do a lively Lithuanian dance can teach it to the others while another contributes a German folk song and still another demonstrates the chip-carving his art-teacher mother has taught him. Farm boys and girls may be far ahead of city cousins in naturelore but lag far behind in executing fancy dives and swimming strokes.

9. *The length of the camping period.* Campers who come for only a week or two will need more or less simple projects which they can complete in a short time. Others doing short-term camping will be putting into practice skills and knowledges acquired under the sponsoring agency back in the city. In short-term camps it will be a question of choosing how much and what can be accomplished in the time available. Eight-week camps can approach the program in a little more leisurely fashion and lay long-term plans which build up to a climax of accomplishment at the end of the season. One group of campers decided they needed a log cabin to shelter their arts and crafts equipment and worked like little beavers to complete it (with help on the heavy work from some older men); another undertook to clear a vista through the underbrush down to the lake. A group of girls planned an exhibit of dolls dressed in the native costumes of various countries and displayed against papier-mâché relief maps of the respective native lands.

10. *Ratio of counselors to campers.* Many children and relatively few counselors mean a preponderance of group activities with little opportunity for small-group and individual instruction.

## CHANGING PROGRAM EMPHASES

Early camps felt that filling every moment of a camper's day was the best way to keep him out of mischief and prevent homesickness and boredom. The camper was registered in a number of activities, selected because they were "good for him" or because of parental request, and, if he found himself in one he heartily disliked, it was just too bad, for the schedule and rules were rigid and permitted no change, forcing the child to keep on in a grim death struggle to see whether he or the summer would come to an end first. Activities were scheduled like school classes with attendance carefully checked each day. Motivation came through achievement charts, testing programs, intense competition between individuals and groups, and elaborate systems of awards. In some cases, regimentation and scheduling were carried to such a degree as almost to obliterate the one thing the camper most wanted—to have fun.

As with most customs in the history of mankind, this period was followed by an equal and opposite reaction which, at its worst, went to the extreme of scheduling nothing at all, leaving the camper free to do whatever he chose the livelong day. This practice was apparently based on the assumption that the best way to teach anyone to make choices and govern himself is to give him an entirely free rein and let him learn by the trial-and-error method. The fallacy in this line of thinking is evident, for the theme song of the school of experience is "ouch" and its path is filled with many pitfalls and side lanes which may lead to undesirable learnings. Programs planned exclusively by campers or those not planned at all but which, like Topsy, "just grow," lack continuity and are likely to degenerate into worthlessness and eventual boredom. Best results come from tempering the impetuousity and daring of youth with the sobering influence of experience and greater maturity, as occurs when campers and counselors cooperatively plan the program.

## THE NEW CONCEPTION OF PROGRAM

Such camp activities as dramatics, swimming and archery are indeed important parts of camp program, but we no longer look upon them as *the* program. Mary's development does not begin with arts and crafts at 8:30, stop for lunch at 11:30 and continue again at 2:30 with nature study, to cease entirely after her 4:30 horseback-riding period. Instead, program is everything that happens to Mary throughout the day, for each single incident, no matter how trivial, is a potential influence for good or bad. Even bedtime hours from taps to reveille have importance, for they are (we hope) teaching her to stay quiet out of consideration for others and because she herself realizes the need of adequate sleep. Can we argue convincingly that archery, weaving, campcraft or canoeing will be of more ultimate worth to her than forming habits of orderliness, cooperativeness and punctuality? Mary's senses remain impressionable at all times, and we can be sure that she is constantly learning something, be it good or bad, from every experience that comes her way. She cannot be closed up like a book and placed on the shelf at 4:30 to remain unopened until 8:30 the next morning.

Program and activities are not ends in themselves, but are the means by which camping objectives are brought to fruition in the lives of campers. Whereas learning to play tennis may bring Tommy hours of pleasure throughout life, we cannot ignore the equal or greater importance of such concomitant learnings as persistence in mastering a difficult task, good sportsmanship, and respect for someone who can play better.

## HOW CAMP PROGRAM IS PLANNED

The new camp program in the better camps is flexible so that it can be altered to fit the changing needs and wishes of those who are to participate in it. This quality makes it readily adaptable to the craving of youth for variety and the need to be up and doing, yet it is by no means haphazard and unplanned, for indeed it takes superior planning of such a program to avoid conflicts over facilities, equipment and the services of the few or many specialists who are on the staff.

Certain hours, as for rising, going to bed, eating, rest hour, swimming, and so on, which affect the whole camp, must be scheduled or at least definitely arranged for so that groups will not interfere with each other. Beyond that, the program of individuals and groups is left pretty much to individual choice within the realm of the possibilities the camp offers.

The program for the entire camp is usually coordinated under one person who may be called the program director, the assistant camp director, or a head counselor. Occasionally, particularly in small camps, the director himself may serve as program director, but it is more common for him to act in an advisory capacity to another who has been allocated this particular responsibility.

In long-term private camps, campers usually largely decide upon their own activities irrespective of what the rest of their living unit may be doing. Various schemes are used for doing this, a common one being to have the program director announce at the end of a meal, breakfast, for example, what activities will be available for the ensuing period; campers then indicate by a show of hands the ones in which they wish to participate. Duplicate lists are made with the original going to the counselor in charge of the particular activity while the carbon is retained in the camp office so that the location of any camper or counselor is always available. It makes for better instruction if participants are classified as to degree of skill, as sailing for beginners only or firebuilding for those who have passed their preliminary tests in the use of the knife and hatchet. In other variations offering still freer choice, the program director simply opens the field for suggestions and, when Jack requests an activity such as fishing, the program director asks how many would like to join him in this project.

The foregoing type of scheduling programs by individual choices seems to be the most prevalent in long-term camps which believe that it (1) really centers attention on the individual rather than the activity, (2) widens the circle of friendships as the campers participate with first one, then another, in mutual interest groupings, (3) allows the campers to do what they actually want instead of being coerced into following the wishes of the majority of their living unit and (4) relieves the boredom and animosities which may develop over a period of eight weeks of continuous eating, sleeping and doing everything with the same companions.

The trend in most short-term and many other camps is to operate on the plan of having the living units plan their own programs. Here the thought seems to be that a camper, especially during a short stay in camp, can get better acquainted and feel more at ease if he carries on nearly all of his activities with a small group of his peers. In this small "family" he is recognized as an individual and has more chance to voice his opinions.

Under both plans of programming, it is customary to hold a number of all-camp events during the period, here again the number and character of them varying with the particular camp. Most camps sponsor some sort of camp council in which representative counselors and campers from the various living units meet with the program director to plan such events. Care must be exercised to see that the group consists of many more campers than counselors for campers usually hesitate to speak up if they feel the group is counselor-dominated.

As wide a diversity of activities as facilities and the talents of the staff

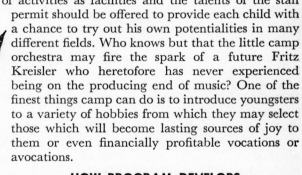

permit should be offered to provide each child with a chance to try out his own potentialities in many different fields. Who knows but that the little camp orchestra may fire the spark of a future Fritz Kreisler who heretofore has never experienced being on the producing end of music? One of the finest things camp can do is to introduce youngsters to a variety of hobbies from which they may select those which will become lasting sources of joy to them or even financially profitable vocations or avocations.

## HOW PROGRAM DEVELOPS

The modern trend in camping is to have the program director, counselors, and campers join in a democratic process of program planning. Counselors act as consultants and advisors, not as dictators, and must avoid superimposing their own ideas yet must guide and control the situation so that wise choices are made. Younger campers need much suggestion, particularly during their first few days in camp for many of them have been quite dependent on radio, movies and television for their entertainment and are at almost a total loss when called upon to make decisions as to how to spend their time. Even older campers often don't really know what they want to do and are inclined to limit their choices to what they already know and are really rather bored with, because they have so little vision of other possibilities. Here is a golden opportunity for you as a counselor to tactfully broaden their interests and open new vistas as you throw in a hint now and then or pick up and help along one of their own. Even when a suggestion is not adopted in its totality, it will stimulate others until the group "catches fire" on something and is off to a truly thrilling experience together. You can often divert impossible or unwise suggestions into something more suitable by coming forth with a still more exciting substitute.

Best practice calls for having a skeleton plan for the day, week or season in the back of your mind or posted on the bulletin board and plenty of possibilities on deck ready to fill in gaps if campers don't supply them. Your sketchy presentation serves as a springboard or take-off point to be altered and elaborated on as your group takes hold and carries the ball. Working out a definite program is extremely important as it keeps the group thinking and anticipating ahead, and details are added little by little with the complete plan usually formulated only about a day or half day ahead of time. Thus you can continuously evaluate and reconsider as you go along.

With youngsters who feel at ease and free to express themselves, proposals literally fly back and forth and it becomes your job to help separate the wheat from the chaff and settle on a few things which give promise of lasting satisfaction. It is an invaluable experience for campers to learn to plan carefully before starting out on an undertaking and to constantly appraise and evaluate what they are doing. Hindsight is notoriously superior to foresight, but a serious attempt at foresight pays big dividends in preventing costly mistakes and disappointments.

It is a tendency of youth to leap breathlessly into anything that sounds new and exciting, then want to drop it without ceremony as soon as the new has worn off or another attraction appears on the stage. Try to lead your group to estimate before they start whether a project has enough true interest to last to a successful completion. Help them see that a good workman does not leave an assortment of half-finished jobs behind him.

Above all, let your campers in on the plan for it just doesn't work to present programs planned from higher up and try to press them willy-nilly on youngsters; the result is rarely more than half-hearted support. When the campers actively have a hand in the planning, they become so excited they can scarcely contain themselves and your worries about discipline problems and problem campers can largely be forgotten.

You must develop keen ears and quick insights to catch program leads.

Often just listening to your group chatter will furnish interesting possibilities. If Jim is describing how his uncle worked on the construction of a city bridge, it may lead to a general discussion of the principles of bridge-building and a suggestion that the group build a bridge across a ravine to save the many steps necessary to go around it. If Susan complains about the prickly brush and rough stones on the way to the waterfront, it's a good time to start a crusade to clear the path. When the Limberlost Unit has just completed a deluxe outdoor shower, promote an invitation for your group to visit it and ten to one you'll soon be helping with plans for a still more luxurious one.

Several stories describe the camping experiences of boys and girls—why not start one during the story hour and watch the account crystallize into action? Step-by-step analyses of how to do things posted in easy-to-read form on a central bulletin board or samples and models placed in conspicuous places ferment brainstorms in young heads. Take a walk and casually mention how certain areas of the campsite could be improved by filling in a muddy place or planting cover crops to control erosion. Make yourself a clothes pole, a no. 10 tin-can cooking outfit or tan a poisonous snake skin and convert it into a belt and watch the interested eyes and eager minds that come to learn. If a canoeing trip is spoiled by a rainstorm that comes up after the hard work of packing, it's a good time to set up a weather bureau and start flying weather flags.

If there is a demand in a field of activity unfamiliar to you, do not discourage it, for research in the camp library will help you, and your fellow counsellors will usually be flattered if you ask their help. If you really want to learn new facts and acquire more skills, you can do so, for it is never necessary to remain like the blind leading the blind.

## Deciding upon a Program

Some projects arise spontaneously, such as the decision to spend the afternoon in cabin clean-up and decoration when rain has spoiled a proposed supper hike. Others, such as a five-day horse-back trip, the camp birthday party, or the stunt for the All-Camp Stunt Night, require long-term planning for the "big event." The pleasures of an undertaking consist of (1) planning for and dreaming of it, (2) actually doing it, and (3) reminiscing over it and basking in the pride of accomplishment.

Facts which in themselves are dry as a bone become alive and fascinating when learned for a definite purpose. It is righteous rebellion when a child objects to learning the technical jargon of sail boating, knowing full well that it will be months or even years before he can pass the tests enabling him even to set foot in one. His attitude does a complete flip flop when he is learning a salty vocabulary to use as he actually helps to manipulate the vessel.

## The Indigenous Program

Most camps now favor what is known as an indigenous program, based upon the resources and unique personality of the camp involved and using native materials for as many camp activities as possible. In arts and crafts, native woods are used for whittling, native vegetation for dyeing, and local grasses for weaving. The folk songs and ballads of the region comprise the singing, and the dances are those of the local inhabitants. Stories, dramatics, pageants and original songs find their basis in the folk lore, legends and history of the locality. Residents of the  area are consulted and brought into camp freely, and the town librarian is consulted for clippings and other materials in her files.

Nature study is an investigation of the flowers, trees and butterflies found on the camp grounds. Starlore, wildlife and forest conservation of the area vie with local lore and history as topics for "program," making it a living, pulsating, vital thing in the daily life of the camper. It is evident that no two indigenous programs would be quite the same, for no two communities offer identical natural resources of historical background.

## The Test of a Good Program Activity

Activities which bear up well under the following tests are likely to be good ones and make a real contribution to the objectives of camping.

1. Is the activity in accord with the idea of simple outdoor living? Does it further an understanding and love of the out-of-doors?

2. Does it answer youth's longing for fun, adventure and dramatic suspense? Do campers *want* to do it or are they merely going through with it to satisfy the whims of adults? Is it interesting in itself without thought of award or other outside inducement?

3. Does it foster camper initiative, resourcefulness and creative expression, or is it a cut-and-dried process where campers follow instructions to cut along the dotted line, then join points A and B?

4. Does it broaden interests and appreciations and help youngsters to see with Stevenson that

> The world is so full of a number of things,
> I'm sure we should all be as happy as kings.

5. Is it free from actual physical danger? Does it contribute to the greater health and vitality of the campers?

6. Could it be done just as well or better in the camper's home community? (This is one of the most important tests and largely rules out the city type of arts and crafts and organized sports such as basketball and baseball if the camper has access to them in his home community.)

7. Does it have carry-over value for use in other situations or after camping days are over?

8. Does it help to develop group consciousness and adaptability to group living?

9. Does it fulfill fundamental desires and help the camper achieve a high state of mental health?

10. Can it be made a true group project to which every member can feel he has contributed, or are all the places of importance usurped by a few of the more aggressive or talented?

## POSSIBLE PROJECTS

### Construction Work

Since a great deal of camp interest is centered around the actual process of camp living, it is only natural that constructing camp fixin's should occupy an important position.

Among possible projects are making a:

Rustic entrance for unit, cabin or camp
Totem pole
Outdoor kitchen
Outdoor theater
Campfire circle
Log cabin
Nature exhibit
Rock garden
Camp craft exhibit
Rustic furniture
Dam up a creek
Rustic bulletin board
Nature aquarium
Green cathedral— outdoor chapel
Improvised camping equipment
Repair of boats, riding tack, tennis courts
Outdoor kitchen

Weathervane
Outpost camp
Tree house
Lean-to
Council ring
Clearing a path
Bows and arrows
Sun dial
Bridge across the creek
Indian tepee
Soil erosion control
Pottery kiln
Nature trail
Fernery
Rock garden
Shelves, tables, benches
Sun dial
Cleaning up the campsite

## Evening Activities

Miscellaneous program of games, singing, stunts, and the like
Informal dramatics
Folk, square or round dancing
Parties—hard times, pioneer, Indian, gypsy, formal (in couples), plantation, masquerade
Old singing school
Spelling matches
Progressive games
Village night (invite the camp neighbors in)
Barn dance
Amateur night

Hay ride
Camp banquet
Moonlight hike
Star hike or study
Lantern party
Poetry, stories
Shadow plays
Torch light or candlelight parade while singing
Quiz show
Discussion groups
Liar's club (see who can tell the biggest whopper)

In many camps the occasional evening campfire program is a tradition dear to the hearts of the campers and can and should be varied enough to lift it above mere routine and anchor it as one of the most meaningful events of the summer. It assumes a more romantic and inspiring air when conducted in beautiful surroundings remote from everyday paths, and many camps have worked out elaborate fire-lighting ceremonies for use with it. Physical comfort warrants attention, for no one can sit in rapt attention to a program while subjected to a fierce bombardment from voracious mosquitoes. Evening programs should be tapered off to a quiet, sleep-inducing conclusion and should end on time even though some part must be omitted. Symbols, though simple, mean much to campers and can be used to stimulate their imaginations and loyalties. Hammett and Musselman* suggest having a town crier call campers together for the Fourth of July program instead of having them just saunter in, and crowning the winner of a swimming meet with a wreath of laurel leaves rather than just announcing that he won.

## Special Days

County or state fair
Camp Birthday
Mardi Gras
Gypsy day
Dude ranch rodeo
Circus day
Holiday of some other nation (costumes, food, dances, games, songs, and so on)
Staff day (when campers and staff interchange roles)
Western barbecue day
Regatta day

Water pageant
Local pageant day
Birthday of some famous person
Clean-up, paint-up day
Story book day (theme of Robin Hood, Paul Bunyan, Robinson Crusoe or other book carried out through the day)
Village day when neighbors from the village visit
Gift day when campers or groups make a gift of something they have constructed to the camp

* Hammett, Catherine T., and Musselman, Virginia: The Camp Program Book, p. 203.

## Rainy-Day Activities

Rainy days always present a problem to the unimaginative counselor, and a steady downpour of several days' duration is enough to tax the ingenuity and resourcefulness of even the doughtiest leader and reduce his spirits to a state of drippy dilapidation. Nevertheless, campers must be kept busy and happy for spells of homesickness are especially likely to sail in with the storm clouds. An A-1 counselor can help his charges turn such an occasion into one of the most satisfying and enjoyable experiences of the summer. If you are a wise leader you will keep the threat of rain ever in the back of your head and steer your group toward outdoor activites which take advantage of balmy weather, literally saving up certain especially appropriate activities for those inevitable rainy days. Here are some possibilities:

Plan a carnival or puppet show

Take a slicker hike in the rain

Compose a cabin or unit yell, song, symbol, slogan, or the like

Learn new songs and sing the old

Work on scrap books and stamp or snapshot albums

Make candy or popcorn, or serve "tea"

Play charades and other indoor games

Plan an open house with simple refreshments for another cabin or unit

Plan stunts for the next all-camp program

Hold discussions

Read or tell stories

Write letters

Listen to recorded music

Plan a future trip, a nature trail, or outpost camp

Toast marshmallows

Hold a convention of the Biggest Liar's Club

Compose a cabin or unit newspaper to be read at supper

Organize a harmonica band or other musical group

Have folk or square dances and singing games

Plan a banquet (with candles or some little extra item of food and program)

Organize Fireside Clubs where small groups can gather in front of available fireplaces to pursue special interests

Arrange a hobby show or other display

Plan a stunt night (keep it on a high level)

Make posters for the bulletin board

Have a pet show—display stuffed animals, etc.

Make puppets or work on a play

Practice camp craft skills such as knots, tincancraft, and so forth

Work on arts and crafts, plan an exhibit

Whittle or carve objects

Mend clothing and get the cabin in apple-pie order

Work on costume box in readiness for the next play

Hold a spelling bee or quiz program

Read or write camp poetry

Make indoor games and play them

Write a dramatic production and prepare to produce it

Make improvised camping equipment such as trench candles and water-proofed matches

Study weather, make weather flags, barometer, and so forth

Play active games to relieve the tension of inactivity

Mark tools and put them in good repair—sharpen knives, axes, and others

Work on riding tack, archery tackle, etc.

Get some extra sleep or rest

Fish, boat or swim in the rain (if no lightning)

Beautify living quarters, by block printing curtains, using natural dyes for materials, adding rustic furniture, and so forth

Hold instruction and practice in Red Cross first aid techniques, study rules for tennis, etc.

Have a talent show

Play indoor nature games or get ready for your next nature hike

You will find other suggestions for programs throughout other chapters of this book and in the program sources listed at the ends of several of the chapters.

## ADDITIONAL READINGS

### ARCHERY

Archery. Boy Scouts (#3381), 1941.
Camp Director's Handbook and Buying Guide: Archery in Camp. (Issued annually.)
Hodgkin, Adrian Eliot: The Archer's Craft. Barnes.
Hunt and Metz: The Flat Bow. Bruce.
Jaeger, Eloise: How to Improve Your Archery. Barnes.
Miller, Myrtle K.: Archery in the Camp Program. C.M., June, 1945.
Miller, Myrtle K.: Archery Safety Rules. Jr. H. and P. E., May, 1952.
Reichert, Natalie, and Keasey, Gilman: Archery. Barnes.
Shane, Adolph: Archery Tackle. Bennett.
Whiffen, Larry C.: Shooting the Bow. Bruce, 1946.

### BICYCLING

Bicycling for Health and Pleasure. Bicycle Institute.
Camp Bicycle Program. C.M., Feb., 1952.
Cycling. Boy Scouts (#3277), 1949.

### EQUITATION

Anderson, S. W.: Heads Up—Heels Down. Macmillan, 1944.
Drachman, Albert I.: How Good Is Your Riding Program? C.M., April and June, 1948.

Hope, C. E. G.: Riding. Pitman, 1948.
Horsemanship. Boy Scouts (#3298), 1951.
Kays, D. J.: The Horse. Barnes.
Orr, Jennie M.: A Manual of Riding. Burgess, 1945, 22 pp.
Self, Margaret Cabell: Horseman's Encyclopedia. Barnes.
Self, Margaret Cabell: Horsemanship. Barnes.
Self, Margaret Cabell: Horses, Their Selection, Care and Handling. Barnes.
Self, Margaret Cabell: Riding Simplified. Barnes, 1948.
Slaughter, Jean: Horsemanship for Beginners. Knopf, 1952.

### FISHING

Bucher, Charles A. (Ed.): Methods and Materials in Physical Education and Recreation. Mosby, 1954, pp. 111–116.
Burns, Eugene: Fishing for Women. Barnes, 1953.
Burns, Eugene: Fresh and Salt Water Spinning. Barnes, 1952, 96 pp.
Caine, Lou S.: North American Fresh Water Sport Fish. Barnes, 1949, 212 pp.
DesGrey, Arthur V.: Camping. Ronald, 1950, pp. 129–135.
Evanoff, Vlad: Natural Fresh Water Fishing Baits. Barnes, 1953.
Evanoff, Vlad: Surf Fishing. Barnes, 1948.
Fishing. Boy Scouts (#3295), 1951.

Gregg, E. C.: How to Tie Flies. Barnes.

Hammett and Musselman: The Camp Program Book, pp. 159–161.

Hollis, Harold G.: Bass Tackle and Tactics. Barnes.

Leonard, J. Edson: Bait Rod Casting. Barnes, 1953.

Leonard, J. Edson: Flies. Barnes, 1950, 352 pp.

Leonard, J. Edson: Fly Rod Casting. Barnes, 1953.

Michael, William W.: Dry Fly Trout Fishing. McGraw-Hill, 202 pp.

Outdoor Life's Fisherman's Encyclopedia. Grosset and Dunlop, 1953, 256 pp.

Plug Casting. C.M., March, 1953.

Tappley, H. G.: Tackle Tinkering. Barnes.

Zarchy, Harry: Let's Fish: A Guide to Fresh and Salt Water. Knopf, 1952.

## GAMES

Ainsworth, Dorothy, and Others: Individual Sports for Women, 2nd ed. Saunders, 1949, 414 pp.

Athletics. Boy Scouts (#3324), 1943.

Bancroft, Jessie H.: Games, 2nd ed. Macmillan, 1937, 685 pp.

Blanchard, Fessender S.: Paddle Tennis. Barnes.

Borst, Evelyne: The Book of Games for Boys and Girls. Barnes, 1953, 256 pp.

Camp Director's Handbook and Buying Guide: Field and Court Dimensions. (Issued annually.)

DePew, Arthur M.: The Cokesbury Game Book, rev. ed. Abingdon-Cokesbury.

Dewitt, R. T.: Teaching Individual and Team Sports. Prentice-Hall, 1953, 497 pp. (25 sports.)

Games for Boys and Men. NRA.

Games for Boy Scouts. Boy Scouts (#3412), 20 pp.

Games for Children. NRA, 1943.

Games for Girl Scouts. Girl Scouts (#20–632), 1949, 70 pp.

Games for Handicapped Children. NRA.

Games for Quiet Hours and Small Spaces. NRA, 1938. (160 games and stunts.)

Harbin, E. O.: Games for Boys and Girls. Abingdon-Cokesbury, 1951.

Hindman, Darwin A.: Handbook of Active Games. Prentice-Hall, 1951, 436 pp.

Horowitz, Caroline: 40 Rainy Day Games (9–14 yrs.). Hart, 1950, 96 pp.

Hunt, Sarah, and Cain, Ethel: Games the World Around, 2nd ed. Barnes, 1950, 269 pp.

Macfarlan, Allan A.: New Games for 'Tween Agers. Ass'n Press.

Make Your Own Games. NRA. (16 games.) (MP 332.)

Make Your Own Puzzles. NRA. (10 puzzles.) (MP 333.)

Mason, Bernard, and Mitchell, Elmer D.: Active Games and Contests. Barnes, 1935, 601 pp. (1800 games.)

Millen, Nina (Ed.): Children's Games from Many Lands, rev. ed. Friendship Press, 1951, 214 pp.

Mitchell, Elmer D. (Ed.): Sports for Recreation and How to Play Them, rev. ed. Barnes, 1952, 512 pp.

Mulac, Margaret E.: The Game Book. Harper, 1946.

Reiley, Catherine C.: Group Fun. Dodd, Mead.

Richardson, Hazel A.: Games for the Elementary School Grades, rev. ed. Burgess, 1951.

Ripley, G. S.: The Book of Games. Ass'n Press, 1952, 236 pp.

Shaw, John H., Troester, Carl A., Jr., and Gabrielsen, Milton A.: Individual Sports for Men. Saunders, 1950, 399 pp.

Smith, Charles F.: Games and Game Leadership. Dodd, Mead, 1937.

Staley, Seward C.: Games, Contests, and Relays. Barnes, 1924, 324 pp.

Stunts, Contests, and Relays. NRA. (MP 326.) (Activities for limited space.)

Tunis, John R.: Lawn Games. Barnes.

Yocom, Rachael D. and Hunsaker, H. B.: Individual Sports for Men and Women. Barnes, 1947, 287 pp.

## GENERAL

Broy, Arline B.: Give Me Counselors with Imagination. C.M., Feb., 1954.

Burns, Gerald P.: Camp Organization for Program. A.C.A., 24 pp.

Burns, Gerald P.: The Program of the Modern Camp. Chaps. 3 and 4.

Camp, Marjorie, and Joy, Barbara E.: You Can Put Real Camping into Your Camp Program. C.M., April, 1952.

Chambers, Robert: Book of Days. Lippin-
cott, 1899, 2 vols.
Cheley, F. H.: Stories for Talks to Boys,
3rd ed. Ass'n Press, 1946.
Douglas, George William: The American
Book of Days. Wilson, 1937.
Gibbs, Howard: Camper Participation in
Program Planning. C.M., June, 1952.
Guide for Day Camping. Camp Fire Girls
(#D 320), 1952.
Hammett and Musselman: The Camp
Program Book. Preface, chap. 1, 2, 3, 4.
Handbook for Guardians of Camp Fire
Girls. Camp Fire Girls, 1952.
Joy, Barbara Ellen: And Gladly Would He
Learn. Jr. H. and P.E., June, 1953.
Joy, Barbara Ellen: And Let the Camper
Choose. C.M., May, 1951.
Ledlie, John A., and Roehm, Ralph D.:
Program Planning Fundamentals. C.M.,
Nov., 1949.
Vickers, Willa: Conversation Creates Good
Program. C.M., April, 1953.
Vinal, William Gould: Let's Take Camping
Back to Nature. C.M., June, 1950.

## INDIAN LORE

Buttree, Julia M.: The Rhythm of the
Redman. Barnes, 1930. (33 dances, cus-
toms, songs and arts of the Indian.)
Campfire, Indian Dance, Game Program
Techniques Revised. C.M., April, 1950.
Following Indian Trails. Camp Fire Girls
(#D 315), 1950. (History and current in-
formation regarding Indians.)
Gallo, Gene J.: Crafts, Nature Study and
Woodcraft Are Combined in Indian
Lore in Camp. C.M., May, 1953.
Hunt, Ben: Indiancraft and Camp Handi-
craft, Bruce.
Indian Lore. Boy Scouts (#3358), 1942.
Mason, Bernard: The Book of Indian
Crafts and Costumes. Barnes, 1946, 188
pp.
Mason, Bernard: Dances and Stories of the
American Indian. Barnes, 1944, 304 pp.
McQuire, Frances: Indian Drums Beat
Again. Dutton, 1953, 123 pp.
Solomon, Julian H.: Book of Indiancraft
and Indian Lore. Harper.
Thoemen, Ethel: Use of Dolls as an Ap-
proach to Indian Lore. C.M., June, 1940.

## MISCELLANEOUS

Activities for Summer Camps. Arts Coop.,
1948, 90 pp.
Berthold, Beatrice: Summer Skiing on Pine
Needles. C.M., June, 1938.
Blue Bird Book, The, Camp Fire Girls,
1954. (Girls ages 7-9.)
Camp Director's Handbook and Buying
Guide. ACA. (Issued annually.)
Chapman, M., Gaudette, M., and Ham-
mett, C.: Program Helps for Camp
Leaders. Girl Scouts (#23-310).
Coin Collecting. Boy Scouts (#3374), 1949.
Easy Stunts. NRA (MP 233), 1947. (10
easy skits.)
Eisenberg, Helen and Larry: The End of
Your Stunt Hunt. Ass'n Press.
Eisenberg, Helen and Larry: The Pleasure
Chest. Eisenberg.
Ford, Mr. and Mrs. Henry: Good Morning.
NRA. (Old time dances.)
Gardner: Handbook for Recreation Leaders.
Graham: The Girls' Camp, chap. 10.
Hammett and Musselman: The Camp
Program Book.
Harbin: The Fun Encyclopedia. Abing-
don-Cokesbury.
Keiser, Armilda B.: Here's How and When.
Friendship Press, 1952, 175 pp.
Ledlie and Holbein: The Camp Coun-
selor's Manual, chap. 25.
Leeming, J.: Fun with Magic. Lippincott,
1943.
Leopold, Jules: At Ease! Whittlesey.
Mason, Bernard S.: Roping. Barnes.
Mulac, Margaret E.: The Playleaders'
Manual.
Musical Mixers and Simple Square Dances.
NRA.
Rainy Day Program for Camps. NRA.
Ripley, G. S.: Fun around the Camp Fire.
Boy Scouts.
Rocks and Minerals. Boy Scouts (#3357),
1937.
Ryan, Grace L.: Dances of Our Pioneers.
Barnes, 1939, 196 pp. (26 dances.)
Spicer, Dorothy Gladys: The Book of
Festivals. Woman's Press, 1937.
Stamp Collecting. Boy Scouts (#3359),
1951.
Suggestions for an Amateur Circus. NRA
(MP 26).

Tolman, Beth, and Page, Ralph: The Country Dance Book. Barnes, 1937, 192 pp.

## PARTIES AND SOCIAL RECREATION

Bowers, Ethel: Let's Plan a Party. Ass'n Press.

Bowers, Ethel: Parties, A–Z. NRA.

Bowers, Ethel (Ed.): Parties for Special Days of the Year. Ass'n Press.

Bowers, Ethel (Ed.): Parties: Plans and Programs. Ass'n Press.

Bowers, Ethel (Ed.): Stunts and Entertainment. Ass'n Press.

Mason, Bernard S., and Mitchell, Elmer D.: Social Games for Recreation. Barnes, 1935, 444 pp. (1200 games.)

Mulac, Margaret, and Holmes, Morean: The Party Game Book. Harper.

Spicer, Dorothy Gladys: Folk Party Fun. Ass'n Press, 1954.

Spicer, Dorothy Gladys: Holiday Parties. Woman's Press, 1939.

Spicer, Dorothy Gladys: Parties for Young Americans. Woman's Press, 1940.

## PHOTOGRAPHY

Deschin, Jacob: Fun with Your Camera. Whittlesey, 1947.

Featherstonough, Diane: Photography for All. Barnes & Noble.

Gottlieb, William: Photography. Knopf, 1953, 44 pp.

Hammett and Musselman: The Camp Program Book, chap. 25.

Haskell, Douglas: A Camper with a Camera. C.M., June, 1948.

Marshall, Lucille Robertson: Photography for Teen-Agers. Prentice-Hall, 1951.

Mayall, R. Newton, and Margaret L.: Skyshooting, Hunting the Stars with Your Camera. Ronald, 1949, 174 pp.

Photograms—Easy Craft with Camper Appeal. C.M., June, 1953.

Photography. Boy Scouts (#3334), 1937.

Photography in Camp—A Manual for Counselors. Eastman Kodak, 1951, 45 pp.

Picture Taking in Camp. Eastman Kodak, 1952, 32 pp. (Camper's Manual.)

Picture Taking Is Important Too. C.M., March, 1954.

## RIFLERY

A Rifle Range Will Do Wonders for Your Camp. Nat'l Rifle Ass'n.

Camp Director's Handbook and Buying Guide, The, Camp Riflery Program. (Issued annually.)

Cardinal, Paul: Easy Ways to Improve Your Rifle Range. C.M., April, 1951.

Daisy Manufacturing Co., Air Rifle Club Dept., Plymouth, Mich.

Damon, G. E.: Gun-Fun with Safety. Standard, 1947, 206 pp.

Fremault, George: Your Camp Riflery Program. C.M., March, 1954.

Hammett and Musselman: The Camp Program Book. Riflery, pp. 157–159.

Haven, Charles T.: Small Arms Manual. Morrow, 1943.

Hicks, Marjorie: Air Rifle Shooting. C.M., May, 1953.

How to Organize a Junior Air Rifle Club. Daisy Manufacturing Co., 10 pp.

How to Shoot a Rifle (Official Instructor's Handbook, Nat'l Rifle Ass'n). Barnes.

Janes, E. C.: A Boy and His Gun. Barnes, 1951, 207 pp.

Junior Rifle Handbook, rev. Nat'l Rifle Ass'n, 1951, 48 pp.

Marksmanship. Boy Scouts (#3338), 1938.

Stephens, William L., Jr.: Rifle Marksmanship. Barnes.

Wilson, R. C.: Rifle Manual, rev. ed. Burgess, 1946, 30 pp.

Of all people, children are the most imaginative.

MACAULAY, Essays: Mitford's Greece

# Chapter 8

# DRAMATICS

## Let's Pretend

EVERYONE loves to pretend, for all of us would like to be and do many more things in life than time will permit. Movies and novels provide an escape into the realm of imagination where we can picture ourselves in the role of the beautiful heroine or the swashbuckling pirate, and this seems to satisfy us temporarily and make us content to return into our prosaic, everyday lives. Though grandfather and grandmother still like to pretend, it is in youth that we find the most pressing urge to "make believe" and dwell in the land of fantasy. Almost every child loves to dress up and "be" all the people his imagination points for him.

Informal skits and stunts for self-entertainment or the enjoyment of friends are perennial favorites in the summer camp. Only the formal dramatic presentation, with its long and complicated parts and its many hours of rehearsal necessary to stage a finished product, palls on all but the especially talented and interested. Some camps put on one or more formal plays a summer, but others feel this practice but duplicates the child's city or school experience and absorbs too much precious time from the outdoor experiences that are unique to camping.

## Standards for Dramatics

The dramatics counselor who best fits into the average camp situation is the one who realizes that most campers cannot and do not even aspire to become stage professionals; they are just average children who can find real values and keen enjoyment in truly informal dramatics. A child's interest is intense but fleeting, making him not want to concentrate too long on any one thing. This does not mean that we need sacrifice quality and high standards or sink to the levels of the slap stick and crude humor which once brought camp stunt night into such ill repute. Seemingly impromptu performances are deceiving, for, when really good, we can rest assured that someone has put real time and thought into them. Hastily thrown together productions invariably reveal themselves as such. Campers enjoy most what they themselves create, writing their own script and using what they have at hand for properties and costumes.

## The Value of Dramatics

Any form of dramatics should, first of all, provide fun for the participants. It should offer a chance to develop poise in front of others and give practice in controlling voice and body. Mumbling or speaking in a low inaudible voice is inexcusable; always strive for good enunciation. Original productions offer great opportunity for creative ability and self-expression, so urge young actors to let their imaginations run riot as they actually *live* the part they are playing instead of being wooden and expressionless and dropping out of character as soon as they have spoken their lines.

Every member of your group can find a place for his talents, for those playing roles must be supported by some members to design and make costumes, to build scenery and paint it, to prompt and to act as property men, ushers, stage hands, and the like. Dramatic activities unite many of the different activities and interests of camp. Dramatizing a story, a bit of local history or legend, camp history, lives and customs of the pioneers, historical events or folk tales or myths will interest campers in much educational research if the dramatic production is made truly authentic.

## Staging the Show

Keep sets and properties simple, often merely suggesting the real thing, with details left to the imagination. A grassy slope will do for seating the audience, although some camps boast of a more permanent outdoor theater with scenery and entrances of planted trees and shrubbery and rustic seats for the audience. Tin-can footlights and blanket curtains serve adequately.

Scenery may be crude and painted on brown paper. It sometimes adds a touch of humor to label a stick, "tree"; a log, "park bench"; and so on. Paint a false face on a paper bag that just fits over your head. Cut out holes for your eyes and nose, paste on paper ears and a false nose and construct hair from yarn, frayed rope or burlap. Create costumes such as pillow-slip aprons, handkerchief collars and sheet angel-robes. Fringed burlap bags will serve as pioneer costumes and acorns, sea shells and no. 10 tin can be made into jewelry. Make animals with blanket bodies, cardboard ears, and tails of frayed rope. Many camps have costume boxes which will transform a camper as magically as Cinderella's godmother changed mice into horses.

## Dramatic Activities

Activities embodying elements of the dramatic come in many forms, as shown by this list:

1. Musical comedy and operettas (Gilbert and Sullivan are particularly liked by youngsters). Combine music, dance and dramatics.

2. Dramatization of ballads, songs or poems as someone reads them.

3. Pageants—based on local history, camp history, etc.

4. Folk festivals.

5. Readings and recitations.

6. Pantomime with modern dance.

7. Choral readings—an old form which is being revived; good at camp-fires, Sunday services or just anytime.

8. Marionette and puppet shows—combine dramatics with arts and crafts. Shy campers often lose their reticence as they manipulate and furnish the voices for their puppets.

9. Charades—an old game in which individuals or groups take turns acting out the syllables of a word such as dandelion (dandie—lyin'), or idolatry (eye—doll—a tree), while the others attempt to guess the word. In another version one group writes out a word and hands it to the captain of the other group who must act it out so that his group can guess it. Time the groups to see which can "stump" the other longest at acting out and guessing their words.

10. Burlesques—take-offs of camp scenes with much exaggeration, such as "the first night out on the soft, downy ground" or "dining with the tender-foot outdoor cook." Be sure it is just good fun with no feelings hurt.

11. Sealed orders. Each writes out a situation to be acted out, such as "an old lady caught in the middle of the block with the traffic light changing." All "orders" are placed in a hat, and each camper draws one which he must act out.

12. Tableaux or "album of familiar pictures." Groups or individuals are posed in characteristic stance when the curtain is drawn or the light is turned on.

13. Shadow plays. Actors carry out actions close to a curtain with the audience seated on the other side. Lights behind the actors cause their shadows to show through. If desired, someone may read a poem or story to accompany the acting. Puppets can also substitute as actors.

14. Pantomime. Action may be with or without accompanying reading. Act out a familiar story or folk tale and see if others can guess it.

15. Reading a play. This offers great possibilities when actors are familiar enough with the lines to be able to put good expression into their reading. They may employ as much or little accompanying action as they wish.

16. New Orleans. An old, familiar childhood game.

17. Dumb crambo. This is the opposite of charades, in that one side chooses a word and tells the other side what it rhymes with. The latter then act out various "guesses" as to what the word is until they finally get it right.

18. Paper-bag dramatics. Give each group a paper bag and allow the members a few minutes to plan a skit using their properties.

19. Write and produce an original playlet based on a Bible story, a familiar folk tale, a well-loved story, camp history, or the like.

## ADDITIONAL READINGS

### BOOKS AND PAMPHLETS

Brown, Mildred H.: Let's Give a Play. Girl Scouts (#23–419).

Brown, Thelma S.: Treasury of Religious Plays. Ass'n Press.

Bucher: Methods and Materials in Physical Education and Recreation, chap. 7. (More formal type of plays.)

Burack, A. S.: One Hundred Plays for Children. Plays, Inc., 1949.

Burger, Isabel B.: Creative Play Acting. Barnes, 1950, 224 pp.

Children Write a Play, The, NRA. (8–13 yrs. old.)

Dramatics. Boy Scouts (#3367), 1936.

Dramatics for the Camp Community. NRA (MP 420), 10 pp.

Dramatics for Girl Scouts. Girl Scouts (#19–750), 1950.

Du Bois, Graham: Plays for Great Occasions. Plays, Inc. (Based on holidays, most not within camp season.)

Easy Stunts. NRA (MP 233).

Eisenberg, Helen and Larry: The Handbook of Skits and Stunts. Ass'n Press, 1953, 254 pp.

Eisenberg, Helen and Larry: Skit Hits. Eisenberg, 1952, 66 pp.

Entertainment Stunts. NRA (MP 170).

Finger Puppets. NRA.

Hammett and Musselman: The Camp Program Book. Ass'n Press, chap. 21.

Harbin: The Fun Encyclopedia. Abington-Cokesbury, 1940, chaps. 14 and 15.

Hark, Mildred, and McQueen, Noel: Modern Comedies for Young Players. Plays, Inc.

How to Produce a Play. NRA.

Kamerman, Sylvia E.: Little Plays for Little Players. Plays, Inc.

Lease, Ruth, and Siks, Geraldine: Creative Dramatics in Home, School, and Community. Harper, 1952, 306 pp.

Macfarlan, Allan A.: Campfire and Council Ring Programs. Ass'n Press, 1951, 155 pp.

Mason and Mitchell: Social Games for Recreation. Barnes, chap. 13.

Monahan, Elaine and Douglas: On Stage, Five Camp Plays with a Purpose. Character Craft Publications.

Mulac: The Play Leader's Manual. Harper, pp. 131–139.

Paradis, Marjorie B.: One-Act Plays for All-Girl Casts. Plays, Inc.

Plays for Teen-Agers. NRA (MP 383). (List of titles and publishers.)

Play Production Made Easy. NRA.

Price, Olive: Debutante Plays. French. (Girls, ages 12–20.)

Silver Bells and Cockle Shells and Seven Other Plays. NRA.

Simon, S. Sylvan: Camp Theatricals. French, 1934.

Simon, S. Sylvan: Easily Staged Plays for Boys. French.

Six More Dramatic Stunts. NRA (MP 168).

Six New Dramatic Stunts. NRA (MP 142).

Ward, Winifred: Stories to Dramatize. Children's Theatre Press.

White, Alice: Anthology of Choral Readings. Girl Scouts (#23–466). (24 choral readings.)

## MAGAZINE ARTICLES

Booth, Judy: Camp Dramatics—A Performance for Stars or a Creative Experience for All? C.M., June, 1951.

Breeser, Bettye: Fantasy in Camp Programs. C.M., Dec., 1953.

Harlor, Betty: Emphasize Fun in Camp Dramatics. C.M., May, 1953.

## PUPPETS

Batchelder, Marjorie: Puppet Theatre Handbook. Harper, 1947.

Blackham, Olive: Puppets into Actors. Macmillan, 1949.

Hetrich, Lenore: Puppet Plays and Peephole Shows. Paine.

Lanchester, Weale: Marionette Charts. Bennett. (Imported.)

Lewis, Roger: Puppets and Marionettes. Knopf, 1952. (Ages 7–11.)

Rasmussen, Carrie, and Slorck, Caroline: Fun-Time Puppets. Children's Press, 1952, 41 pp.

Wright, John: Your Puppetry. Bennett, 1952. (Imported.)

Music washes away from the soul the dust of everyday life.

AUERBACH

# Chapter 9

# MUSIC

## The Place of Music in Camp

It is the most natural thing in the world for happy campers to sing whenever and wherever they are; conversely, campers who sing just naturally can't keep from being happy. Song should burst forth as spontaneously as mushrooms after a rain, for the miles fly by while hiking, dishes seem almost to dry themselves and a group of paddlers can proceed in perfect rhythm when there's a song in the air. Good music is a great morale booster, for few fail to succumb to a catchy tune, a strong rhythm, or the sheer beauty of a lovely melody. No camper should return home without a complete repertoire of good new (to him) songs in his head.

## Kinds of Songs

Most songs can be divided roughly into three types, each having a definite place in camp.

1. *Folk songs* such as "Louisiana Lullaby" and "Walking at Night" cannot be traced to any one composer, for they have been handed down from one generation to the next and sung for many years before anyone ever got around to putting them into writing. They must have had real meaning and worth, for only songs which speak the language of the people can survive for so long. *Ballads*, such as "Barbara Allen" and "The Old Woman's Courtin'," tell a story, and can therefore be dramatized. The *sea chanteys* of sailors such as "Blow the Man Down," various *work songs*, as "Roll the Cotton Down," and the French *voyageur* songs were used to shorten long hours of labor. All types of folk songs, including lullabies, singing games, Negro spirituals,

113

plantation songs, cowboy songs and mountain ballads, hold even more fascination when the singers know the story behind them and the customs, occupations and manner of life of the peoples who originally sang them.

2. In *rounds* or *canons*, the group is subdivided into two or more groups who carry the same tune, but start singing at spaced intervals. Each sings the song through an agreed number of times (usually as many as there are parts), so that they end the song in reverse order. "White Coral Bells" and "Dona Nobis Pacem" are well known examples.

3. *Art songs* are compositions of the masters and are surprisingly often based on old folk songs. They are lovely and offer unlimited possibilities in the way of bringing about a deeper appreciation of really good music. "Prayer from Hansel and Gretel" is of this type.

## Should a General Counselor Lead Singing?

There is a far too prevalent feeling that only counselors with special talent and training in music should lead or teach songs, but this will rob both you and your group of much pleasure. Any person who can carry a tune can learn to teach songs which will be influential in drawing his group together in happiness and good fellowship. Some successful leaders do not even try to join the singing but merely "mouth" the words in good rhythm as they spur their singers on to a worthy rendition. An enthusiastic person with a little musical knowledge can keep a group together and sometimes gets better results than a professional musician who kills spontaneity and joy by his insistance on perfection.

## How Should You Present Songs?

1. You will need tact and patience to wean campers' tastes away from the inferior doggerel and popular tunes of the juke box and transfer them to the abundance of really good music available. It may be wisest to join them at first in the songs they already know, gradually introducing short, catchy new ones, and eventually leading up to more complicated ones. It is surprising how soon the right approach finds campers requesting more new songs and resinging the ones just learned for they find a new source of satisfaction when they learn to sing good songs well.

2. It is easiest to teach songs to a small group whose members can then be used as the nucleus to teach them to others.

3. Know the tune and words thoroughly before trying to teach them. Sing it several times to yourself, perhaps practicing your arm movements for leading in front of a mirror. You may not need arm movements at all, or at least only simple ones, if your group is small for you need only keep them in unison; in fact, it is really detrimental to the spirit of camp singing to use gesticulations approaching those of a symphony conductor. Use your left hand to regulate volume and indicate when certain groups are to start or stop as in rounds. Keep the rhythm with your right hand. A crisp manner

on your part will bring a like response from your singers, whereas a lacka-daisical, spiritless manner will be similarly reflected. Your right arm movements may follow this pattern:

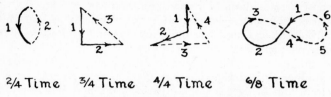

**2/4 Time      3/4 Time      4/4 Time      6/8 Time**

Arm Movements for Leading Singing.

Have some signal to start as "ready," draw in a breath on the next beat, and then give a brisk downstroke of your right arm for the first word or make an upbeat, pause and start the group with a vigorous downbeat. Be sure to hold your hands high enough for everyone to see. Let the vigor of your hand movements show how much volume and accent you want, hold your hand in a fixed position to indicate a held note, and chop it off at the end of the song so all will stop together.

4. Some camps mimeograph or print song books of their own particular favorites or you may print the words of a new song to be learned in large characters on rolled butcher's paper which can be hung where all can see. Most song leaders, however, feel that singers put more thought and feeling into a song if they sing the words from memory and that this also allows them to watch you and so keep together in the pride and thrill of singing in perfect cadence.

5. When teaching a new song, sing it through to give a general idea of the tempo and spirit and set a good mood for learning. If it seems desirable, call attention to the story or background of the song or the sequence of events as you repeat the words and give little cues to help the singers remember. If the chorus is particularly catchy, teach it first, then present the verses one at a time, coming back to the now familiar chorus each time. Watch carefully and present additional parts of the song as fast as the group is ready for them, but don't rush things too much.

6. Iron out mistakes in timing, phrasing, words or pitch before they have become habits and stress good performance and pride in singing well. A good technique is to occasionally send a few of the group a short distance away to make a critical evaluation of how well the rest sing.

7. Have plenty of lively funful singing but never boisterous noise-making with little thought for anything except volume.

8. When starting an already familiar song, sing a line to give the intended tempo and key. It is good to use piano, guitar, accordion, or other instrument occasionally, but tones are truer and singing more spontaneous when

groups are accustomed to singing à *capella* (without instrumental accompaniment).

9. As a leader, you should enjoy singing and show it, for temper and grumpiness are disheartening and fatal to a joyful spirit. Don't be afraid to give a word of commendation for good performance.

10. A variety of songs—happy, sad, plaintive, rollicking, thoughtful, sentimental, nonsensical, and just plain lovely—and such devices as antiphonal singing, part singing, and descants (tenor air carried along by a few high voices) add color and diversity. Try letting one group hum harmonizing chords as another sings and encourage good part singing. Never repeat a song too often, and bring the singing period to a close while enthusiasm is still running high. If a song has been sung to the threadbare, boresome stage, have a mock funeral and "bury it"; then plant a dandelion over the grave and let no one thereafter disturb the body.

11. The mood of a group dictates the singing. Quiet, thoughtful songs are best for vesper programs, Sundays and quieting activities before taps, while happy, rollicking ones fit better for other occasions.

12. Organize glee clubs, solos, duets, trios, quartettes, octettes, and so on, for enjoyment or to perform for special occasions. A choir, approaching tunefully through the woods on the way to the Outdoor Chapel, adds greatly to vesper or Sunday services.

13. Use music just before taps, while waiting to go into the dining room, for graces, campfire programs, serenades and antiphonal singing in which one group answers another from an adjoining hill or from canoes out on the water. There should also be periods when campers can listen to the recordings of the best in music.

14. Encourage campers to bring and play their own instruments. Rhythm orchestras are easy and inexpensive to organize and have a particular appeal to younger campers. Campers can make their own instruments, such as shepherd's pipes and ocarinas as described in the sources at the end of the chapter; some camps have orchestras playing camper-made instruments.

15. Let campers compose their own songs for their groups or units or try to fit a new tune to a favorite poem. Surely it is more fun to be original rather than adopt or paraphrase a song from a school or some other camp.

16. Most informal song sessions should be a mutual give-and-take with both campers and counselors sharing in the choice of what to sing.

17. Don't teach too many songs at once; intersperse the old with the new.

## ADDITIONAL READINGS

### MUSIC

#### BOOKS AND PAMPHLETS

ACA Song Book. Coop. Rec. Service, 66 pp.

Action Songs. NRA (MP 325).

Best, Dick and Beth: Song Fest. Crown, 1948.

Boni, Margaret B., and Lloyd, Norman. The Fireside Book of Folk Songs. Simon and Schuster, 1947.

Bucher, Charles A.: Methods and Materials

in Physical Education and Recreation. Mosby, chaps. 6 and 11.

Carmer, Carl: America Sings: Stories and Songs of Our Country's Growing. Knopf, 1942.

Coleman, Satis: Creative Music in Home and School. Day, 1939, 431 pp.

Dunsmore, J. M.: Songs of Discovery and Exploration. Toronto, Clark, Irvin, and Co.

Felton, Harold W.: Cowboy Jamboree: Western Songs and Lore. Knopf, 1951.

Forty Approaches to Informal Singing. NRA.

Gardner: Handbook for Recreation Leaders, pp. 85–97.

Hammett and Musselman: The Camp Program Book. Ass'n Press, 1951, chaps. 20 and 24.

Harbin: The Fun Encyclopedia. Abingdon-Cokesbury, chaps. 12, 13, and 18.

How to Make and Play a Shepherd Pipe. NRA.

Joyful Singing. Camp Fire Girls, 1949, #D 79. (Folk songs from many lands.)

Music and Bugling. Boy Scouts, 1947, #3336.

Our Songs. Girl Scouts, 1942, #23–464. (Brownie Scouts.)

Roads to Music Appreciation. NRA.

Sandburg, Carl: The American Songbag. Harcourt, Brace, 1927.

Sing Along the Way. Woman's Press.

Sing High! Sing Low! Girl Scouts, 1946, #23–468. (36 songs, ages 7–17.)

Sing Together. Girl Scouts, 1949, #20–196, 128 pp.

Singing America. NRA. (120 folk songs.) Accompaniment book available.

Singing Is the Thing. Ass'n Press.

Songs Children Like—Folk Songs from Many Lands. Ass'n for Childhood Ed.

Starting and Developing a Rhythm Band. NRA.

Tobitt, Janet E.: The Ditty Bag. Girl Scouts, 1946, #23–460, 184 pp. (177 songs.)

Tobitt, Janet E.: A Book of Negro Songs. Girl Scouts, #23–470.

Tobitt, Janet E., and White, Alice: Dramatized Ballads. Girl Scouts, #23–413.

We Sing. Girl Scouts, #23–464. (Over 100 songs for younger children.)

Zander, Carl E., and Klusmann, W. R.:

Camp Songs 'N' Things. Boy Scouts, 1949, #3249, 120 pp.

Zanzig, Augustus D.: Singing America. NRA. (128 songs.)

MAGAZINE ARTICLES

Lushbough, L. E.: Music Hath Power—If It's Good Music. C.M., Dec., 1950.

Wagner, Doris: Let There Be Good Music. C.M., Dec., 1952.

DANCING

Bowers, Ethel (Ed.): Musical Mixers and Simple Square Dances. Ass'n Press.

Chase, Ann Hasting: The Singing Caller. Ass'n Press.

Dugan, Anne Schley, Schlottmann, Jeannette, and Rutledge, Abbie: The Folk Dance Library. Barnes, 1948, 5 vols.

Durlacher, Ed: Honor Your Partner. Devin-Adair, 1949, 286 pp.

Eisenberg, Helen and Larry: And Promenade All. Eisenberg, 40 pp.

Harris, Jane A., Pittman, Anne, and Swenson, Marlys: Dance Awhile. Burgess, 1952, 165 pp.

Kirkell, Miriam H, and Schaffnit, Irma K.: Partner's All—Places All. Dutton, 1949, 129 pp.

Kraus, Richard: Square Dances of Today and How to Teach and Call Them. Barnes, 1950, 130 pp.

Tobitt, Janet E.: Promenade All. Girl Scouts, #23–469. (Singing games.)

I would rather be the author of one original thought than conqueror of a hundred battles.

W. B. CLULOW

## Chapter 10

## CREATIVE WRITING

### WRITING CREATIVELY

TO BE CREATIVE, you must take some old material and fashion it through your own imagination and personality into an entirely new and unique product. If you would foster creative work of any sort in others you must use a cautious and sensitive touch, for dictatorial methods and too many unwanted suggestions soon crush the spark of originality. Your role as a counselor is one of encouraging, giving aid where needed, and in general setting the yeast which in the hands of the camper will foam and bubble over into a true creative product.

Campers are often inclined to dismiss with a shrug the suggestion that they compose a poem or do a piece of creative writing, for some of them have been discouraged by insistence in school upon such mechanical details as neatness, legibility, exact diction, spelling and punctuation. Sincere thought and self-expression are of more importance in creative work, and youngsters should not be expected to attain adult standards. As always, encourage them to do their best, however. Mrs. Cumming tells of a seven-year old who, after insisting that he could not write anything, chattered on in the following soliloquy which she, unknown to him, recorded as he talked.

118

I hear echoes when I walk around hiking.
All the pretty voices I hear in places I go.
I see all the pretty flowers around the lake, in the forest and
   the mountainsides.
You have a good time in camp.
I wish I could stay at camp a long time,
And see all the pretty trees around with pretty leaves on them,
And see the tadpoles in the lake.
I have a good time going in swimming. and have a good time
   horseback riding.
All these things I have fun doing.
I like the cute birds in the trees;
They whistle at me, and I whistle at them.
The bees are funny things;
They sting some children, but not me.
Sometimes they sting me!
There are very funny things around camp.
Some voices sound hummy, and people act very funny some-
   times.
The mountainside sometimes just sings by itself, and no one else
   makes a noise.
The falls make a pretty noise;
There are rocks at the bottom of the falls.
Then you sit down and think about it, and you want to write a
   poem about it.*

Encourage every camper to jot
down his thoughts for his own benefit
if not for sharing with others, and recognize him when he does something
especially well by posting it on the
bulletin board, reading it at the campfire or publishing it in the camp newspaper. Encourage the writing of
poems, plays, pageants, diaries, letters,
and accounts of things seen and done.

### The Camp Paper

It is advantageous to have a camp paper, for it (1) serves to encourage
and recognize creative writing, (2) keeps campers and staff as well as parents
and friends informed of the doings of the whole camp, (3) fosters good camp
morale and (4) serves as a souvenir to recall many pleasant memories of the
summer.

* Conversation of Charles Mitchell, recorded and submitted by Mrs. Ely C. Cumming
of Mary Gwynn's Camp, Brevard, North Carolina.

Camp papers vary greatly as to frequency of publication. Some put out a short edition every day, others go to the opposite extreme and publish only one or two during the entire summer. A few camps are financially able to print their paper, but most are satisfied to use mimeograph; some type only one copy to read before the assembled campers. It is fun to put out an occasional "extra" to celebrate some important camp event.

Mimeographers, editors, reporters, copy readers, artists, make-up editors, typists, stencil cutters, staplers and circulation managers are all essential, giving opportunity to utilize a wide variety of talents.

To avoid inaccuracies, sloppy appearance and last minute rush, non-current material should be written, cut on stencils, and run off ahead of time. The staff members should critically evaluate each issue to see how they can improve the next one and should set high standards for all types of work so that they can take pride in the finished product. Post assignments for the next issue as early as possible, and run everything in a business-like fashion that does credit to a juvenile newspaper office.

Make a point of including each camper's name frequently in some connection. Give contributors of articles "by lines" to stimulate high standards and give recognition where it is due.

You can help the staff by encouraging your campers to submit material and aid in the actual production of the paper when asked. Keep the staff representative of the whole camp, and avoid letting the paper fall into the hands of a little clique. Wholesome, kindly humor adds immeasurably, but anything that might hurt or serve as a personal "axe to grind" is strictly taboo.

## ADDITIONAL READINGS

Dillon, C.: Journalism for High School. Barnes & Noble.

Greenawalt, Lambert: A Student's Journalism Laboratory. New York, Thomas Nelson.

Hyde, Grant M.: Newspaper Editing. Appleton.

Jeffries, David L.: Publishing a Camp Paper. C.M., April, 1948.

Journalism. Boy Scouts (#3812), 1943.

Knapp, G. L.: The Boy's Book of Journalism. Dodd, Mead.

Art is not a thing: it is a way.
ELBERT HUBBARD "Epigrams"*

"Ah, ha! a cattail for my torch!"

## Chapter 11

## ARTS AND CRAFTS

IT HAS BEEN said that the word "art" is like a woman's mother hubbard; it covers everything, yet touches nothing. The truth of this statement is clearly shown in this book, for nearly all phases of camping have some part which can be classed as art. Tincancraft, nature study and map-making are but a few examples.

Art is where you find it, and in camp it is found right on the campsite by the campers and counselors themselves. The arts and crafts byword might well be, "Stop, look and listen," for far too many of us pass unseeingly by wonderful supplies of native clay and tall reeds and tread upon nuts, acorns and pine cones on our way to mail an order to the nearest craft supply house.

To begin, let us stop for a moment to consider the aims and purposes of arts and crafts in the camping program. Arts and crafts give an opportunity for self-expression, a growing appreciation of beauty in the things of every-day life, a recognition of beauty in the commonplace, and a chance to be-

* Reproduced by permission of Elbert Hubbard II.

come alertly aware of surroundings. Art is merely the best way of doing a thing which needs to be done, be it scouring the kitchen sink, arranging flowers, setting the dinner table, or laying brick for a clay oven.

John Galsworthy said, "In these unsuperstitious days no other ideal seems worthy of us, or indeed possible to us, save beauty—or call it, if you will, the dignity of human life . . . the teaching of what beauty is, to all . . . so that we wish and work and dream that not only ourselves but everybody may be healthy and happy, and, above all, the fostering of the habit of doing things and making things well, for the joy of the work and the pleasure of achievement." * This message indicates the need to find beauty, not only in the things we make and use, but in the relationships we have with one another.

In striving for the ideal through arts and crafts, the foremost idea should be, not to think of what the youngster does to the material with which he works, but of what effect the material has on the youngster.

By now you may be justified in saying, "All this talk and philosophical chatter is fine, but I want to know what to do and how to do it." Of course you do, but you must be patient and try to realize from past experience that you can be told little, but must largely find things out for yourself, and you will see this same principle manifested in the youngsters with whom you work. The following anecdote illustrates this point and, even though from a formal school situation, is just as likely to occur in a summer camp, where it is equally important to give campers credit for independent thought and having the courage to back up their beliefs.

After a visit to a farm, members of the second grade were asked to paint farm pictures. Brenda had painted a huge barn on the left hand side of her paper with a big fence running horizontally across the paper. Being earnest, if not wise, the teacher suggested that she put a cow in the picture. Some few minutes later the teacher came back to see Brenda and her masterpiece, but still no cow had been added. Thinking that more urging was needed, the teacher commented again on how much a cow would improve the general aspects of the composition. Brenda looked up and flatly stated, "The cow is in the barn." Now anyone would expect this to end the discussion, but not with this persistent teacher, who came back a third time to Brenda and began, "A cow . . ." She got no farther, for Brenda straightened up, propped her hands against her hips, and announced through gritted teeth, "I told you the cow is in the barn and the door is shut!"

Without a basic understanding of children and materials, no creative work will be produced. No set of rules, but only suggestions can be given for working with such highly specialized and individualized beings as children, for it is the counselor's job to point out, guide and expose his group to the possibilities nature has to offer.

* John Galsworthy, *Candelabra*, Scribners.

The arts and crafts program should stem from the campers, the camp environment and camp situations. The free method of "Here is the material, do whatever you want with it" doesn't work, for some will say, "Do we *have* to do what we want to do today?" Arts and crafts are the most reasonable thing this side of mathematics, and, unless there is purpose in making a thing, the finished product—if it is ever finished—will be only a dead thing.

Nor are arts and crafts limited to the few who can be branded as "talented" or "artistic." Art is for everyone who has eyes to see, ears to hear, or any other of the senses.

The arts and crafts program should be directed as a man drives a wagon. He gives the mule his head and, with reins firm but relaxed, puts the mule on his own, except for a few "gees" and "haws" here and there. It is indeed a rare thing to see a man leading a mule and wagon and an even rarer one to see them being *driven*. With the same delicacy of touch, the counselor guides his artists and craftsmen to see and use the materials they find in their environment.

In a camping program it is well to avoid the use of such overworked city techniques as craft strip for braiding and media calling for following the directions of others, allowing little opportunity for the child to express his own personality and originality. Keep the program as inexpensive as possible by using indigenous materials and making your own equipment wherever possible. The "back to nature" movement offers a complete stock of arts and crafts materials for the counselor and camper who has "eyes to see" them. Good conservation practices must always be employed, however, being careful to use only what nature can spare and doing as little damage to the environment as possible.

Art has been defined as "order," and a good craftsman is an orderly person who sees to it that there are definite places for supplies, tools and equipment, and that there is adequate space in which to work. Teaching campers an appreciation of these qualities and of the proper use and care of tools is an important phase of instruction in arts and crafts and is a main responsibility of the counselor.

There must be a clear distinction between "busy work" and creative work as determined by (1) the usefulness of the finished product itself and (2) the effect of the making upon the producer.

## Making Paste

There are many ways of making paste, one being to mix a half cup of flour with enough water to form a creamy mixture and heat over a low flame for about five minutes, stirring constantly to prevent lumping. If you are not going to use the paste immediately, a few drops of glycerine, oil of wintergreen, or alum will preserve it indefinitely.

## Papier-Mâché

Papier-mâché, a gorgeous French word, is a simple arts and crafts medium which adapts itself successfully to all age levels. It is used commercially for figures in window displays, masks, and so on, as seen in the Mardi Gras and the animals prevalent at Easter.

Papier-Mâché Animals.

HAND PUPPET
CHOIR BOY                                                    ARMATURE

Papier-Mâché Figures.

There are almost as many ways to make papier-mâché as there are people to make it. Newspapers torn into small bits, paper towels, or packing excelsior can be soaked in warm water for a few hours until they can be easily mashed into a pulp. Then add enough paste to give the pulp the consistency of clay.

You can use papier-mâché to build animals on a paper armature by applying and shaping the papier-mâché with your hands. When dry, sandpaper the animal, then paint and shellac it.

Relief maps are lovely when made with this medium and, unlike clay, permit pins to be stuck into the surface. They are much lighter in weight than is clay and so are more practical for hanging purposes.

When you use white paper as a bases, you can divide it into proper proportions and mix with the colors desired for each section. For example, you estimate the amount of material you need for the ocean and mix blue with it, and so on.

Another way to make papier-mâché is to cut bias strips of paper 3 by 4 inches long and 1 inch wide, dipping them into a thin solution of glue, and applying each slightly overlapping the other and carefully smoothing over a thoroughly petrolateumized or oiled mold such as an apple, orange, bowl, jar or bottle with smooth sides. You can also make masks.

Make head puppets by forming a model of clay or plastiline with the neck large enough on the inside to admit the finger with which you manipulate the puppet. Coat the model with some type of lubricant, and apply the strips of paper criss-cross until the entire head and neck are covered. When dry (which takes a varying length of time, according to weather conditions), cut the head in half, remove the clay, and tape the two halves together with strips of paste-covered paper. When the joining is dry, the head is ready to paint and the puppet to dress as desired.

Cows, horses, ducks, in fact the whole animal kingdom, can be made by first crumpling newspapers to form a body and then attaching rolled newspapers for neck, head and legs, tying them securely in place. Then cover this form with strips of paper as previously described. It is an advantage to cut the strips on the bias, since the aim is to keep the paper as smooth as possible when fitting it over the rounded form.

## Clay Modeling

Ceramics or clay modeling provides great opportunity for creative work. Clay is found in all parts of the world and ranges from white, yellow, green, gray, and even blues and blacks which result from the presence of such impurities as organic matter or iron oxide. You may often use native clays successfully, and can make the search for them the occasion for an exciting excursion, thus adding materially to campers' sense of achievement. You can construct a potter's wheel and a kiln inexpensively with the aid of good instructions such as those given in the sources listed at the end of the chapter. They add to the permanent equipment of the camp. Whittle the few tools needed from sticks.

Figurines, animals, tiles and bowls are quickly made and bring out all the creative imagination of the most inhibited. As one child ungrammatically said, "I closed my eyes and seen an angel and made one like I seen it."*

* Cole, Natalie Robinson: *The Arts in the Classroom*, Day, 1940, p. 39.

## Tops

Tops are fun to make, and play with or give as gifts. Form them from acorns by inserting a match stick about $1\frac{1}{2}$ inch long into the top; fasten the stick with glue, attach a string to the match stick, and dip the acorn into bright-colored enamel, and hang by the string to dry. Vary the color by dipping the top halfway into another color after the first is thoroughly dry.

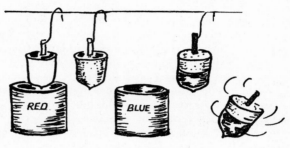

Acorn Tops.

## Portfolios

Portfolios are handy things to have at camp, home and school for keeping correspondence, notes or pictures. You can make one of good size from two pieces of cardboard, each 12 by 9 inches, and a strip of cloth 4 by 16 inches.

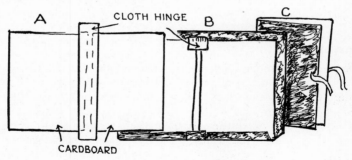

Portfolio.

Join the cardboards as shown in *A*, with the cloth acting as a hinge. Then turn in the ends of the cloth and paste down the inside as shown in *B*. Cut decorated paper (marbelized, finger painted, shadow printed or block printed) 1 inch larger in all dimensions than the cardboard, and spread paste smoothly over its entire surface (wrong side). Then paste to the cardboards to form a cover for the portfolio, and fold the edges in and paste as shown in *B*. Paste a piece of paper $\frac{1}{4}$ inch smaller in all dimensions than the cardboards inside as a lining. Cut a slit about 1 inch from the outside edges of the cardboard and half way down and insert a piece of tape or ribbon through it to tie the portfolio shut.

To prevent warping, use only the amount of paste actually necessary. Insert a piece of paper between the sides of the portfolio to keep them from sticking together, and press it under a heavy weight until absolutely dry.

Marbelizing paper is fun, because, like finger painting, it completely defeats those who say, "I can't even draw a straight line," for even they can turn out something lovely. Use any kind of paper which is not too absorbent. Mix a little oil paint (any color) with kerosene, turpentine or some other oil and pour onto a large pan of water. Since water and oil do not mix, the oil remains floating on top, and you marbelize the paper by laying it on top of the water. Draw bright, varicolored fish on the paper with wax crayons, scrubbing the colors on vigorously to produce the most highly decorative type of fish imaginable. Make a solution of blue-green oil color and pour on the water, stirring or breathing on it to make it swirl, and dip the picture in the water. The fish look as though they are in the water and in your imagination you can even hear them swishing about!

## Block Printing

Block printing is an old art which appeals to individuals of all ages and is useful in producing personal cards, gift wrapping paper, menus or program covers in quantities. You can use linoleum, cork, soap, scrap rubber, erasers, wash-basin stoppers, dowels, or even potatoes, turnips and apples. Make small designs on the heads of wooden clothes pins and stamp them on cloth with textile paint.

Block Printing.

Cut firm, eyeless potatoes or turnips in half and draw a simple design on the flat surface with a brush and water colors. Extend the design to include even the edges. Incise the outlines of the design about $\frac{1}{4}$ inch with a small knife and lift it out of the background.

You can potato print on colored construction paper, wrapping paper, cellophane or tissue paper, but not cloth. Potatoes will not take printer's ink or oils. Paint the embossed design on the potato with a brush, or make a stamp pad by folding a piece of cloth or felt and spread paint on it. Blot out the moisture as much as possible before applying the paint.

*Inner Tube Prints.* Make a cut paper design, either bisymmetric or asymmetric, and trace the pieces of the design onto the tubing and cut out with scissors. Use strong vegetable glue to fasten the smooth side of the rubber design to a background of cardboard or wood. Leave almost no wood or cardboard background extending beyond the design, lest it show in the print.

*The Block Printing Process.*

1. Draw a simple design with definite lines.
2. Transfer the design with carbon or by thoroughly blacking the back of it by tracing over it with a pencil.
3. Remember to make the design on the block in reverse, so that when it is printed it will reproduce the original drawing. This is especially necessary to watch with lettering.
4. Put a portion of printer's ink (comes in oil or water forms) on glass (window pane) or any smooth surface.
5. Use a brayer, rolling pin or smooth bottle (such as an olive bottle) as a roller to roll the paint onto the block.
6. Apply the block to the cloth or paper and press hard with hands or feet to secure a good print.

## Chip Carving

Chip carving requires precision and patience and is therefore not suitable for younger campers. Most designs are based upon geometrical patterns, and the "chips" themselves are triangular pieces of wood removed from a board by means of slicing knives; a razor blade may be used as an emergency tool. Chip carving requires a gradual slope and not a gouge. A ruler, compass and pencil are necessary to lay out the design.

Basswood (linden) is best to use because it is soft and workable, yet fine-grained and finishes nicely. Pine or apple wood is also recommended.

The simplest way to finish woodwork is to mix oil paint (burnt umber, burnt sienna, mahogany, walnut) with turpentine and rub it on with a rag which leaves no lint. When the paint is thoroughly dry, shellac it and let dry before again sandpapering and shellacking it. (Sandpaper and elbow grease are important constituents for all woodwork.) A good floor wax makes the best finish. Use chip carving to decorate boxes, albums, scrap books, coasters, trays, letter knives, checkers, belt buckles, costume pins and carved buttons.

## Dyeing

Dyeing is an art, not a science. As in other arts, there are several ways to arrive at the same result, but all involve thought, care and patience. Silk, chiffon or cheese cloth are exciting and beautiful when tied and dyed, and curtains and bed spreads or costumes for camp use are easy to make. Natural dyes from berries, bark or roots of plants are soft and attractive and compare favorably with commercial dyes.

To make vegetable dyes, steep the plants in water overnight and then boil them slowly until you obtain the desired intensity of color.

Tie Dyeing.

You must use a large enough container (copper or enamel preferred) to cover the material in the dye bath entirely, and must stir it and move it freely with blunt, smooth sticks.

To insure a good dye job, wash the material thoroughly to remove all the starch. Boil the wet material slowly for an hour in water in which you have dissolved some *mordant* such as alum, cream of tartar or tannic acid (or barks or woods containing it). This mordant is a chemical which helps to fix or charge the color. After boiling, rinse the material well, immerse it in the dye bath, and boil from one-half hour to an hour or until you obtain the desired shade. (Remember that it will appear much darker when wet than after it dries.) Add salt or vinegar to the dye bath to set the color and continue to boil it for another ten minutes. Then remove the material, rinse it and dry it in the shade. Thorough washing and rinsing are most important and must not be neglected. The following are indigenous sources of the principal colors:

*Blue:*

- Hazel roots
- Larkspur flowers
- Sunflower seeds
- Shrub indigo—roots
- Red maple—bark, boiled with copper sulphate
- Blue ash—boiled with copper sulphate

*Black:*

- Field sorrel leaves
- Sumac and gallberry leaves
- Maple—inner bark and leaves
- Flowering dogwood—branches and bark
- Black walnut—roots
- Elderberry stems

*Brown:*

    Alder bark
    Red oak bark
    Maple bark
    Hickory bark
    Butternut—hulls and bark
    Walnut—hulls and bark
    Onion skins
    Coffee bean—inside

*Purple:*

    Purple flag—petals
    Blueberries—berries
    Barberries—berries
    Maple—rotted wood
    Elderberry berries
    Sumac berries
    Pokeberry berries
    Cedar—tips of branches
    Red cedar—rootlets

*Gray:*

    Sumac leaves
    Butternut bark
    Maple bark

*Green:*

    Water scum (algae)—whole plant
    Giant arbor vitae—twigs and leaves
    Spinach leaves

*Red:*

    Alder—inner bark
    Amaranth seeds
    Coreopsis flowers
    Red dogwood—inner bark
    Pokeberries—berries; boil with alum
    Cedar—inner bark
    Bloodroot—root
    Hemlock bark
    Beets, boiled with alum
    Cleavers—roots, extracted with alcohol
      or oil
    Sycamore—old, half-rotten roots
    Red sumac berries

*Yellow:*

    Celandine poppy
    Alder—inner bark
    Goldenrod flowers
    Sassafras bark
    Onions and their skins
    Balsam—flowers
    St. John's wort—flowers
    Saffron—dried stigmas
    Cottonwood—seed vessels or leaf buds
    Thistle—flowers
    Sumac roots
    Lichen—whole plant
    Holly—boiled with alum
    Smartweed—boiled with alum
    White mulberry—roots and leaves
    Black oak—inner bark
    Pignut hickory—inner bark
    Shiny sumac

## Basketry

Basketry is such an old art that we do not know its origin or native country. Many and foreign-flavored materials such as rattan from India, raffia shredded from a Madagascar palm, hemp from the Philippines, and bamboo from China and Japan are used.

Native to our country are such materials as willow branches, cut in the spring when the sap is running, cattail leaves from low, damp places, flags, rushes, straw, wire grass, sweet grass, sedge, broom wheat, rye, corn husks, and so on. Vines of the honeysuckle and Virginia creeper, when peeled and allowed to dry for two years, work up fast and make an even coil. Wood splints from hickory, ash, oak and maple trees require more experienced hands than those of the average beginner.

## Nuts

A hike will disclose large acorns, hazel nuts, and the like, to use in making lapel pins, buttons, bracelets and tops. You may paint a face on an acorn, remembering to place the eyes directly at the center between top and bottom

Mammy Doll.

and the mouth half-way between the eyes and chin. Attach a safety pin for fastening with a good grade of airplane or china cement, and complete the decoration with ear rings and a hat.

## Pine Cones

Pine cones are beautiful in themselves and can be used to make many interesting objects. Large ones with painted tips form lovely tree ornaments to hang by tying a string around the core between the scales, or by inserting a small screw eye into the cone at the top.

Big cones can be used as candle-stick holders by slicing off the pointed end to make a flat base and inserting a candle in the top.

All kinds of animals can be made from cones, their success depending largely upon the maker, as revealed in the story of the wood carver whose artistic output ran heavily to horses. He carved them swiftly and unerringly from almost any sort of wood, and rough and crude as they were, each had a remarkable individual "horsishness." He explained his gift for carving so easily and quickly by, "I jest look at the piece of wood till I see the horse and then I carve away the wood and there's the horse."

Likewise, you must look at a cone or stick until you clearly see what it is to become. Crafts are logical in that they consist of three steps: (1) thinking of all the possible things which you can make out of a material, (2) choosing the one which seems to fit the material best, and (3) then doing it.

Birds are made by gluing an acorn with eyes painted on it for a head, to the top of a pine cone. Matchstick legs may be glued between the scales in the middle of the cone and stuck in a glob of clay for feet (remember that the clay feet must be made rather big to balance the bird). A feather glued to the cap completes a well-dressed dodo bird.

Woodpeckers are composed of a maple seed, shaped to form a head, a beak, a cone body, a feather tail, and a forked stick tree to peck on. To assemble these various parts, press a pin through the top of the head and into the cone where you removed the stem. A little quick-drying glue around the pin helps fix the head to the body. If any of the pin is left showing, you can snip it off with cutting pliers. The tail is glued on at the proper place.

Woodpecker.

To mount the bird on a perching twig requires a little care. Press another pin a short distance through the twig or perch in an upward, slanting direction. You then rest the head of the pin on a hard surface, and press the body of the bird downward onto the pin point until it has penetrated about $\frac{1}{4}$ inch or more into the cone. Add glue where the perch and cone meet to strengthen the pin. Snip off the head of the pin with a pair of cutting pliers. Too much pressure may cause the pin to bend; you must then remove it and repeat the process with a fresh pin.

An ordinary cork cut off to $\frac{1}{2}$ inch thickness may be used as a base by boring a hole into its center and filling it with glue before inserting the perch. A clay base can also be used. Eyes for the maple seed head can be painted on, small seeds may be pasted on, or a pin may be inserted through the head and the ends snipped off.

Penguins made with acorn bodies, maple seed heads, and beads for eyes, may be balanced on feet made from the scales of a pine cone.

The difference between a pine cone and a turtle is a knife, some glue, and a little time and imagination. Cut a slice from the stem end of a large cone (this is a rather difficult job, for it is very tough in texture). The turtle's feet are scales torn from the other section of the cone, the head is an acorn, the neck a twig, and the eyes are beads. Bore holes into the cone to receive the feet and neck, which are held in place with glue. This makes a sturdy turtle which would stand up well in a race with any pine cone rabbit.

Flying Fish.

A flying fish can be made from a long pine cone with the fins and tail cut from maple wings and glued into slots made in the cone with a pen knife.

Gallnut people with twig arms and legs can be dressed in all types of fancy gear and made to represent any one from Little Lord Fauntleroy to Little Black Sambo.

An armadillo has a head made of a small chestnut burr, a pine cone body, and a tail and feet made from twigs; it is mounted on a strip of bark.

Shells, bits of sponge, coral, dried seaweed, sharks' teeth or fish fins, when combined with pipe cleaners and liquid glue, make many beautiful and useful objects such as earrings, pins, brooches, hair pins, and designs for boxes, place cards, and so on.

Animals and dolls of all kinds can be created by using various sizes of shells for heads, bodies and legs.

Other camp arts and crafts projects are:

Papier-mâché
 Puppets
 Masks
 Bowls
 Jewelry
 Animals
 Relief maps

Plaster of Paris (see p. 161)
 Plaques
 Tile
 Fossils
 Nature prints
 Sculpture

Silk screen process
 Posters
 Hand bills
 Scarves

Finger painting
Camp furniture
Camping utensils
Archery equipment
Leather work
Terrariums
Fishing flies and lures

## ADDITIONAL READINGS

### BASKETRY

Basketry. Boy Scouts (#3313), 1937.

Christopher, F. J.: Basketry. Dover.

Couch, Osma P.: Basket Pioneering. Judd, 1940.

Crampton, Charles: The Junior Basket Maker. Bennett, 1952, 35 pp.

Roffey, Mabel: Simple Basketry. Pitman.

### BLOCK PRINTING

Polk, Ralph W.: Essentials of Linoleum-Block Printing. Bennett.

Rice, William S.: Block Prints, How to Make Them. Bruce, 70 pp.

Rice, William S.: Block Printing Designs. Bruce, 16 pp.

Tanner, Robin: Children's Work in Block Printing. Bennett, 51 pp. (Imported.)

### BRAIDING AND WEAVING

Allan, Edith Louise: Weaving You Can Do. Bennett, 1947, 118 pp.

Atwater, Mary Meigs: Byways in Hand-Weaving. Macmillan, 128 pp.

Atwater, Mary Meigs: Card Weaving. Universal Handicrafts.

Baillie, Kenneth: Homespun Crafts. Bruce, 160 pp.

Belash, Constantine A.: Braiding and Knotting for Amateurs. Branford.

Brown, Harriette J.: Hand Weaving. Harper.

Clifford, Lois I.: Card Weaving. Bennett, 40 pp.

Coates, Helen: Weaving for Amateurs. Studio.

Cooke, Viva, and Sampley, Julia: Palmetto Braiding and Weaving. Bennett.

Faber, M. E.: Knots and Braids. Hand-crafters.

Gallinger, Osma Couch, and Benson, Oscar H.: Hand Weaving with Reeds and Fibers. Pitman, 1948, 199 pp.

Grant, Bruce: Leather Braiding. Cornell Maritime.

Graumont, R., and Hensel, J.: Square Knotting, Tatting, Fringe and Needle Work. Cornell Maritime, 1943.

Hooper, Luther: Hand-Loom Weaving. Pitman, 1948.

Knots and Braids in Handicraft. Hand-crafters, 30 pp.

Lewis, Roger: Weaving. Knopf, 1953, 48 pp.

Simpson, L. E., and Weir, M.: The Weaver's Craft. Bennett, 1949, 198 pp. (Imported.)

Worst, Edward F.: Foot Power Loom Weaving. Bruce, 278 pp.

### DYEING

Arts and Crafts with Inexpensive Materials. Girl Scouts, 1941.

Dyeing from Native Materials. NRA.

Home Dyeing with Natural Dyes. Supt. of Documents, Washington, D.C.

Sager, Azalea: The Use of Natural Dyes in Home Crafts. Corvallis, Oregon State College, Extension Service, 1934.

Thurstan, Violetta: The Use of Vegetable Dyes for Beginners. Bennett, 52 pp.

### GENERAL CRAFTS

Anderson, Florence C. E.: Try It Yourself. Woman's Press.

Arts and Crafts for the Recreation Leader. NRA.

Arts and Crafts with Inexpensive Materials. Girl Scouts (#19–303), 1942.

Bacon, Eleanor T.: Preparation and Careful Inventory Will Help You Determine Craft Shop Needs. C.M., Nov. 1952.

Bjoland, Esther M.: Things to Make and Do. Standard Education Society, 1953, 192 pp.

Blide, D. C.: Elementary Hand Craft Projects. Pitman, 1946, 92 pp.

Breeser, Bettye: Let's Make Something. C.M., May, 1953.

Burns, Gerald P.: The Program of the Modern Camp, chap. 9.

Carlson, Bernice: Make It Yourself. Abingdon-Cokesbury.

Champion, Paul V.: Creative Crate Craft. Bruce, 1942, 110 pp.

Cooper, Marjorie: Creative Arts Crafts. Davis, book II.

Corke, Lois: Crafts with Nature Materials. Woman's Press.

Cox, Doris, and Warren, Barbara: Creative Hands, 2nd ed. Wiley, 1951, 381 pp.

Craftsman's Instruction Handbook. Ass'n Press.

Dank, Michael Carlton: Adventures in Scrap Craft. Greenberg, 1946.

Dow, Emily R.: What Can I Do Now? Aladdin Books.

Dryad Handicrafts: Handicrafts for Children. Bennett.

Everybody's Handicraft Handbook. Progress, 1946.

Glantz, Evelyn: Scrap Fun for Everyone. Ass'n Press.

Green Book of Designs. Handicrafts.

Grimm, Gretchen, and Skeels, Catherine: Craft Adventures for Children. Bruce, 110 pp.

Griswold, Lester: Handicraft: Simplified Procedure and Projects, 9th ed., Prentice-Hall, 1951, 480 pp.

Haines, Ray E.: The Home Crafts Handbook. Van Nostrand, 1948.

Hammett and Musselman: The Camp Program Book, chap. 16.

Hening, Viola: Fun with Scraps. Bruce, 1947, 185 pp.

Hughes, F. Clarke: Amateur Handcraft. Bruce, 128 pp.

Hunt, W. Ben: Indian and Camp Handicraft. Bruce, 1938, 180 pp.

Ickis, Marguerite: Arts and Crafts; A Practical Handbook. Barnes, 1943.

Ickis, Marguerite: Handicrafts and Hobbies for Pleasure and Profit. Crown, 1948, 310 pp.

Ickis, Marguerite, and Esh, Reba Selden: The Book of Arts and Crafts. Ass'n Press, 1954.

Jaeger, Ellsworth: Easy Crafts. Macmillan, 1947.

Knapp, Harriet: Design Approach to Crafts. Holden, 1945.

Let's Make Things! (A Handcraft Party.) NRA (MP #274).

McFarlan, John W.: Popular Projects. Craft Service, 20 pp.

Meixner, Mary: Art in the Camp Environment. C.M., April, 1953.

Parkhill, Martha, and Spaeth, Dorothy: It's Fun to Make Things. Barnes, 1941.

Roberts, Catherine: Make It—and Make It Pay. Houghton, 1949, 120 pp.

Robinson, Jessie: Things to Make from Odds and Ends. Appleton, 1945.

Shanklin, Margaret E.: Use of Native Craft Materials. Bennett, 1947.

Showalter, H.: Small Creatures for Your Tools. Bruce, 1942, 224 pp.

Spear, Marion R.: Keeping Idle Hands Busy. Burgess, 1950, 100 pp.

Staples, Frank A.: Arts and Crafts for the Recreation Leader. Ass'n. Press, 1943.

Sweet, Herb and Dee: Try It Just for Fun (Boys). Holt, 1951, 66 pp.

Sweet, Herb and Dee: Try it Because It's Fun (Girls). Holt, 1951, 66 pp.

Tinsley, Eleanor: How to Get More from Your Craft Program. C.M., May, 1950.

Victor, Marllys: Music and Crafts Can Go Hand in Hand. C.M., Nov., 1950. (How to make various musical instruments.)

Zarchy, Harry: Creative Hobbies. Knopf, 1953, 303 pp.

Zarchy, Harry: Here's Your Hobby. Knopf, 1950.

Zarchy, Harry: Let's Make a Lot of Things. Knopf, 1948, 156 pp.

## LEATHER

Cherry, Raymond: General Leathercraft, 3rd ed. McKnight, 1949, 128 pp.

Christopher, F. J.: Leather Work. Dover.

Cromlet, Ross C.: Fundamentals of Leathercraft. Bruce, 64 pp.

Dean, John W.: Leathercraft Techniques and Designs. McKnight, 1950, 256 pp.

Doughterty, Betty: Your Leatherwork. Bennett. (Imported.)

Groneman, C. H.: Applied Leathercraft, rev. ed. Bennett, 1952.

Leathercraft Methods. Boy Scouts (#3167), 20 pp.

Leatherwork. Boy Scouts (#3310), 1951.

Lewis, Roger: Leathercraft. Knopf, 1953, 44 pp.

Mannel, Elise: Leathercraft is Fun. Bruce, 96 pp.

## MARIONETTES AND PUPPETS*

Beaton, Mabel, and Beaton, Les: Marionettes: A Hobby for Everyone. Crowell, 1948.

Lanchester, W. S.: Hand Puppets and String Puppets, rev. ed. Bennett, 54 pp.

## METAL WORK

Dronquist, Emil K.: Art Metalwork, A Manual for Amateurs. McGraw-Hill, 1942.

Hunt, W. Ben: Indian Silversmithing. Bruce, 160 pp.

Lewis, Roger: Metalcraft. Knopf, 1953, 48 pp.

Lukowitz, J. J.: Interesting Art Metalwork. Bruce, 1938.

Metalcraft Methods. Boy Scouts (#3168), 20 pp.

Metal Foiling, Tooling, Book of Designs. Am. Handicrafts.

Metalwork. Boy Scouts (#3312A), 1952.

Payne Arthur F.: Art Metalwork with Inexpensive Equipment. Bennett, 1929, 176 pp.

Smith, Robert E.: Etching, Spinning, Raising, Tooling Metal. McKnight, 1951, 88 pp.

## MISCELLANEOUS

Ackley, Edith Flack: Dolls to Make for Fun and Profit, rev. ed. Lippincott, 1952, 126 pp.

Art. Boy Scouts (#3320), 1944.

Bayley, Thomas: The Craft of Model Making. Dryad, 1950.

Bollinger, J. W.: Simple Bracelets. Bruce, 80 pp.

Bookbinding. Boy Scouts (#3378), 1940.

Champion, Paul V.: Games You Can Make and Play. Bruce, 128 pp.

* See also page 111.

Crafts Projects That Can Be Made with Inexpensive and Discarded Materials. NRA (MP 256).

Ellis, Clifford, and Ellis, Rosemary: Modelling for Amateurs. Studio.

First Book of Feltcraft, The—Fun with Felt, 1951, 32 pp.

Fowler, H. Waller, Jr.: Kites. Barnes, 1953.

Hammett and Musselman: The Camp Program Book, chap. 16.

Hunt, W. Ben: Indiancraft. Bruce, 124 pp.

Hunt, W. Ben, and Burshears, J. F.: American Indian Beadwork—Designs and Methods. Bruce, 1951, 64 pp.

Hunt, W. Ben, and Metz, John J.: The Flat Bow. Bruce, 1936, 72 pp.

Jaeger, Ellsworth: Bark Crafts. C.M., March, 1950.

Kalmbach, A. C.: Model Railroad Handbook. Kalmbach, 1952.

La Berge, A. J.: Boats, Airplanes, and Kites, rev. ed. Bennett, 1950.

Lewis, Roger: Sculpture. Knopf, 1952. (Ages 7–11.)

Lionel Corporation Editorial Staff: Model Railroading. Bantam, 1950.

Make Your Own Games. NRA (MP 332).

Make Your Own Puzzles. NRA (MP 333).

Moritz, La Verne: Papier Mâché. LaVee Studio, 1953, 48 pp.

Painting. Boy Scouts (#3372), 1940.

Sculpture. Boy Scouts (#3322), 1945.

Shellcraft Instructions. Cleveland Crafts Co.

Smith, F. R.: Small Jewelry. Pitman.

Staples, Frank A.: Water-Color Painting Is Fun. NRA or McGraw-Hill, 1948, 127 pp.

Walworth, Ruth Lippincott: Shellcraft. Bruce Humphries.

## PLASTICS

Cherry, Raymond: General Plastics—Projects and Procedures. McKnight, 1948, 160 pp.

Staples, Frank A.: Plastics for the Beginner. NRA, 24 pp. (23 articles.)

Walton, Harry: Plastics for the Home Craftsman. McGraw, 1951, 191 pp.

* See also page 258.

## POTTERY

Dougherty, John W.: Pottery Made Easy. Bruce, 1945, 192 pp.

Honoré, York: Pottery Making. Viking.

Jenkins, R. H.: Practical Pottery for Craftsmen and Students. Bruce, 204 pp.

Lester, Katherine M.: Creative Ceramics. Bennett, 213 pp.

Lunn, Dora: Pottery in the Making. Bennett, 96 pp.

Pottery. Boy Scouts (#3314). 1932.

Sanders, Herbert H.: Sunset Ceramics Book. Lane, 1953, 96 pp.

Taylor, Keith: Pottery without a Wheel. Bennett, 1953.

Turoff, Muriel P.: How to Make Pottery and Other Ceramic Ware. Crown, 1949, 145 pp.

## TINCANCRAFT

Cook, Sherman R.: Tin Things We Like to Make. Bruce, 112 pp.

Groneman, C. H.: Ornamental Tin Craft. Bruce, 160 pp.

Hamilton, Edwin T.: Tin Can Craft. Dodd, Mead, 1935.

Lukowitz, Joseph J.: 55 New Tin Can Projects. Bruce, 1936, 80 pp.

## WOODWORK, CARPENTRY, CARVING, WHITTLING*

Aller, Doris: Sunset Wood Carving Book. Lane, 1951, 95 pp.

Dank, Michael C.: Creative Crafts in Wood. Bennett.

Gottschall, Franklin H., and Hellum, Amanda W.: You Can Whittle and Carve. Bruce, 1942, 96 pp.

Gottschall, Franklin H.: Woodwork for the Beginner. Bruce, 162 pp.

Hunt, W. Ben: Ben Hunt's Whittling Book. Bruce, 1945, 127 pp.

Hunt, W. Ben: Indian and Camp Handicraft. Bruce, 180 pp.

Jaeger, Ellsworth: Making Belts and Necklaces from Twigs. C.M., Jan., 1950.

Jaeger, Ellsworth: Wildwood Wisdom, chaps. 13, 18, and 19.

Katchina Dolls and the Indian Give Away. NRA, p. 12.

Lacey, J. C., and McBride: The Audubon Book of Bird Carving. McGraw-Hill.

Lacey, John: Book of Woodcarving. Prentice-Hall.

Lewis, Roger: Woodworking. Knopf, 1952.

Mankin, Vic: Modernistic Chip Carving. Bruce.

Mason: Woodcraft, chaps. 10, 14, 15, 18–22 and 24.

Pynn, Leroy, Jr.: Let's Whittle. Bennett, 1948, 128 pp. (Small animals.)

Sowers, J. I.: Wood Carving Made Easy. 1948, Bruce, 96 pp.

Stieri, Emanuele: Woodworking for the Home Craftsman. Barnes and Noble, 1953, 376 pp.

Tangerman, E. J.: Whittling and Woodcarving. McGraw-Hill, 1936.

Van Tassel, R.: Woodworking Crafts. Van Nostrand, 1948.

Victor, Marllys: Campers Love Cedar Jewelry. C.M., March, 1952.

Waltner, Elma and W. H.: Carving Animal Caricatures. McKnight, 1951, 104 pp.

Woodwork. Boy Scouts (#3316 A), 1952.

You cannot tell a good story unless
you tell it before a fire. You cannot have a complete fire unless you
have a good story teller along.
                    Dr. G. Stanley Hall

## Chapter 12

## STORY TELLING

### An Ancient Heritage

The art of story telling is probably almost as old as man, for history tells us
that from the advent of speech, primitive peoples loved to cluster about one
of their most esteemed and beloved members, the story teller. From 8000 b.c.,
when the blind bard Homer was recounting the Iliad and Odyssey, down
through the Minnesingers, troubadours and traveling minstrels, men have
loved to gather to hear once again the oft-repeated tales of courage and adventure which doubtless lost nothing in the telling under the golden tongue
of the skilled narrator. The American Indians, likewise, made much of story
telling, their legends serving to entertain, carry on tradition, and instruct
the younger members of the tribe in geography, history and biography.
What golden spells their tales of bravery and daring must have woven!

To this day, the fat, the lean, the dark, the fair, in fact everyone from the
toddler to grandfather and grandmother loves a well-told tale. Though
radio, movie and "funny" book may have largely impaired the interests and
abilities of both "teller" and "listener" in the home and various gathering
places of the gang, not so in the summer camp, where "Tell us a story" is
just as frequent and fervent a plea as ever. True, some campers may need to
be encouraged to participate the first few times the story hour comes along,
but a few sessions will usually convert them into just as avid listeners as the
old-timers.

No counselor worthy of his hire will fail to have a few good stories up his sleeve for that inevitable moment when nothing else will quite fill the bill. None worth his salt will meet a request by saying, "Oh, I can't tell stories." Almost anyone can learn to be a "good" story teller, even though not all of us may become supercolossal spinners of yarns.

## The Why

There are numerous reasons for telling stories in camp; here are four of the most important:

1. *Enjoyment.*     Hearing a *good* story is fun, and that is almost important enough in itself to warrant its inclusion. It is hard to think of anything we can do that would be more helpful for boys or girls than teach them to enjoy good literature, for it is foolish to content oneself with trash when so much worthwhile writing exists that we could not read it all if we devoted a lifetime to the task.

2. *Reliving Great Moments.*     Who among us does not thrill to the adventures of the pioneers or the doings of such imaginary heroes as Paul Bunyan or the characters in the Uncle Remus stories? Many historical events and personalities provide excellent subject matter for the story period. Local tales, as learned from the residents or from the clipping file or books and pamphlets of the local librarian, furnish a true gold mine of source material. W.P.A. State Guide Books are also valuable sources of such information and may lead to enthusiastic planning for a gypsy trip to a nearby locality to see what has been read about.

3. *Gaining New Friends.*     Though we are not privileged to know Franklin, Gulliver, Robinson Crusoe, or Huck Finn or Paul Bunyan in person, we can form their intimate acquaintance through the story teller.

4. *Moral and Character Values.*     Since youth is the age of hero worship, there is no better way to teach that "virtue has its own reward" and "crime does not pay" than through the stories of the great and good of all ages.

## The When and Where

Almost any time is "story time," but there are occasions which just seem to beg for a story. A camp fire, a lovely hilltop at sunset, or a peaceful dell are "naturals," and a circle of blanket-rolled listeners under a starlit sky forms a perfect setting for star study and retelling the same star myths heard by Indian, Greek and Roman boys and girls of many centuries ago. A rainy day seems less dreary when there's an open fireplace and an exciting tale; camp disappointments and minor tragedies fade under the spell of a Kipling adventure. A good story will often keep restless youngsters relaxed during the rest hour or put them in a mood for quickly going to sleep at night.

## The Who

Though everyone likes to hear stories, not everyone likes the same story, for the teen-ager is bored beyond words with the adventures of Billie Goat

Gruff or Jimmie the Jumping Frog; consequently it is best to have listeners of approximately the same age.

It should be understood from the very start that there is to be no disturbance of any sort until the story is finished; therefore, "it's all right to sit with your pal as long as you don't bother anyone, and you must save any questions and comments until the story is finished."

Encourage campers who "don't like stories" to sample them a few times. If you choose appropriate stories and tell them well, few will fail to succumb to their charms; if some still resist, it may perhaps be better to excuse them to follow "safe" activities more to their liking.

### The What

There are a few sure-fire stories which appeal to almost everyone, but, in general, "the group dictates the story," and what would be adored by one gathering may fall perfectly flat with another. You must learn to know your group and pick your story for *them*.

Boys and girls ordinarily like the same stories until they are about ten, when the boys begin to crave real he-man stories and disdain "kid" or "sissy stuff." Tales of Indians, cowboys, pioneers, pirates, aeroplanes, football and baseball now appeal. Girls are not quite so exclusive, being satisfied with many of the same stories previously liked as well as some of those now chosen by the boys.

A good story teller paints a mental panorama of peoples, places and action for his listeners; he must deal, therefore, in things familiar to them so that the picture will seem vivid and lifelike. Suit the tale to the general background and intelligence of your listeners.

Small children like stories containing alliteration and nonsensical jingles as well as those about animals and people they know. They are particularly fond of the ludicrous and illogical, such as "Corabelle Cow Who Goes Shopping on Roller Skates" or "Dulcimer Duck Who Carries a Pink Silk Umbrella and Wears Green Spats When She Goes to the Beach." Youngsters of all ages have a good sense of humor, though what strikes them as funny may seem silly or flat to adults, and vice versa.

Dulcimer Duck.

You may tell several short stories at one sitting, particularly if they vary in style and subject matter, but one long story may be enough, since the story period should never exceed twenty to thirty minutes for small children and forty-five to sixty minutes for older ones. A book or long story may be condensed by an expert, but it is risky business for an amateur. He had better divide it into parts, like a serial, each ending at some natural break which temporarily satisfies his listeners, yet leaves them curious about what will happen next. Books, long stories or stories depending on the style of the author for their effectiveness are most successful when read rather than told.

For the novice at choosing, many lists are available which classify stories as to their type and age appeal. Some such lists will be found in the sources given at the end of the chapter. Another safe way of picking a story is to recall one of your own childhood favorites.

Not every story that makes good reading is equally good for telling. Rapidly moving action stories without long descriptions of people or situations are usually best. Poetry written especially for children is definitely popular with them, and you should include some of it.

The inevitable cry, "Tell us a ghost story," sometimes poses a problem, for there are bound to be some campers in almost any group who want nothing else. Certainly no one can question the mental indigestion possible from a diet of gruesomeness and horror, and it may even prove quite upsetting to some of the more sensitive campers. There are *some good* ghost and mystery stories which may be used to quench the thirst for the mysterious and supernatural, and the best procedure is perhaps a gradual weaning process brought about by interspersing a *good* ghost story occasionally among stories of other types. They should, of course, never be told just before going to bed.

As you read for your own pleasure, be ever on the lookout for stories which would be good to tell. Augment your list of suitable selections by consulting lists and talking with people experienced in working with children.

## The How

After you have selected your story, read it carefully for general plot and action and decide upon the best method of presenting it. Then read it again several times, even as many as ten or fifteen, until you are on the verge of memorizing it, for there is much more danger of failing through not knowing your story well than of going "stale" through knowing it too well. Nothing is so disconcerting to listeners as a faltering "er" interjected to give you time to think of what comes next, or an "Oh, I forgot to tell you," as you go back to insert something you should have told five minutes before. Practice telling the story to yourself until you are positive of every character and bit of action.

When the fateful moment arrives, gather your little group of not more than twenty-five or thirty about you, minimizing squirming and wiggling by seeing that all are comfortably seated. Have all located where they can see and hear you clearly.

If the setting is to be an open fire, build it of hardwood sufficiently early to let it die down to coals. Appoint one person to inconspicuously keep it going, for a spluttery, smoky fire or one throwing out alarming sparks provides too much competition for any teller.

If your listeners are excited or full of pent-up energy, try bringing them to an attentive mood by playing a quiet game or two. Compel attention with the very first sentence of your story by saying, for example, "Do you know how the rabbit got his powder-puff tail?"

Since your voice is the center of attention, try to make it pleasant with clear and distinct enunciation. A low tone forces close attention, but use care to have your voice loud enough to be audible to those on the outskirts. Check this by asking them if they can hear you. Straining your voice, shouting, and using poorly chosen words and trite phrases detract much. Youngsters dislike being "talked down to," and a sing-song manner with no variation in tone or timing soon becomes monotonous. Vary your tone; get excited when the story calls for it; talk in a tired or dispirited tone if that is the mood of what you are relating. Pick a story you thoroughly enjoy, so that your natural facial expressions and gestures attract your listeners. Change your voice or turn your head to indicate when different characters are speaking and pause subtly for effect or change your timing to suit the action of the story and build up suspense. Mimicry and dialect, where indicated, add much if you can give the rendition without sounding stilted or forced. Overdramatizing and such mannerisms as dandling something in your hands or slicking down your hair divert attention from the story to you and are therefore undesirable.

Look at your listeners and talk to them instead of mumbling down your shirt collar. Watch their faces for their reaction, making a mental note of the effectiveness of various techniques. If one or two of your audience seem inattentive, bring them back to you by talking directly to them. Quell disturbers with a sharp glance.

Dressing in costume and using sketches previously drawn with crayon on large sheets of paper or pictures drawn in the dirt help to produce a vivid mental image.

If your story has a moral, do not overstress it; it is better to pay your hearers the compliment of letting them grasp it by their intuition. When you reach the climax, conclude with what few words are necessary. If they ask, "Is it true?" answer them honestly.

Encourage your campers to use the camp library by telling them sections of books suggesting that they read the rest of the book for themselves. Let good story tellers among them carry on other sections of the story you have started at a later time. It is often good fun for a small group to set aside a certain time each day for the continuation of a long story, with each member of the group taking a turn at telling it.

There is no secret formula for telling a story, for all good story tellers develop their own techniques. The embryo teller should never miss an opportunity to study a skillful performer or gain experience for himself, for each occasion teaches you much and you will find that the technique of telling stories is like a piece of good leather: it improves with use.

# ADDITIONAL READINGS

## BOOKS AND PAMPHLETS

Adams, Ramon F.: Come and Get It. University of Oklahoma Press, Norman, Okla. (Trials and tribulations of old range cooks.)

Barrel, Lloyd (Ed.): American Indian Tales. Devin-Adair, 1954.

Bibliography of Books for Children. Ass'n for Childhood Ed.

Breen, Mary J.: For the Story Teller. NRA, 1938.

Bryant, Sara Cone: How to Tell Stories to Children. Houghton, 1924.

Feasts and Frolics, Knopf, 1949. (Stories for every holiday; ages 8–12.)

Hamilton, Charles: Cry of the Thunderbird. Macmillan. (The telling of Indian stories.)

Harbin: The Fun Encyclopedia. Abingdon-Cokesbury, pp. 850–860.

Johnson and Scott: Anthology of Children's Literature, Houghton, 1940.

Lantz, J. Edward (Ed.): Stories to Grow By. Ass'n Press.

Leach, Maria (Ed.): Standard Dictionary of Folklore, Mythology, and Legend. Funk & Wagnalls, 1949, 531 pp.

Lotz, M. M., and Monahan, Douglas: Twenty Tepee Tales for "Y" Indian Guides. Ass'n Press. (Boys 7–9.)

Macfarlan, Allan A.: Campfire Adventure Stories. Ass'n Press, 1951.

Rugoff, Milton: A Harvest of World Folk Tales. Viking.

Shedlock, Marie L.: The Art of the Story Teller. Dover Publications, 1951.

Steinmetz, Eulalie: A List of Stories to Tell and Read Aloud. N.Y. Public Library.

Stewart, George: Fire. Random, 1948.

Storytelling. Ass'n for Childhood Ed., 1942.

Strong, Joanna: Favorite Folktales and Fables. Hart. (Ages 7–12.)

Strong, Joanna: Legends Children Love. Hart. (Ages 8–13.)

Strong, Joanna, and Leonard, Tom B.: Treasury of Hero Stories. Hart, 1949, 191 pp.

Treasury of the World's Great Myths and Legends for Boys and Girls from 8–13. Hart, 1951, 319 pp.

Wiley, Farida A.: Ernest Thompson Seton's America: Selections from the Writings of the Artist-Naturalist. Devin-Adair, 1954, 444 pp.

## MAGAZINE ARTICLES

Cumming, Elizabeth Chandler: Creative Reading at Camp. C.M., May, 1954.

Horn Book, The — magazine guide to children's books. The Horn Book, Inc., or NEA, 1942.

Mansur, Alice: Wanted—A Camp Story Teller. C.M., Oct., 1940.

Walp, Esther Spargo, and Walp, Russell Lee: The Wonderland of Books. C.M., April, 1953.

Consult your local librarian for other stories to tell.

Unto those who talk and talk,
This proverb should appeal,
The steam that blows the whistle
Will never turn the wheel.

AUTHOR UNKNOWN

## Chapter 13

# LEADING A DISCUSSION

DISCUSSING is such a favorite American pastime that it is difficult to imagine two or more people assembling for even a few moments without engaging in it. Campers, being human, discuss, too, and this interchange of opinion is doubtless influential in shaping their thinking. Besides the informal discussions which go on perpetually in camp, there are also planned discussions which are more or less scheduled as to time and place, and often arise out of the felt needs or wishes of the group. Such discussions fit naturally into rainy days, late afternoons after swimming, or the period just before taps.

### Why the Discussion?

Discussions are often motivated by a simple desire to exchange opinions or acquire information by chatting with others, often with those who are older and more experienced, as counselors and other staff personnel. Such topics as college life, vocations, love and marriage, Indians, fishing, camping techniques, cheating, religion, Alaska, and so forth, interest boys and girls and serve as the basis for many sessions.

Discussions may serve as clearing houses for matters of unhappiness or concern to the group, such as how to divide cabin duties so as to eliminate "work horses" and "shirkers," campers in general (not individuals) who lie, steal, or gossip, or why taps must sound so early.

144

Discussion is the best way to plan such group projects as an overnight hike, a three-day canoe trip, a cabin name and slogan, a camp safety week, a stunt for stunt night, or ways of beautifying unit and unit grounds.

Current events prove interesting, too, and everyone should keep aware of the more important news as expressed by radio and newspaper so he will not appear like Rip van Winkle awaking from a long sleep when he returns to "civilization."

## How to Conduct a Planned Discussion

The how, when and what of a planned discussion are important considerations. Groups of six to eight, never more than fifteen, work best, for they are small enough to eliminate embarrassment and stage fright at speaking up before others and permit close grouping so that each may hear and be heard.

Seat all comfortably, and, if there is to be a fire, place an extra supply of wood conveniently near to avoid the interruption of foraging for more.

Either a counselor or capable camper should act as leader or chairman. His function is to launch the discussion, then retire into the background; if conversation starts to lag, he must revive it with a thought-provoking comment or question calculated to bring about a lively response from several. Though it may occasionally be wise to let the group stray from the question at hand, it is the leader's job to determine just how far and how long such ramblings are advisable and, at the proper time, tactfully bring the discussion back to the topic at hand. If needed, appoint a secretary to take notes on the proceedings.

An informal atmosphere sets everyone at ease and encourages all to speak freely and openly. On the other hand, you must exercise enough control to keep the discussion from degenerating into a gossip session or a chat about trivialities. You must see that order is maintained and that no one person monopolizes an undue share of the time. Campers who are busy whittling or working on some arts and crafts project often find themselves more relaxed and ready to enter into a friendly give and take.

See that meetings end on time even though argument is still waging hot and heavy, but a postponment to some future date is in order if desired. You may ask campers to volunteer or appoint someone to look up data or consult experts for additional information, and surveys may be made or questionnaires filled out if a decision hinges on what the "camper thinks" or "wants." When a decision has been reached or interest seems to wane, the leader should promptly bring the meeting to a close.

## Characteristics of a Good Leader

A good leader is like a good basketball referee: he keeps the situation well in hand, yet keeps himself in the background. Express your opinions like any other member of the group, but never use your office as an excuse to force your will or overrule majority opinion. Keep the discussion between the members of the group—not between you and the group.

Use democratic procedures and encourage *every* member of the group to participate, for the quiet individual who spends his time thinking instead of talking often has a most worthwhile contribution to make. Be particularly attentive to the unpopular camper whose every opinion is scoffed at just because it is *his*, for, if others are permitted to dash cold water on his efforts, he soon stops trying to contribute and fit in with the group. Tactfully call attention to any merit his suggestion may have and supplement it with a private talk in an effort to show how he might present his ideas in a more favorable light in the future.

Keep things moving, for discussions should be virile and lively, not soothing like a bedtime story. Undue attempts at haste, however, cause some to feel hurried and unable to express themselves fully.

Be friendly and informal, yet maintain the dignity of your office. Do not try to cover up your embarrassment or ineptitude by giggling or making wise cracks, but remain poised and well in control of the situation.

Be broad-minded and able to see all sides of a question and bear constantly in mind that thinking people often change their minds. Above all, don't take advantage of your position by sneering, wise cracking or laughing at any ideas seriously expressed by others.

It may be advisable to spend some time in preparing for the discussion, reading or consulting others on topics about which you feel insecure and jotting down suggestions to rejuvenate the discussion when it lags.

## Why Discussions Fail

You may find some groups unable to carry on a worthwhile and satisfying discussion, for, even with good leadership, all must have a minimum of instruction and practice in it. Such a group might well plan an early consideration on "How to Participate in a Discussion."

Make each member of the group feel it is his duty to contribute, for those who say nothing add as little as the perpetual talkers whose ideas apparently originate in their mouths instead of their brains. Members should always refrain from garrulousness, for, as George Eliot said, "Blessed is the man who, having nothing to say, abstains from giving us wordy evidence of the fact."

Some people in a group often apparently feel called upon to comment on every point made, while others are "know-it-alls" who pose as authorities on every topic. Some ramble about and get off the subject, while others are apparently so busy planning their next remarks that they do not realize someone else has just expressed the thoughts they have in mind. For these, we would like to recommend the "South African treatment," which limits a speaker to what he can say while standing on one foot, with his speech automatically ending the instant he has to touch his upraised foot to the ground.

Some want their specific problems solved, apparently feeling that, like an automat, it ought to be possible to drop in a question, push a certain lever, and get an answer like magic. A group can do no more than open up various lines of thought for others to use as tools in arriving at their own solutions.

Every group is likely to contain biased, opinionated persons who look upon discussion merely as a sounding board for displaying their own pearls of wisdom to the hungry multitudes of the ignorant. Such is the intolerant camper or counselor who "only listens when he speaks" and furiously attacks any who dare to differ with him. They should recall the Chinese saying that getting angry is a sign one has run out of arguments.

## Benefits of a Discussion

Although the discussion method is a slow and somewhat inefficient way to cover material, it has undeniable advantages. It is a democratic procedure, for each person has the privilege of expressing his own thoughts and feelings and so the danger of hearing only one side of the argument is minimized. Each also has the opportunity to ask questions and get further information about any points not clear to him, and the very act of participating tends to keep people alert and interested.

Since youth tends to resent having ideas and opinions crammed down their throats by older people, the discussion method gives them a chance to share ideas with their peers and elders. Increased understanding and appreciation will result if they can learn to respect the opinions of others even though not endorsing them. It is often a revelation to see what deep and interesting thoughts lurk in the minds of our everyday companions. You, as a counselor will likewise gain new insights about your little brood, and they in turn should emerge with a changed feeling and understanding of you.

## ADDITIONAL READINGS

### BOOKS AND PAMPHLETS

Bucher, Charles A. (Ed.): Methods and Materials in Physical Education and Recreation. Mosby, 1954, pp. 240–250.

Hall, D. M.: The Dynamics of Group Discussion, a Handbook for Discussion Leaders. Interstate.

Johns, Ray: The Cooperative Process among National Social Agencies. Ass'n Press, 1946.

Parliamentary Procedure. Denver University Press, 1950. (A pictorial presentation on how to conduct a meeting.)

Roberts, General Henry M.: Parliamentary Practice. Century, 1921.

Talking It Through, A Manual for Discussion Groups. Nat'l Ed. Ass'n, Department of Secondary School Principals.

### MAGAZINE ARTICLES

Fox, James Harold: The Use of Group Procedures in Problem Solving. Jr. H. and P.E., Nov.–Dec., 1950.

I Give My
Pledge As An American
To Save And Faithfully To
Defend From Waste The
Natural Resources Of
My Country—Its Soil
And Minerals, Its
Forest, Waters,
And Wildlife.*

## Chapter 14

# NATURE AND CONSERVATION

A RETURN to the simple life and its intimate contact with nature has always been a stated purpose of camping, but the methods used have not always brought the love of nature hoped for. Campers have victoriously displayed badges and ribbons won by learning the scientific names of twenty insects or mounting twenty flowers, and have returned to the city bearing such live pets as squirrels, turtles, grasshoppers, snakes and even skunks to foist upon long-suffering parents or let die of neglect and mistreatment. Only an occasional camper acquired enough interest in nature to make it a lifelong hobby, for, like human friends, plants and animals become friends only through long and personal acquaintance. Learning a name or viewing a still, cold corpse impaled upon a mounting pin will never bring about such a result.

Dragon Fly.

It may bolster one's ego to identify a giant dragon fly as *Epiaeschna heros*, but it cannot compare with the enchantment of watching this evil-looking, blood-

*This pledge originated in a national competition conducted in 1946 by *Outdoor Life Magazine*.

thirsty creature zoom and bank through the air, using its basketlike under-carriage of legs to scoop up flies, mosquitoes and other insects which it later crams into its capacious mouth. Its appetite is enormous, and it has been known to bolt down forty-two flies topped off with large quantities of its own tail which had been bent around and fed into its mouth. Its needle is only an elongated stomach, and its huge eyes have 30,000 facets which enable it to see in all directions. These, with its fierce expression, give it a truly sinister look, but it is quite harmless to man and does not merit its common names of devil's darning needle, horse killer, and snake feeder. Perhaps it is unfortunate that its long "darning needle" does not have its reputed power to sew up the lips of liars.

Nature in camp should not be conducted as an isolated class, for it is at its best only when made a part of each child's experience in the out-of-doors. It can be interwoven with all phases of the indigenous program and should be thought of as what one experiences by touch, taste, smell, sound and sight. It should consist of studying nature's creatures as they carry on their normal activities in their natural habitats, and not of studying dead, dried-up skele-tons.

Naturelore should not be knowledge acquired to pass tests or pose as a walking encyclopedia, but should come rather as the inevitable result of widened visions and deepened appreciations. Specimens are not the smelly laboratory variety nor the foreign imports of zoo and circus, but are those things which we encounter every day, but have failed to notice up to now. Aided by such inexpensive pieces of equipment as a homemade butter-fly net and a little pocket microscope, the field of exploration is unlimited.

Instead of being bookish or formal, nature should be an active, doing process in which children venture forth to look at whatever lies beside the path, under the rocks, in the trees, or at the bottom of the pond. Campers should unite minds, hearts and hands to explore, uncover, mount specimens, make insect dip nets, splatter prints, and indigenous arts and crafts projects. If their group is building an outdoor camp site, they must never become too absorbed to stop and watch the antics of a venturesome squirrel or listen to a noisy jay. A night of restless slumber under a quaking aspen creates a real interest in seeing how the flat, wide stem is set "on edge" against the broad leaf so that the least breeze keeps leaves stirring, producing the rainlike patter so disturbing the previous night. Like opportunity, nature experiences often knock but once and we must seize them whenever and wherever they appear. We cannot schedule them for definite times and places, for Mother Earth's children are too busy carrying on their daily activities to be amenable to man-made schedules. Let us not be like the poor, misguided nature counselor who said, "Now children, come away from that porpoise washed up on the beach! Remember, we're studying birds today and won't get around to porpoises until two weeks from Tuesday."

A child's feeling of confidence and security in the out-of-doors increases as he learns that nearly all animals are timid and much prefer to stay out of his path and sight, attempting to harm him only if cornered or frightened. He makes friends with chipmunks, squirrels, toads and birds as he discovers that nearly all woodland creatures readily respond to kindly overtures. His appreciation makes him enjoy doing a good turn for smaller, weaker woodfolk instead of tormenting or killing them just for the fun of it. His spiritual self gets uplift from the wonders and beauties of nature and since love comes from the feelings rather than the mind, the result is a genuine and abiding "love" for all living creatures.

Tests and ranks depend on information secured by first-hand observation rather than learned from a book. Books, though, are important, as they answer queries about things the camper has seen but doesn't understand or better prepare him for a future excursion.

## Conservation

Campers need to comprehend the interdependence of all forms of life. All living things are dependent upon plants, for every animal, including man, either dines directly upon some form of plant life or upon some other animal which, in the final analysis, does so. Everything looks like a delectable dietary tidbit to something else, so that each is simultaneously engaged in a struggle to secure its own food and avoid becoming the food of another. Each has its own means for securing food, and some methods are unique and most interesting. The opposite leaves of the teasel are joined into a small cup at the stem which catches water and drowns minute ants for its banquet dish. The rare Venus's flytrap has a hairtrigger mechanism which causes the sharp teeth along the edges of its leaves to instantly interlock and trap any insect unlucky enough to merely brush against them.

Everything also has a way of protecting itself. Deer can outrun most of their enemies, and cats climb trees to evade dogs. Porcupines pursue their leisurely way, secure in the knowledge that their barbed quills will deter most attackers; skunks make amiable and affectionate pets, but nature has given them the power to exact a fiendish revenge on whatever frightens or attacks them. The chameleon changes color, the rabbit "freezes," the rosebush has thorns, and the thistle has prickles to help protect them against their enemies.

Nature provides each variety of life in abundance, so that, though some may become food or succumb to disease, wind, flood or unfavorable climatic conditions, there will always be enough left to carry on the species. The female frog lays 20,000 eggs, but only 200 develop into adult frogs, while the other 19,800 lose their lives by accident or become food for fish and water insects. Nature, if left to her own devices, keeps all species in balance, so that none either die out or become so numerous as to overrun the earth, and every single form of life has its own role in maintaining this balance. Enough birdlings are created to spare a few for the snake, just as enough lettuce, green beans, and pork chops grow to supply our needs. We must rid our minds once and for all of the idea that certain forms of life are more worthy than others, for man's efforts to kill out what he considers an unworthy species has sometimes backfired in a most unfortunate way. A concentrated drive to eradicate "chicken-killing" hawks, for instance, may bring about a huge oversupply of rats, mice, snakes and frogs which really constitute over 90 per cent of their diet in contrast to the occasional chicken they eat.

Almost everything we do affects plant or animal life in some way. Picking berries in the fall cuts down on the supply of winter food for some bird or animal, and squirrels lose out when we gather nuts. Draining a swamp to provide more farm land kills thousands of plants and animals which cannot survive without a wet environment. Spraying trees kills the insects and grubs which provide food for certain birds. Killing squirrels will eventually mean fewer trees, for dead squirrels cannot bury nuts to sprout and grow into future forest monarchs.

Man, in his greediness to sell beaver pelts, thinned out these little animals until no more beaver dams were built in certain areas. When hard rains came, water rushed down the open streams, causing floods to destroy both property and life; between rains, the creek bed dried out so that water life could not survive, and land animals went thirsty.

Man has used the rivers as garbage tanks and open sewers, and as drains for the various chemicals and waste products of manufacturing; as a result, they are no longer fit for swimming, and even plant and fish life sometimes cannot survive in them.

Man has cut down the trees and shrubs which used to provide food and shelter for animals and birds. He has shot and trapped so many animals for food, furs or sport that some, such as the buffalo, are scarce, while the great auk and passenger pigeon are extinct.

Forest preserves, the requiring of hunting and fishing licenses, open and closed seasons, bag limits, and the nurturing and "planting" of young birds, fish and animals are making feeble strides toward preserving the remnants of our natural heritage, but the understanding and loyal support of thousands of persons are needed if satisfactory progress is to be made. Camping can do much by spreading information and enlisting the cooperation of the youngsters who will be the citizens of tomorrow.

One of man's most myopic perspectives has been with regard to the conservation of the soil upon which all plant and animal life depends. Topsoil consists of a mixture of minerals and the remnants of animals and plants which is admirably suited for plant growth. It lies above the nonfertile subsoil, and varies from a depth of a few inches on hill tops to several feet in the valleys. When on the floor of the forest, it is known as *humus*.

When our ancestors came to America, they were delighted with the rich topsoil they found after they had cleared away the trees and shrubs. When they had quickly worn out the land, through replanting the same crop over and over again, they cared little, for more land could be had for the taking, so that they simply moved on to repeat the same process all over again. Progressive farmers now plant crops in rotation so that one crop helps to restore the fertility lost to the previous one.

Vegetation keeps soil porous and loose, enabling it to absorb and hold large quantities of water which is gradually absorbed by the plants and returned to the air by evaporation. Without plant growth, rains quickly run off down sloping surfaces, forming ever-enlarging gullies and carrying off large quantities of the topsoil. When the farmer makes his plow lines straight up and down the hillsides, he but adds to this wastage so that every year 25,000,000 cubic feet of our richest topsoil are being washed away and eternally lost for cultivation. This is not a cheering picture when we stop to think that from 500 to 1000 years are required to create an inch thickness of fertile topsoil.

The rapidly draining slopes cause swollen streams and eventual floods which menace the plant and animal life along the banks. Campers will be interested in making a tour of their own camp site to find examples of erosion and plan for its elimination.

The topsoil in dry areas, where there are no roots of vegetation to hold it in place, is carried away as dust, leaving behind whole areas of infertile and desolate dust bowls. Many farmers still burn off their land each year in an attempt to kill off weeds and get the ground "ready" for spring crops, but this practice damages their precious topsoil.

Testing the soil and supplying needed chemicals, rotating crops, planting cover crops to hold moisture and prevent erosion, and using terraced and contour plowing on hillside areas are valuable steps in soil conservation.

True conservation is based upon an appreciation of the value of each living thing in maintaining the balance of the whole. It tells us that we are free to use the surplus which nature lavishly supplies, but that we must always carefully leave enough of everything to insure its continuance for our own future use and that of coming generations. We may liken it to an investment at the bank where the interest always continues to come as long as we leave the principal intact. When man, in his infinite short-sightedness, sets himself up to decide which varieties of life are worthy to continue, he is likely to upset nature's nicely poised balance in ways difficult to foresee. It is much wiser to take the attitude that any wanton destruction of wild life is extremely undesirable.

## THE NATURE COUNSELOR

Each counselor must, in a sense, be a nature counselor if camp is to make an appreciation and understanding of the out-of-doors a vital part of camp living. This does not mean that each is expected to be an authority on naturelore, but rather that the individual counselor will be interested in it and willing to start with whatever meager knowledge he has and add to it as he learns with his campers. He need not be ashamed to admit he doesn't know all the answers, for even experts at one time started with absolutely no knowledge in their chosen field. He will gradually need to say, "I don't know, but let's find out" less and less often as he explores with his campers and consults the nature counselor or source books about what campers cannot learn by observation.

Nature, like happiness, lurks in most unexpected places, disclosing itself most often to those alert enough to notice rather than to those who go out consciously seeking it. A ten-mile hike may end up a hundred yards from the cabin as a fascinated group watches a spider weave its web or a trip to gather wood for camp construction turns into a study of different woods and their uses, and who can say that these side excursions are not more valuable than the original objectives?

The main requirements for you if you want to help with a real nature program are curiosity, enthusiasm, and an insight into the possibilities for integrating nature with many camp experiences and, most of all, interest in and love of *human* nature. You must not let nature study become a boresome tedious thing, but must keep it ever a pulsating, vibrant answer to your campers' query of how, when, where and why?

A trip offers a wonderful opportunity to acquire information about the world in which we live. What camper is not interested in nontechnical information about the different terrains and soils and their effect upon flora and fauna, and about watersheds, rivers, drainage, currents, water life, and the hundreds of displays Dame Nature has set up along the way? When carried on with naturalness and enthusiasm, you can make nature study one of the most interesting activities in camp. Carry it on in the out-of-doors under the sun and skies and winds and rain of nature's own laboratory whenever possible.

Such pieces of equipment as microscopes, pocket magnifying glasses, butterfly nets and attractive nature books stimulate youngsters to want to use them. Hands and imaginations occupied in making cages, arranging bulletin boards, mounting displays, and planning museums and nature trails result in interested, happy campers. They may keep such creatures as frogs, salamanders, ants, nonpoisonous snakes or larvae as pets for a few hours if they know how to make them comfortable. This provides an opportunity to observe them closely.

Many excellent slides and movie films are now available free or at nominal cost and there is a multitude of good literature now on the market.

## NATURE WALKS

Nature walks are not hikes, but must be taken leisurely enough to allow time to look, listen, smell, taste, touch and investigate. Keep the group small (six to eight) and travel slowly and quietly so that you do not scatter your wild friends in terror. Proceed with your back to the sun so colors will show up more brightly.

Take pocket magnifying glasses, binoculars, sacks or boxes for bringing back unusual "finds," a few good identification books, and a notebook and pencil to jot down points of interest.

## COLLECTING

Though making collections still has its place, it does not occupy the pinnacle it once did. One reason for this is that previous collectors, in their zeal to get "just one more specimen," all but annihilated some of our rarer species of wildlife. Before picking a flower or other specimen, apply the principles of conservation by glancing about to see that there are ample quantities left to carry on the species.

Collections also sometimes become ends in themselves, with the collector heaving a satisfied sigh each time he has corralled another specimen, fastened it on paper and labeled it with a polysyllabic title. He neither knows nor cares anything about Exhibit X beyond having a mere nodding acquaintance with its name; in fact he may completely overlook it the next time he pursues his one-track search for some new vicitm to add to his store. This sort of collecting becomes busy work, contributing nothing whatsoever toward furthering a real love of nature.

When properly regarded, collections of rocks, minerals, flowers, leaves, seeds, insects, shells, ferns, mosses, and the like, add to a nature program. Accompany each mounting with its name, date, locale, your name as collector, and chatty data concerning its life and place in the balance of nature and its commercial value to man to help you achieve real nature appreciation. Be sure to practice good conservation in all you do.

Reproducing actual specimens with water color or sketching, or taking photographs with the aid of a camera portrait attachment, is even better than mounting actual specimens.

### Pressing Plants

It is easy to make a press to prepare leaves, ferns, and flowers for mounting. One 10 by 12 inches will meet ordinary needs and should be constructed so as to simultaneously dry and flatten the plants. Two pieces of board, approximately 10 by 12 inches and about $\frac{1}{2}$ inch thick, are needed for the outside covers. Cut a dozen or more sheets of blotting paper and half as many sheets of corrugated cardboard from packing boxes to fit and complete the outfit with two web or leather straps.

Place each plant between sheets of blotting paper (or newspaper) and separate from the others by the sheets of corrugated paper. Place the covers on the top and bottom, draw the straps tight to hold the whole thing com-

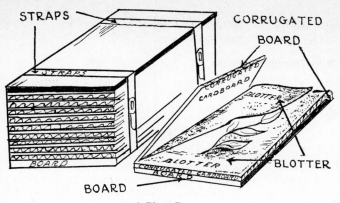

A Plant Press.

pact, and leave for several days while the plants dry and flatten. If desired, a weight can be placed on top of the press. Beware of picking rare specimens or large quantities of even the plentiful. A hundred campers make a serious inroad if each picks only one leaf. It is usually better to learn to look at nature's exhibits as they grow, leaving them intact for the pleasure of others.

## MUSEUMS

Camp museums may be located in the nature house, under a tree near camp, or along a nature trail. You may use them to display such camper activities as a nature bulletin board, mounted specimens, indigenous arts and crafts projects, trail maps, creative writing on nature topics, papier-mâché relief maps, live pets, weather predictions and equipment, knot display boards, friction sets made from camp materials, mats and baskets woven of native materials, articles fashioned from local clay, and so forth.

The craft house itself should be supplied with guide books, displays, tools, storage facilities, working space at tables, and other things. A fireplace provides a cheery environment on damp days. Campers should plan and keep up all exhibits themselves with all on the lookout for interesting materials. Maintain a "What Is It?" shelf or corner for unidentified curios with the name of the person who first correctly identifies them given a place of honor on the bulletin board. Change the display frequently so that campers do not pass it by because "it's just the same old thing." Make a terrarium and stock it with such inhabitants as frogs, toads and salamanders.

### Useful Plants

Collect samples of medicinal and other useful plants and label them with their names and uses. It is interesting to gather and serve a meal composed exclusively of wild foods (but be sure you get expert help to avoid eating something harmful or poisonous). Use native dyes, and make elderberry wine, blueberry pie or wild strawberry shortcake.

### Raising Wild Things in Camp

A fernery or wild flower garden, an insect cage, an aquarium for water life, or a terrarium for things that live on land may be made. Make outdoor feeding stations to attract wildlife where you can watch them firsthand.

## MAKING A NATURE TRAIL

Laying a nature trail is an interesting and educational experience, for it requires careful consultation and planning to include as many worthwhile things as possible. Ideally, the trail should be narrow and about one-half to a mile in length and should include sections of meadowland, woods, a stream or pond, and the edge of a swamp to bring in a variety of life. You may indicate such interesting side trips as a visit to a rare flower, a spring or a beaver dam.

Make all labels brief but interesting and informative. If a lot of information is desirable, it is best to distribute it on several short labels, for people will not bother to read anything at all if they are discouraged by undue lengthiness. Bristol board tags or pieces of filing card are satisfactory for temporary use, but when more durable labels are called for, you can use bits of tin, enameling them and printing on them with India ink and then protecting them with a coat of shellac or Valspar. Short poems, photographs, bulletin boards, displays, and trailside museums add interest. The changing season calls for new labels and a rerouting of the trail every now and then.

You can sharpen the campers' observations by giving them sheets to fill out as they move along the trail. Invitations to listen, taste, smell or feel help to bring all the senses into play.

You may need to clear the trail somewhat for easy passage, but be sure to keep it woodsy and natural. You can lay flat stepping stones or brush across wet places, or even construct a rustic bridge across a stream. Be careful not to make your trail so it results in erosion.

## BIRDS*

Bird study has a larger following than any other phase of nature, and these projects for carrying it on are suggested.

Birdwalks—best carried on in early morning or late evening when the birds are most active. Learn to identify by nest, color, sound, and manner of flight. Move slowly and quietly.

* Write to the National Audubon Society, 1000 Fifth Avenue, New York 28, N.Y., for information about the Audubon Junior Clubs for Summer Camps.

Attract birds by planting shrubs and trees near camp to provide food and cover. Supply short pieces of string or yarn (3 to 4 inches) for nesting material during the nesting season. Bird houses placed this summer will attract birds next spring for next summer's camp. Bird baths and feeding trays also help.

Collect feathers. Collect old nests (no birds except hawks use them a second time) and dissect them to see what materials were used in their construction. Place modelled eggs painted the proper colors in whole nests and display them on branches arranged to resemble trees.

Contrast the bills and feet of birds to see how they are adapted to their diet and habits. Listen to the bird's song and watch its pattern of flight.

Take a bird census or keep a record of all the birds you see in camp.

Make a bird scrapbook of pictures, stories, anecdotes and poems.

Make plaster casts of tracks in mud or at the beach.

## PLANTS

Make a wild flower garden or fernery. (Ferns and wild flowers will only grow with soil and other conditions similar to those of their natural habitat.)

Draw or paint pictures of wild flowers, adding name, date, where found, and such information as native country, seeds and their dispersal, pollination and uses (medicinal, dyes, and so on). In mounting specimens, use small pieces of Scotch tape or dip the specimens in a mixture of glue and vinegar spread evenly on glass, and transfer them to heavy paper.

Study seeds and their dispersal by barbs, parachutes, or other means. Collect some and keep them for making a wild flower garden. Glue them on mounting boards and label.

Make a plant gall collection.

Study lichens, mosses and ferns. Look at them through a microscope.

Identify nut-bearing bushes and trees. Learn when the nuts ripen.

Study flower arrangement for indoor decoration.

Identify poison ivy, oak and sumac.

Identify different types of mushrooms, particularly the morels which are safe to eat. Do not trust other kinds, for even experts have difficulty in distinguishing the poisonous ones.

Learn which plants are edible; prepare and eat some of them (be sure to get expert advice).

## TREES

Identify trees by contour, color, leaf, bark, flower, seed and wood structure. Then learn all you can about them: what they are used for, how they burn, and so on.

Press and mount leaves, using the methods suggested for flowers.

Photograph trees; make sketches or water colors of them.

Carry on a tree conservation program, thinning out dead, diseased and crowded ones, and pruning off dead or diseased branches as close to the trunk as possible and covering the scar with paint (brown or green blend in well). Clear out obstructing brush and vines which are choking young trees.

Learn how individual trees serve for shade, beauty, soil conservation, firewood or commercial products. Learn their early uses by the Indians and pioneers. Identify the kinds found in camp furniture, walls, and so forth.

Study stumps to learn the life history of the tree such as its age, injuries, insect damage, favorable and unfavorable seasons, and the like.

Learn the uses of different kinds of woods in fire-building (tinder, kindling, heat, light, fire dogs, and others). Which ones are best for whittling? Notice how the growth of trees is affected by those surrounding them.

## INSECTS

Learn the distinguishing characteristics of insects, spiders, bees, wasps, grasshoppers, bugs, beetles, flies, moths, butterflies, and the like. Identify the various sorts and learn their habits, food, life cycles, and use or destructiveness. Watch them in their native habitat.

Make sketches of common varieties.

Prepare and mount specimens, adding pertinent information about them.

Raise families of butterflies, moths, ants, insects.

Photograph spider webs and other photogenic things.

Watch an ant colony at work.

## ROCKS AND MINERALS

Distinguish between minerals and rocks.

Visit a quarry, a fresh road cut, a dried-up stream bed, or a mine opening.

Gather specimens, using a geology hammer (a regular hammer will serve) to prepare uniform sizes (about $1\frac{1}{2}$ by $2\frac{1}{2}$ inches) for collections. Wash carefully and label. Keep the specimens in boxes with compartments of cardboard; mount small samples on a mounting board or in plaster of Paris. Enter dates, places and interesting facts about the find.

Study the characteristics of rocks, determining which are best for use in fireplaces, as kettle supports, and so on.

## FISH

Make your own poles, baits (flies and lures), and lines.

Learn to recognize the different species and learn their life histories.

Prepare and mount an especially good specimen.

Learn about state fishing laws, fish hatcheries and efforts at conservation.

Learn to clean fish and study their structures as you are cleaning them.

## ANIMALS

Keep an animal a *short* time (not over twenty-four hours) for observation. Be sure you know how to feed and care for it.

Take close-up photographs. Use a portrait attachment.

Make plaster casts of tracks.

Make a wildlife sanctuary. Put out some foods animals like to attract them, never frighten them and see how tame they get.

Play stalking games.

Stalk animals with a camera (takes patience and skill). Lie or sit still and watch them. If you wait long enough you may be able to discover where they live.

## STARS

It is best to study stars on a clear evening when there is no moon to detract from their brightness.

Use the beam of a focusing flashlight to help point them out.

Learn the folklore regarding the stars and constellations.

Paint diagrams of the heavens on dark blue or black paper with luminous paint so you can use them at night.

Take time exposures of stars with your camera.

Binoculars make the observation of stars more interesting.

## MAKING PRINTS

There are several methods of printing flowers, leaves and ferns. Better results are obtained if you first press the specimens flat. Use them to decorate your memory book, place cards, invitations and stationery.

### Ozalid and Blue Prints

These give beautiful results, but are slightly more expensive than other prints and require some skill to make well.

### Crayon Prints

Place a leaf, vein side up, on a flat surface, cover it with a sheet of unlined paper and, holding leaf and paper firmly in place, rub a soft crayon over the paper with parallel strokes until the edges and veins stand out clearly. Outline the edge with a firm black line and cut out the print and mount it or use it for decorating menus or stationery (see page 160).

### Ink Pad Prints

Lay a leaf, vein side down, on an ink pad, cover with a layer of newspaper cut to fit the ink pad, and rub thoroughly. Transfer the leaf, inky side down, onto a piece of paper, cover it with a fresh newspaper, hold it firmly in place, and rub until the ink pad print appears clearly on the paper.

### Printer's Ink Print

Spread a small quantity of printer's ink of any desired color on a piece of glass and run a rubber photographic roller through it until it is thinly and evenly spread. Place the leaf, vein side up, on a newspaper and rub the inky roller over it, transferring a uniform coating of ink. Reverse the leaf, place it on a fresh sheet of paper, cover with newspaper and, holding it firmly in place, rub over it with a clean roller until the transfer is completed.

### Smoke Prints

Many consider smoke prints the most attractive of all. Candles (plumber's

Smoke Print Stationery.

are best) and some grease such as lard or petroleum jelly are necessary. Spread a small quantity of grease evenly over a fourth of a sheet of newspaper and pass it through the candle flame (being careful not to let it get close enough to burn) until it is uniformly coated with carbon. Then lay it on a flat surface, place the leaf, vein side down, on it, cover with a clean piece of newspaper, and rub over the newspaper, holding the leaf firmly in place. Transfer the leaf, carbon side down, to a fresh sheet of paper, again cover with newspaper, and rub until the smoke print is transferred.

### Spatter Prints

An old tooth brush and some India ink or diluted poster paint are neces-

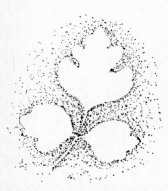

A Spatter Print.

sary for this method of printing. Protect the scene of operation by spreading newspapers about and place the leaf on a plain sheet of paper. Pin the edges flat so that no paint can get under them and slant the heads of the pins slightly toward the center of the leaf. Dip the toothbrush into the paint to get a thin but uniform coating on it. Holding the brush at a 45-degree angle and about 2 inches from the paper, use a knife, nail file or thin, flat stick, to scrape *toward you* across the tooth brush. Continue the process until a sufficiently heavy "spatter" has been deposited around the leaf. Do not remove the leaf until the paint is dry.

# PLASTER CASTS

Inexpensive plaster casts of flowers, animal tracks, leaves, and the like, are simple to make and are quite attractive when used as paper weights, book ends or wall plaques. They may be tinted in natural colors if desired. Plaster of Paris may be purchased at the hardware or drug store and should be mixed in an old container such as a tin can, using a stick for stirring (it is practically impossible to remove the plaster from anything with which it has come in contact). Estimate the amount of plaster needed for the cast desired and place three-fourths of that amount of water in the container. Pour in as much plaster of Paris as will sink to the bottom, then add a trifle more for good measure. Put in a pinch of salt to hasten setting and stir thoroughly. A good mixture has about the consistency of pancake batter.

If an animal track is to be cast, dust it lightly with talcum powder and place a circular or rectangular collar of cardboard of the size desired for the finished cast around it. Pour in the plaster of Paris and let it harden. Then lift the cast carefully, remove the cardboard collar, and scrub it well with water. Plaques should have a screw eye or paper clip for hanging inserted in the edge before they are dry.

To make a positive cast (with the track in relief), powder the negative cast lightly, place a collar about it and pour in more plaster of Paris. When dry, carefully separate the two casts.

To make casts of leaves, ferns, flowers, seeds, and so forth, pour the plaster of Paris into a mold, dampen the specimen and place it on the plaster of Paris, brushing it with a paint brush to make a tight contact over its entire surface. When about half dry, remove the leaf and let the plaster continue to harden.

Obviously, superfluous plaster of Paris should never be poured down the drain.

# NATURE GAMES

*Starvation Hike.*     Go out and cook a meal, using only things found growing in the woods. Be sure you *know* what is safe to use.

*Nature Quests.*     See who can bring in and identify a square stemmed plant; a lady beetle; a piece of wood that is shaped like an animal; and such. Be careful not to cause harm or destruction.

*Nature Treasure or Scavenger Hunt.*     Give each group, person or pair a list of nature objects to bring in, such as leaves of certain trees, common flowers, certain kinds of rocks, and so forth. The first back with the correct and complete list wins. Some of the items should be easy to find, others hard. Avoid poor conservation practice by not tramping over and collecting items which should be conserved.

*Nature Quiz Programs.*     Carried on like "Information, Please," with small prizes for winners.

*Leaf Relay.* Give each team a list of trees. The first one in line runs to get a leaf of the first tree on the list, returns, and gives the list to the second in line, who then reads the second kind of tree and runs to get a sample, and so on. The first group through wins.

*Identification.* Have pictures of animals, trees, birds, insects, and the like, pasted on cards. Flash them. The first person who correctly identifies the picture receives the card. The person with the most cards at the end of the playing time wins.

*Touch, Taste, Smell Identification.* Blindfold players and pass around objects for them to identify, designating whether they are to do so by tasting, smelling, or feeling.

*Tree Identification.* Make a tour, stopping at various trees, so that each person can fill in the name of the tree on his numbered chart. The person with the most correct identifications wins. When first learning, participants may take their tree identification books along and be given three or four minutes to identify the tree with the assistance of the book. Ferns, flowers, birds, sea shells, animals, or any other kind of wildlife desired may be identified in this game.

*Trailing.* "It" walks carelessly through the woods, making no effort to conceal his footprints or avoid breaking branches. Ten minutes later, a small group or an individual tries to follow his trail and spy him where he is hiding beside it. A variation is to have two persons walk in single file through the woods. At a given signal, they reverse, and the one originally in the rear tries to lead the way back over the same trail. He may be given a start of twenty-five points, with two deducted each time he wanders off the trail and one each time he hesitates more than a minute in determining the correct course.

*Nature Sounds.* Each listens for five minutes, listing all the nature sounds heard and identified. This is a particularly good game to play at night.

*Upside Down Hike.* Turn rocks and large sticks over to see what is living underneath. Be sure to restore them without harming any living inhabitants.

*What Is It?* Have a number of clues describing a nature object written on a card, with the least well known first. Read them one at a time until someone is finally able to guess the object and receives the card as his reward. A variation is to let campers take turns, giving oral clues until a fellow camper is able to guess what he has in mind.

*What's Wrong with This Picture?* Announce that a certain nature object is to be described, and that, although most of the characteristics given will be true, a few erroneous ones will be included. See how many can detect the incorrect ones.

*Quiet, Please!* The members of one group sit blindfolded with some designated object located about 6 feet in front of them. The idea is for the second group to creep stealthily in and steal the object without being detected. When members of the blindfolded group hear an opponent approaching and point directly at him, he is eliminated. A variation is to have only one member blindfolded while the others are scattered in various directions and at different distances from him. They take turns whistling, rustling leaves, or stamping a foot, and so forth. If he can judge the direction and point directly to the person, the two exchange places.

## ADDITIONAL READINGS

### BIRDS

Allen, Arthur A.: Book of Bird Life—A Study of Birds in Their Native Haunts. Van Nostrand.

Bird Study. Boy Scouts (#3282), 1938.

Chapman, Frank M.: Color Key to North American Birds, rev. ed. Appleton.

Forbush, Edward Howe: Natural History of the Birds of Eastern and Central North America. Houghton, 1939, 400 pp.

Griscom, Ludlow: Modern Bird Study. Harvard University Press.

Hoffman, Ralph: Birds of the Pacific States. Houghton, 1938, 353 pp.

Hoffman, Len: Birds As Individuals. Doubleday.

Lemmon, Robert S.: Our Amazing Birds. Doubleday, 1952, 239 pp.

Mason, C. Russell: Picture Primer of Attracting Birds. Houghton.

Pearson, T. Gilbert (Ed.): Birds of America.

Peterson, Roger Tory: A Field Guide to the Birds, 2nd ed. Houghton, 1948, 290 pp.

Peterson, Roger Tory: Birds over America. Dodd, Mead, 1948.

Peterson, Roger Tory: How to Know the Birds. Girl Scouts (#23–545).

Pickwell, Gayle: Birds. McGraw-Hill.

Pough, Richard H.: Audubon Bird Guide; Eastern Land Birds. Doubleday, 1946.

Pough, Richard H.: Audubon Water Bird Guide. Doubleday.

Saunders, Aretas A.: The Lives of Wild Birds. Doubleday.

Zim, Herbert S.: Owls. Morrow.

Zim, Herbert S., and Gabrielson, I. N.: Birds (A Golden Nature Guide). Simon and Schuster, 1949, 157 pp.

### COMPREHENSIVE

Andrews, Roy Chapman: Nature's Ways. Crown, 1951.

Asch, John: The Story of Plants. Putnam, 1948, 415 pp.

Bauer, Margaret J.: Animal Babies. Donohue.

Brown, Vinson: The Amateur Naturalist's Handbook. Little, 1948, 475 pp.

Buck, Margaret Waring: In Woods and Fields. Abingdon-Cokesbury.

Burt, William H.: A Field Guide to the Mammals North of Mexican Boundary. Houghton, 1952.

Colby, Carroll: Who Lives There? Aladdin Books, 48 pp.

Colby, Carroll: Who Went There? Alladin Books, 48 pp.

Comstock, Anna Botsford: Handbook of Nature Study, 24th ed. Comstock, 1948, 957 pp.

Devoe, Alan: This Fascinating Animal World. McGraw-Hill.

Devoe, Alan, and Devoe, Mary Berry: Our Animal Neighbors. McGraw-Hill, 1953, 278 pp.

Fenton, Carroll Lane: Along the Hill. Day, 1935, 96 pp.

Fenton, Carroll Lane: Along Nature's Highway. Day, 1943, 96 pp.

Fenton, Carroll Lane: Life Long Ago. Day, 1937, 299 pp.

Fenton, Carroll Lane: Wild Folk at the Pond. Day, 1948, 127 pp.

Fenton, Carroll Lane: Wild Folk in the Woods. Day, 1952, 128 pp.

Graham, E. H., and Vandersal, R.: Wildlife for America. Oxford U.

Guberlet, Muriel Lewin: The Seashore Parade. Ronald, 1942, 197 pp.

Hausman, Leon A.: Beginner's Guide to Fresh-Water Life. Putnam, 1950, 128 pp.

Hausman, Leon A.: Beginner's Guide to Seashore Life. Putnam, 1949, 128 pp.

Hegner, Robert W.: Parade of the Animal Kingdom. Macmillan, 1942, 675 pp.

Hogner, D. C., and Hogner, Nils: The Animal Book. Oxford U., 1951.

Hylander, Clarence J.: Sea and Shore. Macmillan.

Jaeger, Ellsworth: Land and Water Trails. Macmillan.

Jaeger, Ellsworth: Tracks and Trailcraft. Macmillan, 1948, 381 pp.

Jacques, H. E.: Plants We Eat and Wear. Jacques.

Martin, Alexander C., Zim, Schubert S., and Nelson, Arnold L.: American Wildlife and Plants. McGraw-Hill.

Marx, David S.: The American Book of the Woods. Botanic Publishing Co., 1940.

Miner, Roy Waldo: Field Book of Seashore Life. Putnam, 1950, 630 pp.

Moore, Clifford B.: Book of Wild Pets. Putnam.

Moore, Clifford B.: Ways of Mammals— in Fact and Fancy. Ronald, 1953, 273 pp.

Morgan, Alfred: Pet Book for Boys and Girls. Scribner, 1949.

Morgan, Anne, Haven: Field Book of Ponds and Streams. Putnam, 1930, 464 pp.

Nature. Boy Scouts (#3258), 1953.

Packard, Vance: Animal IQ. Dial, 1950.

Palmer, E. Laurence: Fieldbook of Natural History. McGraw-Hill, 1949, 664 pp.

Parker, Bertha Morris: The Golden Treasury of Natural History. Simon and Schuster.

Peterson, Roger Tory: Wild Life in Color. Houghton, 1952, 192 pp.

Platt, Rutherford: This Green World. Dodd, Mead.

Sanderson, Ivan T.: How to Know the American Mammals. Little.

Scout Field Book. Boy Scouts (#3649).

Selsam, Millicent: A Time for Sleep, How the Animals Rest. Scott, 1953, 57 pp.

Seton, Ernest Thompson: Wild Animals I Have Known. Bantam.

Shaw, Margaret, and Fisher, James: Animals As Friends. Didier. (Rearing camp pets.)

## CONSERVATION

Bassett, Ray E.: Protect Your Camp against Erosion. C.M., April, 1949.

Beard, Ward P.: Teaching Conservation. Am. Forestry Ass'n, 1948.

Clark, Wilson F.: Teach Conservation to Campers. C.M., May, 1952.

Conservation Education in American Schools. Am. Ass'n of Sch. Administrators, 29th Yearbook, 1951, 527 pp.

Conservation in Camping. (A Workshop on Conservation.) ACA, 1952, 26 pp.

Gabrielson, Ira N.: Wildlife Conservation. Macmillan.

Hall, William B.: Teach Conservation with A Forestry Program. C.M., April, 1953.

Kauffman, Erle: The Conservation Yearbook, 1952. Conservation Yearbook.

Our Land—Conservation Activities for Camp Fire Girls. Camp Fire Girls (#D 313), 1949.

Soil and Water Conservation. Boy Scouts (#3291), 1952.

## FLOWERS

Armstrong, Margaret: Field Book of Western Wild Flowers. Putnam.

Hausman, Ethel H.: Beginners Guide to Wild Flowers. Putnam, 1948, 376 pp.

Kiernan, John: An Introduction to Wild Flowers. Hanover House, 1952, 77 pp.

Mathews, G. Schuyler: Field Book of American Wild Flowers. Putnam, 1929, 558 pp.

Rickett, H. W.: Wild Flowers of America. Crown, 1953, 432 pp.

Stefferud, Alfred: How to Know Wild Flowers. Holt, 144 pp.

Walcott, Mary Vaux, and Platt, Dorothy Falcon: Wild Flowers of America. Crown, 1953, 400 pp.

Zim, Herbert S., and Martin, Alexander C.: Flowers, A Golden Nature Guide to American Wildflowers. Simon and Schuster.

## INSECTS, SPIDERS, BUTTER-FLIES, ETC.

Crompton, John: The Life of the Spider. Houghton.

Duncan, Winifred: Webs in the Wind, the Habits of Web-Weaving Spiders. Ronald, 1949, 387 pp.

Insect Life. Boy Scouts (#3348), 1944.

Klots, Alexander B.: A Field Guide to the Butterflies of North America. Houghton, 1951, 349 pp.

Lutz, Frank E.: Field Book of Insects. Putnam, 1935, 510 pp.

Needham, James G.: Introducing Insects. Ronald, 1943, 129 pp.

Neurath, Marie: The Wonder World of Insects. Lothrop, 36 pp.

Teale, Edwin Way: The Junior Book of Insects, rev. ed. Dutton, 1953, 249 pp.

Williamson, Margaret: First Book of Bugs. Watts, 1949.

Zim, Herbert S., and Cottam, Clarence: Insects—A Guide to Familiar American Insects. Simon and Schuster, 1951.

## MISCELLANEOUS

Bronson, Wilfred S.: Turtles. Harcourt, Brace.

Chase, Agnes: First Book of Grasses. Silveus.

Durand, Herbert: Field Book of Common Ferns. Putnam, 1949, 219 pp.

Medsger, Oliver Perry: Edible Wild Plants. Macmillan, 1945, 323 pp. (Identification, preparation and cooking of wild vegetation.)

Morris, Percy A.: A Field Guide to Shells of Our Atlantic and Gulf Coast, 2nd ed. Houghton, 1951, 236 pp.

Ramsbottom, John: Mushrooms and Toadstools. Macmillan, 1953, 306 pp.

Schrenkeisen, Ray: Field Book of Fresh Water Fishes of North America. Putnam, 1938.

Thomas, R.: Field Book of Mushrooms. Putnam.

Thomas, William S.: Field Book of Common Mushrooms. Putnam, 1928, 384 pp.

Verrill, A. Hyatt: Shell Collector's Handbook. Putnam, 1950, 265 pp.

Wiley, Farida: Ferns of the North Eastern United States. American Museum of Natural History.

## NATURE PROGRAM

Adventuring in Nature. NRA, 96 pp.

Botany. Boy Scouts (#3379), 1941.

Breeser, Bettye: Finding Nature's Treasures. C.M., March, 1953.

Brown, Vinson: How to Make a Home Nature Museum. Little. (Ages 9 and up.)

Burns, Gerald P.: The Program of the Modern Camp, chap. 5.

Enjoying Nature—Nature Centers, Nature Trails, Trailside Museums. NRA, 1946, 40 pp.

Eshmeyer, R. E.: How to Display Nature Lore Collections. C.M., June, 1953.

Fuller, Raymond T.: Nature Quests and Quizzes. Day, 1948, 64 pp. (Ages 12 and up.)

Gaudette, Marie E.: Leader's Nature Guide—How to Do Nature before She Does You. Girl Scouts (#19–205), 1942, 94 pp.

Gehr, Frank: Adventures in the Dark. C.M., March, 1952. (Night hiking.)

Green, Ivah: Partners with Nature. International Textbook Co., 1950.

Hammett and Musselman: The Camp Program Book, chaps. 10 and 11.

Hillcourt, William: Along the Nature Trail. C.M., May, 1951.

Hillcourt, William: Field Book of Nature Activities. Putnam, 1950, 320 pp.

Hillcourt, William: Show-Offs for the Nature Museum. C.M., March, 1954.

Jaeger, Ellsworth: Nature Crafts. Macmillan, 1950, 128 pp.

Jaeger, Ellsworth: Wildwood Wisdom. Macmillan.

Joy, Barbara Ellen: Bibliography on Nature Education. Camp Publications no. 36.

Joy, Barbara Ellen: Bibliography on Wild Foods and for Native Materials for Craft Use. Camp Publications, no. 35.

Joy, Barbara Ellen: Projects for a Camp Nature Lore Program. Camp Publications no. 10.

Leader's Nature Guide. Girl Scouts (#19–205), 1942.

Mulac: The Play Leader's Manual, pp. 140–175.

Nature Adventuring. Boy Scouts (#9253), 12 pp.

Nature Games for Various Situations. NRA, MP 357.

Nickelsburg, Janet: Capture Your Campers' Interest in Nature. C.M., Jan., 1954.

Nickelsburg, Janet: Nature Counselors—
Need They Be So Rare? C.M., Feb.,
1951.

Pettit, Ted: The Book of Nature Hobbies.
Didier, 1952, 280 pp.

Price, Betty: Adventuring in Nature. Girl
Scouts (#23–305), 1939.

Shuttleworth, Dorothy Edwards: Exploring
Nature with Your Child. Greystone,
1952, 448 pp.

True and False (Nature Game). Girl
Scouts (#19–202), 1937. (160 questions
and answers.)

Valett, Robert: Is Your Nature Program
Too Exclusive? C.M., March, 1951.

Victor, Marilyn: There's Magic in Blue
Printing. C.M., March, 1951.

Vinal, William Gould: Nature Recreation.
McGraw-Hill, 1940.

Vivian, V. E.: Interesting Nature Activities
with Real Purpose. C.M., Feb., 1953.

Vivian, V. E.: Let's Put Nature in the
Center of Camp Programming. C.M.,
Jan. and Feb., 1953.

Wildlife Management. Boy Scouts (#3300),
1952.

Zoology. Boy Scouts (#3356), 1941.

## REPTILES AND AMPHIBIANS

Ditmars, Raymond L.: Reptiles of the
World. Macmillan, 1936, 321 pp.

Morris, Percy A.: Boy's Book of Snakes—
How to Recognize and Understand
Them. Ronald, 1948, 185 pp.

Morris, Percy A.: They Hop and Crawl—
Reptiles and Amphibians of the U.S.
Ronald, 1944, 253 pp.

Reptile Study. Boy Scouts (#3813), 1944.

Schmidt, Karl P., and Dwight, D. Dwight:
Field Book of Snakes of the U.S. and
Canada. Putnam, 1941, 378 pp.

Wright, Anna Allen, and Hazen, Albert:
Handbook of Frogs and Toads. Comstock.

Zim, Herbert S.: Snakes. Morrow, 1949.

Zim, Herbert S., and Smith, H. M.: Reptiles and Amphibians. Simon and
Schuster, 1954.

## ROCKS

Cormack, M. B.: The First Book of Stones.
Watts.

Crowell, V.: Activities in Geology for Children. State Teachers' College, Trenton,
N.J.

Geology. Boy Scouts (#3284), 1953.

Loomis, Frederick B.: Field Book of Common Rocks and Minerals, rev. ed. Putnam, 1948, 370 pp.

Pough, Frederick: A Field Guide to Rocks
and Minerals. Houghton.

Rocks and Minerals. Boy Scouts (#3357),
1937.

Williams, Henry Lionel: Stories in Rocks.
Holt, 151 pp.

## STARS

Astronomy. Boy Scouts (#3303), 1944.

Baker, Robert H.: When the Stars Come
Out. Viking.

Bennett, H. J., and others: New Handbook
of the Heavens. Whittlesey, 1948.

Bernhard, Bennett and Rice: New Handbook of the Heavens, 2nd ed. McGraw-
Hill, 1948, 368 pp.

Dipper Full of Stars, A—Girl Scouts.
(#23–543).

Fenton, Carroll Lane, and Adams, Mildred:
Worlds in the Sky. Day, 1950.

Freeman, Mae and Ira: Fun with Astronomy. Random, 1953, 58 pp.

Harding, A.: Astronomy. Garden City Pub.
Co.

McKready, Kelvin: A Beginner's Star
Book. Putnam, 1937, 162 pp.

Olcott, W. T., and Putnam, E. W.: Field
Book of the Skies, rev. ed. Putnam, 1954.

Pocket Planetarium. Girl Scouts (#23–
542).

Rey, H. A.: The Stars, A New Way to
See Them. Houghton, 1952. (New
graphic way to present constellations as
forms which correspond to their names.)

White, W. B.: Seeing Stars. Harter.

Zadde, A.: Making Friends with The
Stars. Barnes & Noble, 1948.

Zim, Herbert S., and Baker, Robert H.:
Stars, A Golden Nature Guide. Simon
and Schuster, 1951.

## TREES

Collis, John Stewart: The Triumph of the Tree. Morrow, 1954.

Curtis, Carlton and Bausor: Complete Guide to North American Trees, rev. ed., New Home Library, 1943.

Forestry. Boy Scouts (#3302), 1943.

Harlow, W. M.: Trees of Northeastern U.S. Whittlesey.

Hazard, Joseph T.: Our Living Forests. Superior, 1948.

Hylander, Clarence J.: Trees and Trails. Macmillan.

Lane, Dr. Ferdinand C.: The Story of Trees. Doubleday.

Managing a Small Forest. U.S. Dept. of Agriculture (Farmers Bulletin no. 1989).

Marx, David S.: Learn the Trees from Leaf Prints. Girl Scouts (#23–526). (Nearly 200 trees.)

Mathews, F. Schuyler: Field Book of American Trees and Shrubs. Putnam, 1915, 554 pp.

Peattie, Donald Culross: Natural History of Trees. Houghton, 1947.

Teale, Edwin: The Lost Woods. Dodd, Mead, 1945.

Watts, Mary T.: Tree Finder. Ass'n Press

Zim, Herbert S., and Martin, Alexander C.: Trees—A Guide to Familiar American Trees. Simon and Schuster.

I wish that I'd been born a fish
So I could swim when'er I wish.
Then mother would not have to say
It is too cold for you today.

THE EAVESDROPPER

# Chapter 15

# AQUATICS

WATERFRONT activities are among the most popular in camp, and little artificial motivation is needed to enlist the wholehearted participation of the campers. The aquatic program ordinarily consists of these divisions: (1) swimming (instructional and recreational), (2) diving, (3) life saving, (4) boating (canoeing, sailing, rowing, surf boarding, and the like), and (5) trips by water.

Aquatic pursuits encourage sociability and provide enjoyment both for camp days and for many years thereafter. Since most people at some time in their lives venture into or on the water, it is an excellent thing for them to learn correct techniques, for both pleasure and safety increase in direct proportion to the skill and confidence of the participant. Many of the 7000 to 8000 deaths which occur each year in water accidents could be prevented by proper instruction in water skills and safety procedures.

## THE WATERFRONT STAFF

### The Waterfront Director

All aquatic activities are in charge of the Waterfront Director, who organizes and coordinates the various phase with each other and with the entire camp program. He trains and supervises his staff of assistants, assigns responsibilities and checks on their successful completion, and makes suitable reports on the progress of his department. He sees that all equipment is adequate in quantity and quality and that the highest type of safety precautions are carried out.

He must have a current Water Safety Instructor's certificate in swimming and life-saving skills from the American Red Cross, the Y.M.C.A. or the Aquatic School of the Boy Scouts of America and should be a college graduate and over twenty-one years of age. Although his many duties usually exempt him from cabin responsibilities, he should be a trained camper and in sympathy with all the phases of camp so that he sees the waterfront in its proper perspective to the total program. He must know his subject matter thoroughly and must constantly strive to learn while on the job, for he has one of the biggest tasks in camp and is at one time or another likely to be responsible for the life of every member of the personnel. He must have presence of mind, sound judgment, and the ability to remain calm, even when faced with an emergency.

## Waterfront Assistants

Waterfront Assistants should have at least a Senior Life Saving Certificate, although counselors with Junior Certificates may sometimes serve an auxiliary staff. They may or may not have cabin responsibilities, and their waterfront duties are determined by the Waterfront Director in accordance with their various abilities in swimming, diving or boating. They also should be trained and interested in the whole camp program and should consider their activities only as integral parts of it. All waterfront staff should expect, and, in fact, be eager to help out with general camp program on rainy days and when waterfront duties permit.

## General Counselors

A counselor who does not accompany his campers during their periods at the waterfront is missing a golden opportunity to know them better as they engage in joyful and uninhibited behaviour.

The immense popularity of waterfront activities sometimes makes it imperative that all personnel help in the way best qualified during the peak periods of the day. Cabin counselors usually accompany their groups to the swimming period and assist in any way suggested by the Waterfront Staff.

All counselors should serve as models of proper conduct at the waterfront, diligently observing the rules themselves and helping to interpret them to their cabin group. Never knowingly let a camper get by with disobeying a rule; waterfront rules must be kept inviolate.

Counselors who wish to participate in waterfront activities will, like the campers, need to pass classification tests. Though you may sometimes be able to get instruction to improve your own skills, you must remember that

this is a privilege and is possible only when it can be carried on without interfering with your regular duties or those of the Waterfront Staff.

## THE SWIMMING, DIVING, AND LIFE-SAVING PROGRAM

Early in the camp season, all campers are tested and classified as non-
swimmers, beginners, intermediates, swimmers or life savers, according to
their proficiency in the water. Instructional periods, ordinarily a half hour
in length, are usually scheduled in the morning and, in camps where the
decentralized or unit system is in operation, are carried on by unit groups.
The different classifications separate upon arrival at the dock, each going to
its respective area for instruction. Each group is under the supervision of a
Senior Life Saver, who has enough assistants to make a ratio of approximately one waterfront staff for each ten campers. Recreational periods, also
a half hour in length, are customarily held in the afternoon.

### Water Safety

Vigilance every single moment is necessary, for one accident during the
summer can cause untold grief and force a camp into bankruptcy. Three
safety devices are in common use:

1. *The Buddy System.* Each camper chooses a companion of about his own
ability, and the two stay constantly near each other, each being responsible
for the other's safety. When the signal is given for "buddy call" (about every
ten minutes), they quickly raise their joined hands in the air. They always
enter and leave the water together. Failure to stay close to and watch over a
buddy means prompt banishment from the water for the rest of the day, or
even longer.

2. *The Check Board System.* As each swimmer enters the water, he turns
over the tag on the check board bearing his name so that the red side is
uppermost. When he leaves the swimming area, he turns it back to expose
the white side again. Station a counselor near to see that no tag is forgotten.
Some camps use pegs bearing the camper's name which they insert into a
peg board in a similiar manner.

3. *Colored Caps.* Colored caps denote swimming ability so that Waterfront
Staff can immediately spot a camper out of his proper swimming area or one
taking chances too hazardous for his ability. The following colors are suggested:

> Nonswimmer—red (danger)
> Beginner—yellow (caution)
> Intermediate—green
> Swimmer—blue
> Lifesaver—white

Waterfront counselors must keep their eyes on the swimmers at all times;
knitting, chatting, reading, or basking in the sun are definitely out of place.

When on duty, they never enter the water except to rescue a swimmer (and this is recommended only as a last resort) or when necessary for some particular phase of teaching.

Docks are not lounging places; use them only as directed by the Waterfront Staff.

Sunburn is an ever-present danger for waterfront counselors who must spend long hours exposed to the sun rays, and they should wear long trousers and long sleeves, at least during a portion of the hours on duty. See that campers also take precautions. Recent studies have shown that getting too tanned permanently harms the complexion and may even predispose to cancer.

As in all camp activities, informality and fun are of supreme importance, but rules must be rigidly enforced, for there is too much at stake to brook even minor breaches of discipline. Campers readily respond if shown the wisdom and justice of requirements and, in the long run, will respect and like best the counselor who is friendly and kindly, yet just and firm in discipline.

Though opinion seems to have changed concerning the danger of cramps from swimming too soon after eating, it may still be advisable for psychological and health reasons to wait for an hour or two after eating before going into the water.

Campers and counselors never go swimming alone or at times when the Waterfront Staff is not on duty. On trips, they swim only in approved areas and when at least one Senior Life Saver is on guard. Never dive into unknown waters which have not been thoroughly investigated for sufficient depth and hidden obstructions. Visitors use the waterfront only when they meet the requirements set up for staff and campers.

Campers enter the water only on signal and come out again promptly at signal. They will respond more willingly if warned by "one more dive and out" instead of a "sudden death" blast announcing the end of the period and "out right now."

Wear shoes and robes to and from the bathing area. Prevent chilling by hurrying back to the cabins, followed by a brisk rub down, being careful to dry between the toes and sprinkle with talcum to discourage athlete's foot. Immediately hang wet suits and towels out to dry.

Thunderstorms are a serious menace, particularly to those near water, and all who are swimming or out in boats should immediately get on land.

For sanitary and esthetic reasons, we do not take soap and water baths in the swimming area, nor permit such animals as horses or dogs to swim or drink there.

Night swimming is rarely if ever permissible and then only under the careful arrangement and supervision of the Waterfront Staff. Powerful focusing beam flashlights and white swimming caps greatly reduce hazards.

Before-breakfast dips, if permitted, should be optional, for not everyone reacts favorably to them.

Distance swimming is allowed at the discretion of the Waterfront Staff, if each swimmer is accompanied by his own row boat, oarsman and Senior Life Saver.

Whereas swimming in moderation is invigorating and conducive to good health, too frequent or long periods are debilitating and lay the foundation for colds, sinus infections and other ailments. Two half-hour periods (even less if the water is cold) are usually enough. Campers with open sores, skin infections, or colds should not go into the water, and those who develop blue lips or nails or a pale face, who shiver or whose teeth chatter must come out immediately.

## BOATING

The popularity of boating almost equals that of swimming. It not only provides present and carry-over pleasure, but also serves as a means of transportation to outlying regions, on fishing or other trips, and as a means of rescue for those in distress.

Contrary to popular opinion, properly constructed and maintained boats do not capsize when used with common sense and some degree of skill. Most catastrophies result from boats in poor condition or from such misuses or indiscretions as overloading, going into dangerous or rough water, fooling around, standing up, rocking the boat, or changing positions improperly. Therefore it is time well spent to test all small craft for seaworthiness and steadiness, and to instruct users in proper handling with actual practice in recovering from capsizing or swamping (carried on in shallow, safe water) so that they could meet a real emergency with coolness and efficiency.

Always keep the center of gravity in a canoe low; remove the seats and kneel on a light kneeling pad on the bottom rather than sit on the seats. Some prefer to kneel on the paddle-side knee, stretching out the opposite foot and bracing it against a rib of the canoe and resting the back against a thwart. Sit on the floor or even lie flat in the canoe to still further increase stability if you should inadvertently be caught in rough water. Avoid getting your weight off center by stepping or sitting over on one side in either canoe or rowboat. In two-man paddling, the bowman uses a straight stroke while the stern man, who is responsible for steering, paddles on the opposite side with a straight stroke ending in a "J."

Rowboats are safest in respect to upsetting, canoes less so, and sailboats least of all. All tipped boats, usually even if submerged, will float and support their occupants; therefore, if you are thrown into the water, you should swim to the boat and hang on until help comes instead of striking out for shore. For this reason, endurance and the ability to tread water and float occupy a place of prominence in boating tests.

The dangers of lightning and rough water make it imperative to head for the nearest land and get out of the water when you sight an approaching storm. Stay close to shore on trips, even though it necessitates covering more distance than a straight course. To change positions in a boat, maintain one or both hands on the gunwale for balance and keep your weight low. It is safest to pull into shallow water before attempting the transfer.

Neither visitors, counselors nor campers use boating equipment unless they have passed appropriate swimming tests and have been granted permission each and every time from the Waterfront Staff. Even then they must state where they are going and how soon they will be back. Boating after dark is permissible only in case of emergency or for an occasional moonlight cruise under the immediate supervision of the Waterfront Staff.

Those who do not swim well enough to quality as boaters often find the waterfront only a tantalizing but forbidden temptation and would appreciate an occasional excursion, which some camps permit under the careful supervision of the Waterfront Staff and with one Senior Life Saver and a life belt for each nonswimmer.

Stow all waterfront equipment neatly away; never leave it carelessly lying about to be stumbled over or misused. Keep it in good repair, and teach campers to respect such equipment as they would fine tools, repairing damage themselves or instantly reporting it to the proper person when it occurs. Thoroughly ground campers in the care of boats, giving practice in launching and taking them from the water, entering and disembarking, and so forth. Real boaters are never satisfied just to splash about any old way but pride themselves on neat and exact manipulations performed with perfect timing and skill. Never drop or drag canoes over the ground in launching them or removing them from the water. Carry them when on land, and wade in shallow water to keep from dragging them on the bottom.

## ADDITIONAL READINGS

### BOOKS AND PAMPHLETS

Ainsworth, Dorothy S., et al.: Individual Sports for Women, 2nd ed. Saunders, 1949, pp. 296–354.

American Red Cross: Life Saving and Water Safety. P. Blakiston's Sons and Company, Inc., 1937.

Aquatic Games, Pageantry Stunts. Book Dept., Beach & Pool, 1947.

Aquatic Standards for YMCA Camps. Ass'n Press.

Armbruster, David A., and Morehouse, Laurence E.: Swimming and Diving, 2nd ed. Mosby, 1950, 302 pp.

Bearse, Richard H., and Hazelton, Sidney C.: A Camp Aquatic Program. Hazelton, 1952.

Bourgaize, Eidola Jean: More Fun in the Water. Ass'n Press, 1951.

Brown, R. L.: Teaching Progressions for the Swimming Instructor. Barnes, 1948.

Bucher, Charles A. (Ed.): Methods and Materials in Physical Education and Recreation, pp. 34–59.

Camp Director's Handbook and Buying Guide, The. ACA. (Issued annually.)

Camp Safety Digest, pp. 36–44.

Comedy Diving, NRA (F 12).

Cureton, Thomas K., Jr.: Fun in the Water. Ass'n Press, 1949, 143 pp.

Cureton, Thomas K., Jr.: How to Teach Swimming and Diving. Ass'n Press, 1943.

Cureton, Thomas K., Jr., and Pohndorf, Richard H.: Aquatic Programs for Camps. Ass'n Press.

Curtis, Katharine Whitney: Rhythmic Swimming. Burgess, 1942, 140 pp.

Hammett and Musselman: The Camp Program Book. Ass'n Press, chap. 13.

Hazelton, S. C.: A Method of Teaching Swimming to Young Children. Hazelton.

Hazelton, S. C., and Pulis, C. A.: Diving Manual for Instructors. Hazelton, 1950.

Karpovich, Peter J.: Adventures in Artificial Respiration. Ass'n Press.

Kiefer, Adolph, Gabrielson, Milton, and Gabrielson, Bramwell: Learning to Swim in 12 Easy Steps. Prentice-Hall, 1951, 256 pp.

Kiphuth, Robert: Swimming. Barnes, 1942.

Kiphuth, Robert, and Burke, Harry M.: Basic Swimming. Yale U., 1950, 125 pp.

Life Saving. Boy Scouts (#3278), 1944.

Lipovetz, Ferd John: The Teaching and Coaching of Swimming, Diving and Water Sports, rev. ed. Burgess, 1950, 172 pp.

Lukens, Paul W.: Teaching Swimming. Burgess, 1948, 40 pp.

Mason, Bernard S., and Mitchell, Elmer D.: Active Games and Contests, pp. 515–553. (Aquatic games.)

Safety-Wise. Girl Scouts, pp. 60–68.

Scout Field Book: Fun in the Water. Boy Scouts.

Shaw, John H., Troester, Carl A., Jr., and Gabrielson, Milton A.: Individual Sports for Men. Saunders, 1950, pp. 262–313, 399 pp.

Silvia, Charles E.: Manual of Lifesaving and Water Safety Instruction. Ass'n Press, 1950, 175 pp.

Spears, Betty: Beginning Synchronized Swimming. Burgess, 1950, 94 pp.

Swimming, Water Sports and Safety. Boy Scouts.

Torney, John A., Jr.: Swimming. McGraw-Hill, 1950.

U.S. Naval Institute: Swimming and Diving, A Naval Aviation Physical Training Manual, rev. ed. Barnes, 1950.

Water Games and Stunts. NRA (MP 158).

Yates, Fern, and Anderson, Theresa W.: Synchronized Swimming. Barnes, 1951, 160 pp.

## MAGAZINE ARTICLES

Camp, Marjorie: Learning to Breathe Correctly. C.M., March, 1953.

Heath, Cherry: Buddy Board Deluxe. C.M., March, 1952.

Newer Methods of Resuscitation. C.M., March, 1952. (Back-pressure arm lift method.)

Roberts, Catherine T.: How to Build a Crib Dam. C.M., Nov., 1949.

Swimming for Beginners. C.M., March, 1950. (Instruction on how to construct a "swim easy.")

## BOATING

### BOOKS AND PAMPHLETS

Aymar, Gordon C.: Start 'Em Sailing. Barnes.

Bodin, Arthur: Bibliography of Canoeing.

Brindze, Ruth: Boating is Fun. Dodd, Mead.

Calahan, H. A.: Learning to Sail. Macmillan.

Calahan, H. A.: Sailing Technique. Macmillan.

Camp Director's Handbook and Buying Guide, ACA. (Issued annually.)

Canoeing. Boy Scouts (#3811), 1952.

Canoeing Manual, 3rd ed. New England Section of ACA, 1952, 84 pp.

Canoeing Standards of the ACA. ACA, 1947.

Canoeing Standards and Graded Classifications, Report of the Committee on Canoeing of the New England Section of the ACA. ACA, 16 pp.

Carter, Samuel, III: How to Sail. Leisure League of America, 30 Rockefeller Plaza, New York, N.Y.

Elvedt, Ruth: Canoeing—A–Z, rev. ed. Burgess, 1953, 43 pp.

Lee, Joseph: How to Sail a Boat. Waverly.

Lineaweaver, Marion: The First Book of Sailing. Watts, 1953, 72 pp.

Moorehouse, Lanore, and Fancher, Leonard: Know Your Canoeing. Am. Canoe Asso., 1950, 40 pp.

Quirke, Terence T.: Canoes the World Over. U. Ill.

Rowing. Boy Scouts (#3392), 1952.

Rutstrum: Way of the Wilderness, chap. III.

Sail Boating (Mechanics Illustrated): Fawcett, 1952, 144 pp.

Sailing Standards and Graded Classifications. New England Section of ACA, 11 pp.

Schock, Edson I.: How to Build Small Boats. Barnes, 1952, 137 pp.

Seamanship. Boy Scouts (#3332), 1940.

Varney, Russell, and Varney, Margaret A.: A Manual of Sailing, rev. ed. Burgess, 1948, 39 pp.

White, Charles D.: Handbook of Sailing. Crowell.

Zarchy, Harry: Let's Go Boating. Knopf, 1952.

### MAGAZINE ARTICLES

Canoe Trailer, A. C.M., April, 1951.

Claussen, W. Van B.: Boat Mooring Layouts for Lakes. C. M., Mar., 1951.

Claussen, W. Van B.: Camp Seamanship. C.M., May, 1945.

Claussen, W. Van B.: How to Choose Your Oars. C.M., May, 1951.

Joy, Barbara Ellen: An All-Weather Canoe Shed. C.M., Jan., 1945, Camp Publications, No. 11.

Proper Care of Canvas Canoes. C.M., Feb., 1953.

Sanborn, Marion A.: Sailing on a Budget. Jr. H. and P.E., June, 1953.

Simone, Irv: Method of Teaching Sailing. C.M., March, 1954.

Waterfront, Craft Skills Used in Boat Building. C.M., March, 1953.

Weber, Ann Elizabeth: Care of Waterfront Equipment. C.N., Nov., 1952.

Weber, Ann Elizabeth: Safe Canoe Programs. C.M., May, 1953.

God's Out-of-Doors. The cease-
less march
Of sun and stars from night to
dawn
Trace for our eyes the dome's high
arch,
Show us what it is builded on,
Hymn, anthem and recessional
The shouting, storm in grandeur
pours.
Mute worshipers, we hear His call
In this great house of Out-of-
Doors.

AUTHOR UNKNOWN

# Chapter 16

# SPIRITUAL LIFE

ALTHOUGH camps have different practices in regard to the spiritual life of campers, they almost without exception feel deeply their obligation along this line and have as an important aim the furthering of spiritual growth through an appreciation of the higher values of life.* Most have daily or weekly all-camp periods of devotion supplemented by various cabin or unit endeavors highlighting a deeper sense of spiritual values as expressed in all phases of daily living.

Such experiences ordinarily consist of some combination of the following: (1) grace before meals (oral, spoken in unison, sung, silence maintained during an appropriate musical selection, or a period of silent prayer), (2) outdoor vespers, or serious programs of some sort, (3) sunrise services, (4) cabin devotions or meditations just before taps, (5) Sunday services in neighboring churches of the individual's choice or on the campsite in a "Woodland Chapel" conducted by visiting members of the ministry or by camp personnel.

* Camp Leadership Courses for Colleges and Universities, p. 9, II B.

## DIFFERENT FAITHS TOGETHER

In many camps, those of various faiths are encouraged to attend and live in a spirit of broad-minded tolerance, and appreciation of each other and of the right of each to worship as he chooses. There should be no attempt to indoctrinate, but, on the other hand, each should be encouraged to become a better member of his own faith. In such nonsectarian camps, it is likewise customary to hire counselors of different faiths. If you accept a job in such a camp, it is most important that you believe in and practice wholeheartedly this attitude of tolerance and understanding. Encourage each of your campers to observe such practices as he is accustomed to, such as a moment of silent grace before meals, Catholic children making the sign of the cross before eating, and individual prayers before retiring. Your personal conduct typifies what your own spiritual convictions mean to you as best exemplified by a constant attitude of kindliness, tolerance, fairness to and respect for every individual in camp.

In a large camp it is customary to arrange separate services for the three major groups, Catholic, Jewish, and Protestant. The following remarks concerning each are extracted from a more detailed discussion in a free booklet, *Suggestions for Camp Directors.**

### Catholic

Each Catholic child is required to attend Mass on Sunday and Holy Days (the only Holy Day falling within the usual camp season of June to September is the Feast of the Assumption of the Blessed Virgin Mary on August 15). It is forbidden by the laws of the Church that Catholic children participate in nonsectarian services or religious services of other faiths. A priest should be sent for in case of serious accident to a Catholic camper.

Camps usually take their Catholic campers and staff to the nearest Catholic church for Mass but arrangements are sometimes made to celebrate Mass at the camp if a priest is available and the Bishop of the Diocese approves. Arrangements should be made for Catholics to go to Confession and receive Holy Communion at least once a month. Catholics eat no meat on Fridays and other days of abstinence.

### Jewish

Those of the Jewish faith observe Saturday, the seventh day of the week, as Sabbath, the day of rest. The Jewish Sabbath begins at twenty minutes past sunset on Friday evening and ends at sunset on Saturday. Sabbath candles should be lit at or before the beginning of the Sabbath and the service usually follows immediately. Personnel may attend a nearby synagogue or the services may be conducted by an older counselor or other lay-leader who understands the spirit and mode of Jewish worship.

* *Suggestions for Camp Directors.* The National Conference of Christians and Jews, 381 Fourth Avenue, New York 16, N.Y.

Campers of Jewish faith who come from homes of traditional observances will want to adhere to the Jewish dietary laws. No pork in any form should be served; if meat or fowl is on the camp menu, there should be an alternative menu of vegetables, salads, eggs or fish (not shellfish) for those who wish it.

The Jewish Holy Day, *Tishoh B'ab*, usually falls during the camp season; the date varies each year. Those from homes where there is strict traditional observance will wish to observe it as a fast day and will refrain from swimming and festive activities.

## Protestant

There are three ways of providing Sunday worship services for Protestant campers: (1) taking them to a nearby Protestant church which meets with the approval of their parents, (2) inviting a local minister to conduct service at camp, or (3) having a worship service conducted by a lay person or by staff and campers. Camp personnel often enjoy choosing and constructing their own "Woodland Chapel" or "Woodland Cathedral." Most worship services include:

1. Invocation
2. Hymns
3. Scripture
4. Prayer
5. Talk
6. Benediction

Few Protestant denominations observe dietary restrictions although some abstain from eating meat on Fridays. There are no Protestant Holy Days during the camp season.

## Informal Worship

Spiritual experiences, of course, are not at all confined to formally arranged times or places. Instead, we might think of them as times of the day when our thoughts and very souls rise to unusual heights as we contemplate the way in which some power almost beyond human comprehension has arranged this wonderful universe. Sometimes it may be simply a deep and abiding appreciation of the real goodness and kindliness of our fellow men as we see a companion do a truly noble and unselfish deed or as we note a perfect stranger extend a helping hand to someone younger or weaker or "down on his luck." Occasions for sharing our deeper and more serious thoughts with others may come most unexpectedly as when sharing a brief time off with a fellow counselor, as you look out over the countryside from a vantage spot high on a hill, or as a small camper slips a hand trustingly into yours and confides some inner thought or small trouble (but not to him). Others may be quiet periods of meditation as you lie flat on your back and enjoy the beauties of a sky full of stars or the call of a lone whip-poor-will in the distance. How true that "The Heavens declare the Glory of God; and the firmament showeth his handiwork."

## CAMP SERVICES

Having a special committee of campers and counselors plan a camp spiritual program is a democratic procedure and one most likely to insure wholehearted camper interest and participation. Make the program acceptable to all the creeds that will attend and alter the procedures at different times so campers will never know quite what to expect. Gear any service planned for campers to their age level and couch it in simple, understandable language with illustrations and events common to their experience. Think of spiritual experiences as brief respites from the busyness of the day which offer a chance for quiet, thoughtful consideration of the deeper meanings of life.

Campers often like to hunt for and select some special nook for these occasions and many feel that an out-of-door setting is particularly appropriate. If there is to be an outside speaker, campers and counselors may contribute such parts of the service as scripture reading, special prayers, a short dramatization of a Bible story or antiphonal reading. Special music always adds an enjoyable part and may be in such a form as special music by the choir, a selection sung by a living unit or vocal or instrumental solos, duets, quartets, or octets. Choral reading is appropriate, particularly if it has been practiced with the intent to read with feeling and comprehension.

Talks by staff or campers in lieu of an outside speaker may be built upon any topic of interest or worth to camp and camp living. Representative topics are kindness to animals, the high ideals and objectives of the organization sponsoring the camp, true democracy which realizes the worth of *all* individuals regardless of appearance, talent, race, or creed and the application of the Golden Rule to camp life as shown by consideration for others, generosity, helpfulness, and the like.

Above all, keep the program short and to the point. Since it is hot at the usual church hour, camp worship services are often held in the cool of the early morning or evening. If a collection is taken, it is usually designated for some charitable purpose.

## SUNDAY IN CAMP

"Sunday is the golden clasp that binds together the volume of the week."—LONGFELLOW

Sunday is a "special" day in camp; the regular program is dispensed with and campers are given much free time to engage in quiet, restful activities, although tennis courts, boats, waterfront and other facilities are available to those who want them. Breakfast is usually served a little later than usual and may consist of some extra touch such as eating in a special place, eating in pajamas, or with service cafeteria style. It is a day for dressing in best camp clothes and for spending time together as a cabin group listening to music, singing, holding discussions, telling stories, or writing letters. It is often designated as Visitor's Day with the camp playing host to parents and friends. A cold supper or outdoor cooking is sometimes customary to give the kitchen staff extra time off; this also provides opportunity for small groups to enjoy eating together in a secluded spot of beauty.

Sunday can and should be the most cherished day in the week. In planning for it, we must remember to look at it through the eyes of youth, for if we fill it with taboos, stuffy pursuits, unnatural quiet, and lengthy talks, we will build up rebelliousness, distaste and entirely unchristian attitudes. Campers should know it as a day especially devoted to renewing strength of mind and spirit for the coming week. Observing it in the wrong way can do a great deal of harm to their developing spiritual consciousness.

## ADDITIONAL READINGS

### BOOKS AND PAMPHLETS

Auch, Myrtle: Adventuring Together As Christians. Judson.

Bowman, Clarice M.: Spiritual Values in Camping. Ass'n Press, 1954, 240 pp.

Britten, Rodney: Adventure into Friendship. Judson.

Camping with Juniors. National Council of Churches of Christ in the U.S.A.

Cheley, F. H.: Stories for Talks to Boys, rev. ed. Ass'n Press, 1946.

Gaudette, Marie E.: You and the Other One. Girl Scouts (#23–326). (Gives insight into the field of relationships with other races and creeds.)

Gilbert and Britten: Adventures on the Way. Judson.

Gilbert, Clark R.: Devotions for Youth, Ass'n Press.

Gibson, H. W.: Five Minutes a Day. Ass'n Press, 1946.

Going Camping with Junior High Boys and Girls. National Council of Churches of Christ in U.S.A.

Graham: The Girls' Camp, chap. 11.

Hammett and Musselman: The Camp Program Book, chaps. 38 and 39.

Kelsey, Alice Geer: More Stories for Junior Worship. Abingdon-Cokesbury. (35 stories.)

Kruse, Lenore: Outdoors with God. Judson.

Mattoon, Laura I., and Bragdon, Helen D.: Services for the Open. Ass'n Press, 1947, 211 pp.

Pineo, Caroline C., Blankenship, Lois, and Whitmore, Martha J.: We Work with God. Judson, 1949, 119 pp. (How to fit religion into daily camp program for juniors.)

Porter, David R.: Worship Resources for Youth. Ass'n Press.

Rice, Rebecca: Exploring God's Out-of-Doors. Pilgrim Press, 1935.

Suggestions for Camp Directors. National Conference of Christians and Jews, 381 Fourth Ave., New York 16, N.Y., 12 pp.

Wickenden, Arthur C.: Youth Looks at Religion, rev. ed. Harper, 1947.

Woodall, William L.: Devotions for Boys and Girls. Ass'n Press.

### MAGAZINE ARTICLES

Allen, Hope: When Sunday Comes Around. C.M., Dec., 1949.

French, Mary Margaret: Planning for Sunday. C.M., March, 1942. (Camp Publications, no. 4.)

Hazzard, Lowell B.: Spiritual Values in Camp. C.M., June, 1952.

Holroyd, A. Waldie: Learning Spiritual Values in Camp. C.M., Jan., 1950.

MacMillan, Rev. A. M.: Spiritual Values in Every Camp. C.M., June, 1952.

Munson, Howard E.: Can Religion be Handled in Camp? C.M., Nov., 1950.

# PART IV

# Campcraft and Woodcraft

## Chapter 17

## SOME CAMP PESTS

### POISONOUS PLANTS

POISON IVY, poison oak and poison sumac are the three plants poisonous to touch. It is interesting to note that they do not affect animals other than man, although cases have occurred from contact with the fur of dogs or other animals which have rubbed against the plant. Symptoms of itching and burning with the appearance of little white blisters may occur from a few hours to as long as five days after exposure. Some people continually travel the woods without ever contracting a case, but they can never be confident for, after years of apparent immunity, some suddenly become susceptible.

### Poison Ivy

Poison ivy is perhaps the most widespread of the three and is potent at any season, for cases have occurred from mere contact with the smoke as it is being burned in winter or early spring. For this reason, you should be especially careful not to get it mixed in with your firewood. However, poison-

182

ing from it occurs most frequently from May to August when it is actively spreading. This may be partly due to the fact that more people are out-of-doors, tramping around where they encounter it during these months.

The ivy plant may climb as a vine or stand as an erect shrub, 2 to 3 feet high, and is found in woods, open fields or pastures. It has three shiny, greenish-white leaves and is often confused with the harmless Virginia creeper, or woodbine, which has five leaves. An easy way to distinguish the two is to remember the saying, "Leaflets three, let it be." In the fall, poison ivy bears clusters of white berries, and its leaves turn beautiful colors. It is more poisonous than poison oak, but less so than poison sumac. The plant sweats or bleeds its poison, which may be carried for some little distance

SMOOTH-LEAF
POISON IVY          POISON IVY          VIRGINIA CREEPER

through the air where its sticky, oily droplets adhere to the skin and start their deadly work if not removed fairly soon. Teach campers to recognize and avoid this plant when traveling about; the safest way to hike is to cover the entire body, including hands and arms, so that there is no possibility of contact. Rid your campsite and more frequented trails of it by using a good commercial spray.

Immediately after returning from a hike, scrub all exposed parts of the body with warm water and a strong solution of yellow (laundry) soap. Then apply alcohol. This takes but a few moments and is a small price to pay to avoid from seven to ten days of utter misery. Clothing, also, should be washed and sunned for the oils can remain active for weeks.

There is no magic cure but only treatment to minimize the discomfort.

If symptoms of poisoning appear, you should immediately consult the camp physician or nurse. You can get temporary relief on a trip by applying one of the following:

Ferric chloride, calamine lotion, weak solution of potassium permanganate, photographic hypo, wet dressings dipped in a solution of Epsom salts.

Some advocate applying heat as by hot applications, a heat lamp, or exposure to the sun's rays. For an extensive irritation, it helps to soak the part in a vessel of water in which a mixture of baking soda and cornstarch has been dissolved.

### Poison Oak

Poison oak is found west of the Rocky Mountains along the Pacific slope. It bears three leaves and is an erect shrub which never climbs. Prevention and treatment are the same as for poison ivy.

### Poison or Swamp Sumac

**POISON OAK**

Poison or swamp sumac is the most poisonous of the three and is found all over the Eastern half of the United States. It grows as a shrub a few feet high, and its leaves turn to a beautiful scarlet in the fall, to the undoing of many who are poisoned when they pick them for inside decoration. It is easy to confuse with harmless

POISON SUMAC     STAGHORN     DWARF SUMAC

staghorn sumac, which gets its name from the fact that its branches are covered with a fuzzy velvet like the new horns of a deer. A little study of the characteristics of the two makes it easy to distinguish them.

|  | *Poison or Swamp Sumac* | *Staghorn Sumac* |
| --- | --- | --- |
| Branches...... | Smooth | Covered with fuzz |
| Leaflets....... | No so pointed | Acutely pointed |
|  | Edges smooth | Edges serrated (toothed) |
|  | 7–13 in number | 11–35 in number |
| Berries........ | White or greenish-gray | Scarlet |
| Found........ | Marshy ground | Dry uplands |

## SNAKES

There are probably no more feared or despised creatures in the world than snakes, yet of the hundred or more varieties living in the United States, only four are poisonous. All are helpful to man, particularly to farmers, for they live on mice, rats and other pests which destroy crops. The non-poisonous varieties, which are much more plentiful, should therefore never be killed. No snake will bite a person unless it is frightened or cornered, and the bite of the nonpoisonous varieties is no more dangerous than any puncture wound and needs only the usual treatment to prevent infection.

Snakes do not charm birds, none have "stingers" in their tails, nor do they swallow their young to protect them against an approaching enemy. Their forked tongue is entirely harmless and is protruded as a sort of antenna to detect the presence of an intruder by "feeling" its "vibrations." Snakes are covered with perfectly dry scales and are neither slick nor slimy.

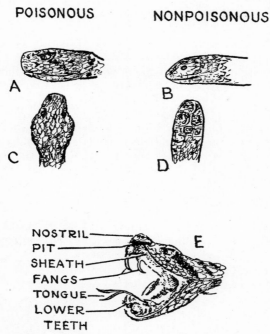

Heads of Poisonous and Nonpoisonous Snakes.

Three of the four poisonous varieties (the *rattlesnake*, the *copperhead* and the *cotton mouth moccasin*) are known as *pit vipers* because they have two deep pits, located one on each side of the face between the nostril and eye, making them appear to have four nostrils. The pupil of the eye is upright and elliptical, and the head is angular and somewhat wider than the narrow neck, making a definite angle where the two join. These snakes have two hollow fangs in the upper jaw which they use like hypodermic needles to inject poison into their victims. These ordinarily rest flat against the roof of the mouth, coming to an erect position only when the snake strikes. If the fangs are extracted or broken off, new ones grow within a few days, for several half-grown substitutes are always present. Harmless snakes have no pits, round pupils, teeth but not fangs, and heads that gradually taper off into necks.

The fourth variety of poisonous snake, the *coral snake*, is like the non-poisonous varieties in that it has neither pits nor an angle where the head and neck join. Its fangs remain always erect and it must get a good hold on and chew its victims instead of striking as other poisonous varieties do.

Miraculous tales as to the ability of a snake to leap through the air and fasten its fangs in its victim are untrue, for no snake, even when coiled, can strike for more than one-third to one-half its length and when not coiled, none can strike so accurately or far. It is claimed that the strike of a snake is so swift that no creature can dodge it.

Though there are only four varieties of poisonous snake, they are so wide-spread that there is probably no state without at least one variety of them.

### The Coral or Harlequin Snake

The coral or harlequin snake is long and slender, with a *black* nose and bright coloring of broad scarlet and black bands, separated by narrow yellow ones. Although there are several varieties of harmless snakes with similar bright-colored bands, they can be readily distinguished by their *pink* or *yellow* noses. It is a Southern snake, found only as far north as North Carolina and the lower Mississippi Valley.

The coral snake is rarely seen, for it stays in the shade during the day, coming out for food only in the cool after a rain or at twilight.

Its venom affects the nervous system, whereas the poison of the pit vipers affects the circulatory system. Although serious and painful, its bite is fatal to only about 20 per cent of those bitten, even when no treatment is given.

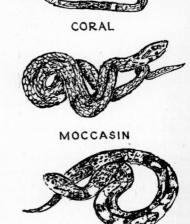

**CORAL**

**MOCCASIN**

**COPPERHEAD**

Poisonous Snakes.

### Water or Cotton Mouth Moccasin

The cotton mouth moccasin is usually found in swampy territory or in the trees and bushes overhanging streams and marshes. It is 3 to 6 feet long and has a dark muddy or olive-brown color with eleven to fifteen inconspicuous dark bars on its short, thick body. It is also a Southern snake, found only as far north as Southern Illinois and West Virginia.

Its name comes from the fact that it "threatens" before striking by opening its mouth to show the ugly white "cotton mouth" interior.

## The Copperhead

The copperhead (also called the Northern moccasin or pilot snake) is found chiefly in the eastern and southern states, being present from Massachusetts to Florida and west as far as Illinois and Texas.

**RATTLESNAKE**

Poisonous Snake.

It is hazel or pinkish-brown in color, with cross markings of darker reddish-brown in the form of an hourglass or short-handled dumbbell, and its head has a distinct copperish tinge. It is 2 to 4 feet long and usually prefers rocky, wooded terrain.

## Rattlesnakes

It is estimated that there are sixteen to twenty-six varieties of rattlesnakes in the United States, with each of the forty-eight states having at least one type. They range in size from the little 8-inch pygmy rattlers to the giant diamond backs. They are variously marked and colored, but all have the characteristic rattle on the end of the tail, with which they usually warn their victim before striking. The tail and rattles vibrate so rapidly that they can scarcely be seen, making a unique sound like the ticking of an alarm clock or the sound of a locust. It is not true that you can tell the age of a rattler by the number of rattles on its tail, for it sheds its skin as often as two to five times a year, leaving a little cap of the skin near its tail each time to harden into another "rattle."

## Treatment for Snake Bite

Snakes are said to be so shy that they will inevitably try to slither away unseen if they hear a person approaching, striking only when surprised or cornered. Therefore, when you travel in snake country you are urged to carry a stick and make a noise with it to avoid the danger of frightening a snake or sneaking up on it while it is asleep. Boots 10 inches or more in height give at least partial protection, for most bites occur below the knee. When climbing ledges, you should be careful where you put your hands, for snakes often hide out or sun themselves in crevices. Use care in striding over logs if you cannot see what is on the other side. Keep your eyes open and watch where you step and sit.

Not many cases of snake bite are reported each year, and few of these prove fatal when proper treatment is given immediately. Ross Allen, famed expert, reports the following percentage of fatalities from snake bites: cotton mouth moccasin, 5 per cent; timber rattler, 4 per cent; copperhead, 1 per cent.* Someone has said that there is more danger of choking to death from eating popcorn in a movie than of dying from snake bite. Nevertheless, any group hiking through "snaky" territory should take along a snake-bite kit consisting of a tiny steel scalpel, a piece of rubber tubing, a rubber suction pump, and an antiseptic.

If bitten, try to recognize the snake or at least tell if it is poisonous, for, if so, you must start treatment immediately for the poison will spread throughout the system by way of the blood stream within a few moments. The venom of a poisonous snake instantly causes a painful, burning sensation which is quickly followed by discoloration and swelling. One or two deep fang marks will probably show, whereas only a round set of teeth marks characterize the bite of a nonpoisonous snake.

If the first aider has a companion, he should start in search of a doctor or nurse right away. Have the patient lie down and keep still, for movement of any sort stimulates the circulation and spreads the poison faster. Do not permit him to see his injury or the treatment given, for the shock may prove detrimental.

Direct your efforts toward (1) keeping the poison from spreading and (2) getting as much of it out of the system as possible. Speed is essential, for every second counts.

Apply a tight bandage a couple of inches above the wound, using the rubber tubing from your snake kit or a bandana or other strip of cloth folded to about a 2-inch width. Do not twist the bandage with a stick, for it must not be as tight as a tourniquet; the idea is to slow the circulation down, not entirely stop it. Loosen the bandage for a few moments every thirty minutes; if the swelling moves up, move the bandage up ahead of it. Do not give stimulants of any sort, particularly alcohol; they but speed up the circulation and cause the poison to spread faster.

Just as soon as possible, sterilize a razor blade, sharp knife or the scalpel from your kit in alcohol or flame and slash an "X" about $\frac{1}{2}$ inch long and $\frac{1}{4}$ inch deep through each fang mark. Take care not to cut across an artery or tendon, but make the cut deep enough to produce an adequate amount of bleeding. Then apply the suction cup to the cut for at least twenty minutes; and keep the wound open and draining freely for several hours in order to get rid of as much of the venom-containing blood as possible. When you have no suction pump, it is best to suck with your mouth if there are no lesions or open sores in it. If the swelling and discoloration move to a new location, it indicates the poison has moved there; make a new incision and apply the suction cup. Replace the bandage up ahead of the new swelling.

* Byron, Dalyrymple: Fishing, Hunting, and Camping. Pocket Books, New York, 1950, p. 330.

The superior treatment for snake bite is, of course, to introduce antivenom into the body of the victim to counteract the poison no matter where it has located. Make an attempt to get this treatment just as soon as possible, for it greatly minimizes the pain and discomfort of the patient.

## OTHER UNFRIENDLY NEIGHBORS

### Woodticks

These are very thick in some areas and have a way of getting under your clothing and hanging on in a most unpleasant way. Have a tick inspection for everyone after traveling or sleeping in the woods. If you find one attached, don't try to pull him off for his head is probably embedded in your skin where it will remain and cause a serious infection, especially if you scratch the irritation. Touch a drop of alcohol, hot water or a lighted match to him and he'll release his grip in a hurry.

### Chiggers (Chigoes)

These small, red spider-like insects constitute one of the worst nuisances for the camper, especially in the Southern states. The best cure is to prevent them from biting by mixing flowers of sulphur with alcohol and rubbing this on your wrists, ankles, belt line, and like areas. If they do bite you, wash the area thoroughly with hot, soapy lather and swab the bites with kerosene or apply a drop of colorless fingernail polish over each.

### Bees, Wasps, and the Like

The bites of these insects are not serious unless you are unfortunate enough to get into a large nest of them and acquire a great many stings. They are, however, quite painful. Apply ammonia or wet baking soda to the site of the sting.

### Spiders

The only really dangerous spider is the female black widow. She can be identified by her shiny black body resembling a shoe button, the bright red hourglass spot on her abdomen, and her distended, round, oversized abdomen. You should get to a doctor immediately if bitten, for a bite can make you seriously ill and one in twenty bites ends fatally.

### Kissing Bug or Assassin Bug

This little bug is largely found in the Southern states. Its bite, often blamed on a spider, may, at times, make the victim quite ill. The symptoms are severe itching, burning and swelling. In more severe cases, red blotches occur, followed by nausea, rapid breathing and palpitation of the heart. Get the patient to a doctor or nurse right away.

## Centipedes and Scorpions

These are particularly dangerous in the Southwest. The scorpion stings with its poison tail and the centipede bites with its poison fangs. Be sure to inspect your bedding well before retiring and fresh shoes and clothing thoroughly before donning them.

## Caterpillar (Larva) of Io Moth

This beautiful and showy specimen can be identified by its light-green coat with two pink and white stripes zigzagging down each side. Its back is a wilderness of spines which give off a substance poisonous to touch. The sting causes pain, irritation and swelling.

### ADDITIONAL READINGS

BOOKS AND PAMPHLETS

Camp Safety Digest, pp. 28–30.
Kephart: Camping and Woodcraft, vol. 1, chap. 14.
Morris, Percy A.: Boy's Book of Snakes. Ronald, 1948, 185 pp.
Reptile Study. Boy Scouts (#3813), 1944.
Weaver and Merrill: Camping Can Be Fun, chap. 10.
West and Hillcourt: Scout Field Book, Pow-wows 34, 35 and 36.

MAGAZINE ARTICLES

Carlson, Dr. A. E.: Licking Those Weed and Brush Problems. C.M., March, 1952.
Schwardt, H. H.: First Line of Defense against Insects. C.M., May. 1954.

The healing fragrance of the wood; the beauties of lake and of coastline; the open air; the clean blue skies—these belong to all people, and the right to enjoy them is the heritage of every child.

<small>CAMPING FOR CRIPPLED CHILDREN *</small>

# Chapter 18

# ROPES AND KNOTCRAFT

## Why Learn to Tie Knots?

FROM TIME immemorial man has needed some medium to join things together. Early man made his "rope" from such things growing about him as thin strips of bark and small branches. The Indians applied wet thongs made from the skins of animals which contracted and became tight as they dried. Campers still use such materials when commercially made rope is unattainable or when they want to be really "woodsy." You will find a knowledge of how to tie a few simple, serviceable knots indispensable for such tasks as joining a broken shoestring, lashing camp furniture, suspending a lighted lantern between two trees, tying a bedroll, making a temporary clothesline, or tying up your boat.

### ROPE

## How Rope Is Made

A close inspection of a rope shows that it consists of many individual *fibers* twisted to the right to form *yarns*, a few yarns twisted to the left to form

* Permission by The National Society for Crippled Children and Adults, Inc.

191

*strands*, and three or more strands twisted together again to the right to form the *rope*. This twisting in alternate direction holds the fibers compact when stress is applied. However, it may cause a new rope to curl and be hard to handle.

Most of the rope we use is made of sisal, which comes from Central America. Manila hemp rope (named after its chief city of export in the Philippines) wears better, though it is stiff, heavy and more expensive. Inexpensive Indian jute or cotton rope is also used and ropes of nylon and other synthetic materials are now appearing on the market. A rope is usually measured by its diameter in inches; sailors, however, designate the size by the measurement of its circumference in inches.

### The Camper's Rope

For ordinary purposes, a rope about 5 to 6 yards long and $\frac{3}{8}$ inch in diameter is the most useful for a camper. You will need additional pieces, smaller in diameter, for practice in knot tying and lashing.

Do not needlessly expose your rope to weather or dampness, for alternate wetting and drying greatly shorten its life. Keep it in a neat, compact roll when not in use. If your rope breaks, learn how to splice it instead of knotting the two ends together. A good splice makes the rope as strong as ever.

How to Carry Your Rope.

### Knots

There are said to be about 4000 different kinds of knots in existence, but many of them are quite specialized. A camper will find the few presented here adequate for his ordinary needs and can find others described in the sources listed at the end of the chapter.

### Relaying a Rope

A rope which has not been whipped sometimes untwists and must be relaid before it can be whipped and put to use again. To do this, hold the rope in your left hand and twist the fibers of strand 1 tightly and pull it into place with your right hand; move your left thumb up to hold it firmly as you now twist strand 2 and pull it into place. Continue this process, twisting and pulling strand 3 into place, then strand 1 again, strand 2, and so on, until the relaying is complete.

Relaying a Rope.

## Whipping the End of the Rope

You whip the end of a rope to keep it from untwisting or ravelling. Use a piece of common grocery string about a foot long for the average camp rope. Lay the string in a loop, "y," along the end of the rope as shown in A, holding it in place with your left thumb. With your right hand, wind end "z" in tight coils about the rope, with the standing part away from end "x" and going toward loop "y" as shown in B. When you have used almost all of the string, insert end "z" through loop "y" as shown in B. Then grasp end "x" in your right hand and pull it gently until the point where "x" and "z" cross is about midway under the coils made, as shown in C. Snip off ends "x" and "z" fairly close to where they emerge from the rolls, and your whipping is complete. Test for permanence by trying to push the whipping off over the end of the rope.

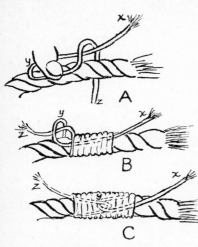

Whipping the End of a Rope.

## SOME TERMS USED

*End*—just what the name implies; the short part of the rope with which you lead in tying knots.

Some Rope Terms.

*Standing Part*—the remainder of the rope.

*Bight*—made by bending an end back to lie alongside its standing part.

*Overhand Loop*—made by crossing an end *over* its standing part.

*Underhand Loop*—made by crossing an end *under* its standing part.

## CHARACTERISTICS OF A GOOD KNOT

A good knot should (1) be easy to tie, (2) do its job well, and (3) be quick and easy to untie.

Packages are often tied with inefficient knots which slip at the wrong time and are so complicated that the average person loses patience in trying to untie them and resorts to the scissors, thus ruining the cord for future use. Whereas this may be satisfactory in city life, no good camper would even consider cutting his faithful camp rope, and even smaller cords are saved for they are precious around camp. A camper ties a good knot which he can easily untie when he is through with it.

## STOPPER OR END KNOTS

Stopper or end knots are used to enlarge the end of a rope so that it will hold in a hole or ring, will provide a good grip for holding onto, or will stop a rope end from sliding through the loop of another knot and thus prevent untying.

Overhand Knot.

### The Overhand Knot

This is one of the simplest knots, and is made by making a loop and drawing the end back through it, and pulling the whole thing tight. If a larger knot is desired, you may pass the end through the loop several times before pulling it tight. It holds well, but tends to jam after stress has been put on it, making it hard to untie. It is sometimes substituted for whipping on the end of a rope, but is inferior to it and should serve only temporarily until you can whip the end properly.

### Figure-of-Eight Knot

This knot is similar to the overhand, but is slightly larger and more easily untied. Besides serving the uses of the overhand knot, it is sometimes used to attach

Figure-of-Eight Knot.

a line to a fish hook. Its name comes from its appearance. To untie it, push end A to loosen it so that you can easily pick it apart.

## KNOTS FOR JOINING TWO ROPES

### Square or Reef Knot

This knot is excellent to join two ropes of equal size, for the stronger you pull the tighter it holds. Make a bight in rope B. Then pass end A down through the bight and bring it up and across both the standing part and end of B, then up and through the bight and pull your knot tight. Notice that end A and its standing part lie parallel above the loop, while end B and its standing part come out parallel below it.

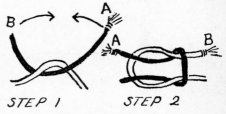

STEP 1    STEP 2

Square or Reef Knot.

To untie the knot, loosen it by a hard simultaneous pull on end A and its standing part; then pick it apart.

Can you see how the square knot gets its name from its appearance?

Granny Knot.

When tying it, avoid tying a granny, which is quite useless since it pulls loose whenever stress is applied. In the granny, an end comes out above the loop, while its standing part comes out below, and vice versa.

### Sheet Bend (Weaver's Knot or Becket Bend)

Use this knot to join ropes of unequal size. It is quickly tied, holds securely

A Sheet Bend.

as long as there is stress on it and is easily picked apart when the stress is removed. Make a bight in the larger rope B. Bring end A of the smaller rope up through the bight, pass it over and down below both the end and standing part of the larger rope and up and under its own standing part. Leave both ends long, hold bight A in your left hand and pull both the end and standing part of B tight about it. Notice that one end of the small rope B is on top and the other end on the bottom of the bight in A. Pull on end A and its standing part simultaneously to loosen it.

## KNOTS TO ATTACH A ROPE TO AN OBJECT

### Slip Knot or Teamster's Hitch

This knot is excellent to tether a horse to a tree, to suspend a bucket by its bail, and similar purposes.

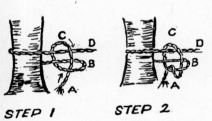

STEP 1        STEP 2

Slip Knot.

Pass end A (Step 1) around the tree and make a small underhand loop, B, near the end of it. Then bring end A up behind and across standing part D, and down through loop B, then up around and down through loop B again (Step 2). When pulled tight, it holds well but tends to tighten and jam as more stress is applied. It also has a tendency to be hard to untie after being subjected to strain.

### Clove Hitch

This is one of the simplest and
most useful knots known to make fast
the end of a rope. Do not use it for
tying such things as horses or boats
for their movements might loosen it.
Hold standing part B in your left
hand and bring end A around the
object in an overhand loop; then
pass end A around again in an underhand loop under its own standing
part. Although not usually necessary,
you can make this knot still more secure by finishing off with one or two
half hitches.

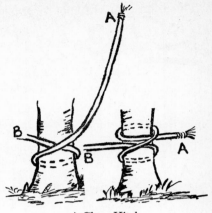

A Clove Hitch.

To pick it apart, push simultaneously on end A and its standing
part B.

A clove hitch is used to start and end most lashing, to anchor a tent to a
tent stake, and like purposes.

You will find it a very useful knot to master. Practice until you can tie
one easily.

### The Half Hitch and Two Half Hitches

Half hitches (several for maximum security) provide the easiest and
quickest way to fasten a rope to a post, but, when subjected to great strain,
may jam so tightly as to make untying difficult.

A Half Hitch.

Two Half Hitches.

### Slippery Hitch

This is an excellent knot to provide a temporary fastening, for it can be

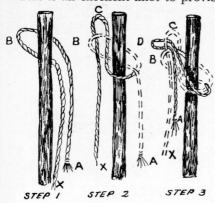

*cast off* (untied) in a hurry, even though held taut at the time. Gather up the standing part to make bight B (Step 1); then gather it up again and take it around the post and up through bight B just made to make bight C (Step 2). Then gather up a third bight of rope next to end A and pull it through bight C to make bight D. When pulled tight it will hold, but a yank on end A loosens the whole thing in a jiffy and explains why it is also called the Highwayman's Hitch.

A Slippery Hitch.

## TO MAKE A PERMANENT LOOP IN A ROPE

### Bowline (pronounced bō-lin)

A bowline will neither slip nor jam and, unlike a slip knot, its noose remains the same size regardless of how much stress you put on it. It is useful in the end of a boat painter, in a bedroll rope or any place where you want a permanent loop to drop over a post or nail and lift off again in an instant. It is easy to untie when you are through with it.

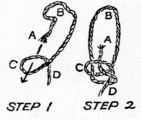

A Bowline.

Make an underhand loop, C, leaving end A a little longer than the circumference of the desired noose. Bring end A up through the loop, around behind the standing part and pass it down through the loop again. Tighten the turns on the standing part. It is an added accomplishment to learn to tie this knot with one hand as sailors do while holding on to the ship's rigging with the other hand.

## TO SHORTEN A ROPE

### Sheep Shank

A sheep shank shortens a rope, may be left in as long as desired, then

quickly untied, leaving your rope the original length and completely un-
damaged.

Fold your rope to the desired length (Step 1). Make an underhand loop with end A around one folded-over portion (Step 2). Repeat with end B. Pull the loops tight and your rope will hold as long as there is stress on both ends of it.

For a more permanent shortening, pass ends A and B down and up respectively through the bights in the folded portion of the rope (Step 3).

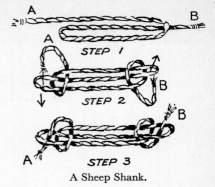

A Sheep Shank.

## TO SUSPEND AN OBJECT

### Barrel Hitch

When you want to suspend a handleless object, such as an outdoor cache, a barrel hitch will do the job nicely.

Set the object on your stretched-out rope and bring the two ends up and knot them loosely above (Step 1). Then spread the knot as indicated by arrows so that one side goes down on each side of the object (Step 2). Bring

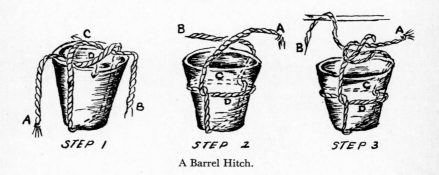

A Barrel Hitch.

both the end and standing parts up on top of the bucket and pull them tight with an overhand knot. The weight of the bucket and its contents keeps the knot secure as you suspend it by standing part, B.

# LASHING

Lashing is a way of fastening various objects, such as sticks or poles, together. Use it when no nails are available, when it would be objectionable to mar or damage the objects by driving nails into them, or when you need only a temporary joining.

Any kind of cord that is heavy and strong enough to hold securely is suitable. *Binder twine* is recommended for ordinary use, for it is tough, cheap and easily obtained. In lashing, you manipulate the standing part of the rope instead of the end as in knot-tying, and you start all lashing with a clove hitch around one of the objects.

*Frapping* is a method of tightening lashing by wrapping the end of the cord around its own turns and is the secret of a good, firm piece of work.

*Square lashing* joins sticks together at right angles. Make a clove hitch around one of the sticks, and bring the standing part, B, across the horizontal stick, around behind the vertical stick and up across the horizontal stick again, then around behind the vertical stick (Step 2). Repeat the whole

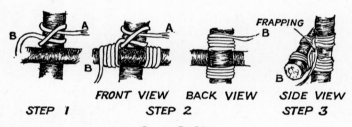

Square Lashing.

process as many times (usually four or five) as needed and tighten with frapping (about three turns) between the two sticks (Step 3). Finish off by tying a square knot with ends A and B or by making a couple of half inches with end B.

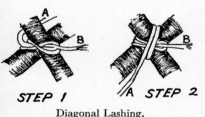

Diagonal Lashing.

*Diagonal lashing* joins sticks diagonally in the form of an "X." Start it with a clove hitch around the two sticks (Step 1). Make about four turns around the joining in one direction, then four in the opposite direction (Step 2). Frap it tightly with about three turns between the two sticks and finish off with a square knot made with the two ends of the cord or with a couple of half hitches made by end A.

*Shear or round lashing* joins two short poles into a single long one or lashes two poles together when laid parallel. Make a clove hitch around one of the poles, and then wrap the cord tightly around both. Finish off with the usual frapping and a square knot or half hitches. Three such lashings make the joining extra strong.

A *pole splice* repairs a broken pole or unites two poles of approximately the same diameter into one long one. Place the two pieces end to end and place splints (A and B) of smaller sticks or pieces of board along the joint. Make a clove hitch around the whole at the top, and wrap the cord tightly about the joint for some distance. Finish off with frapping between the splints and poles and the usual square knot or a couple of half hitches. Let the splints extend for some distance on each side of the joint so that you can make several such wrappings.

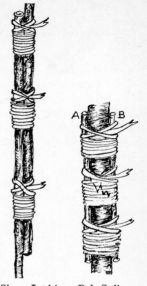

Shear Lashing. Pole Splice.

A *malay hitch* quickly joins wisps of grass, reeds, and the like, into mats for a cabin floor, table, or outdoor mattress.

*Continuous lashing* enables you to lash small sticks into a table top, and so forth. Notch a long stick to receive the short sticks at desired intervals. Use short sticks of the same length and approximately the same diameter.

Anchor the middle of a piece of string about four times the length of the long pole by a clove hitch around the long pole

A Malay Hitch.

just above the first notch. Bring one end of the string diagonally across the back of the long pole and up and across the first short stick. Carry it tightly around behind the long pole again and up and over the second short stick on the opposite side of the long stick. Continue until all of the short sticks have been anchored. Repeat with the other end of the string, anchoring the short sticks on the opposite sides of the long stick and the two ends of the string with two half hitches. Note that the bends in the ends of the string lie

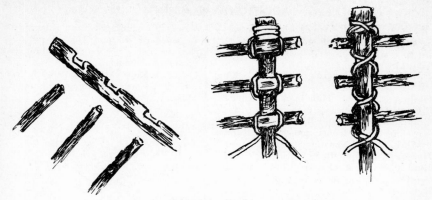

Continuous Lashing.

parallel to the long stick in front and cross each other in the back. Now lash the other ends of the short sticks to a similarly prepared long stick and your table is complete.

You can use lashing in many ways around a campsite, to fashion all kinds of simple furniture and camp "fixin's."

## ADDITIONAL READINGS

Abraham, R. M.: Winter Nights Entertainment. Dutton, 1933, pp. 105–116.

Campcraft Skills. Flip Charts (Lashing). Girl Scouts.

Directions for Square Knotting. NRA (MP 316).

Graumont, Raoul: Handbook of Knots. Cornell Maritime.

Graumont, Raoul, and Hensel, John: Encyclopedia of Knots and Fancy Rope Work. Cornell Maritime.

Hammett: Campcraft A B C's, pp. 17–36.

Illustrated Knot Folder. Boy Scouts (#1057). (39 useful knots.)

Kephart: Camping and Woodcraft, vol. 2, chap. 16.

Knots and How to Tie Them. Boy Scouts (#3166), 56 pp.

Mason, Bernard S.: Woodcraft, chap. 11.

Verril, A. Hyatt: Knots, Splices and Rope Work, 5th ed. (revised and enlarged by E. Armitage McCann. Henley, 1946.

Write the following for information and possible free booklets:

Columbia Rope Company, Auburn, N.Y.

Plymouth Cordage Company, Plymouth, Mass.

"Whatever the weather may be," says he,
"Whatever the weather may be,
It's the songs ye sing, an' the smiles ye wear,
That's a makin' the sun shine everywhere."
JAMES WHITCOMB RILEY*

# Chapter 19

# THE WEATHER

A CAMPER is always interested in the weather, for nearly everything he plans depends upon its suitability. It becomes of particular importance when he is on the water in a canoe or sailboat, for the winds and waves developed by a severe summer storm are stronger than the paddling or swimming of the hardiest "old salt." When he is on a trip and recognizes signs of an approaching storm, he will want to make camp immediately, erecting the best shelter he can and stowing himself and duffel as snugly as possible.

Since he is often too far from "civilization" to tune in on the latest radio report, he must become his own forecaster, depending upon a barometer, thermometer, and trained eyes and ears to tell him what to expect. He should be able to predict accurately at least 80 per cent of the time, but he must be prepared to be drenched, frozen or stewed, according to the caprices of Old Man Weather the remaining 20 per cent.

## Air

We are surrounded by air, which extends many miles above us, becoming thinner and thinner as we go farther above the earth's surface until it hardly exists at all about 200 miles up. Near the ground, it is composed of 20 per cent *oxygen* (essential for animal life), 0.3 to 0.03 per cent *carbon dioxide* (necessary for plant life), 78 per cent *nitrogen*, minute quantities of invisible gases, and 0 to 5 per cent *water* in the form of invisible vapor.

* From *Pipes O'Pan at Zekesbury*, Published by The Bobbs-Merrill Co.

The amount of water in the air is expressed as *humidity* and is derived by evaporation from the rivers, lakes, oceans, soil, and even trees and other vegetation. A perpetual interchange takes place with the air drawing moisture from the earth to form clouds which eventually pour it back again onto the earth as rain or snow.

We are seldom aware of the moisture in the air except on a hot, muggy day when the humidity is so high that the perspiration cannot evaporate from our bodies. We speak of such a day as a *humid* one.

## SOME PHENOMENA OF THE WEATHER

*Fog* appears on a clear, still night, particularly around rivers or lakes where the humidity is high. The air cools toward morning; and since cool air cannot hold as much water vapor as warm air, part of it condenses as infinitesimal drops which hang suspended in the air as fog. Our eyes cannot penetrate these millions of tiny droplets, thus limiting our visibility to only a few feet in front of us. This explains why the driver of a car has better visibility when using his "dims" which direct the light low and close to him instead of his "brights," which throw it high and far ahead.

*Dew* results when moisture collects as droplets on such objects as grass or trees. During the night, as the grass and trees cool off, warm air coming in contact with them is likewise cooled beyond the point where it can retain all its water vapor (*dew point*) and part of it condenses on them as dew. The condensation of warm air as "sweat" on a pitcher of ice water and the clouding up of a window pane when one's breath is blown on it in winter time are examples of the same thing.

*Clouds.* Air which has been heated close to the earth rises, becoming thinner and lighter as it ascends. It also comes under increasingly less pressure from the air above and so expands.

Floating about in the higher regions are infinitesimal bits of dust which give the sky its blue appearance on a clear day or, when very numerous, cause it to appear gray or hazy. The ascending air cools as it rises until it finally reaches dew point and condensation like that of a fog occurs on the bits of dust. The droplets, becoming electrified, attract each other and join to form larger and larger droplets until they eventually become raindrops (composed of 7,000,000 or more of them) which in turn form clouds. The raindrops finally become so heavy that they can no longer be air-borne and fall to earth as rain. Clouds, then, like dew and fog, result from condensation when the cooling air cannot contain all its moisture in vaporous form.

*Snow* is rain which has come from a cold, upper region which freezes the droplets into icy crystals, hundreds or even thousands of them uniting in the beautiful designs of snowflakes.

*Sleet* results when snow is partially melted as it falls through a layer of warm air, then freezes again in a layer of cold air just above the ground.

*Glaze* results when freezing takes place just as the half-melted snow hits the ground.

*Hail* occurs when rain from a rather low-lying cloud is caught in a strong uprush of air and tossed back up into a higher freezing area and coated with snow. It descends again to gather more moisture from the low-lying cloud and is again swept back up into the freezing air to acquire another layer of ice and snow. This process may be repeated many times until it finally becomes too heavy to be carried upward and crashes to earth as hail. It is claimed that hail stones as big as baseballs with twenty-five layers of ice and snow fell at Annapolis, Maryland, on June 22, 1915. Hail is a freak which insolently disregards the calendar, for it is said to be most common in June.

*Frost* occurs when the temperature drops below freezing under conditions which would ordinarily produce dew.

A *halo* or *ring* around the sun or moon occurs when its light is seen shining through a surrounding ring of ice crystals.

*Lightning.* Mythology explains lightning as the War God, Thor, sending bolts of fire to paralyze the earth people, but we know from the experiments of Benjamin Franklin that it is really electricity. It usually passes harmlessly from one cloud to another, but occasionally comes from a cloud to the earth with enough power to kill men or animals, start fires or uproot trees. The safest place to be during an electrical storm is in a cave or ravine between two hills or embankments. The most dangerous places are near a fence, on a high hill, or under a tree which is especially tall or is standing alone. Water is a good conductor of electricity, so that anyone swimming or boating should get on land just as quickly as possible.

*Thunder*, although alarming, is perfectly harmless and is thought to result from the rapid expansion of air as it is heated by the passage of lightning through it. It is possible to estimate roughly the distance of lightning by counting the time between its flash and the sound of the thunder, for the flash appears almost instantaneously, while sound travels only about 1100 feet per second. Therefore an interval of five seconds would indicate that the lightning was about a mile away (since there are 5280 feet in a mile).

A *rainbow* occurs when we see the sun's rays through rain which is falling off at one side. The water, like a prism, breaks the rays into the colors of a rainbow.

## CLOUDS

The sky, nature's roof, forms a backdrop for the clouds. Cloud names are of Latin derivation and there are four basic types of them with nine combinations of these types.

### Basic Forms or Families of Clouds

1. *Cirrus* are the "lock" or "curl" clouds and are highest of all (5 to 10 miles). They are always white, composed entirely of ice crystals, and are sometimes called "witch's broom" or "mare's tail." If the sky is bright blue

Cumulus Clouds.

Cirrostratus Clouds.

Cirrus Clouds.

Stratus Clouds.

Cirrocumulus Clouds.

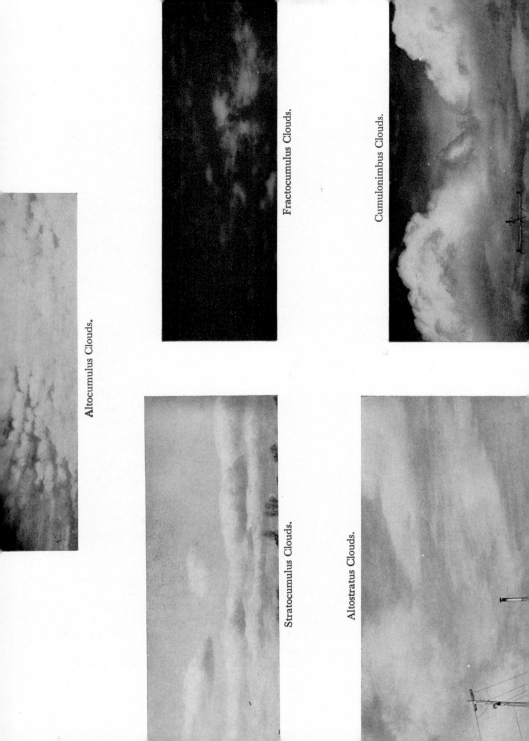

Altocumulus Clouds.

Fractocumulus Clouds.

Cumulonimbus Clouds.

Stratocumulus Clouds.

Altostratus Clouds.

above and the wind is from the north or northwest, they indicate fair weather for twenty-four to forty-eight hours. However, if the sky is gray-blue, and they are moving swiftly, especially from the west, they will likely turn to cirro-stratus clouds with later rain or snow.

2. *Stratus* or "spread sheet" clouds are a horizontal overcast of "fog" high (about 2100 feet) in the air. They are always a shade of gray, some-times being dark enough practically to conceal the sun or moon. Rain usually, but not always, follows.

3. *Cumulus* are the "heap" or "wool pack" clouds which are dark on the bottom and rise to a high, dome-shaped mass of white. They are the lowest of all, being only about a mile above the earth, and usually indicate fair weather, except that on a hot, muggy day, if massed near the horizon or becoming increasingly larger, they may indicate rain.

4. *Nimbus* clouds are the low-lying "umbrella" clouds. They are dark with ragged edges and no definite shapes and usually indicate steady rain or snow. *Scud* clouds are the small, ragged pieces frequently seen traveling rapidy across the sky below them.

### Variations and Combinations

*Alto* means high: *fracto* means broken by the wind.

5. *Cirrostratus* are whitish, veil-like clouds which form a milky, tangled-web sheet over the sky (about $5\frac{1}{2}$ miles up). They sometimes mean nothing in the morning, but, when they persist or appear in the afternoon, are likely to be a sure forerunner of rain or snow within twenty-four hours, particularly if they started as cirrus clouds and are coming from the west.

6. *Cirrocumulus* clouds or "mackerel" sky have a rippled appearance somewhat like sand on the seashore and are about four miles up. They usually indicate fair weather.

7. *Altocumulus* are small, high, white clouds which may lie close together in rows or lines giving a dappled appearance to the sky. They are also called "sheep" clouds and usually indicate fair weather.

8. *Stratocumulus* are the dark-colored twist-shaped clouds (about a mile up) which ordinarily thin to cumulus or fractocumulus later on and seldom bring the rain they threaten. They are likely to be accompanied by high winds, especially in the fall.

9. *Altostratus* are thin, gray, curtain-like clouds (about 3 miles up) and often show a bright patch where the sun or moon hides behind them. They are sometimes followed by squally weather.

10. *Fractonimbus* clouds follow nimbus and generally break up to disclose patches of blue sky indicating clearing weather.

11. *Fractostratus* clouds follow on the heels of fractonimbus and commonly clear into a blue sky with cirrus tufts scattered about.

12. *Fractocumulus* are cumulus clouds which have been broken into some-

what thinner clouds of irregular appearance. They usually indicate clear weather.

13. *Cumulonimbus* are the "thunderhead" clouds, which are most spectacular of all. They have dark bases and light tops and tower into the air like mountains. When they appear in the west, a thunderstorm will likely occur within a few hours.

Clouds moving in different directions at various levels foretell rain.

## PREDICTING THE WEATHER

Man has always been concerned with weather. Sailors, especially, in the days of sailing vessels when no progress could be made without a wind to fill the sails and when severe storms meant possible shipwreck and death, grew expert at foretelling the weather.

The multitude of proverbs about the weather bear mute testimony to man's interest in it. Many of these sayings were, of course, mere superstitions, but others are of actual value, for they are based on factors which really "cause" the weather to be whatever it is. The following seem to be somewhat reliable. Can you explain why?

Red sky (or rainbow) in the morning, sailors take warning.
Red sky (or rainbow) at night, sailor's delight.

Evening red and morning gray,
Sets the traveler on his way;
Evening gray and morning red,
Brings down rain upon his head.

(Rain drops are caused by the condensation of water around a grain of dust, and humidity allows the red rays of the sun to pass through and be more clearly seen.)

Rain before seven,
    clear before eleven.

(Rains seldom last longer than five hours anyway.)

When the dew is on the grass
Rain will never come to pass.

When grass is dry at morning's light,
Look for rain before the night.

When the stars begin to huddle,
The earth will soon become a puddle.

A red sky has water in his eye.

Sound traveling far and wide
A stormy day will betide.

(Mist forms over the sky and causes the smaller stars to cease to be visible. The brighter ones shine through dimly with a blur of light about them, each looking like an indistinct cluster of stars. This, therefore, indicates an increase in humidity.)

The higher the clouds, the finer the weather.

Mackerel scales and mare's tails
Make lofty ships carry low sails.

When the wind's in the south the rain's in his mouth.
When the smoke goes west, good weather is past.
When the smoke goes east, good weather is next.

The weather will clear when there is enough blue sky to make a pair of Dutchman's
breeches.

A ring around the moon means rain;  (Cirrostratus clouds are around the
The larger the ring, the sooner the rain.  moon and are the forerunners of unsettled weather.)

## WIND DIRECTION

The direction and force of the wind are important in weather prediction. A wind from the east or southeast usually brings rain within twenty-four hours. If from the northeast, the rain will be chilly and the temperature cool. A wind from the west or northwest will probably be followed by fair weather. The stronger the wind, the more likely it is to bring the weather indicated.

## BAROMETER

Drawing
Liquid
Through
a Straw.

The name *barometer* comes from two Greek words, one meaning "weight," the other "measure." Air is heavier when it has a low humidity (little moisture in it) and lighter when its humidity is high. At sea level it weighs or has a pressure of approximately 15 pounds per square inch. A barometer determines the humidity of the air by measuring its weight or pressure.

Your ability to drink soda through a straw is due to the weight or pressure of the air, for, when you draw up through the straw, you remove the air from it and create a vacuum. The weight of the air pressing down on the liquid in the glass then forces it up into the straw and, encountering no resistance there, it is forced on up into your mouth.

Aneroid Barometer.

Several types of barometers are available, the commonest being the *aneroid barometer* (meaning without liquid), which consists of a hand or needle that moves around a marked dial owing to the pressure of the air on a sensitive box within it. This type of barometer is accurate but rather expensive.

A *mercury barometer* consists of a column of mercury which rises or falls in a graduated tube. The tube is closed at the top, and has a vacuum in it above the mercury. Its open bottom end is immersed in a vessel of mercury and air pressure on the mercury in the vessel causes the column of

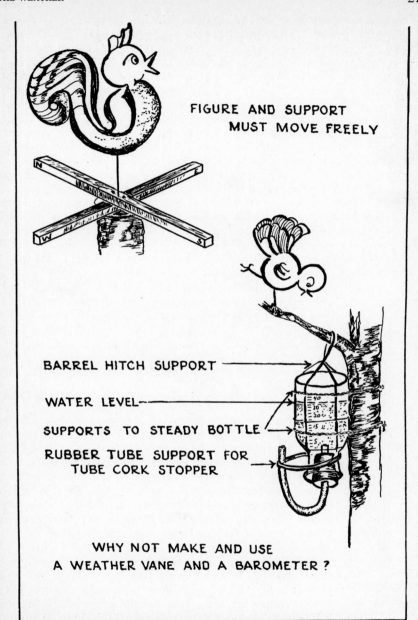

FIGURE AND SUPPORT
MUST MOVE FREELY

BARREL HITCH SUPPORT

WATER LEVEL

SUPPORTS TO STEADY BOTTLE

RUBBER TUBE SUPPORT FOR
TUBE CORK STOPPER

WHY NOT MAKE AND USE
A WEATHER VANE AND A BAROMETER ?

Weathervane and Clipper Ship Barometer.

mercury in the tube to rise or fall, just as in drinking through a straw. Inexpensive barometers operating on this same principle, but using water instead of mercury, are available, or you can make one yourself.

Most commercial barometers bear such notations as "change," "fair," "stormy," and so on, which are based on the rising or falling of the barometer. In general, a reading of 30 or over may be considered high; below 30, as low.

You can make a clipper ship model barometer accurate enough for camp purposes. Fit a bottle with a tight cork and insert a piece of rubber tubing through the cork as shown.

Mercury
Barometer.

Make the union between the tubing and cork air- and water-tight by covering it with melted paraffin or candle wax. Fill the bottle almost full of water, and invert it, making sure that no air is allowed to get into the top. Always suspend a barometer out of the sun's direct rays; and, after it has remained stationary for a day or two to adjust itself, you can estimate the humidity by the rise or fall of the liquid level in the bottle. When the air is dry or heavy, it presses down forcibly on the water in the rubber tube, pushing the liquid back up into the bottle. When the humidity is high it exerts little pressure and the liquid rises and, in extreme cases, may even come out of the tube. You must hang your barometer where it will not be jostled by the wind or by people bumping into it, for it will be inaccurate for a day or two after it has been disturbed.

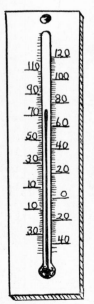

A falling barometer indicates that the air is full of moisture and rain likely. A rising barometer signifies fair weather.

## TEMPERATURE

Temperature is measured by means of a thermometer (coming from Greek words meaning "heat" and "measure"). Thermometers are inexpensive and are indispensable to the amateur weather forecaster. If possible, place your thermometer facing north and out of the direct sunlight. A rising temperature accompanied by other favorable signs, indicates stormy weather. A thunderstorm never occurs when the termperature is below 60°, is possible between 60° and 70°, and extremely likely above 70° F. if other signs of rain are present.

A drop in temperature to 40° to 50° F. at the end of a calm, clear day in spring or fall when no wind or clouds are present indicates a probable frost before morning.

Thermometer.

You can rather accurately determine the temperature if it is between 45° and 80° by catching a cricket and counting the number of times he chirps for his rate increases in almost exact proportion to the rise in temperature. Count his chirps for 15 seconds, add 37 and you will know just about what the temperature is.

## INDICATIONS OF STORMY WEATHER

Wind lacking to moderate, and from southeast or east.
No dew at night.
Atmosphere muggy and sticky.
Temperature 70° F. or above, especially if rising.
Falling barometer.
Smoke not rising straight up in the air.
Crickets and other sounds seeming extra loud (the atmospheric conditions cause sounds to travel farther).
Rapidly moving cirrus clouds, especially from the west.
Dark clouds gathering on the horizon to the west.
Cumulus clouds in masses near the horizon.
Stratus, nimbus, altostratus, cirrostratus, or cumulonimbus clouds.
Clouds moving in different directions at various heights.
Clouds becoming more numerous and nearer the earth.
Red sunrise.
Gray or dull sunset.

## INDICATIONS OF FAIR WEATHER

Gentle winds, especially from the west or northwest.
Heavy dew at night.
Fog in the morning.
Temperature below 70° F., especially if falling.
Steadily rising barometer.
Smoke rising straight up.
Spiders spinning new webs (if they continue spinning during a shower, it indicates clear weather soon).
Cloudless skies.
Cumulus clouds or stationary cirrus clouds.
Stratocumulus, altocumulus, cirrocumulus, fractonimbus, fractostratus or fractocumulus clouds.
Red sunset (sun goes down like a ball of fire).

No one sign is infallible when predicting the weather; note all and take an average when making a prognosis.

### CHART FOR RECORDING WEATHER PREDICTIONS

| DATE | TIME | WIND DIR. | VEL. | CLOUDS | TEMP. | BARO METER | WEATHER SAYINGS OR OTHER SIGNS | PREDICTIONS | WHAT WAS IT ? |
|------|------|-----------|------|--------|-------|------------|-------------------------------|-------------|---------------|
|      |      |           |      |        |       |            |                               |             |               |

# WEATHER FLAGS

INDICATES FAIR WEATHER

INDICATES LOCAL SHOWERS
OR SNOW FLURRIES

INDICATES RAIN OR SNOW

INDICATES A COLD WAVE

THE BLACK TRIANGULAR TEMPERATURE
ABOVE ANY OTHER FLAG MEANS "WARMER";
BELOW, COLDER

IT'S FUN TO HOIST A WEATHER FLAG
INDICATING YOUR PREDICTION OF THE WEATHER.
WEATHER FLAGS CAN BE MADE OF BUNTING
AND SHOULD BE ABOUT 12" SQUARE.

MAKE AND FLY WEATHER FLAGS.

# ADDITIONAL READINGS

## BOOKS AND PAMPHLETS

Cloud Forms According to the International System of Classification. Supt. of Doc., 1941. Catalogue no. C 30.22: C 62/11/938.

Cloud Forms: Chart Prepared with View of Aiding Observers in Identification of the Several Cloud Forms According to International System of Classification of 1932. Supt. of Doc., Catalogue no. C 30.22: C 62/942.

Codes for Cloud Forms and States of the Sky, According to the International System of Classification. Supt. of Doc., 1938, Catalogue no. A 29.11:5.

Fisher, Robert Moore: How About the Weather. Harper, 1951.

Hamilton, Andrew: When Lightning Strikes. Popular Science Monthly, Aug., 1952.

Humphreys, W. J.: Ways of the Weather. Ronald, 1942, 400 pp.

Kimble, George, and Bush, Raymond: The Weather. Penguin.

Pickwell, Gayle: Weather. Newman, 1937.

Price: Adventuring in Nature, chap. 7.

Schneider, H., and Burdick: Everyday Weather. Whittlesey.

Spilhaus, A.: Weathercraft. Viking.

Weather. Boy Scouts (#3816), 1943.

West and Hillcourt: Scout Field Book, Pow-wow 31.

Williams, Lou: Weather Handbook. Girl Scouts (#19–503), 1942.

## MAGAZINE ARTICLES

Berke, Jacqueline, and Wilson, Vivian: Weather and You . . . or Why Spoon Rhymes with June. Colliers, June 23, 1951. (Discussion of the effects of weather on moods and personality.)

Hamilton, Andrew: When Lightning Strikes. Popular Science Monthly, August, 1952.

Kolar, Edward A.: Is Your Camp Weather-Wise? C.M., Feb., 1951.

Miller, R. De Witt: Cosmic Jester. Coronet. April, 1948. (Tales of strange tricks played by lightning.)

Williams, Lou: Camp Weather Bureaus. C.M., June, 1938.

The Amateur Weathermen of America was established in 1947 and, since 1948, has published the magazine, *Weatherwise*, which now comes out six times a year. The address is Weatherwise, Franklin Institute, Philadelphia 3, Pa.

Afoot and light-hearted, I take to the open road,
Healthy, free, the world before me,
The long brown path before me, leading wherever I choose.

WALT WHITMAN*

## Chapter 20

# GETTING ABOUT IN THE OUT-OF-DOORS

### The Compass

THE ONLY way to tell directions accurately, either when making or following a map, is by using a reliable compass. Compasses come in several different styles. Some are set in the ends of waterproof matchboxes; others have a ring for attaching them to a chain or thong and fitting them into your pocket; a third is worn on a strap like a wrist watch. Still another type has a metal cover like a hunting-case watch and, although more expensive, is superior in that the cover protects the crystal and keeps out dust and moisture. The least moisture inside a compass causes the needle to catch or bind, and you must then dry out your compass with *gentle* heat.

### The Compass Card

The directions are printed on a dial called a *compass card*, two forms of which are common. One divides the circle into the *quadrants* (or fourths) North (N), East (E), South (S), and West (W), called *cardinal points*. These quadrants are in turn divided into fourths as N, NNE, NE, ENE, E, and so on. A reading such as NNE combines the names of the points on either side of it (e.g., North and Northeast, lie on either side of the point of which we are speaking, expressed as NNE; North and East, lie on either side of NE, and so on).

* From *Leaves of Grass*. Permission by Doubleday and Co., Inc.

The second and increasingly common way of marking a compass card gives the directions in terms of degrees; that is, North lies at 360 (or 0) degrees, NE at 45 degrees, East at 90 degrees, SE at 135 degrees, S at 180 degrees, and so on.

In most compasses used in camping the compass card is fixed and the needle moves about over it, but, in what is known as the *floating dial compass*, the needle is fixed and the compass card does the moving. The latter is easily read and handier to use in map-making, but is larger and more cumbersome to carry on a trip.

Some compasses have a moveable arrow which you can set in the direction you want to go so that you merely keep facing toward the arrow to stay on course.

## Using a Compass

The blue end of a compass needle is magnetized so that it always points North regardless of how you turn the compass. This magnetic attraction, however, causes any steel or iron close to it to deflect it, making it read inaccurately if you have a knife, hatchet or other piece of metal on your person or nearby. To test for such disturbance, lay the compass flat on the ground and walk a short distance away to see if the reading changes. Your compass is likewise inaccurate when you are near the metal in an overhead bridge, railroad tracks, or even an automobile.

To *orient* your compass, unwind the stem to allow

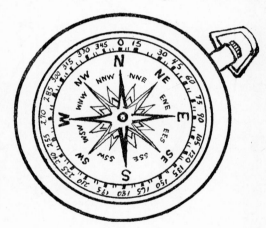

Compass.

the needle to move freely and hold it level in your hands and turn it until N on the compass card lies directly under N on the needle (the needle never becomes absolutely stationary, but continues to move about nervously). To take a *bearing* on an object, hold a pencil or knife blade across the face of your compass and point it directly toward the object, then read the direction on the compass card.

When you travel by compass, do not keep your eyes glued on it or you will stumble over everything in your path. Orient the compass, locate the desired direction on it and pick out some distant object such as a distinctive tree in direct line and start walking toward the object. When you get there, take a new bearing on another object and repeat the process.

Your compass probably has a way to lock the needle so that it does not swing freely; be sure to use it when you are through with the compass so that it will not be injured by rough jostling about.

## True North and Magnetic North

The needle of a compass is always attracted or points to a region about 1400 miles south of the North Pole along the northern edge of Canada called *Magnetic North*. In most regions of the United States *Magnetic North* and *True* or *Geographic North* do not coincide. The only exception is along a wavering, wandering line beginning approximately at Mackinac Island in Lake Michigan and passing diagonally downward across the United States just a

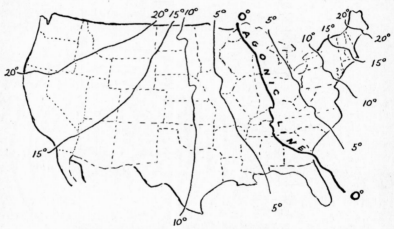

The Agonic Line and Compass Declinations.

little east of Florida. This is called the *Zero* or *Agonic Line*. In regions west of this line, the compass points increasingly east of North, while in regions east it points west of North. As we go farther from the Agonic Line, this *variation* or *declination* increases until it amounts to as much as 20 degrees in the extreme northeastern and northwestern sections of the country. The compass declination of a region is usually indicated on a map by two arrows, one pointing to Magnetic North, the other to True North. In camp trail mapping, you can ordinarily ignore the difference, and use Magnetic North as you read it on your compass. It is interesting to note that the Agonic Line is slowly moving westward, so that, as the years pass, points in the West will gradually coincide more nearly with True North, while those in the East will diverge farther and farther from it, but this will not happen in our lifetimes.

## FINDING YOUR WAY WITHOUT A COMPASS

When exploring unfamiliar territory, always carry a compass and carefully note the direction you take so that you can find your way back without wandering for hours worrying yourself and everyone back at camp as to your whereabouts. Most people become confused in trying to maintain a straight course through territory with no well-marked trails or with several trails, each looking equally inviting and "right." The harder you look, the more confused you become, for your intense scrutiny now causes you to see details not even noticed in your casual glance as you first came along.

Many seasoned explorers and wilderness guides claim to have developed a sixth sense for direction which instinctively tells them how to go. Rutstrum* refutes this by describing how a certain southern university proved that none of a goodly sample of explorers, guides, seamen and others could actually keep on a straight course without the use of their eyes. When blindfolded they, without exception, followed a more or less circular course, some circling to the right, others to the left, with none able to walk directly to the target as they had claimed. Some attributed this circling tendency to the fact that nearly everyone has one leg slightly shorter than the other, which would naturally cause him to circle toward the shorter leg, but the same circling persisted when they swam, drove a car, or directed the driving of a car from the back seat. Thus it appears that their ability to find their way probably depends on their unconsciously noting such things as the direction of the sun and the lay of the land.

This same circling tendency is seen in the old game in which a blindfolded person is turned about and then told to "pin the tail on the donkey." The poor donkey usually ends up with his tail fastened to most unlikely parts of his anatomy.

Woodsmen have long observed this tendency on the part of a person lost in the woods to circle about for days, gradually coming back to his approximate starting point. To avoid this, they advise picking out two trees in the direction chosen, walking straight toward them and picking out another in line with them before reaching the first so that three trees are always in view.

If you inadvertently stray from your group while wandering in the woods, don't get panicky but stop and think the situation over. Use your head and save your legs. Climb a high hill or tree and try to recognize landmarks to orient yourself again. If that doesn't help, follow a creek or river downstream, or a telephone or electric light line and you will surely come to human habitation before long. Look for smoke for it will indicate there is someone nearby. Go downhill rather than uphill. If it is getting dark don't wander around but settle down as comfortably as possible to wait for morning.

For those who lack a compass, old Mother Nature gives directions if we can but understand her language.

* Rutstrum, Calvin: *Way of the Wilderness*, rev. ed. The Burgess Publishing Company, 1952, pp. 5–6.

## Using Your Watch as a Compass

We know that, roughly speaking, the sun rises in the East and sets in the West, but we can tell directions even more accurately by means of a watch and the sun. Stand with your left shoulder toward the sun and hold your watch flat in your palm. Point the hour hand directly toward the sun and south is now located halfway between the hour hand and 12 o'clock the shortest way, clockwise (forward) in the morning and counterclockwise (backward) in the afternoon. If you are on Daylight Saving Time, be sure to allow for it for the preceding reckoning is based on Sun Time. On a cloudy day or if you want to be still more accurate, stand a knife blade or match up along the side of the watch and move them about until the shadow of the match falls directly along the hour hand; the hour hand is now pointed directly at the sun and you can proceed as before. Incidentally, you can set your watch fairly accurately by using a compass and reversing this process.

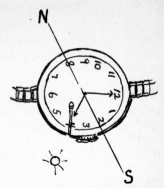

Finding South at Four o'Clock in the Afternoon.

## Telling Directions by the Stars

The stars are our oldest and most faithful guides to direction. When ancient literature speaks of "being guided by a star," it doubtless refers to the *North Star*, which is an even more accurate guide to direction than a compass, for it never varies more than one degree from True North no matter where you are in the United States.

To locate it, find the *Big Dipper* and *Little Dipper* in the sky. Stationed at the front edge of the Big Dipper are two stars known as the *Pointers* because they point directly to the North Star (also called the *Pole Star* or *Polaris*) in the tip of the Little Dipper's handle. The North Star always points due North and the Little Dipper makes a complete circle about it every twenty-four hours while the Big Dipper circles around the Little Dipper in the same length of time. The bowls of the two Dippers face so that they always seem to be pouring into each other.

There are many interesting myths about the stars. One tale relates how many years ago a tribe of Indians was living happily in the midst of good hunting and plenty until an extremely large mother bear and her cub came to the vicinity and frightened away all the small game. This brought famine to the Indians and they decided to send out their best hunters to kill the bears. After being pursued through many miles of wilderness, the bears finally climbed to the top of a tall mountain, where the mother bear, followed by

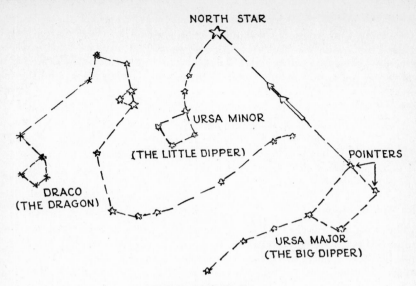

Finding the North Star.

her cub, leaped in desperation into the sky. The hunters began to shoot, and one arrow entered the cub's tail and pinned it fast in the Northern sky. This arrow is the North Star. The cub began running around its tail, and has continued to do so ever since, making one complete circuit each day. The mother bear's wounds show as the seven stars of the Big Dipper, and she remains to this day in the sky, running around her cub and likewise making one complete circuit a day. The Indians called the Big Dipper the Big Bear (Ursa Major) and the Little Dipper the Little Bear (Ursa Minor).

## The Moss on Trees

Everyone has no doubt heard that moss grows on the north side of trees, but we would stray considerably if we took the saying too literally. This sign does have a grain of truth in it, but, to rely on it, we must first make sure we are not mistaking the gray-green lichen commonly found growing on rocks and trees for true moss.

We must also learn to select the trees we inspect, for we can certainly not rely on *every* tree. Moss grows on any side of a tree where conditions are favorable, that is, where the tree holds moisture. Therefore, we must not depend on trees that are leaning or broken over or those with unusually rough spots on their bark. We must count only straight trees with a fairly smooth bark and not located in a heavily wooded section where they are shaded on all sides. The trees we examine must be normal ones where the moss tends to grow on the north side because the sun's rays reach it there for only a short time each day. Still we must not be satisfied until we have inspected several, taking the average and being careful not to be influenced by the bottoms of the trunks, where the moss grows more or less all around the tree.

## Tree Growth

A tree usually grows thickest and most luxuriantly on the south or sunny side and, in general, the annual growth rings on a stump are wider and the bark thicker on the north or northeast side, but here again we must take the average of several stumps.

N ᴛᴏ NE

Annual Rings are Usually Wider and Bark is Thicker on the North Side of a Tree.

## The Tips of Pines

The tip-top branches of pines, hemlocks and spruces ordinarily point slightly Southeast (toward the rising sun), but this is not necessarily true when they grow in deep valleys or on windswept hill tops where strong winds may distort them.

No one sign of nature is infallible, but the average of a number of them is reasonably reliable.

## MEASURING INACCESSIBLE DISTANCES

### To Measure the Height of a Tree or Cliff

If you want to measure the height of cliff, $ZY$, cut a small pole, $AC$, to your exact height, marking your eye level $B$, on it, and sharpening the end from $B$ to $C$. Estimate the height of the cliff and walk away the estimated distance, $XY$. Now lie prone with your head at $X$ and your feet toward the cliff, and mark the spot where your feet rest, $C$. Then drive in the stake at $C$ up to your eye-level mark and lie down again with your feet against the stake and look at the top of the cliff over the top of the stake. If your estimate was correct, the top of the stake and the top of the cliff will be in direct line with each other. You will no doubt have to make several adjustments, however, continuing to move the stake backward or forward and resighting over it until they are in line. Now apply the geometric formula, $AB{:}XC = ZY{:}XY$; since $AB$ and $XC$ were made equal, the height of the cliff, $ZY$, is equal to $XY$ and can easily be measured.

Preparing a Pole for Measuring Heights.

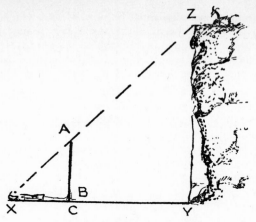

Measuring the Height of a Cliff.

An Indian method, not quite so accurate, but giving as exact a figure

Indian Method of Measuring Heights.

as is usually needed is to walk away from the object you want to measure until you can just see the top of it as you look through your legs while bent over with your hands on your ankles. The height of the object, $XY$, is, roughly, the same distance as $YZ$.

## Measuring the Width of an Object

To measure the width of an object such as a river or gorge, select a landmark easily distinguishable on the other side, such as tree, $Z$, and mark spot $X$ at a 90-degree angle directly opposite it. Now walk down the river bank until you reach a compass bearing of 45 degrees with the tree and mark spot $Y$. You have now outlined an isosceles triangle with $XY$ equal to $XZ$ and can determine the width of the river by measuring $XY$.

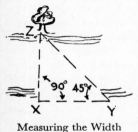

Measuring the Width
of a River.

## To Measure Depth

You can determine the approximate depth of a river, lake or chasm by dropping a rock and timing it until it hits bottom. Multiply the square of the number of seconds that elapse by 16, and the result is the approximate depth in feet.

## Learning to Estimate Measurements

Many boys and girls are notoriously poor at judging distances and heights, owing probably more to lack of practice than to any innate inability to do so. It is handy to be able to make such estimates, and the best way to acquire skill is by estimating simple things you can actually weigh or measure to check on your accuracy. Practice should give you ability to judge within 10 per cent of the correct answers most of the time.

In judging long distances, it sometimes helps to divide them mentally into short, well-known distances and then count the number of shorter distances in the long one. For instance, use a mental image of a yardstick to estimate the number of "yards" in an unknown distance.

In making rough estimates, it is useful to know some of your own measurements such as:

1. The length of your ordinary hiking pace.
2. The length of your foot in the type of shoe you ordinarily wear.
3. Your exact height and the distance from finger tip to finger tip with both arms outstretched (these distances are usually approximately the same, so that you can use one for measuring vertical heights, the other for horizontal ones).
4. A finger joint exactly an inch long.

## MAPS

A map is a bird's eye view of an area and there are many kinds, ranging from the complicated and detailed auto maps of the leading oil companies, to rough, homemade sketch maps designed to guide a person through relatively rough and unsettled country.

It is easy to understand how early peoples, even before they had any system of writing, made crude maps, for, in the main, they were migratory hunters who moved on to a new location when they had exhausted the supply of food where they were. Indians, particularly the Aztecs of Mexico, made such rough maps.

The most complete maps are those published by the Topographic Division of the United States Geological Survey; they are inexpensive and are excellent for all who travel on foot, on horseback or by canoe, for they give a graphic picture of what we will see on such a trip. They tell us where the hills are and how steep and high they are. They show streams and we can quickly determine the direction of their flow, for water always flows from small tributaries into larger main bodies of water; in fact, by reading the changes in elevation as the stream progresses, we can even estimate how swiftly the water will be flowing. Marshlands are indicated so that we can avoid camping near them and their mosquito inhabitants. Every valley and lake, as well as such man-made "improvements" as houses and bridges, are depicted. These maps are often available at local stores; if not, write to the United States Geological Survey, Department of Interior, Washington, D.C., and ask for a free "Index to Topographic Maps" of the state in which your area is located. This will show the various regional maps available so that you can select the one you want and send the small sum necessary to purchase it. Regional maps come on sheets approximately 30 by 38 inches.

The Coast and Geodetic Survey supplies similar maps for water travel, each showing about 40 miles of seacoast. Some of the larger inland bodies of water such as the Ohio and Mississippi Rivers have also been mapped.

Interesting maps are usually available from National Parks* and National Forests† and sometimes at State Parks. State Highway Departments often have detailed county maps.

### Getting Acquainted with a Map

A map usually contains many bits of information in one corner such as:
1. *Name or title* of the region depicted.
2. *Name of the person or firm* who made the map and *date* made (this is important, particularly in well-settled regions, where construction may entirely change the appearance of a locality within a few years).
3. *Compass direction* (maps are ordinarily laid out with North at the top, but the particular contour shown or the shape of the map sometimes makes it more convenient to do it otherwise; there will usually be two lines, one indicating True North and the other Magnetic North).
4. *A scale of distances* (the usual scale ranges from $\frac{1}{2}$ mile to the inch to 20 miles to the inch, depending on the map. It may be given by (1) words and figures, as 1 inch = 24,000 feet; (2) in the form of a ratio, as 1:24,000; or (3) as a fraction, 1/24,000. For making your own camp trail map, a ratio of 200 to 1000 feet to the inch is satisfactory. The scale is usually given also as a graphical scale or measuring bar; this is convenient, for you can quickly transfer it to a scrap of paper and lay it on the map to estimate distances between points).
5. *A key or legend* explaining the meaning of the various symbols used on the map.

When reading a map, you must first orient it by laying it flat on the ground or table and turning it until North on the map lies parallel with North as shown on your compass.

### Principles of Making a Map

A person who draws or makes maps is known as a *cartographer;* campers sometimes enjoy becoming amateur cartographers. Before starting, it is wise to make a brief study of the principles of map-making and get several types of maps and study them carefully. Map study is a fascinating hobby for many.

---

* National Park Service, U.S. Dept. of the Interior, Washington 25, D.C.
† Forest Service, U.S. Dept. of Agriculture, Washington 25, D.C.

*Rough-Sketching Your Map.*    When making a map, it is more interesting to travel cross-country, choosing a route not more than a mile or two in length and with a variety of things to show along the way. Take a compass, a pencil, and notebook or a few sheets of paper tacked on a piece of thin board or held on a clip board to make a rough sketch map as you hike along. Quadrille or cross-section paper is convenient, since you can let each square represent a certain number of feet or strides.

The traditional way to measure distances for a trail map is to count strides, for, when you know the length of your average stride, you can easily change your total strides into feet or yards.

A *step* and a *pace* are the same thing, and a *stride* equals two steps. In counting strides, then, you need only count each time your left foot contacts the ground.

To determine the length of your stride, lay off a distance of 100 yards with a tape measure or yard stick, and, starting with your toe at the starting line, count your strides as you walk exactly as when on a cross-country hike of several miles' duration. Make several trials and find the average number of strides you took. Now divide 3600 (the number of inches in the 100 yards) by the number of strides and you will know how many inches you cover at a stride. Some advocate cultivating a step of a yard, but this would be an unnatural and fatiguing pace for many.

To avoid having to count high numbers when striding off distances for a map, you can count out a certain number of pebbles, throwing one away each twenty to fifty strides so you need only count the remaining pebbles to find the number of strides you took. Some measure their average hiking speed and estimate distance by the time elapsed when hiking steadily.

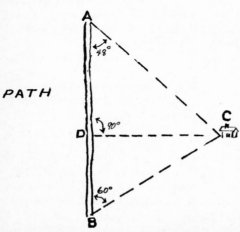

When estimating distances, you must remember that your step is shortened when going up or down hill, particularly if the hill is steep.

When you are ready to rough draft your map, mark your starting point on the paper, pick out an object some distance away on your path, take a compass bearing on it and start out, counting your strides as you go. If you see objects you want to include along the way, jot them down in your sketch map, making any notes you think will be helpful later on. When you reach the object

Locating an Object at the Side of the Road.

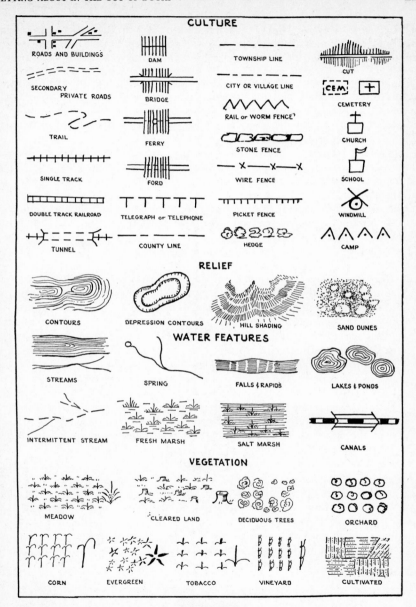

Map Symbols.

sighted, pick out another, take the new compass bearing and proceed as before.

When there is an object off at the side you want to show, such as the old deserted house, *C*, take a compass bearing some distance from it, *A*, and count strides to *B*, and take another bearing. By projecting the two angles on the map and properly plotting distance *AB* to scale, you can locate the old house at *C*, where the lines intersect. If you want to know how far back from the path the old house sits, you need only measure perpendicular distance, *CD*, on the map and translate it by scale.

A *pedometer* is a small instrument, looking somewhat like a pocket watch, which, when worn freely suspended so that it is jostled at each step, measures distances covered. It is adjustable so that you can set it according to the length of your step.

*Map Symbols.*     Certain symbols are in general use on maps and make it possible for one person to understand maps made by others. These symbols are of four types:

1. *Culture,* or the works of man, such as bridges, houses, dams, and so forth, which are done in black.
2. *Relief,* or relative elevations and depressions, above or below sea level, sometimes drawn in brown. These are indicated by *contour lines,* explained in the legend in the lower right hand corner of the map. All points on a single contour line are the same elevation, and each line indicates a rise or fall of a certain number of feet (from 5 to 250 feet, depending on the map). To estimate the height of a hill, you need only count the number of contour lines to the top and multiply by the number of feet represented by the distance between each line. When contour lines are widely spaced, they indicate a gradual slope; when close together, a steep one; lines falling practically on top of each other indicate a cliff or mountainside. Large numbers of contour lines widely spread over the countryside signify that the whole region is hilly.
3. *Water features,* such as lakes, are always done in blue if colors are used.
4. *Vegetation,* such as woods and crops, are shown in black, blue, or green.

For convenience, maps are often drawn in black instead of colors. Common map symbols are simple and bear a rough resemblance to what they depict. You may have to invent symbols for unusual objects; make them bear likeness to what they represent and explain them in your legend. Just for practice, start in the lower right corner and take an imaginary trip around the path indicated in Camp Idlewilde. Write out what you would see.

## Making the Map

When you have completed your rough sketch map, translate it to your real map as soon as possible while the details are still fresh in your memory. Use a ruler, compass and protractor to insure accuracy and don't worry if the path on which you finish fails to exactly coincide with the point from

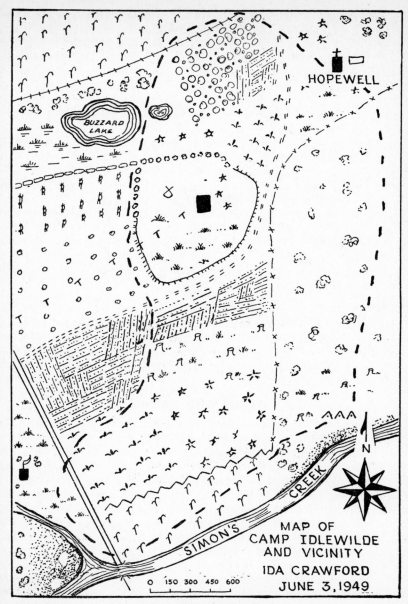

A Trail Map. (Scale in Feet.)

which you started for such a deviation is common with the crude instruments and measurements used and is called the *error of closure*. Keep your symbols small. Use black India ink, supplementing it with colors if you wish.

Keep the purpose of your map in mind. If it is intended for others to follow, too many details will only be confusing. If it is to be principally a decorative wall map, make it a gaily colored "romance" or picture map. You can give it a parchment-like appearance by daubing it lightly with a bit of linseed oil or painting it with yellow shellac. The shellac will also help to preserve it if it is to see actual use on the trail.

A papier-mâché *relief map* is even more decorative and far more realistic than a flat map. To make it, tear a quantity of old newspapers into small scraps and soak them for several hours in hot water. Then mix and press them in your hands until they are assimilated into a "gooey" mixture. Squeeze out all the water possible, and mix in some soft library paste. Model on a piece of stiff cardboard or board previously laid off to scale and make hills, valleys and gentle slopes to scale and finish them just as realistically as possible. When dry, apply a coat or two of enamel or poster paint and draw in details with India or colored ink. If desired, you may add tents, buildings, trees and other forms of vegetation made out of suitable materials and glued on.

### Orienteering

This is a game imported from the Scandinavian countries and becoming increasingly popular in this country. It combines cross-country travel with the use of map and compass and can be adapted to the abilities and interests of both younger and older campers. Write the Silva Company, LaPorte, Indiana, for further information.

### TRAILS AND SIGNALS

Trails are as old as mankind, for it is impossible for any creature to go through wooded territory without leaving some trace. Such obscure signs as a track in the mud or sand, a branch accidentally broken off, or a vine carelessly torn by the foot, though easily overlooked by the tenderfoot, are quite obvious to one skilled and practiced in following trails or *stalking*.

The first trails were made by the big game animals when going to and from their favorite feeding grounds, water holes or salt licks. The Indians, then the pioneer trappers and explorers on foot or on pack horse, and, finally, covered wagons and stage coaches followed these same trails making them ever wider and better established with each passage. We still find many of them preserved in the routes of our railways and superhighways.

The original paths were seldom made in valleys, but kept to the ridges in hilly or mountainous country where there were few streams to ford and the traveler could command a wide view of the surrounding countryside and thus protect himself from a surprise ambush.

## Blazes

The favorite pioneer method of marking a trail through the wilderness was by *blazing*, which meant going along and periodically using an axe or sheath knife to take a chip out of a tree. This exposed the white surface under the bark which was easily apparent from some distance.

There were several ways of blazing trails. One, called the *line blaze*, faced the traveler so that, as he came to one blaze, the next appeared ahead of him. An extraordinarily long slash indicated a change in direction. The line blaze was used when others were to follow the trail blazer. If he wanted to avoid being followed, he merely reversed the process, making the blazes on the other side of the trees where no one would be likely to see them but he as he retraced his steps over the trail. This was known as a *blind trail*.

Blazes are still used in certain sparsely settled regions. One form is seen in the *lop sticks* of the Northland, where the lower branches of tall, straight trees are cut away, leaving peculiar specimens which stand out at great distances.

When our forefathers came to America they found so many trees that they looked upon them as a nuisance and their only thought was to get rid of them just as quickly as possible. Of course we would not even consider using any of these types of blazing today in the regions of organized camping, for trees are far too precious to be mutilated in this way. We now know that such a wound to the bark of a tree is just as injurious as a cut or break in our own skin, for it makes an opening for parasites and disease to initiate their damaging, perhaps even fatal attacks.

## Modern Methods of Laying Trails

1. *Brush Blazes.*    The brush blaze was a favorite Indian way of trail marking. It consisted of breaking a branch of a shrub every hundred yards or so, leaving it still attached with the lighter, under sides of its leaves exposed to attract the attention of the traveler. The branches were left pointing in the direction to be taken. An abrupt change in direction was indicated by breaking the branch completely off and laying it so that its butt end pointed in the new direction. The butt was sometimes supported in the fork of a crotched stick to make it still more evident.

It is still permissible to use this method in regions where the underbrush is heavy and a few broken branches will never be missed.

2. *Grass.*    In prairie regions, where fairly long grass is abundant and trees and shrubs are scarce, tie wisps of grass in a knot, leaving the heads straight up if the trail lies straight ahead, and breaking them over in the correct direction if a change is to be made.

3. *Rocks.*    Along the seashore or in arid regions where there is practically no vegetation, use rocks to mark a trail. A small rock on top of a large one indicates "this is the trail"; a smaller rock placed at one side of these

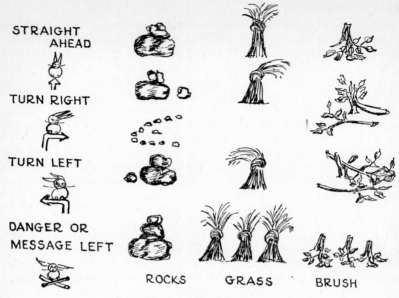

STRAIGHT AHEAD

TURN RIGHT

TURN LEFT

DANGER OR MESSAGE LEFT

ROCKS        GRASS        BRUSH

Common Trail Signs.

two means turn in the direction of the smaller rock. Pebbles are sometimes placed in the form of a "V" to show directions.

4. *Other Ways.* Paper or chalk are sometimes used for trail marking, but, in order not to mar nature's beauty, those following the trail should be instructed to gather them up or erase them as they come along.

Another way of trail marking, which requires keen powers of observation, is to have the leader or trail maker wear a shoe with some distinguishing mark such as a brad or a peculiar heelplate. Following such a trail makes an interesting game to test and train one's powers of perception.

Original ways of marking a trail are sometimes used to suit a particular purpose; if you want those following to do so quickly and easily, make your signs obvious and frequent. If you are testing their powers of observation, make the signs just clear and frequent enough to be barely discernible to a keen eye.

It is fun to have a progressive supper hike with the trail blazers going ahead to lay the trail while the rest of your group follow it to find first course, main dish, dessert and finally the rendezvous for program. Use codes or methods of laying a trail as you wish or prepare cards, giving compass directions and distances which the group (small) must follow accurately to find their suppers. Plan alternate routes and divide the group up if there are many members.

## Danger or Distress Signals

Three of anything has been long and widely known as a signal of danger or distress. Three rocks placed on top of each other, three clumps of grass, three blazes on trees, three smudge fires, three steamboat whistles, or three gunshots are examples. Note that the Morse code applies this principle in its call for help, SOS, which consists of three dots, three dashes, and three dots.

Make a *smudge* fire as a smoke signal for help by placing three fires just far enough apart to be distinguishable at a distance. Build a good fire and get it going well. Then pile noninflammable materials such as green or rotten wood or wet leaves on it to make it "smudge" or smoke. Friends in camp or the everwatchful fire warden in his fire tower will soon see the signal and send help. Never give a distress signal just for fun, lest it be ignored in time of real need like the plea of the little boy who cried "wolf" too often.

## SIGNALING

### The Morse Code

The most universally used and understood code is the International Morse Code, which uses dots and dashes to spell out messages. It may be adapted to many means of communication giving the dot by a short flash or sound and the dash by a long one (held about three times as long).

Wireless telegraphy uses this system, and you may also send messages with a lantern, flashlight, torch, whistle, drum, a blazing fire (hidden periodically with a blanket), or a mirror used to reflect the sun's rays. When using a smudge fire for transmitting smoke signals in Morse code, two persons hold a blanket above the fire, removing it periodically to allow large billows of smoke to rise and spell out the message.

Pause and count three to indicate the end of a letter; pause and count five at the end of a word, and pause still longer for the end of a sentence. Work for accuracy and clearness rather than speed. When first practicing receiving the Morse code, it is best to use two persons, one for calling out the dots and dashes as they come in, the other writing it down for later decoding. The Morse code can also be used to signal with flags.

*Alphabet*

| | | | |
|---|---|---|---|
| A | .— | N | —. |
| B | —... | O | ——— |
| C | —.—. | P | .——. |
| D | —.. | Q | ——.— |
| E | . | R | .—. |
| F | ..—. | S | ... |
| G | ——. | T | — |
| H | .... | U | ..— |
| I | .. | V | ...— |
| J | .——— | W | .—— |
| K | —.— | X | —..— |
| L | .—.. | Y | —.—— |
| M | —— | Z | ——.. |

*Numerals*

| | | | |
|---|---|---|---|
| 1 | .———— | 6 | —.... |
| 2 | ..——— | 7 | ——... |
| 3 | ...—— | 8 | ———.. |
| 4 | ....— | 9 | ————. |
| 5 | ..... | 0 | ————— |

International Morse Code.

### Written Codes

It is fairly simple to work out a secret code for a cabin or group of campers to write messages which cannot be interpreted by others.

Here are three examples of codes; use your ingenuity to make up your own original one.

| | 1 | 2 | 3 | 1 | 2 | | 3 | 1 | | 2 | 3 | 1 | 2 | 3 | | 1 | 2 | 3 |
|---|---|---|---|---|---|---|---|---|---|---|---|---|---|---|---|---|---|---|
| *Message* | S | H | A | L | L | | W | E | | S | L | E | E | P | | O | U | T |
| *Code* | T | J | D | M | N | | Z | F | | U | O | F | G | S | | P | W | W |

Add one, two or three letters in sequence as indicated to each letter of the real message.

| | −1 | +1 | −1 | +1 | −1 | +1 | −1 | +1 | −1 | +1 | −1 | +1 | −1 |
|---|---|---|---|---|---|---|---|---|---|---|---|---|---|
| *Message* | W | I | L | L | W | E | H | I | K | E | O | U | T |
| *Code* | V | J | K | M | V | F | G | J | J | F | N | V | S |

Alternately subtract one letter, then add one, to the real meassage.

Angle Code.*

You can write an invisible note to a friend, using pure lemon juice. The paper is apparently blank and only he knows how to bring it out by pressing over it briefly with a warm iron.

## ADDITIONAL READINGS

Art of Living Out of Doors in Maine, The. Maine Camp Directors' Association.

Campcraft Skills Flip Charts (Compass and Maps). Girl Scouts.

Hedenstrom, Stig, and Kjellstrom, Bjorn: The Sport of Orienteering. Silva, 1948.

Jaeger, Ellsworth: Tracks and Trailcraft. Macmillan, 1948.

Jaeger, Ellsworth: Wildwood Wisdom. Macmillan, chaps. 15 and 16.

Kephart: Camping and Woodcraft. Macmillan, vol. 2, chaps. 2–6.

Larson, E. F.: Orienteering in Camp. Silva.

Mustard, Major C. A.: By Map and Compass—An Introduction to Orienteering. Silva, 1950.

Rutstrum, Calvin: Way of the Wilderness. Burgess, chap. 2 and pp. 91–93.

Signaling. Boy Scouts (#3237), 1940.

Surveying. Boy Scouts (#3327), 1942.

Weaver, Robert W., and Merrill, Anthony F.: Camping Can Be Fun. Harper, chap. 13.

West, James E., and Hillcourt, William: Scout Field Book, Pow-wows 4–8, 10.

* Gibson: Recreational Programs for the Summer Camp, p. 51

There are camp fires unkindled
and songs unsung,
And the untraveled miles of the
trail.
There are unbroken dreams 'neath
whispering trees,
Till the stars of the morning grow
pale.

CHART PITT*

# Chapter 21

# HIKING

HIKING is fun and almost everyone enjoys it, whether for the purpose of getting somewhere, exploring a particular spot, or just taking a ramble like the bear's trip over the mountain "to see what he could see."

The wise hiker wears clothing which is both comfortable and appropriate (see Chap. 27).

## How to Hike

*Your Feet.* Since each of your feet comes down and momentarily bears your weight about a thousand times for each mile, they deserve a maximum of care and attention. Never start on a long hike without having gradually toughened yourself to it by a series of shorter hikes.

Blisters are caused by friction as shoes rub over skin, and it is far more satisfactory to prevent than to treat them. Soaping the backs of your heels and inside heels of your socks and dusting your feet and the insides of your socks with talcum or foot powder help immensely. At the first sign of redness or soreness at any point, apply a piece of adhesive tape to take the friction and save your skin. However, never apply tape over a blister that has already started to form.

* From *Field and Stream:* Romany Road.

*Using Your Body.*    Walk with a rhythmic swing of your whole body, not with a city sidewalk swing from your hips as you hold your upper trunk motionless. Point your toes straight ahead (Indian style), not out like a duck in a way both fatiguing to you and hard on your arches. When you toe out, you may shorten your stride by an inch or more and so have to take several hundred extra steps on a five-mile hike.

Walk Like an Indian,
Not Like a Duck.

Do not make a hike a speed or endurance contest; what you do and see along the way is far more important than how far you go. Strike a steady pace that you can maintain indefinitely and rest five or ten minutes out of every hour when on a long hike. Avoid resting too long lest your leg and back muscles stiffen, and relax completely, lying flat on your back with feet propped up on a convenient rock or tree so that the blood which has collected in your legs and feet will drain away.

If your group hikes ten miles in three or four hours it is making good progress. The *Scout's pace*, which consists of dog trotting for a certain number of paces (thirty to fifty), then walking the same number of paces, eats up the miles steadily and rapidly. You can cover a mile in ten to twelve minutes in this fashion without undue fatigue. Although swift Indian runners were said to cover one hundred or more miles between dawn and dusk, fifteen or twenty will usually be sufficient for even the oldest and most seasoned hikers in an organized camp. Unless you are really trying to cover a certain distance in a limited time, it's more fun to hike at a moderate pace, allowing time to stop and examine anything that looks interesting along the way.

Place a good, but not the fastest hiker ahead as pace setter having him strike a medium pace suitable for even the weaker ones. Groups are most successful when composed of those of approximately the same age and physical stamina, so that the strong do not have to wait for the slow or the latter overdo in an effort to keep up.

A good woodsman never steps on anything he can step over or go around and thus avoids undue fatigue and sprained ankles.

## Where to Hike

Stay off main highways whenever possible for cross-country hiking is less dangerous, the soft ground and grass of field and forest are less fatiguing on your feet and it is more interesting to ramble off the beaten path where you can see nature's handiwork unmarred by man. Hold low-hanging branches aside for the person following you.

When traveling in groups on a busy highway, divide into twos or threes and spread out in single file or walk not more than two abreast and entirely off the pavement on the left side of the road so as to face oncoming traffic. Walking on a highway at night is particularly dangerous; avoid it except in emergency and then wear something white and carry a lighted lantern or flashlight to warn approaching vehicles. It is dangerous to walk along a railroad track and perfectly foolhardy to walk over a railroad trestle at any time.

Hitchhiking is, of course, taboo for hikers. Not only is riding with strangers extremely dangerous and even against the law in some states, but, if you are a red-blooded camper, you will want to be independent enough to go the whole way on your own two feet.

When hiking cross-country show due respect for the property of others, for every stick, stone, flower and fruit tree is someone's property and he may feel about it like the old farmer who said of his wife, "She ain't much, but she's mine!" Respect "no trespassing" signs—they have been put up because of damage done by previous travelers and may be assumed to mean just what they say. Close gates behind you if you found them that way, and avoid climbing fences for it is easy to break them down and permanently damage them.

Do not walk across cultivated fields, but stay close along the edges where no crops have been planted. Pick fruit or flowers only when given express permission to do so.

## Don't Cool Off by Evaporation

To remain in perspiration-soaked clothing is just as dangerous as to stay in rain-soaked clothing insofar as bringing on a cold is concerned. When on a trip of any length, always carry a change of clothing with you and do not hesitate to take time to slip into it if you get wet. This applies particularly to wearing wet socks and wet shoes. They will make your feet sore and tender and may cause you to catch cold. If no change is possible, it is well to stop, build a fire, and dry out thoroughly before proceeding.

## When Dry Enough to Spit Cotton

Thirst is often due to a drying out of the tissues lining your mouth rather than to any real need for water, and so is best relieved by merely rinsing your mouth instead of gulping down large quantities of water. Candy eaten along the way is sure to induce thirst; munching raisins or other dried fruit or sucking on a prune pit is preferable. Carry your own canteens of water unless you know there are *safe* sources at frequent intervals along the way (see p. 376).

## Make the Miles Fly

Think of interesting things to do to make the miles go faster. A continuous round-robin story with each unexpectedly called upon to take up the story at a given signal, singing merry hiking songs, marching in strict "military fashion" for variation, and engaging in hiking games serve this purpose. Sing sweetly and talk quietly; don't annoy others by loud, boisterous conduct.

## Kinds of Hikes

Every hike should have a purpose, so that all will return with a feeling of mission accomplished. The following are examples.

1. *Carefree Hike:* to some interesting or beautiful spot where you meet to cook an outdoor meal, hold a program, or carry on some other project.

2. *Breakfast Hike:* to a good vantage point to see the sun rise and to cook breakfast. You can also take supper or lunch hikes.

3. *Star Hike:* to a hill on a clear evening to study the stars and their legends. Take your blanket rolls for an overnight sleep-out.

4. *Fishing Trip:* to fish in a nearby stream or lake. Take a lunch and, with luck, supplement it with fresh fish.

5. *Bee Line or Crow Flight Hike:* follow a compass bearing as closely as possible to see what interesting scenery you encounter on the way.

6. *Historical Hike:* to some historical place on which you have previously briefed yourself by reading or consulting local people.

7. *Moonlight Hike:* to see how entirely different nature folk live at night.

8. *Camera Hike:* to see who can snap the most interesting photographs.

9. *Nature Hike:* to study interesting flowers, trees, animals, insects, and the like, along the way.

10. *Map Hike:* use a compass and map and collect notes for use in constructing a trail map or try to follow a trail map someone else has constructed (see Chap. 20).

11. *Rain Hike:* waterproof yourselves thoroughly and go out to see how animals and plants conduct themselves in the rain.

12. *Creek's or River's End Hike:* follow a creek or river to its origin or mouth.

13. *Overnight Hike:* find a good place to spend the night, cook breakfast, and return to camp.

14. *Sealed Orders Hike:* give the group a set of sealed directions with a new one to be opened each time the previously designated spot is reached. You can give the clues in poetry form or in riddle or code so that the group must decipher them. Do not make them so difficult that the hikers lose interest or lose their way completely. It is best not to have more than five or six in a group.

15. *Progressive Supper Hike:* lay a nature trail which hikers must follow in order to find their suppers. Serve different courses progressively along the way, with desert at the last station where the evening program is to be held.

16. *Trail Clearing Hike:* find and clear a new trail and establish an outpost camp at the end. Leave a supply of wood for the next group.

17. *Hare and Hound Hike:* the "hares" start out, leaving some not too conspicuous trail signs (see pp. 231–232) along the way. The "hounds" leave later at a specified time and try to follow the trail of the "hares." The object is to spot the hares, who may hide any place within 50 feet of the trail. If a hare is able to stay out of sight until all the hounds have passed him on the trail, he gets in "free." Hares seen are "caught." Use small groups, separating them and laying several trails if there are too many for one.

18. *Hold the Front:* the participants draw for places and assume that order in single file. The object is to get and maintain the position at the head of the line. The leader asks the head to identify a nature object seen along the way; if he does it correctly, he holds his position; if not, those behind him are given a chance in turn to identify it, the one who finally does so passing all those who failed and so automatically pushing them all back one place in line. The leader then asks a new question of the person just behind the one who answered correctly. If he misses, those behind him have a similar chance to advance to his place in line. The person at the head of the line when the game ends, wins.

19. *Roadside Cribbage:* give each player the same number of counters (ten to twenty acorns, pebbles, or such). Then give each a list of objects, such as specific kinds of birds, trees or flowers. As they hike along, each looks for the specified objects, and the first to see one calls "pegs" and throws away one of his counters. The player who first gets rid of all his counters wins the game. If a player doubts that the one who called "pegs" really saw the object he claimed or that he identified it correctly, he can challenge him; if correct, the challenger must accept the other's counter; if not, the player takes back his counter and also receives one from the challenger.

20. *Hike to Another Camp:* this would be done, of course, only by invitation or previous arrangement.

21. *Ride out by Bus or Camp Truck:* then hike back.

22. *Conservation Hike:* discover places where erosion or other examples of poor conservation are taking place. Return and remedy them later.

No matter what kind of a hike you take, do not let it degenerate into a prosaic walk. Cloak it in an aura of glamour and adventure for small children by pretending they are a band of giants, little elves, colorful gypsies or bold, swaggering pirates. Whatever the realm of fancy of the campers, it is much more fun to hike in the land of "let's pretend." You must, of course, adapt your methods to the ages of the group. Plan your hike, no matter how short it is. Meet as a group to decide where to go, what to do, what to wear, and what equipment to take, how to pack it, and how to divide up the jobs on the way and at your destination. Avoid returning over the same territory, if you can.

## ADDITIONAL READINGS

Geist, Roland C.: Hiking, Camping and Mountaineering. Harper, 1943, chaps. 1 and 3.

Hammett, Catherine T., and Musselman, Virginia: The Camp Program Book, chap. 12.

Hiking. Boy Scouts (#3380), 1944.

Hiking—In Town and Country. Girl Scouts (#19–641), 1952, 47 pp.

Hiking. NRA (MP 85).

Progressive Suppers. Camp Publications, No. 61.

Treasure Hunts. NRA.

West, James E., and Hillcourt, William: Scout Field Book, Pow-wows 3 and 11.

First the thought, and then the act,
Before the dream becomes a fact.
H. S. WALTER*

## Chapter 22

## TINCANCRAFT

A TIN CAN is one of the most versatile objects conceived by the human mind. Washed out, it can be used for a cup; turned upside down, it acts as a stove; flattened out, it becomes a tray, a shade or anything that your creative mind designs. So, the next time you start to throw away a tin can, stop to consider how very easily a little time and effort could convert it into a useful object.

The tools you need for working with tin are few and inexpensive, and so common that most homes or camps already have them. Tin snips, cotton gloves, pliers, hammer, file, and nails or nail sets are all that are really essential. If decorative articles are your goal, you will need steel wool to polish the metal.

It is possible to purchase sheet tin at a hardware store, but it is simple to get your own free by cutting and straightening out a tin can of suitable size. Incidentally, tin cans are really misnamed for they are only about 2 per cent tin found in thin layers coating both sides of a layer of steel. You can make helpful and attractive things from them, and they will also give you preliminary training in using tools and patterns preparatory to working with such relatively expensive metals as copper, aluminum, silver and brass. If you make a mistake, you can simply throw it away and begin again with the loss of nothing more serious than a little time. Scrap wire for handles is free for the picking up in neighboring scrap heaps.

* Permission by The Indianapolis News.

Tin cans are available in almost any shape and size desired, varying from the small, flat tobacco tins which make good match cases to large oil cans. The standard sizes used for canning fruits and vegetables are as follows:

> #1—large evaporated milk cans
> #2—most canned vegetables
> #3—canned tomatoes
> #5—twice the size of a #3 can
> #10—gallon size, available from restaurants, dormitories, camps, and elsewhere

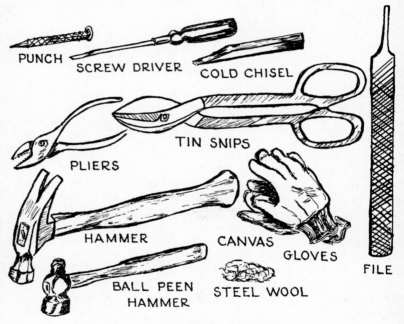

PUNCH    SCREW DRIVER    COLD CHISEL

TIN SNIPS

PLIERS

HAMMER    CANVAS GLOVES

FILE

BALL PEEN HAMMER    STEEL WOOL

Tools for Tincraft.

## Safety

Always wear cotton gloves when working with tin, for there is great danger of cutting yourself on the jagged, sharp edges, and also of getting blisters from the unaccustomed use of heavy tin snips.

It is wise to first make a paper pattern of the object you want to create, fitting it together and altering it until it meets your complete approval. Then trace it on the tin and begin to cut. Work slowly and carefully to insure a more finished product and to avoid injuring your hands. Smooth jagged edges with a file or snip back the edge a short distance every $\frac{1}{4}$ to $\frac{1}{8}$ inch, place a circle of wire around to stiffen it and turn back the edge over the wire with pliers. It is then best to fit the object over a wooden post or butt of a small log and pound the turned over edge flat with a hammer.

### General Hints

To pierce holes, place the article over a tree stump or block of wood, and use a hammer and nail set, ice pick or other sharp object of appropriate size. Use holes for decoration, for inserting a wire handle, or for suspending the object from a nail.

### Cooking Utensils

You can make a complete set of nested cooking utensils by choosing tin cans of appropriate sizes as shown in A in the figure on page 244. Be sure to equip them with detachable handles so that they will nest compactly. You can also make many other useful camp "fixings" as shown in the drawings. Kettles, stew pans, plates, and frying pans are best made from no. 10 or gallon tin cans cut to appropriate depths. Cups are made from no. 2 or no. 2$\frac{1}{2}$ cans, while no. 2$\frac{1}{2}$ or no. 5 cans are about right for cereal bowls. Heat all tin-can cooking or eating utensils and scrub them thoroughly with hot water and a good scouring powder to remove the lacquer usually present on them. Use only cans that have contained food, not paint or oil, for cooking utensils.

### Hobo Stoves

Hobo stoves (C, page 244) are handy little cooking devices that will heat up in no time at all with just a handful of

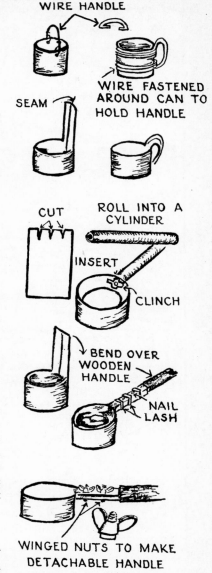

WIRE HANDLE

SEAM

WIRE FASTENED AROUND CAN TO HOLD HANDLE

CUT

ROLL INTO A CYLINDER

INSERT

CLINCH

BEND OVER WOODEN HANDLE

NAIL LASH

WINGED NUTS TO MAKE DETACHABLE HANDLE

Ways of Adding Handles.

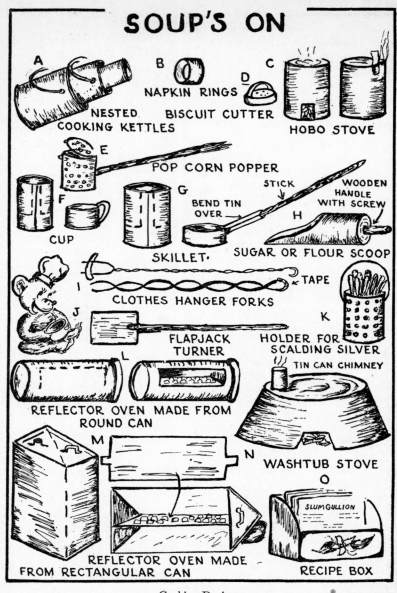

Cooking Devices.

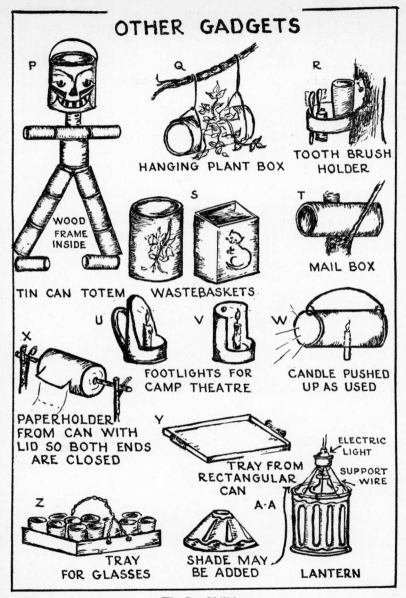

# OTHER GADGETS

P

Q

R
TOOTH BRUSH
HOLDER

HANGING PLANT BOX

WOOD
FRAME
INSIDE

S

T
MAIL BOX

TIN CAN TOTEM    WASTEBASKETS

X

U

V

W
CANDLE PUSHED
UP AS USED

FOOTLIGHTS FOR
CAMP THEATRE

PAPERHOLDER
FROM CAN WITH
LID SO BOTH ENDS
ARE CLOSED

Y

ELECTRIC
LIGHT

SUPPORT
WIRE

TRAY FROM
RECTANGULAR
CAN

Z

A-A

TRAY
FOR GLASSES

SHADE MAY
BE ADDED

LANTERN

Tin Can Utilities.

twigs for fuel. Before you cook on them, heat them and thoroughly scrub the tops to remove the lacquer. An excellent stove large enough to support several pots and pans can be made from an old wash tub or wash boiler.

You can make a compact hobo stove* by cutting off the top of a no. 10 tin can and slicing the sides into three or four strips which will pack almost flat; when ready to use, merely stick the sides solidly into the ground and balance the top over them.

## Other Articles

To make a useful and decorative set of kitchen containers, select tin cans of the right size and enamel them (two coats, for permanence) in any color scheme desired. Paint the name of the contents on the outside, and further decorate them with decalcomania designs. If you wish, you can buy glass or wooden knobs at the ten cent or hardware store. Waxing or painting the outside with clear lacquer further preserves them.

If you want a bright metal finish instead of an enameled one, burnish the outside with steel wool. Another method of finishing is to hold the object over the fire until it assumes a cloudy dullness, then quickly burnish it with a brush and a good scouring powder.

To make an anchor for the candle in a candle holder, cut an "X" in the bottom and bend the edges up until they are the right size to fit snugly around the candle.

### ADDITIONAL READINGS

Also see page 136

Bell, Enid: Tin-Craft as a Hobby. Harper.
Hamilton, Edwin T.: Tin Can Craft. Dodd, Mead, 1935.
Jaeger, Ellsworth: Wildwood Wisdom, pp. 190–195.
Lukowitz, Joseph J.: 55 New Tin Can Projects. Bruce, 1936.
Mason, Bernard S.: Junior Book of Woodcraft, pp. 90, 91.
Mason, Bernard S.: Woodcraft, chap. 23.

* "Suggestions for Improvised Camping Out Equipment," Camp Publications.

The Yankee boy, before he's sent to school,
Well knows the mysteries of that magic
    tool,
The pocket-knife. To that his wistful eye
Turns while he hears his mother's lullaby;
His hoarded cents he gladly gives to get it,
Then leaves no stone unturned till he can
    whet it;
And in the education of the lad
No little part that implement hath had.
His pocket-knife to the young whittler
    brings
A growing knowledge of material things.
                              JOHN PIERPONT

# Chapter 23

# KNIFEMANSHIP AND TOOLCRAFT

THE KNIFE, along with the gun and the axe, was an important tool of the pioneer. It is also important to the camper, for its usefulness ranges from making fuzz sticks or clumps to start a stubborn fire and handy gadgets to use around the campsite to the making of such decorative articles as totem poles, lapel pins, and so forth, and girls become quite as skilled as boys in its use when carefully taught and enthusiastically encouraged. No one who has observed the promiscuous carving of initials and designs in places where they don't belong can doubt that the urge to carve is deep. It is just as easy to channel it into constructive rather than destructive paths.

## Choosing Your Knife

A knife on the order of the Boy or Girl Scout knife with its several blades is usually best for general camp use. It should be strong and fit well in your hand. A certain amount of roughness on the handle is necessary for a firm grip, but too much may cause blisters if you use the implement extensively. You can locate your knife more readily if you should happen to drop it in the duff if it has a brightly colored handle.

A cheap knife is poor economy, for it is likely to be of inferior quality and fail to give satisfactory and long performance. It seldom has good steel in its blade so that no amount of vigorous and skillful sharpening will keep it keen. Blades made of soft steel will not hold an edge, and those which are too hard will chip easily.

Keep your *reamer* on your scout knife sharp, for it is used to bore holes in leather and other substances.

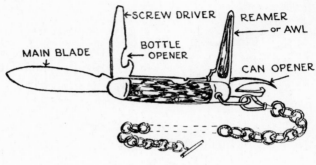

Scout Knife.

Since the usual camp knife has only one blade suitable for whittling, an advanced whittler may prefer to own a special whittling knife with two or three blades of various shapes and sizes which are better adapted to intricate carving. However, it is amazing what work a skilled workman can do with an ordinary jackknife.

## Caring for Your Knife

A knife is a high-class tool and, as such, deserves the best treatment. Keep it clean and dry at all times, and immediately remove all rust and stain with scouring powder or ashes from your campfire dampened with a little water.

Never use your knife to poke in the fire or to stir hot food, for extreme heat ruins the temper of the blade so that it will never again hold a sharp edge. Warm the blade on a cold day by holding it in your hands a few moments so that it will not chip.

Never leave a knife lying carelessly around. Keep it in your pocket, fastened by a chain, leather thong or stout cord long enough to permit using it without detaching.

The blades on a new knife are often stiff and difficult to open. The best remedy is to apply a few drops of lubricating oil to the stubborn springs and repeatedly open and close each blade, using some sort of metal pry for the purpose. The springs will gradually loosen up with continued use.

## Opening and Closing Your Knife

To open your knife, grasp it between your left thumb and index finger and pull the blade open by placing your right thumbnail in the notch, being careful never to get the fingers of your left hand across the slot into which the blade fits. Often the spring on the blade of a new knife is so strong that it will snap the partly opened blade shut again with disastrous results to any finger that should happen to be lying across the slot.

Close your knife the same way, again being careful not to get your fingers across the slot at any time during the process.

## Sharpening Your New Knife

Strange as it may seem, a bright and shiny new knife isn't at all ready for use. The manufacturer has purposely left it dull so that its new owner can sharpen it to suit his own particular taste and needs.

The edge on the blade is called the *bevel*. If it is too rounded, the knife is dull; if too thin, it is sharp but weak and likely to chip if used on other than soft materials. A medium bevel is best suited for ordinary camp use and should extend only a short way back from the edge of the blade so as not to weaken it too much.

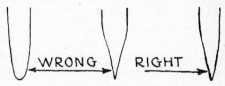

Getting the Proper Bevel.

A new blade or one with a nick in it requires a lot of grinding, and the preliminary work should be done on the fast-grinding surface of a file or hand-turned grindstone. Unless experienced, never use a power grindstone for it cuts away too fast and is likely to overheat the blade and spoil its temper.

Finish sharpening your blade on an oilstone or Carborundum stone (whetstone). The Carborundum has one point in its favor in that the water used with it is always available, unlike oil for the oilstone. The usual Carborundum stone has a medium side for preliminary, faster grinding and a finer side for putting on the finishing touches. Hold the stone in your left hand with the coarse side up, and grasp your knife in your right hand and hold it crosswise of the stone with the back of the blade raised to a 20-degree angle. Maintaining this uniform angle throughout the sharpening is the secret of getting the proper bevel on the blade.

Draw the blade toward you across the stone with a straight stroke, then away from you; continue your strokes, one toward you and then one away,

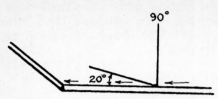

Twenty Degree Angle for Sharpening.

a few times. Keep plenty of water or oil on the stone to offset the heat created by the friction. Then reverse the blade and repeat the process on the other side. When both sides are finished, remove the *wire edge* or hooked roughness from the blade by stroking it on both sides on a piece of oiled leather such as a razor strop, belt, or leather shoe sole.

A sharp blade is much less dangerous than a dull one, for it will bite into the wood instead of sliding off and cutting the user. Test the sharpness of the blade by drawing it downward with a sliding stroke across a sheet of paper held vertically between thumb and forefinger. If sharp, it will cut the paper cleanly and easily; if dull, it will tear it or not even cut it at all. If the knife doesn't meet this test satisfactorily, work on it some more after analyzing what was wrong with your previous technique. You will need much practice to learn to sharpen a knife quickly and well.

Put your knife back in good condition after each use by giving it a few strokes on the fine side of a Carborundum and finishing off on a piece of leather. You should never need to use the file and the coarse side of the Carborundum again unless your knife is misused or gets a nick in its blade. It should be a matter of pride to you to have a well-kept knife.

There is an unwritten law among campers that no one ever asks to borrow another's knife, for one way to quickly sever a fine friendship is to return a knife dull and full of nicks.

## Using Your Knife

You are now ready to pick up some softwood and practice whittling. Hold and use your knife at all times so you cannot possibly cut yourself or anyone else, *even if it should slip.* Keep your thumb around the handle, never on the back of the blade, for if the knife should slip off the object you are cutting, the pressure of your thumb would close the blade right on your fingers.

Cut with a sliding stroke *away* from yourself, using the same spot on the blade throughout the entire stroke, never letting the knife slip to one side as you cut. Cut slowly and deliberately and pride yourself on being a safety artist. Carelessness and overconfidence cause accidents.

You will soon graduate from whittling for the sake of whittling, and can turn out such useful articles as fuzz sticks and fuzz clumps. These are

Fuzz Stick and a Fuzz Clump.

excellent to have ready for use to start a fire in a hurry when firewood is damp and stubborn from a recent rain. When you can make them with fine, close-cut "curls," each just as long as possible without severing it from the stick, you can really be proud of your skill.

Whittle wood which is free from knots, for trying to cut through them will soon dull any blade.

Close your knife if you are going to walk about for even two steps, for bad accidents have occurred from tripping while carrying an open knife in the hand.

You can split fine kindling wood by gripping a piece of wood with your left hand so that the blade of your knife cannot possibly slip and cut your hand, and, with the knife in your right hand, pressing the blade firmly down to split the wood. Take care not to pry or twist with your knife or you will sooner or later chip the blade.

At the first sign of the redness, irritation or other sign of an approaching blister, apply a piece of adhesive tape, a band-aid or a leather finger-stall over your finger to prevent further friction. The usual spot for a blister is on your index finger.

Splitting Kindling
with a Knife.

## Whittling

You are now ready to attempt something a little more difficult. Some "gadgets" are simple and can be made by anyone who has persistence and an average amount of skill. Advanced whittlers use additional tools such as crooked knives, sloyd knives, chisels, wood carving tools, vises, jigsaws, and so on, to save time and produce more finished work. A thorough discussion of their use will be found in some of the sources at the end of the chapter.

Many woods are adaptable to carving, but some are naturally more suitable than others. You can find good wood lying about in almost any wooded

Apply a Pad to Prevent
Blisters.

area, or get bits of scrap lumber at sites where wood is being used in construction. If you want an especially fine piece, purchase it at the lumber yard.

The best wood for whittling is soft enough to cut well, yet has enough "body" to hold it together; it should split straight and smooth, yet not to be so soft as to split ahead of the knife. Avoid brittle woods and those which will not hold together when large sections have been cut away. Wood with large natural rings is usually too coarse-grained for good whittling. Experimenting will soon enable you to choose the most suitable. White pine, oak, white or yellow poplar, cedar, basswood, butternut, maple and holly are all recommended.

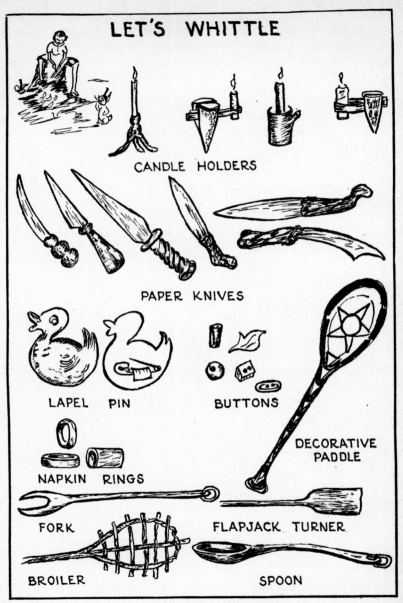

# LET'S WHITTLE

CANDLE HOLDERS

PAPER KNIVES

LAPEL   PIN          BUTTONS

DECORATIVE
PADDLE

NAPKIN   RINGS

FORK                 FLAPJACK   TURNER

BROILER                         SPOON

Try Your Skill on These.

A hiking staff for use over rough or hilly country is both useful and interesting to make. Choose a fairly straight stick about 4 to 5 feet long and about 1 inch in diameter. Decorate it by cutting away sections of the bark, leaving the natural wood exposed in any pattern of initials, faces, figures or spirals which your taste dictates.

Enamel or paint add to the decorative effect, and a coat of clear varnish or lacquer applied over the whole stick helps to keep the bark intact, even after it dries out. Bark carving is best done in the summer or fall, for the bark is inclined to peel off in the spring when the sap is running. Proceed slowly and patiently, for nothing is quite so discouraging as to ruin a "masterpiece" on which you have spent hours of labor by a careless or hasty miscut just as you are adding the last touches. Your staff will become dearer each time you take it on some pleasant expedition and you will find it of real help in making your way over difficult terrain.

Campers and staff members often like to have a name tag to wear the first few days of camp to help get acquainted. The woodsy way is to make your name tag out of a small twig about 2 to $2\frac{1}{2}$ inches long and as big around as your index finger. Flatten one side of it with your knife and sandpaper it smooth. Then print your camp name on it with India ink or burn it in with a woodburning set. Make a small groove in the back and fasten a safety pin in it with plastic wood or household cement. Apply a thin coat of floor wax to it or rub it well with clean hands, continuing the process until it shines from the natural oil of your skin. Make clothespins from pieces of green wood, leaving the bark on the tops or shape into heads, birds, or other object.

Use a small saw to cut off thin slices of wood of interesting cross-section and use your knife to shape into pins or buttons. Finish as above. Make holes in the buttons with a small drill or by driving a small nail through them.

To get campers whittling, just casually let them see you working on some interesting project during rest hour or at odd moments while listening to someone read aloud or tell stories.

## Making a Noggin

A *noggin* is a rustic drinking cup made from a hollowed-out burl of a tree and is designed to be worn on the belt. Making one provides a good many hours of enjoyment for those who like good hard work.

A *burl* results from an injury by insects, animals or man, usually when the tree was young; it is really a scar similar to that which heals an injury on our own bodies.

A Noggin.

The first step in making a noggin is to locate a tree with a suitable burl about 5 inches in diameter. Investigate the burl by removing the bark from its apex to see if the rot at its base has gone all the way through and so would cause your finished noggin to leak.

If the burl is satisfactory, saw it off, covering the exposed area on the tree with paint to protect it from the attack of insects. Include enough of the tree

for a handle on the end of the noggin. You must now laboriously gouge out the inside of the burl with a bit, a chisel or some similar sharp instrument. Continue the hollowing with a sharp knife until a shell not more than $\frac{1}{8}$ inch thick remains. Remove the bark from the outside, and briskly sandpaper both outside and inside smooth. To keep your noggin from splitting or checking as it dries out, keep it submerged in a vessel of linseed oil, grease or bacon fat whenever you are not working on it. Drill a hole in the handle, attach a leather thong or strong cord, polish the wood with a wool cloth, and your work of art is complete.

Removing a Burl from a Tree.

## Making a Whistle

To make a whistle out of willow or basswood, you must remove a section of the bark intact so that you can later slip it back into place; whistles are therefore most successfully made in the spring when the sap is running and the bark is easy to loosen.

Select a straight, smooth shoot, without knots or other blemishes, and about 6 to 9 inches long and $\frac{3}{4}$ inch thick. Slant end *a* (which will be the mouthpiece) and cut notch *b* through the bark and into the wood. Then cut a ring through the bark and around the shoot at *c*, and roll and beat the bark from *c* to *a* with the back of your knife, and "work" it until it is loose enough

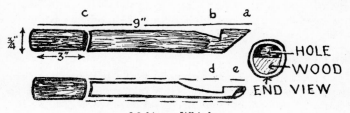

Making a Whistle.

to slip over end *a* by exerting a twisting pull. The beautiful, smooth white surface exposed readily explains the origin of the term "clean (or slick) as a whistle." Enlarge *b* as shown at *d* and thin the area between *d* and end *a* down. Replace the bark on the wood and your whistle is ready for use and should emit a clear, shrill tone.

You can make a two-toned or multi-toned whistle by continuing depression *d* down almost to ring *c*, and cutting one or more round holes through the bark between *b* and *c*. By placing your fingers over these various holes, singly or in combination, you can produce several tones.

You can make a similar whistle from a piece of elderberry branch, removing its pithy center with a long, stiff wire or an ice pick. Whittle one piece of softwood to partially fill the center at the mouthpiece end and another to close the opposite end completely. Cut as many holes as you want tones along the top of the whistle, and it is ready for use.

## Making a Model Totem Pole

Some camps have huge totem poles similar to those of the Indians of long ago. Making a small model (a few inches to a foot tall) gives several hours of fascinating pastime and will reward you with an interesting souvenir for your efforts.

Carefully work out a design on paper and transfer it to a piece of scrap wood of appropriate size and texture, and you are ready to start.

To give the totem pole a real Indian flavor, keep the design merely a rough outline, bizarre in effect, and without attempting to cut away the wood to show intricacies or details. You can best bring out details with enamel or paint. Cut such protruding parts as tails or beaks separately and glue them to the main pole.

## Finishing a Wooden Article

Use fine sandpaper or plain sand held in a piece of leather to smooth down wood to satin finish. It is more "woodsy" and attractive to most campers to leave the article the color Mother Nature gave it; some, however, prefer to add decorative touches of color. Keep whatever means you use simple and make it blend, not clash, with nature. Avoid gaudy paints and enamels. The soft tints of water colors give a delightful effect, if you use plenty of paint and let it soak in well so that you will not have to use two coats. It is still more interesting to use plant dyes as the Indians did (see pp. 129–130).

Bark carving, as described in the section on how to make a walking stick (p. 253), is an appropriate method of finishing the article.

Another Indian method which gives a pleasing effect is to smoke the design on by rubbing the object well with grease, then holding it over the fire until it has become as dark as desired and burnishing it while still warm with a piece of cloth.

You can obtain interesting designs in the original light color of the wood by whittling them from the smoked wood or by cutting a pattern of adhesive tape which you apply to the wood before you smoke it.

To get a dark design on a natural wood background, cut the design down into the wood and hold the object over the fire until the design has been charred or turned as brown as you wish. Then remove the rest of the bark, leaving your design an attractive dark shade.

# TOTEM POLES

Sample Totem Poles:

## The Sheath or Hunting Knife

A hunting knife served many purposes and was an indispensable piece of equipment to the pioneer. The average camper, however, is likely to use it for such menial kitchen tasks as slicing bread, peeling potatoes, cutting up meat, and so on; thus it provides a handy but not essential supplement to his jackknife.

GUARD→

There are many styles, sizes and shapes of sheath knives, but one of fairly small size with the blade moderately thin and not over 4 to 5 inches long is most suitable for a camper. Most modern handles are made of some sort of composition, although those of horn, hair or leather are still sometimes found. Between the handle and the blade is an upright guard which keeps your fore-

Sheath Knife.

finger from slipping forward onto the blade as the knife is used.

Sharpen and care for a sheath knife like a pocket knife, and keep its sharp blade safe in its sheath, wear it on your belt just back of your hip. The rivets along the sides and bottom of the sheath are to keep the sharp blade from cutting through.

## TOOLS

When simple tools are easily available, most campers enjoy using them for repairing and constructing camp furniture and "fixin's." Each living unit should have a set of skeleton tools, painted with the unit's colors or design so that straying tools can be spotted at a glance. Tools are easily lost or mislaid, and a tool board helps to prevent this and keep them orderly and ready

A Rustic Sign.

for use. Place nails on the board so that each tool can be hung in its place, and paint an outline of the tool underneath so that a missing tool will immediately be conspicuous by its absence. Keep a card file near the board with a card for each tool so that when a camper takes a tool, he signs his name on the proper card and hangs it up in place of the tool. When he returns the tool, he replaces the card and crosses off his name. It is an imposition to expect the camp handy man to lend his good tools—campers should by all means have their own.

Remember that a "workman is known by his tools" so learn to care for yours and keep them in good condition at all times. Hold each camper responsible for returning a tool in the same excellent condition it was when he got it. A thorough reconditioning of the tools makes a good rainy-day project.

Cheap tools are usually inferior and will prove a poor investment in the long run. Try to have in your unit or camp as many tools as you can from the following list:

| | | | |
|---|---|---|---|
| Claw hammer | Files | 20″ Camp axe | Pliers (with wire |
| Shovel | Sandpaper | Coping saw | cutter), 6″ or 8″ |
| Saw and saw files | (assorted) | Rope for lashing | Assortment of nails, |
| Cold chisel ($\frac{5}{8}''$) | Rakes | Bit and brace | screws, brads and |
| Machine oil can and | Tin Snips | 4″ and 8″ screw | the like |
| oil | Post hole digger | drivers | Ice pick |
| Bucksaw and sawbuck | Cord | Grind stone | Wheelbarrow |
| Plane | | Binder twine | |

## ADDITIONAL READINGS

### BOOKS AND PAMPHLETS*

Arts and Crafts with Inexpensive Materials· Girl Scouts.

Dank, Michael C.: Adventures in Scrap Craft.

Gottshall, Franklin H., and Hellum, Amanda W.: You Can Whittle and Carve.

Hammett, Catherine T.: Campcraft A B C's, pp. 38–43, 88–89.

Hunt, Ben: Ben Hunt's Whittling Book. Bruce.

Hunt, Ben: Indian and Camp Handicraft.

Hunt, Ben: More Ben Hunt Whittlings. Bruce, 1947.

Ickis, Marguerite: Arts and Crafts.

Maintenance and Care of Hand Tools. U.S. Gov't Printing Office.

Mason, Bernard S.: The Junior Book of Camping and Woodcraft, pp. 4–7, 14, 15.

Mason, Bernard S.: Woodcraft, chaps. 13 and 24.

Parkhill, Martha, and Spaeth, Dorothy: It's Fun to Make Things.

Pynn, Leroy, Jr.: Let's Whittle. Bennett, 1948, 128 pp.

Robinson, Jessie: Things to Make from Odds and Ends.

Tangerman, E. J.: Whittling and Woodcarving. McGraw-Hill, 1936.

Tool Craft. Girl Scouts.

Whittling Is Easy. Boy Scouts (#3165), 16 pp.

Whittling Is Easy with X-acto. X-acto, Inc., 48 Van Dam St., Long Island City 1, N. Y., 40 pp.

Woodcarving. Boy Scouts (#3315).

### MAGAZINE ARTICLE

Cassell, Sylvia: Try Hiking Sticks. C.M. March, 1952.

*See also pages 136 and 137.

Camp is the smooth grip of an axe handle,
The clean bite and the white chips flying.
"OUR AMERICAN HERITAGE"

# Chapter 24

# AXEMANSHIP

THERE ARE many varieties of axes available, perhaps due to the fact that in the early days axes were made in each community by the local blacksmith and consequently were designed to his own particular taste or that of his clients. Each particular axe was named for the region in which it was made, giving us the Maine axe, the Hudson's Bay axe, the Kentucky axe, and so on. Since axes are used for so many purposes, there may be real justification for having so many different kinds.

Axes range in length from the little 13½ inch scout axe to the 33 inch axe of the lumberjack and experienced woodsman, and there is a corresponding variation in weight.

They are of two general types: the double-bitted, and the pole axe.

A *double-bitted* axe is usually full-size and is distinguished by its two blades, one on either side of the head. It is attributed to that legendary hero of the Northwoods, Paul Bunyan, who, of course, couldn't be content to chop like ordinary people, but had to have an axe with which he could chop "both coming and going."

A double-bitted axe ordinarily has one edge ground thin and sharp for felling trees and the other thick and strong for splitting *down* wood.

The champions of the double-bitted axe claim that it is better balanced and easier to handle than the pole axe, but it has no place in the organized camp, for it is far too dangerous for use by any but the most experienced.

A *pole axe* has only one edge and comes in a wide variety of styles and sizes. We shall consider only the two most practical for use in the organized camp, the *scout axe* and the *camp axe*.

## The Scout Axe

This short, 13-inch axe (or hatchet) is recommended for general camp use.

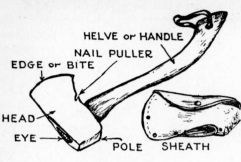

HELVE or HANDLE

NAIL PULLER

EDGE or BITE

HEAD

EYE

POLE     SHEATH

Scout or Belt Axe.

It is sturdy and rugged, inexpensive, light, easy to handle, and meets the needs of the average camper for getting his firewood and doing light construction work about the campsite. It is designed to hold in one hand (hence sometimes called a *hand axe*) and to be carried in a sheath worn on your belt just back of your hip (which accounts for another name, the *belt axe*).

*Selection.*     Scout axes are available in several weights, but the inexperienced should choose one of the lighter models. Get a well-balanced axe with a good grade of steel in the head and test it by grasping it by the head and sighting along its edge or bite to see that it is aligned with the handle.

The grain of the wood should go straight along the handle.

The parts are named as indicated in the figure. The bump at the end of the handle provides a firm grip to keep the axe from flying out of the hand when in use.

## A Camp Axe

A *camp* or *Marble axe* is a light-weight, 18- to 22-inch model with a head the same size and weight as the scout axe, but with a longer handle which gives it more power and speed for cutting firewood at camp. However, because of its length it cannot be worn on a belt and is somewhat cumbersome for trips.

Only counselors and older campers should attempt to use it, for it is potentially dangerous in the hands of the unskilled.

## Care of Your Axe

Be Sure the Handle of the Axe Lines Up with Head.

Regard your axe as a fine tool and keep it in good shape, sharp and ready for use at all times. Like a knife, never borrow nor lend an axe. After once putting in the hard work necessary to get the edge in first class condition, you will certainly understand why no one wants to risk having it nicked or dulled by careless or ignorant use.

The end of the *helve* or handle must fit tightly into the eye and is kept so by means of (1) a wooden wedge, (2) a steel wedge, or (3) a series of screws. No matter how tightly the head fits in a new axe, it will gradually work loose and, as the handle dries out, you must tighten it immediately, for a loose head on a swinging axe is an extremely dangerous thing.

Some may advise you to tighten a loose head by soaking it overnight in a pail of water, but this is only a temporary remedy and will leave the handle looser than ever when it dries out. It is better to soak it in oil which will swell the wood and last for a longer time. The only really lasting remedy is to fit a new wedge into it.

Never leave an axe lying about for someone to cut his hand on or stumble over. Either drive it into dead wood (never a live tree), place it in its sheath and hang it up, or replace it on your belt.

If necessary to carry an unsheathed axe a short distance, grasp it up close to the head and with blade down, so that it can't be deflected into you by collision with some object along your path. When handing it to another person, extend the head for him to grasp.

## Sharpening Your Axe

Since the different uses served by an axe require distinctive types of edge or bite, manufacturers commonly leave a new axe dull, so that it can be sharpened as its new owner wishes.

How to Wear Your Sheath Knife and Hatchet.

If inexperienced, it is best to take your new axe to one who knows how to put it in shape. If doing it yourself, you must first make the edge thinner, for it will not enter the wood at all if left too "stubby" or thick just back of the bite. This is usually done on a hand grindstone, but can be done with a file, though it is a slow, laborious job. Thin in the form of a semicircle, 1 to $1\frac{1}{2}$ inches from edge at its widest portion, for a scout axe. Leave the corners of the blade, which enter the wood first, thicker and more durable than the thin, sharp middle portion.

AREA TO BE SHARPENED
ON GRINDSTONE

Sharpen an Area Like This.

Next, use a 7- to 8-inch *flat* or *mill file* on the edge. Support the axe on a block of wood laid on the floor or table, for it is all important to use the file on the bite at the proper angle. Start the file at the edge and stroke away from it toward the pole. After you finish one side, turn the axe and repeat the process on the other. Like a knife blade, you must keep the edge moderately thick, for it will be dull if too thick and chip easily if too thin. Use the coarse side of the file first, following with the fine side.

You are now ready to *hone* your axe on a Carborundum stone or oilstone, holding it between your knees, and rubbing the stone over its edge in a circular fashion. This turns the *burr* or *"wire edge"* left by the file over to the opposite side, where you remove it when you hone the other side.

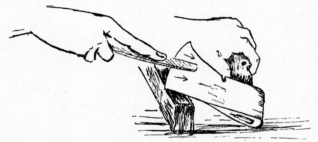

Sharpening the Axe with a Mill File.

Keep your axe sharp enough to bite, not chew, the wood, for it saves work and, as with your pocket knife, is much less hazardous since it bites into the wood instead of glancing off it. Apply the sharpening stone after each use, and you will be repaid by the ease and efficiency with which your axe cuts.

### Using an Axe

Grasp a scout axe in one hand at the extreme end of the handle; many like to squat or kneel while using it.

Swing so that the blade enters the wood at an angle of 45 degrees, for chopping straight down directly across the grain of the wood makes slow progress and quickly dulls your axe. Chop around knots, not through them, for they are very dulling to the blade.

Cut at a 45 Degree Angle.

Direct all strokes so that your hatchet cannot possibly come in contact with any part of you if your stroke is misdirected and misses the wood or hits it a glancing blow.

Work steadily, but not excitedly, practicing until you can hit the exact spot at which you aim and at the exact angle you wish. Keep your eye on the spot you want to hit. You get results from long, rhythmic blows, each landing exactly where you intended and each few taking out sizeable chips. Only a novice pecks away with short, ineffectual blows, each landing near but never exactly on the spot intended, so that he literally chews out the wood in fine bits.

Every campsite should have a good solid chopping block, a foot or two high and as wide as possible and anchored on the ground so that it cannot roll or rock. You may pound stakes in close to the sides to steady it if necessary. Level the top of the block and make a little depression for holding the wood. Direct all swings so that your axe goes on into the chopping block as it severs the wood; never permit your axe to enter the ground, where it is likely to contact small bits of rock to dull it.

Before beginning to chop, look carefully about you to see that there are no vines, underbrush or overhanging branches to deflect your axe on the backswing. No bystanders should be near. These safety precautions are not "just borrowing trouble," for accidents not only can but do happen, and you must take the utmost precautions to see that they do not happen to you.

Use two hands on a camp axe, with the one away from the handle end (the right in a right-handed person) placed fairly well down the helve toward the head as the swing starts, sliding it back toward the other hand as the axe descends, so that both are close together as the axe bites into the wood. Your right hand then slides back up the helve, ready for the next stroke. Keep your left hand close to the end of the helve throughout the swing, guiding the axe and keeping contact with it so that it cannot fly out of your hands. Use all your muscles, particularly those of the back and shoulders, to avoid undue fatigue. Swing the axe to give the stroke real power.

Stand at a comfortable distance from the wood with your feet parallel, comfortably spread, and solidly balanced, and with no sticks or stones which might roll under them.

## Cutting a Log in Two

If the log is small enough to be turned over, cut a "V" on one side about half through; then turn it and cut a similar "V" on the other side to meet the first. Make the top of the "V's" approximately as wide as the log is thick and cut at an angle of 45 degrees or more so that they meet about halfway through it.

Take Out a Chip with Each Two Strokes.

The average beginner makes the top of his "V's" too narrow, so that they soon meet and leave him no room to work, and he must go to the unnecessary work of enlarging the "V" at the top and starting all over again. The better the axeman, the fewer the chips.

Chop alternately from right and left, with well-aimed, decisive blows of a

Severing a Log.

sharp hatchet to take out a sizeable chip with each few strokes, twisting your axe slightly at the end of the blow. When you want to cut a log into several lengths, cut all the "V's" on one side before turning the log over, for the length and weight of a long log make it ride better and have less tendency to roll.

When a log is too large to turn over, stand at one side of it and cut a fairly wide "V" opposite you, then step across the log and repeat the process. If the "V's" are of the proper width, you can finish severing the log with a few well-aimed strokes. An experienced woodsman, when cutting an extremely large log, stands directly on top of it and chops the "V" between his feet, but this is precarious for a novice, whose glancing blow would be sure to land on his foot or leg.

### Felling a Tree

It is often essential to cut down a small sapling for campsite construction, and you will want to make a clean, quick job of it. For the average small tree, make your cuts (called kerfs) nearly straight across at the bottom. Continue them until they meet, and a gentle push will send your tree to the ground.

If the top of the tree is enmeshed in overhanging branches so that there is danger of its getting caught as it falls, decide upon the direction it can fall with least impediment and make your first kerf (A) on the opposite side. Make the second kerf (B) slightly lower so that it will act as a hinge to pull the tree over toward itself.

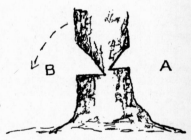

Felling a Small Tree.

You can usually sever small saplings by bending them over and giving them one or two good blows directly on top of the bulge.

Use dead, diseased, crooked or crowded trees which the forest can well afford to lose for practice. Never cut live, sound trees unless absolutely necessary for it takes but a moment to destroy what it will take nature years to replace.

### Lopping off Branches

To remove branches from a down tree, stand on one side of the trunk and lop the branches from the opposite side, carefully protecting yourself by

Limbing a Tree.

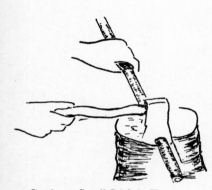

Cutting a Small Stick in Two.

keeping the trunk between you and your swinging hatchet. Start at the butt end and proceed to the top, severing the branches as close to the trunk as possible. Then cross over to the other side and cut the remaining branches.

### Cutting Small Sticks in Two

Hold the stick in your left hand, slant it downward across the chopping block with the point at which it is to be severed resting solidly against the block. Bring the axe down on the stick with good momentum, severing it diagonally with one blow so that it falls close to the chopping block instead of flying dangerously through the air. Keep your left hand high on the stick out of the way and swing your axe so that it will enter the chopping block if you miss the stick. If the stick is too large to be severed by one blow, give it a quarter turn, and repeat the process.

### Splitting Kindling

Since split wood burns much better than whole sticks with the bark intact, it is time well spent to keep a little kindling wood on

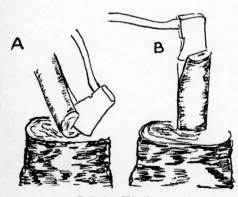

Splitting Kindling.

hand. Standing at the side of the chopping block, grasp the piece of wood in your left hand, place the axe on it and bring both wood and axe down simultaneously on the chopping block several times until you have made a split clear across the end of the wood. With your hatchet still in the split, turn the wood upright, and bring both hatchet and wood down again on the chopping block until the wood splits all the way down. Split the segments repeatedly if you want still finer kindling. Notice again that, when correctly done, the hatchet is directed toward the chopping block so that it can't possibly hurt you.

Stand a stick too large to be split by this method upright on the chopping block. Place your axe on it and drive it into the wood by pounding on it with another stick. Never use another axe for this purpose for there is danger of breaking one or both of them.

Do not hold a stick up against the chopping block with your foot unless you have found ten toes too many and want to get rid of a few.

### Sharpening a Stake

When you want to sharpen a tent stake or pole for driving into the ground, hold it upright on the chopping block and sharpen it on four sides. You can make a four-sided point more quickly and it will drive better than a round point.

Stake Sharpening.

## ADDITIONAL READINGS

Art of Living Outdoors in Maine. Maine Camp Directors' Association.

Des Grey, Arthur H.: Camping. Ronald, 1930, pp. 58–68.

Hammett, Catherine: Campcraft A B C's, pp. 11, 12, 44–47.

Kephart, Horace: Camping and Woodcraft, vol. 2, chaps. 12 and 14.

McLaren, Peter: The Axe Manual of Peter McLaren. Plumb, 1929.

Mason, Bernard S.: The Junior Book of Camping and Woodcraft, pp. 8–17. Barnes, 1943, 120 pp.

Mason, Bernard S.: Woodcraft, chaps. 8, 12, 15, 16 and 24. Barnes, 1939, 280 pp.

Mason, Bernard S., and Kock, Frederick H.: Cabins, Cottages and Summer Homes. Barnes, 1947.

Meinecke, Conrad: Your Cabin in the Woods. Foster and Steward, 1945.

Pioneering. Boy Scouts (#3382). 1941.

Swanson, William: Log Cabins. Macmillian, 1948.

Each color or tint that a tree has known
   In the heart of a wood-fire glows
Look into the flames and you will see
   Blue dusk and the dawn's pale rose,
The golden light of the noonday sun,
   The purple of darkening night,
The crimson glow of the sunset,
   The sheen of the soft moonlight.
Fire brings forth from the heart of a tree
Beauty stored there in memory.

                   MARY S. EDGAR*

# Chapter 25

# FIRECRAFT

WHEN THE early settlers came to America, the whole country, except for the great plains areas, was covered with trees—in fact, there were so many trees that the supply seemed inexhaustible. To the pioneer, the forests must have seemed an abomination, for they sheltered hostile Indians to murder his family, and wild animals to prey upon him and his precious livestock. He could not plant his crops until he had removed the trees by hard work and the sweat of his brow. We can readily understand and sympathize with his fervent desire to "conquer the wilderness" and do away with the trees just as rapidly as possible.

Saving trees was not even thought of in those days. As America became more and more settled, large logging companies sprang up, and they, least of all, had any conception of conservation, for "clean cutting" of everything regardless of size or kind was their general practice. However, a few far-seeing citizens realized where this wholesale destruction was leading; as early as 1653, William Penn suggested, to no avail of course, that one acre of forest be preserved for every five cut.

Now, more and more people are becoming aware of the need to conserve

* From *Wood-Fire and Candle-Light*. Permission by publishers, The Macmillan Company of Canada, Limited.

our rapidly dwindling forests, and many things are being done toward this end. One big improvement has been the controlled lumbering of wise owners who, each year, cut only mature trees which have already attained maximum size and would only age and perhaps become diseased if left standing. With this system, new trees are always coming on to supplant those cut, so that supply and demand are equalized.

Another help has been through research and practice in fighting tree diseases and pests and protecting the birds which eat injurious insects. The public is being educated, not only as to the need for forest conservation, but also as to the best methods for doing it. Much printed material is now available free or at small cost from the United States government and various other agencies.

There are now 161 National Forests, in forty states, mostly located on land unsuited for agriculture anyway, where not only the trees but the animals and other wildlife living among them are well protected and nurtured in the most approved fashion.

The twenty-six National Parks add their bit to this program. Despite these efforts, however, our trees are still disappearing at an alarming rate, and much greater efforts are needed to prevent their wholesale loss.

## FOREST FIRES

### The Problem

Fire is one of the most serious sources of forest destruction, for an average of about 550 forest fires a day occurred in the United States in 1947, burning over 23,200,000 acres or an area approximately the size of the state of Indiana. It would take nature forty to one hundred years to replace the trees on these burned-over areas, but a still more serious result is in the destruction of the *humus* and minerals in the soil which are so essential for plant growth. It is impossible even to estimate the number of forest creatures that lose their homes and even lives to forest fires which travel swiftly enough to overtake a deer running at full speed or a man fleeing on horseback.

A few forest fires are caused by lightning and some possibly by the friction of two trees rubbing together in a severe storm. Some are started from such sources as mills and trains, but at least 90 per cent are caused directly by man. Some result when fires set to burn weeds or debris get out of control, and many are caused by smokers who carelessly flip aside a burning match or a partly smoked cigarette. Far too many are due to ignorant or careless campers who build larger campfires than they can control or who fail to extinguish their fires completely.

### Types of Forest Fires

There are three types of forest fires: (1) *surface fires*, commonly found in sparsely wooded areas where they follow on or close to the surface of the ground; (2) *ground fires*, which burn along the ground through areas abundant in leaf litter and humus; and (3) *crown fires*, which are whipped up into the tree tops by a strong wind, where they travel rapidly along, and are hardest to combat and most destructive of all.

## What Is Being Done

Much is being done to combat forest fires. Aerial patrols fly over the forest and observers keep watch from high lookout towers to spot them while yet in the "baby" stage and comparatively easy to control. Well-trained fire-fighters attack them with chemical barrages from low-flying aeroplanes, while other workers drop by parachute or rush to the scene over carefully maintained fire roads which give ready access to every region of the forest.

An important part of fire prevention comes through the attempt to regulate and control the building of campfires. To build a fire in some state or forest preserves, you must have a permit which is granted only after you have demonstrated a knowledge of proper construction, maintenance and extinguishing of fires. Other areas permit fires only in designated fireproof campsites and fireplaces. Much is being done to educate the public through radio, moving picture, newspapers and educational signs placed throughout forest preserves and along public highways.

## What a Camper Can Do

The first and most important thing you as a camper can do is to see that neither you nor anyone in your party is ever responsible for starting a forest fire.

Next, you can actually help the wooded areas in which you camp or picnic by observing principles of conservation. Dead limbs still on trees or scattered about the forest floor furnish fuel for a potential fire, so that you help when you collect and burn this wood in your campfire.

Never cut a living tree when a dead one will do. If a green one is indispensable, pick out the *worst* tree that will serve your purpose. Select one that is crooked, diseased, of a less desirable species, or in a thicket where none have a chance to grow because of overcrowding.

## CHOOSING THE SITE FOR YOUR FIRE

You must be sure, above all things, that your fire will not spread, so choose your site carefully. If on someone else's property you must always secure permission.

No matter how pleasant and romantic a fire in a deeply wooded area seems, it is always dangerous, for there are dry branches on the bottom of trees to catch on fire, and a roaring fire underneath may even dry out green branches. It is much safer to build your fire in an open space.

If you want to replace the grass so that you do not spoil the appearance of the area, remove the sod with a shovel and replace it after your fire is out.

The floor of the forest is usually covered with a litter of dead leaves, broken branches, and other debris called *duff* and underlying organic matter of the soil in the form of leaf mold and decomposing branches called *humus*. These are combustible and fire may smoulder and break out in them hours after your campfire is forgotten. Clear away all such material down to hard ground for an area of 8 to 10 feet before you build your fire. Use caution

Fireplace Properly Prepared with a Circle of Rocks.

especially with the soil known as "peat" or "muck" for this soil itself is combustible, and fire may creep along it and break out even as long as several days later. Surround your fire site with rocks if available.

It is best to make a foundation of sand, gravel or flat stones for your fire. Avoid using the type of stones which crack and fly like shrapnel when heated and which are particularly prevalent near water or in creek beds where they have become so water-logged that heating creates enough steam to burst them. If *gradually* dry them out by *gentle* heat you may eventually find them satisfactory for use.

Never build a fire against a tree, for, if dead, it might catch on fire; if green, you will injure or perhaps kill it.

### Fire Prevention and Control

Before lighting a campfire, make preparations to (1) quickly handle it if it starts to spread, and (2) put it out when through with it.

Certain tools are useful for this purpose. A shovel is handy for trenching your fire site before building your fire and for shoveling dirt on it if it starts to spread. It also serves to move coals into the exact position needed for baking or cooking and to push blazing firebrands to one side where they will not burn or smoke your food. Lastly, you can use it for burying garbage and extinguishing the fire.

Tools for the Campfire.

When through with your fire, water makes the best fire extinguisher, so, if not close at hand, keep several bucketsful standing by for emergency use. Carefully pick out all blazing pieces and lay them to one side and saturate them with water or place them in the edge of a lake or stream. Then apply a goodly amount of water to the fire bed, stirring it up thoroughly and repeating several times. Sprinkle water on by hand so as to reach *all* surfaces and make it go as far as possible and continue sprinkling until the whole fire bed is cool enough to place your hand comfortably on any part of it.

If water is unavailable, cover the fire with sand or gravel, but use caution in applying other kinds of dirt for they may contain enough vegetable matter to burn. Minimize danger of fire spreading by keeping an orderly campsite with all equipment neatly in its place and all debris promptly disposed of.

Never leave a campfire unattended for even a few moments, for fire can spread and get completely out of control in that brief time. Do not place hot ashes on inflammable material, but wet them thoroughly and place them on a safe surface.

## If a Fire Spreads

When a fire starts to run wild, immediate action is important, for every instant counts and a fire that could easily be controlled by one person who knows what to do, may get out of hand enough to defeat the efforts of many in a short time. Send for help unless you are sure you can handle it alone.

To put out a fire, (1) deprive it of oxygen, for no fire can burn without it, or (2) deprive it of fuel. Douse it with water; beat it with a broom, a green switch of evergreen (with the top branches remaining), or a wet burlap bag; or cover it with sand, dirt or gravel to cut off the oxygen supply. Beat toward the wind so that you will not simply be fanning the fire and spreading sparks on ahead of you. To deprive it of fuel go far enough ahead in the direction the wind is blowing to allow time to dig a trench, 12 to 18 inches wide and deep enough to reach mineral soil and throw the dirt *away* from the path of the fire so that the fire will simply starve to death for lack of fuel when it arrives. Watch over the area long enough to be sure the fire is really out.

## A Camper and His Campfire

A fire out of control is a dreadful thing, yet nothing is quite so helpful to a camper as a controlled campfire, for it cooks his food, warms him when he is cold, destroys his unwanted rubbish, and, most important of all, cheers him and keeps his morale high with its bright, friendly glow. One of your most poignant memories will be of the time you spend in pleasant cameraderie and genuine fellowship around a campfire.

The disappointment and discomfort experienced when no one in a group can produce more than a smudge fire are enough to give a new camper a lifetime dislike for camping. A camper is known by his campfire; therefore you must know about fires and be able to build the right one in the right place and at the right time.

Three components enter into every successful fire: (1) good *tinder* to catch immediately when you apply the match and burn long and strong enough to ignite (2) the *kindling*, which in turn sets fire to the (3) *firewood*, which will continue to burn long enough and with sufficient force to provide the heat, light or atmosphere you want. You must carefully select, prepare and arrange each of these three components to get a "just right" fire. A skillful fire builder does not carelessly pick up any old wood, toss it into a hit-or-miss pile and apply a match. He works quickly and deftly, each movement made for a definite purpose; he carefully selects each bit of fuel to do just what he wants it to. The fuel for a fire which is balky and refuses to burn briskly or which coughs spasmodically a few times and then quietly dies in the middle of the meal is most likely composed of the wrong sort of wood or is arranged in the wrong way.

You must know your wood so that you can make a wise selection from the several kinds available in your particular region. It isn't enough to be able to glibly recite the names of trees when arrayed in all their summer glory, for campers use dead, dry wood which has no leaves and must be identified by its bark and the character of the wood itself.

## Tinder

Many things are suitable for tinder, that highly inflammable material which goes off at the touch of a match. The white birchbark of the Northland is the general favorite since it burns well, even when wet. Never strip it from a living tree, but use the plenteous quantities usually available where it has peeled off and fallen to the ground, or use *dead* curls which can be removed without harming the tree. Black, red or yellow birch are also usable.

Pieces of fat pine are excellent, as are dry evergreen cones, dry weed stalks, dried goldenrod, grape or honeysuckle vines, Queen Anne's lace, old birds' or squirrels' nests, milkweed silk, sagebrush, dried cactus, corn stalks and dry corncobs. The bark of the elm, hemlock or cedar is good if torn into thin strips and fuzzed up a bit.

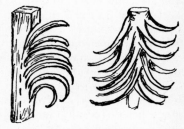

Three fuzz clumps or fuzz sticks pyramided together at the base of a fire, make good tinder and cutting them gives excellent practice in the use of your knife. But, as a matter of fact, woodsmen seldom use them for they take too much time to prepare when so many natural tinders are readily available. Plain shavings, if thin and curly, also serve adequately.

Fuzz Clump and a Fuzz Stick.

A handful of twigs hardly bigger than a match, and broken in the middle, makes good tinder and burns even more readily if the twigs are split.

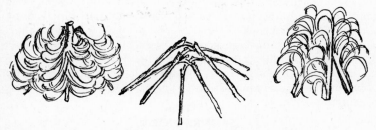

Fuzz Sticks, Broken Sticks and Fuzz Clumps Pyramided as Tinder.

Such things as oiled bread paper, excelsior, or newspapers are good if incidentally taken along as food wrappings, but no camper should ever become dependent on them.

Grass and leaves make poor tinder for, though they burn brightly, they do not last long enough to set anything heavier on fire.

**Kindling**

You will need kindling which will burn briskly and long enough to ignite the firewood. It should be small in size, ranging from just a little larger than tinder to about the size of your little finger. Fat pine or paper birch are best, but all the birches are satisfactory. Split evergreen, basswood, tulip, sumac, white and nearly all other kinds of pine, spruce, balsam or box elder and the frayed bark of cedar or helmock are all good.

## SOFT WOODS

Unlike the lumbering industry, which considers only the *evergreens* or *conifers* as soft woods and all the broad-leaved trees (*deciduous*, or those which shed their leaves annually) as hard woods, campers consider as soft woods all actually softer and weighing less for their size. This includes the evergreens and also some of the broad-leaved trees. Soft woods are usually faster growing.

It is easy to learn to distinguish between soft woods and hard woods by picking up samples and testing their comparative weights in your hand. Soft woods burn quickly and furiously and so are prized as kindling or to provide quick flames for rapid boiling or baking. They have little use beyond this, however, for they quickly burn down to dead ashes with few good coals.

The soft woods include alder, quaking aspen, balsam, basswood (linden), buckeye, cedar (red or white), chestnut, cottonwood, soft or silver maple, pine (jack or Labrador and white or loblobby), pitch pine (fine for kindling, but, even when burning brightly, emits a resin which taints food and coats utensils), spruce, sycamore, tamarack, and tulip (yellow poplar).

## HARD WOODS

You will want hard woods for cooking and warmth. They kindle slowly and require a hot fire of softwood to get them started, but, when once ablaze, are long-lasting and burn down to a bed of glowing coals which continues to throw out steady heat for a long time. Among the hard woods that make good fuel are apple, white ash, large-toothed aspen, beech, all the birches, dogwood, hickory (generally accorded to be the best fuel, whether dry or green), holly, hornbeam (ironwood), locust, sugar maple (one of the best), mulberry, oaks (except the scarlet and willow), pecan, yellow pine, and tamarack (lodge pole pine).

## SPITFIRE WOOD

These are woods which, in general, burn well enough, but tend to spit and make alarming noises. A still worse feature is their tendency to throw sparks which may start a forest fire or burn holes in tents or blankets. Soft woods in this class are alder, arbor vitae (white cedar), balsam, basswood (linden), box elder, red cedar, chestnut, hemlock, all the pines, sassafras, spruce, tamarack, tulip (yellow poplar) and willow (this is also undesirable because it imparts an unpleasant taste to food cooked over it).

Some hardwoods also have a tendency to spit for a few moments while the fire is getting under way; they are especially dangerous since their sparks burn longer and thus increase the fire hazard. Among such woods are beech, hickory, sugar maple or silver maple, and white oak.

## SLOW-BURNING GREEN WOODS

These are woods which, when green, will scarcely burn at all. This quality, though making them practically worthless as firewood, greatly enhances their value as fire dogs, backlogs and fire banks. The following belong in this class: black ash, balsam, basswood (linden), box elder, buckeye, butternut (white walnut), chestnut, cypress, hemlock, red (scarlet) maple, red and water oak, persimmon, pine (black or pitch and white), poplar (aspen), sassafras, sourwood, sycamore (plane tree or buttonwood), tamarack, tulip (yellow poplar) and tupelo (sour gum).

## SELECTING WOOD

You must use discrimination when selecting firewood, for just any old wood won't do. Green wood seldom burns well because it has too much moisture in it. On the other hand, wood that is extremely old has lost some of its most valuable heat-producing qualities. A little intelligent experimentation will help you select the best.

The *duff* of the forest usually consists of a layer of dead and decaying leaves and twigs called *humus*, which varies from a few inches to a foot or two in depth. This forest carpet tends to hold moisture so that, even in dry weather, branches lying on the ground in contact with it are often half rotten and more or less damp, at least on the underside. Therefore, picking up branches from the ground is sometimes a poor way to get firewood. As the trees in a heavily wooded area grow, each is in a constant struggle to reach above the others and so absorb more of the sunlight. The lower branches of all are too shaded to thrive and eventually die, and make especially good firewood when they have hung on long enough for the bark to disintegrate, for they are kept dry by the free circulation of air about them. They seem to have been prized as fuel even in feudal times. The story goes that in those days all the land belonged to the lord of the manor. The peasants were not permitted to cut trees, but could use only such firewood as they found on the ground or could reach in the trees with their pruning hooks and shepherd's crooks (an ingenious way for the lord to keep his trees free from underbrush). It is easy to imagine how a shortage of fuel caused them to invent devious methods to obtain more than was rightfully theirs—thus the expression "by hook or by crook." Branches extending up into the air on downwood also provide dry fuel, and dry, weathered roots and knots make excellent, long-lasting fuel.

You can test wood for dryness for small, dry sticks will break cleanly in two with a snap, while wet ones bend and finally break but with jagged edges. Large dry sticks feel firm and heavy in the hand and will usually snap in two if hit sharply on the edge of a rock; if two are tapped against each other, they emit a clear, sharp sound rather than the dull, muffled one of wet or green sticks. Sticks that crumble or break up too easily when given a sharp blow are rotten and would only smoulder and smoke if put on the fire.

Wood picked up from the ground is called *squaw wood* and should not be ignored, for it makes a valuable contribution to any fire. You are also benefitting the forest by getting rid of it. Undoubtedly the Indians used little else for they had no implement comparable to our sharp hatchet for chopping and splitting. Modern campers differ in opinion as to just how much to use a hatchet in preparing firewood. It is only common sense and not at all unwoodsman-like to break wood instead of chopping it when you can do it easily. It is also sometimes smart to avoid chopping by laying long pieces of wood across the fire to burn in two. On the other hand, the ability to use a hatchet skillfully is a big asset, particularly for splitting wood. Whitman said, "We are warmed twice by wood; once when we cut it and again when we burn it." All pieces of wood over 2 inches in diameter should ordinarily be split before placing them on the fire.

## LAYING A FIRE

Though it may seem like having the wagon before the horse, it is only proper and safe to have considered preparing your site and taking precautions for putting out your fire before proceeding with building it.

A good camper collects a big handful of tinder, about twice as much kindling, and enough firewood to maintain his fire for some time before he applies the match, for no self-respecting fire builder wants to have to scamper about to get fuel to keep his fire going after it is once started. Gather plenty of fuel, selecting it as previously described and stacking it neatly according to size in an out of the way yet convenient pile.

Cross three small sticks as shown and pile a quantity of tinder loosely within them leaving a little tunnel at the bottom on the *windward* side (side from which the wind is blowing) through which to apply your match, so that the flame will be carried upward and into the center. This is what is known as a *basic fire-lay* and is the basis for any type of fire you want. Now lay on some very fine kindling, leaving ample air spaces, for burning consists of *combustion* (the uniting of fuel and oxygen) and many fire failures are caused by dumping the fuel on too compactly.

Foundation for a Fire.

Fire burns up, only material directly in the path of the flame will ignite, and squatty fires will not have enough air to draw well. These are principles to remember when trying to lay a fire that will soon blaze merrily with the application of but one match.

Without a moderate draft, fires smoke and act balky, but avoid strong drafts and counter drafts.

Since boiling takes only a little heat, put the kettle on before lighting your fire so that it will be boiling and ready to push to one side out of the way by the time the hardwood burns to coals for frying or baking.

## LIGHTING THE FIRE

### Matches

Safety and book matches are practically worthless to a camper. *Kitchen* or *torch matches* are best.

Your matches are so essential that when going on a trip you should separate your supply, placing the bulk of them in a waterproof container kept in a well-protected spot in your pack and carry a small day-by-day supply in a waterproof container on your person. Several containers are illustrated: "A" is a metal box such as a typewriter ribbon or bouillon cube box and is

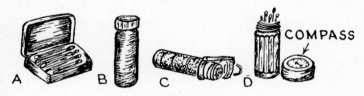

Some Match Cases.

not waterproof so that, for trip use, you must waterproof the matches themselves. "B" is a glass bottle with a screw-on top or tight-fitting cork and is, of course, subject to breakage. "C" represents a common type metal case which you can purchase inexpensively from a supply house or equipment store. It is water-tight and equipped with a screw top which is anchored on to prevent losing it. "D" is a variation, also waterproof, made of hard black rubber or composition. It has a compass in its screw top and sometimes a magnifying lens in the other end. Both "C" and "D" will float if accidentally dropped in the water. A 16-gage shotgun shell slipped over a 12-gage shell makes a serviceable holder.

### Waterproofing Matches

The commonest method of waterproofing matches is to coat them with melted paraffin, which forms a waterproof covering as it hardens. Use a long string to tie them in small bundles far enough back to leave air spaces between the heads and dip them in melted paraffin. Use care in handling hot paraffin, for it may burst into flame if allowed to get too hot, and will burn you severely if you get it on your skin. When needed, pick the matches out of their bed of paraffin and scrape off a little of the excess paraffin; what remains will but help the match to burn more ardently.

You can also waterproof matches by dipping them in a thin solution of shellac, varnish, fingernail polish, or collodion.

### Applying the Match

Pride yourself on laying your fire so well that you need only one match to start it. Only a greenhorn, with poorly selected and arranged material, surrounds himself with a collection of burned matches making his fire site resemble a game of "pick-up-sticks."

Kneel on the windward side close to the little tunnel into the tinder and select one match, closing your container to protect the rest. Grasp the match part way down the shaft to lessen the chance of breaking it and strike it, immediately shielding it from the wind with your cupped hands. Hold the match head down so that the flame will run up the shaft and wait until it is burning through at least a third of its length before *slowly* inserting it through the tunnel to the *bottom* of the tinder.

If you have chosen your material well and arranged it properly you will need do nothing more than stand by to apply more fuel as needed; avoid smothering the fire by putting on too much wood or applying it too compactly. On the other hand, be sure to keep plenty of loosely arranged wood on it to keep it going. If the flame fails to take hold after two or three attempts, don't keep striking more matches, for the trouble is obviously in the fire lay and you'll save time in the long run by tearing it down and starting again from scratch.

Don't toss away burning matches, but use them in the fire or break them and stick the heads in the ground.

## SOME GENERAL HINTS ON FIRES

A novice builds a fire large enough to roast an ox when his menu consists of a few little, insignificent weiners. The disdain the Indian feels for such methods is shown by his remark: "White man big fool; make big fire, can't go near; Indian make little fire and sit happy."

A skillful camper cooks a whole meal over a fire no larger than his hat. Big fires take more work, are hot and wasteful of fuel, and create a dangerous fire hazard. They are called *bonfires* to distinguish them from proper campfires.

Cook over coals, not flames, so that your food cooks slowly and clear through instead of being burned and sooty on the outside and raw on the inside. Coals are also more comfortable to cook over and do not cover your kettle with a black, sooty mask. Good cooking coals result from *hard wood* which is ignited well ahead of cooking time, so build a brisk fire and feed it for a time until it burns down to a thick bed of glowing embers.

Heavy, large sticks burn better if you elevate them on slow-burning green fire dogs (see p. 280) which admit air and fire from below. On damp, muggy days, it helps to elevate your whole fire on fire dogs.

A forked green stick *fire poker* 3 to 4 feet long (see p. 271) is excellent for rearranging fuel and embers to better advantage. You may use a shovel instead, but remove the hot coals quickly before they ruin its temper.

*Fire tongs* (see p. 271) help in rearranging fuel or moving hot rocks about (see p. 337 for directions for making them).

The *inspirator*, attributed to Steward Edward White, is an indispensable device for encouraging a stubborn fire. Make it from a piece of rubber tubing of small diameter and about 2 feet long. When applied to strategic spots *at the bottom* of the fire and blown gently, it supplies the

Using an Inspirator.

extra oxygen needed to make a smoky, smouldering fire burst into flame. It is well worth its slight weight for you can coil it up and carry it inside a cooking kettle.

You may resort to the old-fashioned method of blowing directly on a fire by mouth but turn your head each time you breathe, for inhaling smoke is a mighty unpleasant experience.

## KINDS OF FIRES

### Wigwam or Tepee Fire

This is a quick burning fire, for, being tall and slender, the flames climb right to the top and soon have the whole thing ablaze. Hence a small tepee fire provides a good basis for many other types of fire. Start with a foundation fire and lay on the fuel in tall tepee style with plenty of air spaces between.

It burns with a brilliant, cheerful flame and is consequently a favorite for a small campfire when a few friends gather to chat or hold a short program, but its rapid burning demands frequent fuel replenishment and it does not furnish the coals and steady, long-lasting heat needed for most cooking. Its quick, strong flame is

Wigwam or Tepee Fire.

fine for cooking one-pot dishes or bringing water to a boil in a hurry. Keep it small, 6 inches high or less, when using it as the basis for other fires; make it about 18 inches high for a campfire.

Indian, Star, or Lazy Man's Fire.

## Indian Fire, Star Fire or Lazy Man's Fire

This fire serves about the same purposes as the wigwam fire, but its structure makes it slower-burning and longer-lasting. Start with a small wigwam fire and use long poles, preferably small, as fuel. Overlap the poles in the center to provide better ventilation and radiate them in a wide circle at the outside.

Hunter-Trapper Fire.

The name "lazy man's fire" comes from the easy manner of building and tending it. You use long poles which require no chopping and, as their ends burn, you simply push them farther into the fire with your foot. Extinguish the fire by pulling the poles back out of the flame and dousing their ends with water. You can use the remainder of the poles again another time.

## Hunter-Trapper Fire

This is one of the most thoroughly satisfactory cooking fires. Lay two fire dogs of green, slow-burning wood at an angle into the wind, and just far enough apart to support the smallest cooking vessel at the narrowest end

Stone Hunter-Trapper Fire.                     Log Cabin Fire.

and about 15 to 16 inches apart at the other. Flatten their tops to provide a better support for your kettles.

Build a small wigwam fire between the fire dogs and keep it burning until you have a supply of coals to distribute along under the cooking vessels. Lay sticks of green wood flattened on one side across the fire dogs to support the utensils, if desired. These will eventually burn in two so watch them and replace as necessary. You can keep part of your fire burning brightly at one spot for quick boiling while you keep pulling coals over to another for frying or broiling.

The fire dogs act as reflectors to collect all the heat and throw it up under the vessels, making this an excellent fire when fuel is scarce or the weather hot. Damper sticks under the logs on the windward side intensify the heat and help get the fire started. You can convert this into a reflector fire (p. 284) by slanting some sticks into the ground behind one log and piling the others on top of it.

Nonpopping stones may be substituted for the wooden fire dogs.

## Log Cabin or Criss-Cross Fires

A log cabin fire is also an excellent cooking fire, especially when you need a good bed of coals. Build it around a small wigwam fire which will quickly burn down and set the framework of hardwood sticks ablaze. Its loose structure provides plenty of ventilation, so that it quickly burns down to a long-lasting bed of coals. Use sticks not more than 1 inch in diameter so that they will burn quickly.

## Fire-in-a-Hole

This is an efficient fire for preparing a quick, one-pot meal. Lay it in a small hole about 1 foot wide and 6 to 10 inches deep. The walls of the hole reflect all the heat up onto the kettles, which are supported on two or more green sticks laid across the top of the hole. Place the dirt removed from the

Fire-in-a-Hole.

hole on the leeward side of the fire, where it will not interfere with a free draft and replace it in the hole as soon as your cooking is finished. This is a good fire for hot weather or a windy day. If you dig it deep enough, you can use it as an imu (see p. 359).

## Trench Fire

This is another good fire for a hot, windy day. It is a long fire which provides room for a much more elaborate menu than does the fire-in-a-hole.

Dig a trench about a foot wide and sloping from ground level at the windward end to $\frac{1}{2}$ foot wide and 8 to 12 inches deep at the leeward end. Support your cooking vessels directly on the sides of the trench or on green sticks laid across it. Spread your coals and fire along as needed for individual items on the menu. Be sure that enough air can enter at the front end to keep the fire burning briskly.

If you want to use the trench for more than one meal, it is worth while to line it with nonpopping stones to catch and reflect the heat rays.

Trench Fire.

## The Automatic Stew Fire

Like the other types of fire-in-a-hole, this is particularly good on a hot or

windy day. Its particular advantage is that the sticks, which are 2 to 3 feet long, stand slanting in the hole, dropping farther down and automatically feeding the fire as their ends burn off. It is not an extremely hot fire, but is excellent for slow, steady heat over a long period of time. You can make it hotter by adding a few sticks of soft wood to the hardwood and a lining of nonpoppable rocks helps its reflecting qualities.

An automatic stew fire will pretty much look after itself while you busy yourself with other chores. A glance at it every now and then to see that it is

Automatic Stew Fire.

burning satisfactorily and that the food has enough water on it is about all that is necessary.

## The Reflector Fire

A reflector fire gives steady heat for baking with a metal reflector oven or for reflecting heat into an open tent in cold weather (*B*, p. 297). Make a *firebank* of three or four logs or big stones stacked up against a couple of uprights driven into the ground at a slight angle about 4 feet apart.

WIND

HOT COALS→

Wood Reflector Fire.

Place the reflector on the leeward side of the fire, so that the smoke and flames are blown onto it and only the heat is reflected back to the food or the sleepers basking in their tent.

←FIREBANK

Stone Reflector Fire.

### The Altar Fire

This is a convenient labor-saving fire for a more or less permanent campsite; it saves stooping and bending and is safer since it brings the fire up where there is no danger of its spreading in the duff. Build a hollow framework or altar of rocks cemented together or logs notched and fitted together log-cabin style. Make it a convenient height for those who are to use it, $1\frac{1}{2}$ to 2 feet high for small campers and $2\frac{1}{2}$ feet high for adults. Fill the framework with sand, rocks, tin cans or other noninflammable debris and smooth off a top of water-packed earth, sand, or gravel. Build your fire on top and place a crane or lug pole at the side for supporting your kettles. If you extend one side of the altar up a couple of feet, you will have an excellent reflector fire for baking.

### Council Fires

When a whole group meets in the summertime for an evening program around the campfire, they want a maximum of light and cheer with a minimum of heat. Keep your fire small so that people can gather close without being roasted, and make it longlasting to avoid the interruption of frequent tending. You may want to plan definite breaks to tend the fire during a long program.

Use split, well-seasoned hard wood. It will go off with a flash and burn brightly if you sprinkle it with kerosene a short time before lighting. Keep a reserve of similarly treated wood conveniently but not dangerously near.

1. *Log Cabin.* A small log-cabin fire makes the best council fire for a small group and a tall one serves for a large group. Avoid building too large a fire for it creates a fire hazard and is so hot that no one can be comfortable near it.

2. *Wigwam.* As previously mentioned, a small wigwarm fire is excellent for a small group. A tall bonfire, towering high in the air, though spectacular, is hazardous, for, no matter how well it is wired or otherwise fastened together, there is always danger that the long poles may work loose and fall perilously close to those about it. Besides, it is too hot for comfort in summer.

Log Cabin Council Fire.

## WET-WEATHER FIRES

The novice at fire-making has enough trouble getting a bright, steady flame in clear, dry weather, but that is as nothing compared to his difficulties when the heavens have been pouring buckets of rain for hours and everything is squashy under foot. Then comes the real test for any fire builder, since he needs a fire now more than at any other time, for it is quite as important psychologically as physically to send everyone to bed with warm dry clothing, hot food in their stomachs, and visions of happy faces clustered about a cheerful fire. Going to bed on a dismal night without these comforts is enough to quell anyone's ardor for camping.

If you are a wise counselor you will be prepared for such an emergency. Amidst the deluge you can calmly produce your waterproofed matches and some good tinder you have saved for the occasion, and capably set to work. Whenever you are in camp, always keep a supply of kindling and firewood under a tent or tarpaulin. If caught without it, you will have to search for it under overhanging rocks, fallen trees, or on the dead bottom limbs of standing trees. The dampness of any wood is usually confined to its outer layers which can be quickly shaved off if no completely dry wood is available.

## Trench Candles

Trench candles, carried in a waterproof tin box, are excellent for starting a fire on a rainy day. Make them by tightly rolling and twisting six to ten

sheets of newspaper with a strip of cloth or thick cord down the middle.
Tie string tightly about the roll at intervals of 2 to 4 inches, leaving a length attached for suspending the pieces while dipping. Sever the roll half-way between each two strings and pull out the center cloth or cord of each segment at one end as a wick. Suspend the pieces for a couple of minutes in melted paraffin or old candle wax, bring them out to harden slightly, and redip them several times to collect additional coats of wax.

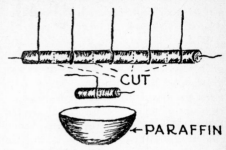

Making Trench Candles.

Trench candles are impervious to rain and wind and burn long enough to start almost any fire. You can use a plain candle stub in the same way, but it isn't nearly so good. Trench candles will provide enough heat for cooking on a hobo stove or furnish a fairly adequate light when burned lying flat in a dish or other container.

## Peas

Barbara Ellen Joy and Jeanne Bassett* describe a method for making "peas" which are also good for starting wet-weather fires. Mix ashes from a softwood fire with kerosene and roll them into small balls about the size of large peas. Carry them in a tin box and they will burn brightly enough to start any stubborn fire.

## Laying a Fire

A fire built on sopping-wet ground can produce enough steam to smother itself. Scoop away the wet top ground and build a little platform of bark, stones or sticks for a base.

A wigwam fire is best on wet ground. Lay the fire with even more care than usual, using only tinder and kindling at first and adding other fuel gradually as your fire gains momentum. Damp fuel dries out with surprising rapidity if you lean it gingerly up against flaming sticks. You can keep other wood close to the fire to gradually dry out.

An inspirator is especially helpful for wet-weather fires.

If moisture is falling, suspend a piece of tarpaulin or an extra poncho on a framework of sticks at least 5 feet above the fire until you get it going well. Since this usage is rather hard on the material employed, some camps keep a few pieces for this specific purpose. If there is an especially strong wind from any direction, build a windbreak of branches or a tarpaulin.

* Barbara Ellen Joy and Jeanne Bassett: Wet Weather Fires. C.M., April, 1939.

## ADDITIONAL READINGS

### BOOKS AND PAMPHLETS

Campcraft Skills Flip Charts (Fire-building). Girl Scouts.

Firemanship. Boy Scouts (#3317). 1945.

Forestry. Boy Scouts (#3302), 1943.

Hammett, Catherine T.: Campcraft A B C's, pp. 49–59.

Jaeger, Ellsworth: Wildwood Wisdom, chap. 6.

Kephart, Horace: Camping and Woodcraft, vol. 1, chap. 13.

Mason, Bernard S.: The Junior Book of Camping and Woodcraft, pp. 46–71.

Mason, Bernard S.: Woodcraft, chap. 6.

Stewart, George: Fire. Random, 1948. (The story of a forest fire.)

Weaver, Robert W., and Merrill, Anthony F.: Camping Can Be Fun, chaps. 1 and 8

West, James E., and Hillcourt, William: Scout Field Book, Pow-wow 15.

### MAGAZINE ARTICLES

Ford, Corey, and MacBain, Alastair: Hell and High Timber. (Forest fires.) Collier's, June 25, 1938, or The Reader's Digest, Oct., 1938.

Hensler, P. C.: Make It a Fire-Safe Summer. C.M., March, 1952.

Joy, Barbara Ellen, and Bassett, Jeanne: Wet Weather Fires. C.M., April, 1939. (Camp Publications, no. 66.)

Worden, William L.: When the Forest Burns. The Saturday Evening Post, Oct. 29, 1949.

Aloft I raise my Shield; the
  pelting Rain
And rattling Hail assault my
  Slope in vain.
The burning Sun, the Weight
  of Winter Snow
Alike I scorn—then rest secure
  below.

FROM MOTTOES*

## Chapter 26

# TENTS AND SHELTERS

THE IDEAL tent would be easy to set up and take down, light and compact to carry, absolutely rainproof and bugproof, and easily heated in winter yet giving a maximum of coolness for summer. Unfortunately, it is impossible to combine all these qualities in one tent, for, as the old farmer said, after several hours of gazing steadfastly at the giraffe in the zoo, "There jest ain't no setch animal." These desired qualities largely account for the many varieties of tents, each with particular features adapting it to certain situations yet making it unsuitable to others.

In this chapter we shall not attempt to consider all types of tents, for many are impractical for use in the average organized camp.

### Materials

The classic material for tents has been canvas or duck—a material with certain serious drawbacks. It is heavy and bulky to pack and carry and is not waterproof in itself, but must be treated by some process which adds further weight and makes it even more stiff and unwieldy to handle. It is usually the cheapest of the materials, however.

---

* Permission by Western Brick Company.

The market has recently been flooded with new materials sold under a variety of trade names, most of them being an outgrowth of experiences during World War II. Several are lightweight and thoroughly waterproof and are thin enough to be rolled into a compact bundle for carrying. They are, for the most part, quite durable and will give years of satisfactory service if carefully handled. Nylon and neoprene-treated materials are increasing in favor. Unfortunately, they are often too expensive to fit into the budget of the average camper or organized camp, and a canvas tent will have to do.

An extremely cheap tent is likely to prove a headache and an expensive one in the long run, for it will be short-lived and give poor service. It is liable to be made of leaky, nondurable material and is often not cut squarely, so that it can never be pitched quite right. The seams may be poorly constructed, failing to brace the material and give it the added strength they should, or they may be sewed with that abomination, the "chain stitch," which ravels out as soon as one thread is broken. The *grommets* (metal rings sewed in to hold ropes) (see p. 293) may be so poorly inserted as to quickly pull out when any stress is put on them, as in a strong wind or after tent shrinkage. It may be possible to get an inexpensive tent which will fulfill ordinary camp needs, but the inexperienced person should not attempt to select one without expert advice.

Tents formerly came in white or very light shades, but new tents that color are rarely seen now. The modern trend is toward a soft brown or green which will blend in well with the forest home, will not collect sun or moon glare, will not soil as easily, nor silhouette the occupants at night, and will not attract bugs and insects as white does. If you have a white tent, you may find it worthwhile to dye it with a good cloth dye.

## Waterproofing

You can waterproof tent material when making your own tent, or you can re-waterproof a tent that has started to leak. The simplest and safest method is with paraffin. Lay the material flat and go over it painstakingly with a cake of paraffin (or candle wax), rubbing carefully until every fiber is evenly and thoroughly coated and the whole surface has a white appearance. Then, with a warm (not hot) iron (a sad iron is superior to an electric iron, which heats too rapidly), rub over the material, melting the wax and causing it to permeate the fibers. This method keeps out moisture by coating the whole surface with wax and will be effective for ordinary rains, but adds materially to the weight and bunglesomeness when handling it. You must keep material so treated away from the heat of a fire or long exposure to the direct rays of the summer sun for these will melt the paraffin.

Another method of waterproofing consists in melting thin shavings of beeswax or paraffin in turpentine (1 pound to a gallon) and painting the surface of the tent with it. Dissolve the mixture by immersing a vessel containing it in hot water, changing the water as rapidly as it cools. This coating is rather dangerous since it may catch fire if direct heat or flame is placed near it. The alum-sugar of lead method of waterproofing is not desirable because it is poisonous. Many patented preparations for waterproofing are available at outfitting stores and are well worth investigating.

Before starting out on a trip with an old tent, pitch it and test it for leaks by pouring buckets of water on it or spraying it with a hose. Mending leaks on a trip is annoying, for they seem never to be noticed until a big juicy drip goes "splotch" in your ear while deep in the arms of Morpheus.

### Ventilation and Insect Screening

Important features in any tent for summer use are the amount and type of ventilation provided. At one extreme is the tarpaulin shelter and the old stand-by pup tent, open at both ends and obviously admitting plenty of breezes as well as various flying and crawling creatures, to enjoy a free lunch at the expense of the occupants. Do not think of going on an overnight trip, particularly in malaria country, without adequate protection against these blood-thirsty creatures—no trip can be fun with them as tentmates.

Three types of materials are commonly used for insect-protection. (1) Mosquito netting is cheap and easy to drape over tent openings, but is fragile and so coarsely woven as to admit some of the smaller insects such as the pestiferous punkies or "no-see-ums." (2) Double layers of cheesecloth screen insects out but at the same time keep out some of the cooling breezes. This material is more durable and less expensive than mosquito netting. (3) Bobbinet, though still more expensive seems to be best as it is fairly durable and finely woven enough to be effective, yet admits plenty of air. The illustration shows a way to provide more ventilation in a tent. The rain flaps should overlap the windows so that there will be no leaks and should be arranged so as to lower from the inside when bad weather sets in. Windows should be at least 12 by 18 inches in size.

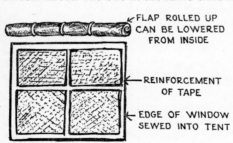

FLAP ROLLED UP CAN BE LOWERED FROM INSIDE

REINFORCEMENT OF TAPE

EDGE OF WINDOW SEWED INTO TENT

Bobbinet Window with Flap.

You can fashion doors in the same way with a center slit for an entrance, bordering it with tape and a zipper. Weight the bottom down with stones or logs, but a better way is to equip it with short tapes which you can fasten to small pegs driven in the ground.

In an emergency, you can drape bobbinet or other material from a forked stick framework over the whole tent, holding it tight to the ground with stones or logs. This is a rather unsatisfactory method, however.

Tent with Side Rails Pitched on a Wooden Floor.

### Flooring

Some tents are pitched on a wooden framework with a regular wooden floor and a wall extending part way up. This is quite suitable for tents which remain more or less permanently in one spot.

Every tent without a wooden floor should be fitted with a *sod cloth*, which

TENT FLY

INSECT SCREEN

GUY ROPES

TRENCH

TRENCH DRAINER

Wall Tent with Tent Fly.

is a strip of material 6 to 9 inches wide sewed to the bottom of the tent wall and arranged to be turned in toward the center so that drafts and insects cannot get in under the bottom of the tent. Weight it down on the inside with rocks or wood blocks.

A floor cloth is also highly desirable and, when laid on top of the sod cloth, removes the danger of invasion by things that fly and crawl and creep as completely as is possible with the movable type of tent. The floor cloth is sometimes sewed directly to the tent

TENT WALL

PLACE FLOOR CLOTH OVER SOD CLOTH

SOD CLOTH

Sod Cloth in Place Inside Tent Wall.

wall, making the sod cloth unnecessary, but this is unhandy since it cannot be taken out to clean.

### Tent Flies (p. 291)

These are extra strips of tent material stretched above the regular tent as an added protection against rain and are almost a necessity with large canvas tents which are often far from waterproof. They also keep a tent cooler by absorbing some of the direct sun's rays in hot weather as well as warmer when the weather is cool. They are fastened by guy ropes to the regular tent pegs or are attached to tent pegs of their own.

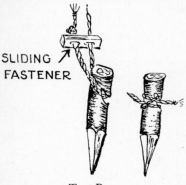

SLIDING
FASTENER

Tent flies are a perfect nuisance unless anchored tightly, for the slightest breeze sets them flapping and booming so that even a dog-tired hiker cannot sleep. They are, of course, seldom used with smaller trip tents, since they increase the weight of the outfit by at least a fourth.

Tent Pegs.

### Tent Pegs

Pegs should be 12 to 18 inches long and $1\frac{1}{2}$ inches in diameter and sharpened on four sides. Shape the notch for fastening the rope as shown and smooth it on the inside to prevent excessive wear on the tent rope. Tent pegs sometimes have an additional upper notch for attaching a tent fly. Insert pegs at a 45-degree angle, sloping them away from the tent wall.

If the ground is too soft or sandy to hold pegs or is so rocky or hard that they cannot be driven in, fasten the guy ropes to logs, stones, or surrounding bushes. An additional method of anchoring a tent peg by means of another peg in soft or sandy soil is illustrated.

Anchoring a Tent Peg in Soft
or Sandy Soil.

### Tent Ropes

Tent ropes need not be large, but must be strong for they are subjected to much stress from wind and storm and deteriorate from the alternate wetting and drying. Number 5 manila or sash cord is good. Periodically rubbing them with a cake of beeswax waterproofs them somewhat.

Large tents with guy ropes are usually supplied with sliding fasteners, which permit you to quickly tighten or loosen them.

Use a clove hitch when tying a tent rope (without a sliding fastener) to a tent peg, with an overhand or figure-of-eight knot in the other end to hold it secure in the grommet. A bowline provides a permanent loop to slip over a peg or stake.

Use your camp rope to anchor light tents as in *A*, *B* and *D*. This saves having to carry poles or to chop them at the campsite. *E* shows a method of support by means of a pole and two forked sticks.

## Ditching

No matter how clear and bright the night, when bedtime comes it is wise to ditch your tent, for there is nothing more disagreeable than to wake in a river of water trickling under the tent walls on its merry way to the ocean. Make the ditch about 4 inches deep and 4 inches wide and extend it all the way around the tent, with "drainers" at low spots to empty it (p. 291). Make the side next the tent straight and the opposite side sloped and place it so the tent wall overlaps the inside edge of the ditch slightly.

Tent Ropes and Supports.

## The Light Trip Tent

When traveling on foot, by canoe or on horseback, when every ounce counts, the most popular tent for camp use is one just large enough to crawl into for sleeping. When made of the new featherweight materials, you can fold it it into a surprisingly small package.

You can convert the familiar poncho or ground cloth, now available in lightweight materials, into several varieties

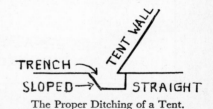

The Proper Ditching of a Tent.

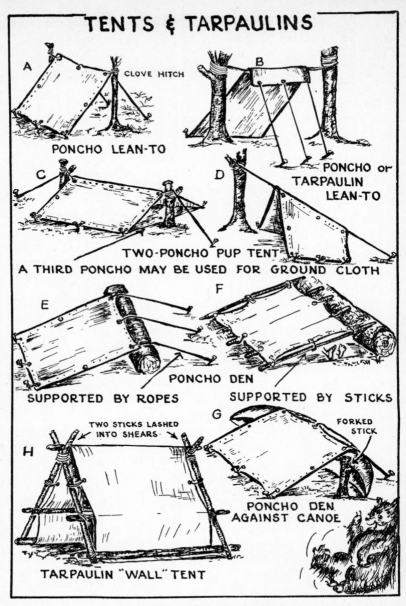

Tarpaulin and Poncho Shelters.

of lean-to or den. A piece of tarpaulin slightly larger than a poncho makes a
roomier type of shelter. Naturally
these do not protect you as well in a
long-continued or driving rain.

When camp overnights or sleep-
outs frequently end at the same spot,
it is helpful to have permanent
shelter frames, so that all the incom-
ing "trippers" have to do is throw
their shelters across the frames and
lash them securely into place.

You can fold blankets or use pieces
of tent cut to fit as ends for a tarpaulin or ground-cloth lean-to.

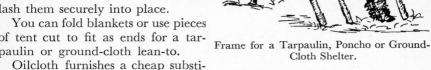

Frame for a Tarpaulin, Poncho or Ground-
Cloth Shelter.

Oilcloth furnishes a cheap substi-
tute for a tarpaulin or poncho, but is not satisfactory or durable for more
than brief use.

Small sleeping tents, each
housing two or at the most three
or four campers, are better than
large tents for trip camping. If
transportation permits, you can
supplement them with one or
two roomier tents to furnish
standing room for cooking, and
other purposes.

Blanket Folded and Used as End for a Tarpaulin.

## Types of Tents

As mentioned previously, there are many varieties of tents, each having
its own points of superiority in certain situations. Most can be classified
roughly into three or four types, according to their general shape. However,
a few do not fall clearly into any one category, for they combine features of
two or more types.

1. *Conical and Pyramidal Tents.*     These, in general, are tall tents, erected
with a center pole (which often gets in the way like a sore thumb) and with
sides which taper down abruptly and are kept in position by tent pegs. They
are suited for open-plains living where the sudden and severe storms char-
acterizing such regions quickly drain down their steep sides like water off
a duck's back. They are substantial and hold firm against anything less than
a severe windstorm.

Their bulk and weight make them impractical for use in light trip camping,
and their shape makes them ill-adapted for small-party use. They work
nicely for a permanent or semipermanent camp, for the large sizes bed down

several campers lying with heads toward the center pole and bodies radiating like the spoke of a wheel. Health authorities, however, might question the advisability of sleeping with heads in such close proximity.

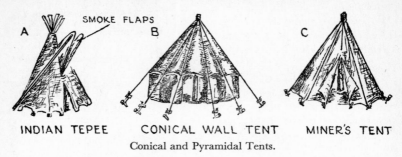

Conical and Pyramidal Tents.

The tepee of the plains Indian is an example of the conical tent with no bothersome pole in the center. The framework is made by lashing together the tops of nine to twenty poles and spreading their ends out in a broad circle. A covering of canvas (the Indians used birch bark, buffalo hides or deer skins) is then spread over the framework. One of the advantages of the tepee in cool weather is the set of adjustable smoke flaps which make it possible to have a small fire on the inside for warmth and cooking. The steep pitch of the walls makes it shed water well without being waterproofed.

Conical tents are distinguished by their circular bottoms, while the bottoms of pyramidal tents are angular and present four or more sides. There are many forms of the conical tent.

2. *Wedge or "A" Tents.*    Wedge or "A" tents are favorites for light trip camping, for many of them are light and convenient to carry, easy to pitch and provide a crawl-in type of shelter which is all that is really essential for the trip camper who is out-of-doors most of the time. Their steep roofs shed rain well, and the absence of guy ropes and heavy poles in the smaller models makes them particularly adaptable to forest country where they can be lashed to trees or tent stakes can be quickly fashioned. Some of the larger models are high enough to permit standing. The wall tent (see p. 291) is a heavy, semipermanent shelter which comes close to affording homelike conditions.

3. *Lean-to Tents.*    Lean-to tents, with an open front for receiving heat from a reflector fire, are favorites for cold-weather camping. They have a sloping ceiling to catch and reflect the heat rays down onto the sleeping occupants and are sometimes available in light models suitable for light trip camping.

Only a few models are arranged to supply the insect protection necessary for summer use.

Wedge or "A" Tents.

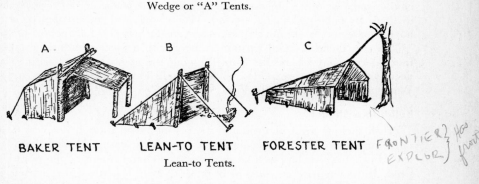

Lean-to Tents.

FRONTIER }
EXPLOR   } HG4
         } front

The Baker tent is really half of a wall tent with a flap which serves as an awning in sunshiny weather, can be lowered over the front when rain comes, or thrown back over the top when you want a reflector fire in front of the tent. It is usually hard to screen adequately.

## Some Pointers about Tents

Your tent will give longer life and better service if you care for it properly. Fold it neatly along the seams to take the wear and roll it tightly and carry it in a bag designed especially for the purpose (a gunny, flour or feed sack equipped with a draw string will do). Dry it out thoroughly before packing, for canvas tents, in particular, are subject to damage from mildew, and never place it where it can rub against hard objects. If you carry tent stakes, never wrap them in the tent, but put them in a separate bag and stow them separately.

Even lightly bumping or rubbing a tent while wet will break the air bubbles which make it waterproof and cause a leak which can't be stopped until the rain is over.

When rolling your tent flaps, roll them with the edges inside so they will not catch and hold the rain. Unroll them occasionally even in dry weather to discourage field mice and other unbidden guests from building nests in them.

If a tent is to stay in the same position for several days, open it as wide as possible and air it thoroughly every sunny day.

Pitch your tent in a tight and workman-like manner to give a neater appearance and prevent it from whipping badly when a breeze comes up. Always loosen guy ropes slightly before a storm, for they and the tent shrink when wet, subjecting them to great strain and sometimes even tearing the tent wall itself or pulling the grommets right out of it.

Never use pins or nails to attach additional ropes, for they make holes which leak and may later develop into rips and tears. Be sure there are no clothes poles or other objects near enough to the walls or roof to wear holes in them by rubbing during a wind. When you need more ropes on a tent have a good tent or awning maker insert steel grommets for anchoring them.

You can mend a small rip temporarily with a piece of adhesive tape. A more permanent job results from drawing the edges together with a large needle and strong thread, taking alternately long and short cross stitches. Waterproof the mend as previously described.

### Building a Shelter

Brush shelters are romantic and interesting, even though not very watertight, and are often a convenience at an outpost camp. Weave them from leafy branches overlapped like shingles, and thatch them at the ends if desired. Indian tepees are easy to build and can be made quite livable, and campers may even aspire to build their own lean-to or log cabin. Directions for doing all these things can be found in the sources given below.

## ADDITIONAL READINGS

Choosing Tents for Camping Out. C.M., April, 1953.

Geist, Roland C.: Hiking, Camping and Mountaineering. Harper, pp. 30–35.

Hammett, Catherine T., and Musselman, Virginia: The Camp Program Book. Ass'n Press, pp. 62–65.

Hammett, Catherine T.: Campcraft A B C's. Ass'n Press, pp. 81–87.

Jaeger, Ellsworth: Wildwood Wisdom. Macmillan, chap. 5.

Jaeger, Ellsworth: Woodsmoke. Macmillan, 1953, 228 pp.

Kephart, Horace: Camping and Woodcraft. Macmillan, vol. 1, chaps. 3, 5 and 6; vol. 2, chap. 13.

Mason, Bernard S.: The Junior Book of Camping and Woodcraft. Barnes, pp. 30–41.

Mason, Bernard S.: Woodcraft. Barnes, chaps. 1–4.

Meinecke, Conrad E.: Cabin Craft and Outdoor Living. Foster and Stewart.

Pashko, Stanley: Boy's Complete Book of Camping. Greenberg.

Rutstrum, Calvin: That Eternal Tent Problem. C.M., April, 1951.

Rutstrum, Calvin: Way of the Wilderness. Burgess, pp. 65–74.

Saloman, Julian H.: One Vote for Tents. C.M., Nov., 1950.

Swanson, William E.: Camping for All It's Worth. Macmillan, 1954, 154 pp.

Tents and Simple Shelters. Girl Scouts.

Wadsworth, William: Do Your Tents Leak $$$? C.M., May, 1949.

Weaver, Robert W., and Merrill, Anthony F.: Camping Can Be Fun. Harper, chap. 6.

West, James E., and Hillcourt, William: Scout Field Book, Pow-wow 13.

Follow the trail to the open air
Alone with the hills and sky;
A pack on your back, but never a care,
Letting the days slip by!
AGATHE DEMING *

# Chapter 27

# DUFFEL FOR CAMPING AND TRIPS

THE NOVICE at camping usually imports all sorts of unnecessary *duffel* (the name given to your equipment at camp), which lies collecting dust and taking up valuable space. When he goes on a trip, he likewise drags along things which add nothing to his comfort and much to his discomfort, for everything taken, even though not carried on your back, has to be handled and moved about many times.

The secret of camping, particularly trip camping, is to take only what you actually need for health, safety and happiness. Yet it is just as grave an error to take too little and try to live like an animal of the woods with only what you wear or can procure from the fields. The ultimate in camping is expressed by the title of Elon Jessup's book, *Roughing It Smoothly*, and its attainment should be the ideal of every camper.

Any sort of trip limits the amount of equipment that can be taken, particularly for adolescent boys and girls, who should never plan to carry heavy packs for more than a short distance. Transportation by canoe, pack saddle or wagon allows a little more latitude, though lightness and compactness are still highly desirable. Some camps minimize the problem on long trips by sending such heavy materials as food and bedding ahead by auto, truck or

* Reproduced by permission of Miss Deming.

pack horse, leaving for the campers to bring only such light equipment as they can easily manage. You can also lighten your trip load by replenishing food supplies at farm houses and stores along the way and by shipping supplies ahead by parcel post or express. Fresh clothing may be supplied in this way and the soiled sent back to camp.

No matter what your means of transportation, keep your outfit just as compact and light as possible without omitting anything you really need. Whenever the temptation to pack some questionable piece of gear arises, recall that each ounce weighs a pound and it is truly the straw that breaks the camel's back on a long trip.

The equipment you will need depends on the season, the nature of the terrain, and the length of the trip.

Camps and counselors should not foster extended expeditions into the woods unless there is enough equipment of the right sort to do it comfortably. However, no great outlay of money is necessary for you can improvise much of the equipment at home. Make your poncho, groundcloth, tent, pack kit and bedroll from waterproof material or waterproof them by the paraffin method (pp. 289-290). Make a paper pattern and adjust it until it is "just right" before cutting into your goods. You can make or assemble cooking utensils, mess kits and many other pieces of equipment.

Cut down on both weight and expense by finding ways to make one piece of equipment serve several purposes and by fashioning what you can at the campsite. For instance, it may be more sensible to make sticks for toasting and tent stakes or small tent poles as needed instead of carrying them along.

Mark each article of equipment, including clothing, with your name, either on a name tape or with India ink or marking pen.

Burn labels into wooden articles such as hatchet or shovel handles with a wood-burning set.

Keep such leather parts as axe sheaths, knapsack straps and sheath knife covers clean and soft by oiling them with neat's-foot oil at least once a year.

## PACKING FOR A TRIP

Even though "camp" is only a few feet from your cabin, take pride in your ability to pack well, for no worthy camper ever forgets part of his duffel. To avoid such a disgrace make a check list and check and recheck it while packing.

Do not include breakables or crushables unless they are well padded and carefully plan every detail of packing, putting heavy things and those not needed until night at the bottom of your pack and keeping such frequently used items as sun glasses, raincoat or poncho, matches, knife, drinking cup, watch, map, money, first aid kit and mess kit near the top.

Place a few small things in your pockets (which should be deep and built for service). Things lost along the trail have an uncanny way of hiding among the brush and leaves so that you cannot find them even if you have enough time for back tracking. Fasten them to your pocket with a safety pin or pin your whole pocket shut.

Attach your knife, compass, and like equipment, to a buttonhole or belt loop by a stout cord or chain which is long enough to permit you to use the object without detaching it.

## PACK SACKS

Traveling on foot with your bedding, food and clothing on your back offers the ultimate in freedom for those who want to get away from man-made things and see nature at its best. When you have learned to walk un-obtrusively through the forest with open eyes and alert mind you will ex-perience scenes of wild life you will never forget. However, a hot, heavy pack is enough to kill the enthusiasm of even the most ardent fan.

Pack all equipment neatly in some type of bag, for only a rank beginner trails along with objects dangling and flapping from his waist and bulging out of his pockets, making him look as bristly as a porcupine. Things sus-pended from your waist pull heavily on your belt and are neither comfortable nor healthful, and objects hanging from one shoulder are but little better. Stow such soft materials as extra clothing and blankets on the side of your pack next your back to forestall being gouged by various odds and ends of hard equipment.

Any heavy pack will feel burdensome but, as you continue to carry it a few days your muscles will strengthen and you will learn how to carry it so that it scarcely bothers at all.

The most comfortable pack distributes the weight to your shoulders and hips without constricting your chest in any way. Many varieties of knapsack are available, but the large-capacity ones weigh too much for adolescent boys and girls. Only the most common will be discussed here.

### A Shoulder Stick Pack

The most picturesque and romantic way to carry your possessions is to tie them in a big bandana, hang it on the end of a stick, tramp-style, and jauntily stride along with it perched over one shoulder. Unfortunately, your jaunty feeling lasts only a short time for this is in reality a most uncomfortable way to carry a bundle.

### Blanket Roll

You may roll your supplies in a blanket, secure it with horse-blanket pins and rope, and wear it in a "U" around your shoulders. This works well enough for a short trip, but the roll becomes hot and sweaty and catches on every tree and branch along the way, making it ill-adapted for long distances.

BLANKET ROLL

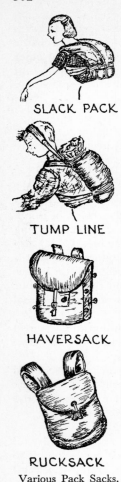

SLACK PACK

TUMP LINE

HAVERSACK

RUCKSACK

Various Pack Sacks.

### Blue Jeans or Slack Pack

Jaeger* describes a novel way to make a pack sack out of blue jeans or slacks. Tie your duffel into a secure parcel and slip into the body of your slacks and secure it by running a rope through the belt loops and up around the crotch. Convert the legs of the slacks into pack straps by bringing them around across your shoulders and under your arms, fastening them to the *middle* rather than the edges of the pack so as to keep the weight centered well over the middle of your back.

### Tump Line

Shoulder straps are used to support most packs, but those who make a practice of carrying heavy packs day after day often use a tump line in conjunction with them. A tump line consists of a narrow strip of leather or webbing about 16 feet long and widened to about $2\frac{1}{2}$ inches at the center where it sits high on your head just above your forehead. Its main use is as a safety precaution when climbing steep mountains or crossing swift steams where your footing is precarious; you then support the heavy pack by only the tump line which you can release by a mere flick of your head if you should start to fall. The tump line also serves to rest you, for, when used alone, it shifts the weight to your neck instead of your shoulders, and, when used with your shoulder straps, it distributes the weight between your neck and shoulders. Tump lines are impractical for girls, but are sometimes used by older boys and men. You can improvise your own by rolling a sock or other strong, soft material and attaching a strong cord to each end of it and fastening the ends to your pack.

### The Haversack

This is perhaps the best pack for an adolescent camper on a long trip when he must take much duffel for it will hold as much as he ought to carry for any appreciable distance. It is large enough to contain a folded blanket next his back, and there are rings around the top and sides for tying on additional blankets. One or more pockets are usually provided for storing things that are used most often.

* Jaeger, Ellsworth: Wildwood Wisdom, p. 64.

### The Rucksack

The rucksack is a small, light type of bag suitable for short trips, but it is not spacious enough for blankets and large quantities of food. The name is of German origin and means "back sack." It is distinguished from other pack sacks by the fact that the shoulder straps come together in a "V" at the middle of the back, causing it to hug the shoulders and ride comfortably on them. Several pockets are usually provided. The Army knapsack and Boy Scout pack are modeled after it.

### Adirondack Pack Baskets

Adirondack pack baskets are woven of ash or oak, shaped to fit the back and equipped with straps for carrying. They are great favorites with many and are rigid enough to hold canned goods and other hard objects without danger of poking you in the back. The disadvantages are that they are awkward to fit into a canoe or automobile, catch on brush and trees when on your back, and can't be folded up for storage when empty. Be sure your basket fits you. They are usually not waterproof so you must pack the contents in waterproof bags.

Adirondack Pack Basket.

### Duluth Pack Sack

The Duluth pack sack is a large bag capable of hauling a week's or more supply of food, bedding, blankets and clothing. It comes in a variety of forms known by various names. The Duluth bag is one of the most popular with strong, brawny men hardened enough to carry it and usually comes equipped with both shoulder straps and tump line.

### Dunnage Bags

Various types of large bags and boxes are available for transporting large quantities of equipment to and from camp. The duffel bag is one of the most widely known. It is made of water-proof material and is designed for ship-ping equipment by automobile, wagon, train, pack horse or canoe, but never for carrying on the back. Protect its contents with a chain and padlock when you ship it by train or common carrier. The original duffel bags had a drawstring at

Duffel Bag.

the top which made them most inconvenient, for the thing most needed seemed always to be at the very bottom, where you could not locate it without emptying all the contents. Modern models have a zipper running down one side so that you can readily locate what you want.

Some prefer wooden lockers with handles and partitioned shelves for transporting their possessions to and from camp. These have an advantage in that they furnish a good storage space for your paraphernalia while in camp.

## Pack Frames

These can be made or purchased in a variety of kinds. They support your pack and keep it away from your back so that it rides more comfortably

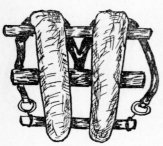

A Pack Frame.

and does not cause you to perspire so much. If you do not have a pack sack, place all of your duffel on your poncho or ground cloth and fold it into a compact package, then lash it to the pack boards. If you have a pack sack with straps, you can usually slip the straps right over the pack frames. Make your own pack frame from pieces of orange crate or scrap lumber and cover them with canvas or other durable padding next your back. The main disadvantages of pack boards is the added expense if purchased and the storage space required when not in use.

## Ditty Bags

A good camper doesn't pack a single thing loose in his pack; he collects things of a similar nature together and puts them in a small *ditty bag*, then

Ditty Bags.

places all his ditty bags inside his pack so that he need not turn everything topsy-turvy while searching for some small object which has dropped to the bottom or been overlooked and left behind at the last stop.

The number of ditty bags you need depends on the length of your trip and the amount of duffel you will take. A minimum is one for toilet articles, one for underwear and clothing, and one for first aid equipment. You may want others for tools and other repair items, shoes, articles of food, and so on.

You can purchase ditty bags from outfitters, but it is easy to make them from waterproof material or strong cloth which you waterproof. In reality, they need not be waterproof at all if the pack containing them is so treated. To determine the size you need for an individual bag, gather all the equipment you want to include in it and make a paper pattern to surround it, allowing extra width for double-stitched seams and extra length for a wide hem with a draw string at the top. Ditty bags with round bottoms, such as the case for toilet articles, will stand open and upright. Those made by simply sewing two straight pieces of cloth together are a bit simpler to make and prove quite satisfactory for most purposes. Letter the name of the contents on the side of the bag with enamel for permanence or with wax crayon which will wash out if it is to be only a temporary receptacle. Making the bags of different colored material will also help you locate the one you want quickly. Regular shoe bags are handy for carrying various pieces of equipment in your pack and may be tied in a jiffy to a tree or the foot of your bed where the contents are easily available.

Shoe Bag Hold-all.

## THE GOOD OLD PONCHO

A poncho is a waterproof cloth available in a variety of sizes; it is a perfect example of a piece of equipment which pays its way by serving many purposes. It is made of rubber, alligator cloth or one of the new featherweight materials. It has a hole near the center large enough to slip your head through so that you can wear it as a large cape, and there are overlapping flaps to cover the hole and make it waterproof when you use it as a flat piece. There are snaps along the edges so that you can fasten it around blankets arranged as a bed roll where it serves both as a waterproof cover and an under layer for the sleeper. The metal *grommets* along the sides are for inserting ropes to convert it into a shelter or lean-to (see p. 294) and it is also useful to shield a fire when you must build it in the rain or in a strong draft.

## GROUND CLOTH

A ground cloth is similiar to a poncho, but does not have a center hole for wearing it as a rain cape. It is even simpler to construct and takes about four yards of material.

In making either a ground cloth or a poncho, wide seams which won't pull out must be allowed for and double or triple stitching must be used throughout. Snaps and grommets (not less than $\frac{1}{2}$ inch in size) may be purchased and inserted.

## WHAT TO WEAR

Take only plain, serviceable, strong and washable clothing. Camp is not the place for fragile or dressy things, for your clothing must wear well and protect you from the weather, be it windy, sunny, cold or hot. It must fit snugly and comfortably, yet loosely enough to permit active use of your body when hiking, climbing or canoeing. It should be loosely woven to permit rapid evaporation of perspiration and should have plenty of deep, secure pockets for holding equipment. Try to find out what kind of weather to expect in the place you intend to camp.

### Shirts

Cotton shirts with open throat and short sleeves make satisfactory camp apparel, but wool flannel shirts are preferable for trip wear in some climates. Although they sound hot and uninviting for summer, they are in reality quite comfortable, for they readily absorb perspiration and just as readily let it evaporate. Cotton shirts absorb moisture until they reach saturation point, then lie like a chilly wet wash, bringing on chills and summer colds. Take at least one extra flannel shirt to wear as a jacket or provide a change if caught in the rain. A shirt with long sleeves is advisable for woods travel to prevent scratches and contact with poison ivy and oak. Deep, buttoned pockets are most useful.

### Sweaters

Sweaters make pretty poor camp attire, for they collect every burr in sight, snag on bushes, stretch out of shape, and become soggy and heavy when wet. Their best use is as a bed jacket or for extra warmth when worn under a more serviceable shirt or jacket.

### Jacket

A windbreaker jacket of waist length is desirable to provide additional warmth when you have no extra flannel shirt.

### Trousers

Blue jeans are the preference of many for general camp wear. They are inexpensive, comfortable, serviceable and washable, and provide ample pockets for storing various items of camp gear. When going through the woods, roll the legs down for protection from branches and poison ivy. If they are too long for you, cut them off instead of rolling them up where the cuffs catch on brush and protruding rocks to trip you and collect dirt and duff. A pair of shorts provides a cool change for wear around the campsite and in a canoe. Riding breeches or jodhpurs should be confined to horseback riding, for they are too tight about the knees for comfort when hiking or stooping and bending around the campsite. Slacks should be of smooth, tough material which will not pick up burrs.

### Belt

You will need a strong belt for attaching your scout axe and clips or safety thongs for your knife, compass, small match box, and similar equipment. You may prefer keeping all except your axe in your pockets to minimize the weight suspended from your belt.

### Hat

A hat or cap with a fairly wide brim will protect you from the sun, wind, cold and rain, and a strap or tie strings for anchoring it under your chin in windy weather is helpful.

### Pajamas

Always take pajamas for sleeping. Do not sleep in your hiking clothes.

### Underwear

Take at least one change of underwear.

### Socks

Socks are one of the most important items for a trip camper (or at any other time for that matter), for they can completely make or mar your comfort and happiness. Light-weight wool socks are the most practical, for they cushion your feet and, like wool shirts, permit the quick evaporation of perspiration. If your skin is sensitive to wool, wear a thin pair of cotton socks underneath. Socks should fit well, for, when too large, they chafe and cause blisters; when too short, they cramp your feet just as ill-fitting shoes do.

Wash and hang your socks and underwear up to dry each night and put on a clean outfit each morning. It is restful to wash your feet and change socks at noon if the hiking has been rough and the weather hot. Mended socks are bad, for, no matter how skillfully darned, they almost invariably irritate and cause blisters. Slipping into an extra pair of wool socks on cold nights is almost equivalent to having an extra blanket.

## Shoes

Flimsy, open-toed shoes are a menace for camp wear. They give little support and slip around so freely that they often cause falls, arch trouble and sprained ankles. They are not even fit to wear around a campfire—leave them in the city.

You will need at least two pairs of shoes—a light pair for resting your feet in the evening around the campfire or in a canoe, and a heavy pair for woods wear.

Moccasins are the woodsman's choice for the light pair. They are so thin and pliable that travel in them is almost like going barefoot, yet you have the added protection of a thickness of leather and the heavy wool socks you should wear with them. They are excellent when in a canoe, though some prefer to slip them off and paddle in their stocking feet. Those whose feet have accustomed themselves to moccasins will have nothing else even when walking through dry woods, for they permit "feeling" your way along the trail with sureness and ease. However, if you have never worn them your feet will be used to the support of hard city shoes. Do not initiate them on a rugged trip but accustom your feet to them around camp and on short hikes. It is easy to make your own moccasins using the many patterns and kits available now.

Rubber sneakers, though light, are not at all satisfactory for hiking; their rubber soles do not permit the perspiration to escape, and they literally steam your feet until they are raw and tender. You may prefer them around the campfire, in the canoe, or as a relief from heavier hiking shoes. Those with leather soles are better for camp wear than those with rubber.

For general woods hiking, strong, sturdy shoes with fairly thick, flexible soles are best. They should be large enough to allow for wearing heavy wool socks and for the swelling of your feet which inevitably accompanies hiking long distances in hot weather. Heels should be low and broad and preferably of leather; rubber heels, though more shock-absorbent for hard city pavements, are not really needed on country trails and are slippery on wet leaves and other damp surfaces. The same can be said of smooth leather or rubber soles, which are treacherous in the woods, where there is always some moisture. Be sure to have heavily corrugated soles or strong rubber cleats.

Pacs are adaptations of the moccasin, made of strong but light leather and with shoe seams on the outside, like moccasins. They are favorites with many campers.

Some prefer light boots, 8 to 10 inches high, into which they can stuff the bottoms of their blue jeans or slacks. These are especially good for snaky territory. Boots higher than this are a nuisance, for they are usually stiff, clumsy and hot, and often cause blisters on the feet and ankles.

Moisten and then tie your shoestrings by pulling one loop through the knot a second time before tightening it. This prevents the strings from coming untied in a dangerous or bothersome way along the trail.

You cannot actually waterproof your shoes with any degree of permanency, and the heavy and frequent applications of oil make them heavy and airtight and cause your feet to become steamy and tender. However, it is a good idea to apply a light application of neat's-foot oil now and then to keep the leather in good condition and make it resistant to moisture.

When your shoes get wet, dry them slowly with gentle heat; rapid drying with intense heat cracks and utterly ruins leather.

"Tenderfoot" has a literal meaning, and a good camper avoids being one by giving proper care and attention to his feet and footwear. New shoes never make good companions on the trail, nor do your old rundown ones. A well broken-in, strong pair is best.

## For Rainy Weather

Getting completely drenched will not cause a cold or any ill effects whatsoever if you immediately change into dry clothing and get thoroughly warm in front of a blazing fire. Even so, it is much better not to take chances on getting wet, and a wise camper always goes prepared for rain. Use waterproof pack sacks and bedrolls and carry extra tarpaulins or ponchos to cover any duffel not so protected.

Keep your own waterproofing close to the top of your pack where you can find it in a hurry when you need it. There is little agreement as to the best rain protection but none disputes the inadequacy of the gossamer, oiled silk cape with hood which is nice for town wear. It would soon be torn to ribbons if subjected to the rough treatment of camp life. Town raincoats, too, prove more or less unsatisfactory.

The general preference seems to be for a "rain shirt" or combination poncho and raincoat with loose raglan type sleeve and a wide bottom which can be spread to cover your duffel when in a canoe.

A regular poncho with a hole in the middle to fit over your head, a "pudding string" around your waist, and snaps down the sides to give it the approximation of a fit is still preferred by some, but it is hot for warm-weather wear.

When made of alligator cloth or one of the new featherweight materials, it is cooler and lighter to wear and carry than the old-style rubber type.

Raincoats, which are too long, are a pure nuisance, for they flap about in your way at every step, tripping you when you climb hills, and constantly flying open to expose the lower part of your body to the elements. They are usually hot and binding and cause profuse sweating.

Poncho Worn as a Raincoat.

Some ponchos are equipped with hoods to keep your head dry. Otherwise a sou'wester or light waterproof hat with a medium brim (which will also serve as a sun hat) and tie strings for under your chin is good.

You will need light rubbers to fit over your shoes or moccasins. Rubber boots are clumsy and tiring to walk in and are recommended only for actually wading through water.

Rain pants and shirts are good if made of strong enough material to stand up under rough treatment.

### Bandana

A large-sized bandana is another piece of equipment which adapts itself to many purposes. You can use it to handle hot pans around the cooking fire, to tie up a home-made mess kit, to hold specimens gathered along the way, to double for a triangular bandage, or to shield your neck and face from sunburn and insects. Carry it in your hip pocket or wear it around your neck cowboy fashion, ready for instant use.

### Canvas Gloves

Cheap, washable canvas gloves are a very important part of your equipment. They are a wonderful aid when handling cooking pots and pans and when building fires or working with brush. They protect your skin from abrasions and keep your hands clean for actually working with food. They must be small enough to fit properly, for large ones are awkward and tend to slip, making them dangerous to use.

### Swimming Suit and Cap

You will need these for refreshing dips or for cleansing purposes when other facilities are not available.

### TOILET ARTICLES

Carry a few well-chosen toilet articles in a ditty bag approximately 9 by 19 inches or in a specially constructed case. The case is particularly handy for you can wear it around your waist while using it, tie it at the foot of your bed, or roll it up and place it in your pack en route. Fashion it from waterproof material or other strong goods. Spread out all the articles you want to include in logical sequence and make a paper pattern to fit, allowing enough space for hems and turning up 6 or 7 inches of the material for pockets (be sure to allow enough fullness to accommodate the thickness of the objects).

For a short trip, you need take only small quantities of toilet supplies (a small piece of soap instead of the whole bar, a small quantity of tooth powder instead of the whole can, and the like). Pack them in nonbreakable containers. Such planning is the secret of successful *Go Light* trips. You may

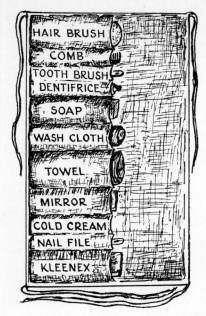

Toilet Case.

sometimes have to pack such articles as toothbrush, toilet soap, wash-cloths and towels wet so it is best to fit them with individual oiled-silk covers. You need take no great supply of washcloths and towels for you can wash them out and hang them up to dry overnight. A small metal mirror is superior to the usual type.

## MISCELLANEOUS EQUIPMENT

Include a few tools in your trip outfit. If several campers are going, you need not burden each member of the party with duplicates; for instance, two axes will serve a whole party, for few will be using them at any one time; one would be inadequate owing to the danger of loss or breakage.

### Axe, Knife and Sheath Knife

The choice of an axe, knife and sheath knife has already been discussed.

Always keep your axe in its sheath, and wear it on your belt or pack it on top of your duffel where you can find it quickly.

Carry your knife in your pocket, attached to your belt or belt loop, or fasten it securely in one of the pockets of your pack sack.

One or two sheath knives for the group are convenient to use as cooking knives or as strong knives for heavy work.

### Tools for Sharpening

Include at least one file and one Carborundum stone for party use.

### Adhesive Tape

Adhesive tape serves many functions in addition to its first aid use in applying bandages and supporting sprains. It will stick to almost anything that is dry, especially if pressed on with a little heat as from a heated spoon or frying pan. You can use it to temporarily mend a leaky tent or canoe, a rip in clothing, or a leak in a bucket or kettle. It will also secure a cork in a bottle, fasten the lid on a box or tin can, and even make hinges for a lid.

### Tools

Such tools as a screw driver, pliers with wire cutter, and so forth, are useful. A compact tool haft is available which you can convert into several tools by fitting it with the different attachments contained in the hollow handle. Carry a trowel or small shovel with detachable handle for trenching your tent and manipulating and putting out fires.

### Camera

Only a really good camera and equipment will give superior results in nature photography, for you must take the shots where you find them, often in the shade or in other spots difficult to photograph. Keep your camera where you can snatch it up and use it in the brief period nature poses. Be sure to take extra films along.

### Purse and Money

You may need a small amount of money for supplies along the way and for emergency use. Pin it fast in your pocket or keep it in a secure place in your pack sack.

### Watch

At least two people in a group should have watches. Luminous dials are an advantage at night.

### Glasses

Campers with bad vision should take along an extra pair of glasses in a strong case on long trips.

### Maps

Even though you do not actually need a map to find your way, a topographical map of the region will be very interesting and will help you choose the most intriguing path. To protect it, make a map case from two sheets of transparent celluloid, joining them on three sides with adhesive or Scotch tape. Slip the folded map into the case and tape it shut on the fourth side. Have the sheets large enough to accommodate the map folded to show the particular region in which you are traveling.

## Compass

You will need a compass to follow or make a trail map. Slip it into your shirt pocket and fasten it with a strong cord or thong.

## Stationery

Never take ink for it is likely to leak and ruin valuable duffel, and anything written with it runs and becomes undecipherable when it gets damp. A hard pencil and postal cards or envelopes already stamped are most suitable in camp.

## Notebook and Pencil

Always keep a small notebook and pencil in your pocket. A hard pencil is best, for it will not smear as the pages of the book rub together.

It is excellent to form the habit of jotting down and filing anything you encounter which might be of later interest. Games, stories, songs, bits of nature lore, and so on are veritable gold mines during counseling days and you may keep them in a file box or large-capacity notebook cover for ready reference.

A loose-leaf notebook, opening on the side, and holding sheets about $3\frac{3}{4}$ by $6\frac{3}{4}$ inches is good, for the sheets are roomy, yet the notebook is small enough to slip into your pocket or store compactly. Before starting on a trip make a few well-chosen selections from your file to use along the way. Provide blank pages for making notes on the trip.

## Protection from Sunlight

You will need a broad-brimmed hat, a bandana for your neck, a *good* pair of sunglasses and some sun tan oil if you are to be much in the open, particularly on water. Carry sunburn ointment, too, in case someone is so foolish as to overexpose himself.

## Protection from Insects

Take a good insect repellent to apply to your face, neck and hands, a head net, and insect protection for your tent. Many good sprays are now available which will aid greatly in keeping your campsite free from irritating insects, but science is still debating and experimenting for the use of some is dangerous under certain conditions. Before purchasing or using them, get expert advice and be sure to follow directions carefully.

## Bed Roll

This includes a poncho or ground cloth, rope, a sleeping bag or a bedroll of blanket pins and rope. Extra socks, underwear, towels, and the like in a bag, make a satisfactory pillow.

## Sit-upons

These inventions of the Girl Scouts are useful when sitting on damp ground and also make good pillows. Make them by placing a few layers of newspaper between two pieces of oilcloth about a foot square and binding the edges together with a blanket stitch. You may paint your name upon your sit-upon. Roll it up and tie it with a string for carrying.

## Tents

Tents or extra tarpaulins and ponchos are necessary in case of rain.

## Flashlight

Take a good flashlight with extra bulbs and batteries. The type with the head on the side is expecially good since it can be hung up to serve as a lantern. Each camper should have his own flashlight.

A Good Type of Flashlight.

## Field Glasses

Good, light-weight field glasses are valuable for nature study. The term "field glasses" is a general one applied to several types of instrument, the most popular being *binoculars*, which permit looking with both eyes simultaneously. The *power* of field glasses, usually printed on them as 6X, 8X, 10X, and so on, indicates the number of times they magnify what you see. For instance, 8X glasses make an object a mile away seem as though it were only $\frac{1}{8}$ mile away because they magnify it eight times its normal size. You might naturally assume that it is best to get the highest powered glasses available, but this is not necessarily true, since they magnify what you do not want to see as well as what you do. Thus they intensify haze, smoke, the trembling of your hands holding them, the movements of the boat, or even a gnat that happens to cross your line of vision. Also, the higher the power, the narrower the field of vision—in other words, you see more and more of less and less. You will usually find it most desirable to get a clear view of a fairly wide field, and so your choice will be a 6X or 8X pair.

## Canteen

If you are not sure there is pure water along your route, purify an adequate supply once a day and carry it in individual canteens or large group containers.

Aluminum canteens are best, for they neither taint the water nor rust. They are ordinarily covered by a thick layer of felt and another of flannel which, when kept wet, cools the contents by evaporation. The canvas keeps the felt from drying out too rapidly and somewhat protects your clothing from dampness. To sterilize water in the canteen, remove the outside coverings and boil it for twenty to thirty minutes. Rinse out your canteen occasionally with boiling water. You can make a canteen by fitting tight covers of flannel (or felt) and canvas over the lower two-thirds of a flat quart bottle and attaching carrying straps. The coverings make the bottle less breakable.

Home-made Canteen.

## Pedometer

This is an interesting instrument to record the distance you cover on foot (see p. 228).

## Fishing Gear

Fresh fish make a welcome addition to your camp menu.

## Toilet Paper

## Books and Pamphlets

Sources for songs, games, nature identification, poetry, or stories are welcome.

## Mending Kit

Pack equipment for construction and repair in a tin box or canvas bag and include such items as needles, pins, a few yards of thread wound on a piece of cardboard, small pointed scissors, buttons, patches of cloth and leather, large rubber bands, adhesive tape, twine, strong waxed linen thread, nails, tacks, strong wire, glue, and a canoe repair kit.

## Candles

Candles are useful for light at night and for getting a stubborn fire started in wet weather.

## Matches

Include a large reserve supply and a small daily supply, either waterproofed or in a waterproof container.

### Equipment for Building Fires in Wet Weather

Trench candles (pp. 285–286) or "peas" (p. 286) and bits of dry tinder will come in handy. An inspirator (p. 279) coiled up in one of your cooking kettles is worth its weight in gold for starting fires in wet weather.

### Extra Paddles

Include them when traveling by canoe in case one is lost or broken.

### Water Purification Equipment

Carry halazone tablets or some other means of purification unless you are going to boil your water (see p. 376), or camp where you know there is safe water.

### Whistle

Wear it on a cord or lanyard and use it to signal anyone who has strayed from the group. This should not happen in a well-organized trip but you can never be too sure.

### Cooking Outfits

When on the move, nested cooking outfits are most economical of weight and space and come in sizes serving up to twelve persons. If you find their regular canvas cover too tight for easy handling, transfer them to a home-made cotton bag or an old flour or sugar sack with a draw string.

Aluminum is perhaps the best light material for kits although light-weight stainless steel has less tendency to cause food to stick and burn. Porcelain will chip when carried on trips. Aluminum drinking cups burn your lips when filled with hot liquids. Enamel cups, especially with the handles open at the bottom so that they do not get too hot to hold comfortably, are better and tin ones will do.

You can make your own cooking or mess kits (Chap. 22) or assemble them at the ten-cent store or hardware store, using a tape measure or the trial-and-error method to insure compact nesting. Carry your cooking kit in a home-made bag as described and your individual mess kit tied up in your bandana. Wire bails make the best handles for cooking pots for they serve to suspend them over the fire and can be folded flat for nesting. Fold down rings on lids instead of knobs and a minimum of spouts and bail ears also aid in compact nesting. Tight-fitting pot covers keep the heat and juices in and dirt and ashes out. The long handles on many frying pans are hollow. Cut them off for ease in packing and attach them with wing nuts (p. 243) or cut wooden handles at the campsite. Low, broad utensils heat faster and are less liable to upset than high ones. Pie tins make good unbreakable plates. Knives, forks, and spoons can be placed inside the kettles or carried inside a bag made like a toilet kit (pp. 310–311). Use the largest pail, which fits outside your kit, for a water bucket so that it will always be clean for contact with the cloth cover.

Some never wash the outsides of any of their cooking kettles, claiming that the accumulation of carbon improves their heat-retaining properties. If you follow this practice you will need to pack them between layers of newspapers.

Individual Mess Kit.

Your reflector oven should fold flat. A Dutch oven is a big convenience, but is cumbersome to transport.

Careful planning of your menu will facilitate your utensil problem, for you can cook many things as one-pot meals, or without utensils in aluminum foil or on sticks or woodland broilers fashioned at the campsite.

If you take individual cooking outfits, the Boy or Girl Scout kits are as good as any.

## FIRST AID KITS

Always be safety conscious so that you will have as little need as possible for first aid treatment. Nevertheless on every trip going out of camp, you should take along a first aid kit complete enough to care for minor ailments and injuries.

Assemble it in a compact container which protects the contents. A flat tobacco tin makes a satisfactory individual kit, and a small-sized tackle box with its several compartments is excellent for a larger kit. Aluminum kits are light in weight. You can make a canvas cover with a carry strap so as to carry it over one shoulder.

Line the kit with corrugated cardboard, sponge rubber or several layers of heavy blotters to prevent breakage. If this is impossible, cover all glass containers individually with a layer of sponge rubber, corrugated cardboard, cotton or tissues held in place by a rubber band or a piece of string. Slip small vials of liquid medicines into old wooden or cardboard pill boxes. You can buy first aid kits, but they are more expensive and often do not contain exactly what you want.

First Aid Kit.

You need take only small quantities of each medication, and you can buy small vials for liquids and tin cans for ointments economically at the drug store or from a doctor's office. Some medications are available in ampules just large enough for a single treatment. The camp doctor or nurse will advise you what supplies to take but the following are suggested:

Instruction booklet
Triangular bandage (you can use a clean bandana for this)
Absorbent cotton
Adhesive tape
Band aids
Gauze squares—roller gauze
Aromatic spirits of ammonia—for bites, stings, and fainting
Boric acid solution—for minor eye irritations
Aspirin
Bicarbonate of soda—for bites, stings, and indigestion
Oil of cloves—for toothache
Tincture of iodine (2% solution), Zephiran Chloride or Merthiolate for open cuts and abrasions (ampules provide the most convenient form)
Tannic acid (jelly or powder) or picric acid—for burns
Tweezers (sharp pointed)
Ferric chloride (5% solution) or calamine lotion—for poison ivy or oak
Snake bite outfit
Scissors
Safety pins
American Red Cross First Aid Textbook.

You can make a temporary crutch as illustrated. The top, which rests under the armpit, should be smoothed with sandpaper or sand held in a piece of cloth or leather, and padded with sponge rubber, gauze or some folds of soft cloth bound on with adhesive tape.

Emergency Crutch.

## CHECK LISTS FOR PACKING EQUIPMENT

Select from the following to make out your own check list. Then check and recheck it to eliminate everything not really essential. Revise it on the basis of your experience when you return and keep it handy for use the next time.

*Personal Equipment*

| ESSENTIAL | OPTIONAL |
|---|---|
| Hatchet | Sheath knife |
| Knife | Field glasses |
| Waterproof match box and matches | Camera and extra film |
| Flashlight and extra bulb and batteries | Map |
| Toilet soap | Nature books |
| Face towels (small, light ones best) | Story books |
| Pocket mirror (metal, preferred) | Money |
| Toothbrush | Sun glasses |

## *Personal Equipment*

| ESSENTIAL | OPTIONAL |
|---|---|
| Toothpaste or powder | Sit-upons |
| Extra shoes | Stationery (already stamped) |
| Extra socks | Canteen |
| Pajamas | Fishing equipment |
| Slicker or raincoat and rain hat | Musical instrument |
| Leather belt for hatchet | Compass |
| Notebook | Watch |
| Hard pencil | Song books |
| Canvas gloves | Bathing suit and bathing cap |
| Bandana | Game books |
| Mess kit, including fork and spoon | Poetry |
| Bed roll | Whistle |
| Washcloths | Sun tan lotion |
| Comb | Rubbers |
| Extra underclothes | Insect shield and repellent |
| Handkerchiefs | Pedometer |
| Leather jacket, wool shirt, or wind breaker | Razor |
| | Eyeglasses and case |
| | Kotex (for girls) |

## *Group Equipment*

Check list of equipment

Scouring powder

Matches—extra supply

Menus and recipes

Food list

Mending kit—buttons, thread, needles, and so on

Washpan or canvas wash basin

Aluminum foil

Paper napkins

Egg beater (for use in mixing dehydrated milk)

Halazone tablets (or other means of purifying water)

Hobo stoves

Cooking forks

Cooking spoons

Spatulas

Cooking pans

Water pails

Dutch ovens

Reflector ovens

Dish towels

First aid kit

Nails, twine, and other tools

Carborundum stone

Adhesive tape

Salt and pepper shakers (fit a piece of waxed paper inside the screw-on tops)

Extra tarpaulins or ponchos

Tents, poles and pegs

Inspirator, "peas," trench candles, and so forth

Extra paddles

Food

#10 tin can buckets

Dishcloths

Yellow soap or soap flakes

Metal sponge for cleaning pans

Camp shovel

File

Can opener

Toilet paper

Candles (plumbers' are best)

Insect spray

Fishing equipment

## ADDITIONAL READINGS

Camping. Boy Scouts (#3256), 1946.

Des Grey, Arthur H.: Camping. Ronald, 1950, pp. 12–35.

Geist, Roland C.: Hiking, Camping and Mountaineering, chap. 2.

Good Idea. C.M., March, 1946. (Directions for making a personal locker.)

Halstead, Homer: How to Live in the Woods. Little, 1948.

Jaeger, Ellsworth: Wildwood Wisdom, chaps. 1–3.

Jessup, Elon: The Boy's Book of Camp Life, chaps. 5, 7 and 8.

Joy, Barbara Ellen: Suggestions for Improvised Camping-out Equipment. Camp Publications, no. 64.

Kephart, Horace: Camping out and Woodcraft, vol. 1, chaps. 7, 9 and 10; vol. 2, chaps. 7 and 8.

Mason, Bernard S.: The Junior Book of Camping and Woodcraft, pp. 2, 3, 21–23, 82, 93.

Mason, Bernard S.: Woodcraft, chap. 5.

Rutstrum, Calvin: Way of the Wilderness, chaps. 8, 9 and 10.

Safety Wise: The What and Why of a First Aid Kit. Girl Scouts.

West, James E., and Hillcourt, William: Scout Field Book, Pow-wow 13.

With never a thought of danger, he lies in his blanket
bed,
His coat of canvas the pillow
supporting his drowsy head
As he watches the white
clouds drifting through lim-
itless azure seas
Where only the stars can find
him as they peep through
the sheltering trees.
JAMES BARTON ADAMS

## Chapter 28

# SLEEPING IN THE OPEN

SINCE A THIRD or more of a camper's time is spent in sleep, his bed is de-
serving of much of his thought and attention. A good night's rest with at
least eight hours of sleep for adults and even more for youngsters is a
"must" for those on a trip.

If you are going by covered wagon or if the camp truck is to transport the
heavy baggage, bulk and weight are not of tremendous importance. But
when you travel entirely on your own two feet with all your possessions on
your back, it is really a problem to provide a comfortable bed that will
weigh little and not be cumbersome to handle. Canoe bedding, too, must be
kept light and compact, although it is possible to take a little more than
when back packing.

One of the most difficult jobs in all the world would be to try to get a
crowd of experienced campers to agree on which type of outdoor bed is best.
One reason for this is, of course, the difference in circumstances and localities
in which they have camped. Obviously, a person who has always bedded
down in the cold Northland, often in the dead of winter, will have entirely
different standards from those that would be applicable or desirable for the
organized summer camp.

A good bed should provide warmth, a reasonable degree of softness,
smoothness and freedom from bumps, and protection from wind and rain,

and you must attain these qualities according to the nature of the particular terrain in which you sleep. Taking into consideration how much you can carry, you must select from the several types of beds available.

Since we are accustomed to sleeping on a mattress which needs practically no attention, most of us are inclined to ignore what is under us and think only in terms of what to use for cover. As you scamper about gathering your duffel in a knapsack ready for an overnight, the sun is shining, warm and cheerful, and it is hard to realize that it will go to bed long before you do and that the air will get increasingly colder as night progresses. The un-initiated will really travel light, but an experience or two will teach you that you need as many or more blankets under as over you. The ground is always damp, even with no recent rain, and the earth is an efficient conductor of heat away from the body so that you will likely spend a chilly night no matter how high you pile the blankets over you if you place too few underneath.

To rest, you must relax, and it's a little difficult to imagine an iceberg relaxing. Incidentally, the padding the extra blankets underneath provide isn't at all objectionable, either.

## Blankets

The finances of the boy or girl in an organized camp often makes the purchase of a sleeping bag or other fancy sleeping equipment out of the question. Blankets are the answer in this case. Indeed, some prefer them to a sleeping bag, for you can easily and quickly adapt them to changes in temperature and they are simple to spread for airing and give thorough cleaning from time to time. Air and sun your blankets everyday to get rid of the night's accumulation of perspiration from your body. Dry blankets are much warmer than clammy ones.

Blankets for outdoor beds should be of a dark, neutral shade which won't easily show soil.

One hundred per cent virgin wool blankets are much to be preferred, for their loose weave and long nap create pockets to imprison dead air and act as insulation against the loss of body heat. They help to cut down the weight of bedding by giving maximum warmth with minimum weight, for one wool blanket is the equivalent of several of part-wool or cotton. Many so-called wool blankets, however, have a percentage of cotton mixed in with them. Cotton blankets are poorest of all, for they gather and retain moisture from the body as well as from the air and ground.

Single blankets are easier to manipulate and several are warmer than one of their combined thickness since they trap a layer of insulating dead air between them.

Hudson's Bay blankets or blankets made of llama or camel's hair are the warmest of all and are the choice of Northwoods hunters and trappers, but they are expensive and provide more warmth than a summer camper ordinarily needs.

Quilts and comforters are bulky and too fragile for trail requirements.

## Making a Bed Roll

Some people simply roll up in their blankets and claim to sleep in perfect comfort throughout the night. This might be possible if we could truly go to bed and "sleep like a log," but scientific studies show that nearly all sleepers turn frequently to lie in many different positions before the night is over. Consequently they are likely to find parts of their anatomy exposed several times during the night and end up with an unhappy, restless time of it.

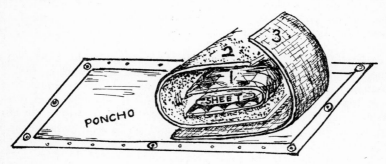

Making a Bed Roll.

It is easy to make an envelope or Klondike bedroll to keep you snug and warm throughout the night. You need four horse-blanket pins and blankets of equivalent size. First, lay your poncho or ground cloth on the ground,

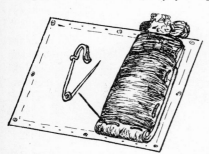

Pinning the Bed Roll.

and place the blanket you want outside (blanket No. 3) with its edge at the middle of the poncho and half of it extending beyond the poncho on one side. Next, place blanket No. 2 with its edge at the center of blanket No. 3 so that it lies directly above the poncho. Lay down as many blankets as you want in this fashion, each lapping half way over on the one beneath. Place your sheet on last and fold it in half lengthwise. Now fold your blankets over, in reverse order, beginning with No. 1 on top, then No. 2, and so on; when all are folded, pin them along the sides and bottom with your large horse-blanket pins if your poncho does not snap along sides and bottom to hold them in place. Make sure the pins go through *all* the blankets. Make your bed roll wide enough to let you turn during the night since confinement in narrow quarters seriously interferes with rest. Roll and tie your bedroll for carrying.

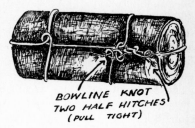

Tying the Bed Roll.

### Sleeping Bags

A sleeping bag consists of a waterproof covering and an inside compact arrangement of blankets or down. The best ones fasten with a zipper down one side and across the bottom so that you can open them out flat for a daily sunning and airing.

A variety of materials is used for filler. Those intended for use in subzero weather are made of eider or goose down; they are entirely too warm for use in summer camping, and their expense would make them prohibitive for many campers anyway. *Kapok* is a favorite, for it is inexpensive, durable, warm and dry. It is heavier and bulkier than down, but does not readily absorb water and is light enough to float and act as a life preserver in case of a canoe upset.

Good quality blankets also make an acceptable type of filler.

Sleeping bags have several points in their favor. They are arranged with no waste corners to add weight and bulk and you are zippered in so that you can't get uncovered and wake up in the middle of the night with a cold breeze blowing in on your back—particularly important with youngsters of camp age, who are often restless sleepers. Good ones also have adjustable awnings to protect you from insects and dew.

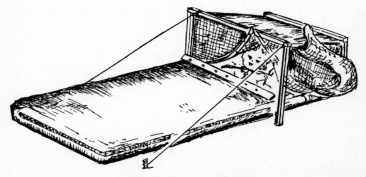

Bed Roll with Insect Shield.

On the other hand, the better bags are rather expensive, and many dislike the feeling of confinement they give. Some have the blankets or other filler sewed in so that you cannot remove them for the daily airing and cleaning dictated by good standards of sanitation. This also makes it impossible to vary the amount of bedding with the temperature. All you can do in this situation is to crawl in under only the topmost blankets, leaving the extra ones underneath for padding. Then, as the temperature falls toward morning, you must emerge from your roll and crawl back in again under a lower layer —a thing not too highly recommended for sound, restful sleep.

Bedrolls are now available with an inner removable section which can be taken out and slept in leaving the outer shell available for a second bed-roll. Both are warm enough for ordinary summer sleeping. In hot weather you may rest on top of your bedroll, using it for softness, and covering your-self with a supplementary blanket.

### Sleeping on the Ground

"Trippers" often make one-night or even longer trips sleeping in their bedrolls with only the ground for a mattess. Pollyanna might find some ad-vantages in this sort of bed, for there are no squeaking bed springs, the sleeper may be sure that the slats will not fall out, and there is no danger whatsoever of falling out of bed. But even Pollyanna would have to admit that softness is not one of its virtues.

It helps to hollow out depressions for your hips and shoulders carefully, repeatedly trying them for "fit," but even then there seems little doubt that the expression "making mountains out of molehills" must have originated with some unhappy outdoor sleeper. If spending the night in this fashion, get down on your hands and knees and go over every inch of the surface where your bed is to lie, removing each twig, acorn and tough weed.

One way to make a ground bed a bit softer is to gather such things as leaves, dry ferns and dry grass to make a mattress. They will spread out from under you until there is hardly anything left as the night progresses unless you "fence" them in by a pen of logs or some similar technique. Hay makes a good mattress and can often be purchased cheaply from a neighboring farmer. Fern and hay "mattresses" are especially good for holding heat.

If the night is particularly cold, you can build a reflector fire so that you sleep between the fire and reflector to be warmed by the fire on one side and the reflector on the other.

### Mattresses

A bed sack about $2\frac{1}{2}$ feet wide and $4\frac{1}{2}$ feet long can be made of bed ticking, strong, unbleached muslin, canvas, drill, burlap or grain sacks. It will weigh only a pound or a little over and can be taken on a trip if not too much

Stretcher Bed with Rain and Insect Shield in Place.

premium is placed on going light. Equip one end of the bag with snaps, safety pins, or strings so that you can open it and stuff it with leaves, grass, ferns, hay or whatever is available at the campsite. Waterproof the under side of the bag unless you are going to use it on top of a tarpaulin, ground cloth or poncho. A mattress of the dimensions given will be long enough to support the upper three-fourths of your body, which is really all that is necessary for com-

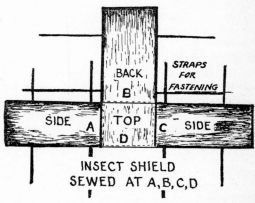

Pattern for a Combination Rain and Insect Shield.

fort. Air mattresses are, of course, very fine for those who want more comfort. Inflate them with the little hand inflater which comes with them but avoid overinflation. Carry a tire patching outfit for mending small leaks.

## Stretcher Beds

A comfortable and light form of mattress is the stretcher bed. Make it of canvas, drill, bed ticking or a doubled piece of burlap or grain sack with 3- to 4-inch seams on each side for inserting sticks to support it as shown. Support the sticks by logs, rocks, or forked sticks about $\frac{1}{2}$ to 1 foot above the ground and pound in stakes just inside the supporting sticks at the

Stretcher Bed.

four corners to keep them from rolling toward the center. You can place the waterproof canopy with a *bobbinet* insect shield shown above over the bed.

## Insect Shields

The rain canopy consists of a top and three flaps to be rolled up when
the weather is nice and lowered
and tied around the supporting
framework when it rains. The
best material to use for the insect shield is bobbinet, and it
is fastened to the top of the canopy where it meets the three
flaps at the seams. Leave it
long enough to tuck in around
the sleeper and under the bedroll.

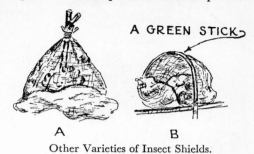

A GREEN STICK

A          B

Other Varieties of Insect Shields.

## Bough Beds

Beds of balsam, hemlock or spruce boughs sound romantic and are no
doubt comfortable when skillfully made, but the camper in an organized
camp will seldom be in a region so plentifully supplied with threse trees that
he can cut them for a bed without irreparably harm-
ing the forest. If you do make one, consult someone
who is an authority for there is a real art to the process. You definitely do not do it by just piling up an
assortment of boughs in haphazard fashion—such
would be worse than sleeping on the bare ground.

## Home-made Pillows

Pillows that are light, soft, and cost practically nothing can be made by
stuffing a bag with the soft down from milkweed pods or with cattail heads
picked when nearly ripe in the late summer or early fall. A pillow for a canoe
can be made in this way. On the trail, campers usually dispense with the
weight and bulk of a pillow, and use a pack sack (with hard objects removed)
or a rolled-up coat or sweater instead.

## ADDITIONAL READINGS

Geist, Roland C.: Hiking, Camping and
    Mountaineering, pp. 29, 30.
Jaeger, Ellsworth: Wildwood Wisdom,
    chap. 4.
Mason, Bernard S.: The Junior Book of
    Camping and Woodcraft, pp. 18, 24, 25.
Mason, Bernard S.: Woodcraft, chap. 5.
Rutstrum, Calvin: Way of the Wilderness,
    pp. 73–80.
Weaver, Robert W., and Merrill, Anthony
    F.: Camping Can Be Fun, chap. 4.

Then after a day filled with pleasure
    and work,
  As you trudge back to camp with
    your trout,
The smell of bacon that's cooking up
    there,
  Is the sweetest of odors, no doubt.
           F. K. BERRY,
          "Cooking in Camp"

## Chapter 29

# KEEPING FOOD COOL AND SAFE

"OH, THIS is the life," you say, as you sink back with a few of your pals on the first night away from permanent camp. Just a handful of friends, a delicious supper under your belt, dishes all washed up and put away, and nothing to do but gather around the campfire and enjoy yourself until time to turn in for the night, away from civilization for a few days with no danger of outsiders crashing in.

You may be right insofar as human intrusion is concerned, but do you realize that hundreds of forest eyes are or soon will be focused upon your camp? Friendly eyes, to be sure, but also curious, and wanting to investigate this strange assortment that has established itself in the midst of their owners' forest home. These creatures are hungry, too, and willing to nibble on anything and everything they can find after you have gone to bed.

Unless you are camping in wild country well toward the borders or clear outside of the United States, you are extremely unlikely to be visited by such animals as wolves, foxes or bears which constantly plagued the lives of the early settlers of the country. But such animals as chipmunks, squirrels, roving dogs, pack rats, and field mice are likely to be your neighbors. In some regions, porcupines are numerous and may prove troublesome, for their sharp teeth can be most destructive. Anything with a salty taste has a fatal attraction for them, and perspiration-soaked paddles, axes, shoes, belts, bridles and saddles must be kept well beyond their reach.

## PROTECTION FROM INSECTS

You must anticipate the ever-present flies, ants and other tiny crawling or flying creatures that love to sample your food and literally get in your hair. There are three chief ways to protect food from ants and other insects: (1) Place it on a table with each leg resting in a small container of water so that the insects cannot get to the food without going through the water. A variation is to suspend the food from a hook made by inserting a strong piece of wire as from a coat hanger through a small hole in a shallow tin can or cup. Solder the joining between the wire and can to make it watertight, turn back both ends of the wire to form hooks, and keep the cup filled with water to provide a barrier in the path to the food. (2) Place small strips of sticky fly paper over all ropes or other approaches to the food. These are messy to carry on trips and dry up so that you must replace them every few days. (3) Keep the food in insect-proof containers such as jars or cans with tight-fitting suction or screw-on lids. Plastic film jar covers weigh practically nothing, take up a negligible amount of space in your pack and can be slipped on as insect-proof coverings. A tight wrapping of cloth, mosquito netting, cheesecloth or waxed paper is likewise effective.

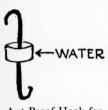

Ant-Proof Hook for Suspending Food.

## PROTECTION FROM ANIMALS

The type of marauders expected will, of course, determine the kind of cache or protection you must provide. Even tin cans are not safe, for some animals, including dogs, can pierce them with their teeth and suck out the contents. The usual method of caching food is to suspend it about 15 to 20 feet above the ground and at such a distance from overhanging branches that neither jumping nor climbing animals can get to it. Attach a rope and throw it across a tree limb to provide a pulley for quickly raising and lowering it. Food hung in the open in this way must have some sort of waterproof covering.

### The Green Sapling Cache

One method sometimes used to cache food is to bend a small green sapling over, attach the food among its branches, and then let it fly back into place. This gives adequate protection from dogs and other land animals, but spreads a bounteous feast for ants and tree-climbing animals unless you place the food in containers which protect it.

## The Peeled-Stick Cache

This is an easily made cache which provides satisfactory protection from any animals likely to be encountered. Suspend the food by a pulley-like rope arrangement from a stick lodged in the crotches of two trees. It is best to

Peeled Stick Cache.

peel the bark from the stick so that its smooth surface will provide poor footing for climbing animals. Use a forked stick to hoist the ends of the pole into place in the crotches of the trees, throw the free end of the rope over the pole and draw the food up as high as desired. Fasten the free end of the rope around one of the trees with a couple of half hitches.

## St. Andrew's Cross Cache

An even safer cache when you have several packages to suspend is provided by the St. Andrew's cross support. It consists of two poles lashed securely together to form a cross from which the various packages of food are suspended. Try to balance the amount of weight hanging from each arm of the cross. The packages are kept safe from prowling animals and sway in the breeze so that even ants are discouraged from climbing to them.

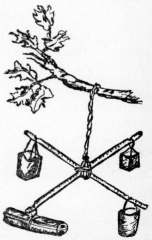

St. Andrew's Cross.

## Cupboard Cache

Make this convenient cupboard from an oblong box such as an old orange or other fruit crate and fit it with appropriate shelves. Make a tight-fitting insect-proof front of canvas, oilcloth or cheesecloth, arranged with tabs to tie into eyes or loops to slip over hooks placed around the bottom and sides of the crate. Anchor a rope for suspending the cache in large screw eyes placed along the top edge, or fasten the ends in holes in the box with overhand or figure-of-eight knots. This cupboard is awkward to take on a hiking trip, but makes an excellent food container when going by wagon or canoe. It is practical to leave at a main outdoor campsite or at an outpost camp.

You can make a similar cupboard to fold or roll up, from canvas. It is more substantial if you leave wide hems at the top for inserting stick supports upon arrival at the campsite.

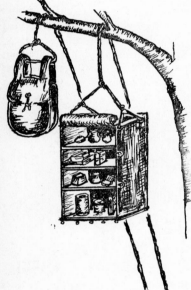

Cupboard Cache.

## KEEPING FOOD COOL

One of the main problems when trip camping is to keep such perishable foods as butter, milk and meat cool. Fresh meat is the most difficult of all, and is probably not safe to use beyond the first meal out with only primitive cooling methods available. You can keep milk for twenty-four hours or a little longer, and butter will remain sweet and relatively firm for two weeks or more if stored in an airtight container of some sort.

As with most things in camping, the particular method of cooling you use will depend largely upon what is available and convenient. Your ingenuity will be called into play to make the most of the possibilities.

## Cooling with Ice

The advocates of the rough and rugged type of camping will consider that taking ice along for refrigeration purposes is entirely too "sissified," but we maintain it to be highly desirable when transporting your trip supplies by automobile or truck. A 50-pound cake of ice will last as long as four days if you properly care for it, and a 100-pound cake will last correspondingly longer.

As soon as possible after the ice arrives at the campsite, dig a hole of ample size to contain it and whatever food you want to refrigerate with it. Put small rocks or gravel along the bottom and sides of the pit and line it with a layer of grass or leaves. Wrap the ice tightly in several layers of newspaper and cover it with burlap to serve as insulation. After thoroughly moistening the insulation, place the package in some container such as an old cardboard box or tin can with holes punched in it to allow the ice water to drain off. Pack the food in close about the ice and lower the container into the pit. Shovel wet sand or gravel in around the container, and cover the whole thing with wet burlap, tree branches, and the like.

If you plan your cooking program so that you need open your "refrigerator" as seldom as possible during the day, the ice will last surprisingly well.

### Cooling with Running Water

When water from a stream or lake is available, you can devise several varieties of satisfactory coolers. If there are strong waves as in a lake or river (either natural or due to passing boats) you must weight your food down with rocks or anchor it to trees or rocks along the shore so that it can't be overturned or washed away. Guard against the danger of contamination from having impure water get into it by placing it in watertight containers made secure from dashing waves.

Spring Box.

*A Spring Box.*      A large box or barrel can be sunk in the edge of a stream or lake with the top weighted down with heavy rocks if necessary to keep it immersed. Lakes are often fed by underground streams and the water in such regions is much cooler; locate one (by feeling the water) if possible. The top of the cooler should be shaded by trees or by a framework of branches built over it and kept wet by frequent dousing with water.

Prepare the box or barrel with a shelf which is above water level and large enough to contain all food not in watertight containers; it is well to leave a part of the container unshelved so that you can immerse tall watertight containers directly in the water. Make large holes near the bottom of the barrel to promote a free flow of water in and out of your spring box.

Anchor the box or barrel in the water under some shade and place the food in it. Then cover the whole with a piece of burlap with its ends hanging down into the water so that it is kept constantly moist and cools the top of the box by evaporation.

*Immersing Directly in the Water.* You may keep your food in a large watertight container such as a five-gallon milk can and submerge it in a cool spot in the lake or stream, using rocks to weight the can down if the contents are not sufficiently heavy to hold it. Place it in the shade or arrange a piece of burlap and brush framework over it as described for the spring box.

When you have no large container available, lash a stick framework and sink it in the water. Then fit your food in watertight containers into the spaces in the framework, and anchor it by means of rocks on the bank, or sharp posts driven into the stream bed at its corners.

**Cooling by Evaporation**

Cooling by evaporation is effective, particularly on a hot day when a fairly good breeze is blowing, but it does not work so well on a still day when the humidity is high. Putting salt in the water hastens the evaporation and so increases the efficiency of the system.

Framework for Immersing Food in the Water.

*An Oriole Cache.* This cache provides one of the best all-around methods for preserving food, for it keeps it cool as well as protects it from animals and all sorts of insects. Lower the cache when you want to take food from it. No waterproof containers are necessary except buckets or no. 10 tin cans.

Make three or four holes near the tops of the cans or buckets. Space the holes evenly so that the cans will hang straight, and join the cans with rope as shown, leaving enough space between them to insert the food into the lower can.

Keep the upper can filled about two-thirds full of water. Cover both cans with a piece of cheesecloth, weighting it down in the water in the top can by small rocks and tying it around under the bottom can to form an insect-proof cover.

This arrangement constantly dampens the cheesecloth from the water in the top can, and the resulting evaporation keeps the whole contents cool if you hang your cache in the shade where a fairly strong breeze has access to it. Swing the rope over a limb and raise the contents where it will be safe as explained for the peeled-stick cache.

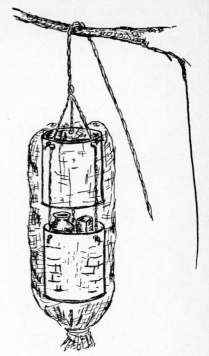

Oriole Cache.

*Other Cooling Devices.*     Another way to cool food is to put it in a bucket or pan which you set inside a larger vessel containing water. Place all in the shade, and cover the vessel containing the food with a cloth with the ends hanging down in the water so as to keep it constantly saturated.

Cool food in a cupboard cache by surrounding it with cheesecloth or burlap weighted down in a pan of water set on top.

If you dig a shallow pit in a bank close to a lake or stream, it will usually quickly fill with underground water which is even cooler than that in the lake or stream. Keep food in suitable receptacles in this pit, shading or covering the top to keep it cool.

Place food in a watertight can or cooking vessel with a tight-fitting lid and keep it cool in a hole dug in a shady place under a tree and lined with rocks, gravel, leaves or grass. Fill in dampened leaves or grass around and over the top of the kettle and dampen the surrounding insulation as needed.

## ADDITIONAL READINGS

How to Preserve Food in Pioneer Units. C.M., Feb., 1945.

Joy, Barbara Ellen: Care of Food and Equipment on Trips. C.M., Jan., Feb., 1941. (Camp Publications, no. 51.)

Mason, Bernard S.: Woodcraft, chap. 9.

None is so poor that he need sit on a
pumpkin; that is shiftlessness.

HENRY THOREAU

## Chapter 30

## COOKING DEVICES

A GOOD CAMPER is able to adapt himself happily to whatever media for camp
life he finds plentiful in his particular region. If wood is scarce or you are
prohibited from cutting green saplings to use as kettle supports, there may be
ample quantities of nonpopping rocks which will do beautifully. A dump
yard in the vicinity may provide flat or odd-shaped bits of metal, old stove
parts, and the like, which you can convert into cooking devices and other
gadgets for use around the campsite. Ingenuity and skill will surprise you
with what you can improvise, and your satisfaction is greatly enhanced by
knowing the origin of your creation "from the ground up."

### THE CROTCHED STICK

Few things are more valuable around a camp site than the good old
crotched stick; there are a thousand-and-one uses for it.
When seeking one, there is no use wasting time in searching for the variety shown in *B* in the illustration, for it is
rare and is unsatisfactory anyway, since it is quite likely
to split when you try to drive it into the ground. If it is
ever necessary to drive one, lay another stick through the
crotch to pound on, but even then your chances of driving
it without splitting are meager. A forked stick like *A* in
the illustration will serve the purpose just as well, is
much easier to find, and eliminates most of the danger of
splitting the crotch, since you pound on the main part
of the stick to drive it. For easy driving, give the stick a four-sided point.

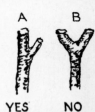

A    B

YES    NO

The Good "Ole"
Crotched Stick.

# CAMPFIRE PARAPHERNALIA

A camper disabled through carelessness is about as welcome around camp as a rainstorm. It is well to take time to prepare properly for work.

Canvas work gloves and a big bandana are useful when handling hot objects around the fire and keep the hands clean for cooking. A green forked-stick fire poker and a shovel are indispensable for manipulating the hot rocks, burning embers and glowing coals into more advantageous positions for cooking.

## Fire Tongs

Hot rocks are often used for cooking or heating purposes and, if no shovel is available, are best moved between a forked stick and another stick, as in *B*.

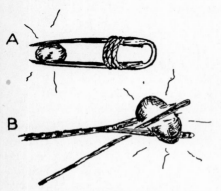

Figure *A* shows a pair of fire tongs made by taking a strong green sapling of hickory or other suitable wood, about 2 to 3 feet long, and shaving away part of it near the center so that you can bend it around in the form of a "U." It bends more easily if you heat it over the fire while working with it. Lash the two ends of the stick into position. These fire tongs are excellent for shifting fire brands about and may even be used for lifting small heated rocks.

Green Stick Fire Tongs.

## Tin Can or Hobo Stove

A hobo stove is made from a no. 10 tin can and provides a fine little stove for frying bacon and eggs or other quickly cooked foods. Cut a 3-inch hole at the bottom for building a fire and a 1- to 2-inch hole on the opposite side near the top for a smoke vent. A fire of small twigs is all you need to heat it; in fact, you must use care to keep the fire small enough not to burn the food. Lay the fire and place the hobo stove in position over it, making sure that the stove is level so the food won't spill. A trench candle can be used under it instead of wood to furnish heat.

## Paraffin Stove or Buddy Burner

The little paraffin stove or buddy burner is excellent for quick cooking, for it will burn several minutes, throwing out enough heat to cook simple dishes.

Hobo Stove.

Make it by melting about two-thirds of a medium or small-sized can full of paraffin or old candle stubs. When the wax begins to harden, insert a piece of cardboard or corrugated paper which has been wound in a loose spiral making sure to leave the edges extending a little above the wax to act as a wick. You can use a paraffin stove in your cooking fireplace just like a small fire. When through with it, smother it by putting a lid over it and save it to use another time. You can also use a buddy burner for light or for starting a stubborn fire.

Paraffin Stove or Buddy Burner.

## SUPPORTS FOR THE KETTLE

Self-reliant campers find many ways to support their cooking utensils over the fire. As previously mentioned, you can build supports of nonpopping stones or green, slow-burning wood, or lay small green sticks across a pit or other support to form a sort of grate.

Scrap heaps often yield iron bars for grates and large pieces of sheet metal for stove tops. An old metal washtub makes an excellent stove when a door for fuel is cut at the bottom of one side and a small hole for a chimney and cross ventilation is placed at the top of the other (*N*, p. 244). A piece of gravel screen makes a fine grate on which to roast steaks and such foods directly over the coals.

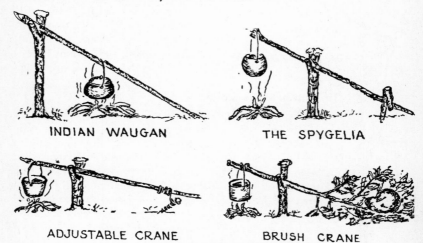

INDIAN WAUGAN                    THE SPYGELIA

ADJUSTABLE CRANE              BRUSH CRANE

Single Pot Holders.

### Single Pot Holders or Dingle Sticks

When you have only one kettle to heat, a variety of *dingle sticks* or *single pot holders* are available. Several types are shown here, and others can be devised from whatever materials you have at hand. The Indian waugan is one of the simplest, especially if you have a large rock or stump available to use in place of the forked stick upright, for you will then need only a long

notched stick for suspending the kettle. The adjustable crane, attributed to Stuart Thompson, is a clever arrangement by which you can raise or lower a kettle over the fire by simply winding or unwinding the string by which it is suspended. The spygelia and brush crane illustrate other single pot holders.

### Pan Tree

Make a handy pan tree by cutting the branches off a dead but solid tree for convenient pegs; then anchor the shaft of the tree into the ground near the fire or work table.

### Kitchen Cabinet

Make a kitchen cabinet of any desired shape and design, combining forked sticks and lashing to suit your own particular taste and needs. Store your dishes on it with a waterproof covering over them to keep them clean and dry for the next meal.

A Pan Tree.

Kitchen Cabinet.

## Chippewa Kitchen

This is another variety of kitchen cabinet which features shelves and protruding ends for suspending things. Make it any size desired, ranging from a small tripod for a few persons to the fairly commodious size shown in the

Chippewa Kitchen.

picture. If desired, you can build your fire right under it, suspending your pots by means of a lug pole across the lower levels of the kitchen as shown.

## The Standard Crane

The standard crane is a favorite for suspending several kettles simultaneously. It consists of a lug pole supported by two forked sticks about 3 to 4 feet above the fire. Hang pot hooks of various lengths on the lug pole to provide for varying the distance of your kettles from the fire. After the meal

LUG POLE

The Standard Crane.

The Victor Auer Crane.

is over, remove the lug pole and build up the fire for the evening program.

### The Victor Auer Crane

The Victor Auer crane serves the same general purposes as the standard crane, but its peculiar method of construction enables the cook to swing the arm and kettles to one side when the food is ready to serve. The arm of the crane is branched, and one branch ends in a long strip of bark which you bring around the upright and lash back to the main stick; the other arm is a forked stick with its crotch resting against the upright. The crane will turn about on the upright so that you can place it in any position you want.

## Pot Hooks

Keep several pot-hooks of varying lengths available to permit choosing one

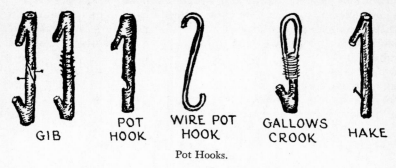

GIB  POT HOOK  WIRE POT HOOK  GALLOWS CROOK  HAKE

Pot Hooks.

Gib, Used as a Pot Lifter.

to suspend your food at just the right height above the fire.

The *gib* is made by splicing two sticks together with their forks facing each other, so that one can be used to hold the handle of the kettle, the other to anchor the gib across the lug pole. Fasten the two sticks together with nails, lashing or a combination of the two. A *pot hook* has a notch cut in it which slants downward and is deep enough to hold the handle of the kettle securely. *Wire pot hooks* must be made of rather heavy material which will not straighten out when supporting a weight. A *gallows crook* is made by leaving a long strip of tough bark to bring up and around and lash down to form a handle. It is the least convenient of the lot, for you cannot remove it from the fire without lifting the end of the lug pole to slip it off. The *hake* uses a large nail for a kettle support. Any of these pot hooks can be used to lift hot kettles from the fire.

## CLAY OVENS

The various sorts of clay ovens are interesting to construct and, if properly made, give excellent results when roasting meats and vegetables, or baking pies, cakes and cookies. They must be made of clay of a good cohesive quality which will bake hard if they are to be durable and satisfactory. No one except an earthworm would want little pieces of clay oven dropping into his food as it cooks.

Satisfactory clay is available in most regions. Consult published geological surveys or with persons in the neighborhood who are interested in geology to help locate it. If such is unavailable, seek the clay in cellars, road cuttings, and other places of excavation, and along the banks of running streams. Test it for cohesiveness and workability by allowing it to dry out for a little, then knead it thoroughly and curl it around your finger. If you can curl and un-curl it without breaking or cracking it, it will probably be satisfactory.

Dig enough clay to make your oven, using care not to mix any dirt with it. Leave it to dry for a while and then work and knead it until it is quite pliable. If it does not seem to stick together well, weave a little hay or grass into it to give added body.

To make a clay oven from an old wash boiler such as you can pick up in a junk heap, cut a hole in the top for a chimney, and build up a platform of clay or rocks for it to rest on. Lay a layer of rocks over the sides, ends and back of the boiler and cover it with clay to the depth of about a foot, making sure

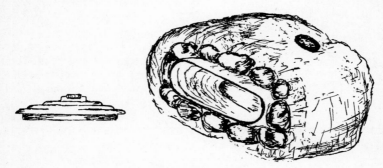

Clay Wash Boiler Oven.

NO. 10 TIN CAN CHIMNEYS

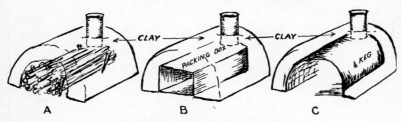

Other Varieties of Clay Ovens.

to leave the chimney hole uncovered. Bake the clay in the sun for a couple of days, and then build a slow-burning fire of partly green wood inside it and keep it going for two or three hours to bake it hard and firm; the fire must not be too hot or it will cause cracks to appear.

There are other forms over which to build a clay oven. One form is of small sticks bound into a round bundle of the desired size and shape, another uses a wooden packing box, and a third uses a half-keg. Make the chimney hole by inserting a tin can with both ends removed or by inserting a small wooden box or a bundle of sticks of the appropriate size. Cover the forms with clay and bake as previously described, with the fire inside burning out the wooden form as it hardens the clay. If cracks appear, fill them with new clay and let it harden the next time you use the oven. Make the oven just large enough to accommodate the baking for the group it is to feed.

When ready to bake, build a hot fire in the oven, and keep it going until your oven is as hot as desired. If the fire does not burn well, you can improve

Oven Door.

the ventilation by raising the wood on rocks or green stick firedogs. When the proper temperature has been reached, rake out the fire from the oven, place the food inside, and close the oven up tightly by placing a flat stone over the chimney and fitting a tight door into place. The figure shows how to make a door by joining a few pieces of wood together. The lid of the wash boiler makes an excellent door for a wash boiler oven and a large flat stone also works well.

A Campsite.

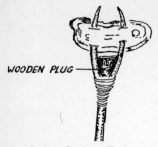

WOODEN PLUG

Rustic Cooking Fork.

## COOKING FORK

You can make a handy cooking fork from a sweet-tasting stick of fire-resistant wood. Point the end, split down the middle to make tines, and insert a small piece of wood to keep the tines apart. Lash the fork for a short distance below the split to keep it from splitting too far.

## ADDITIONAL READINGS

Bassett, Jeanne; Young, Monroe; and Joy, Barbara Ellen: Device for Barbecuing C.M., April, 1942. (Camp Publications, no. 52.)

Hammett, Catherine T.: Campcraft A B C's.

Jaeger, Ellsworth: Wildwood Wisdom, chap. 9.

Mason, Bernard S.: Junior Book of Woodcraft.

Mason, Bernard S.: Woodcraft, chap. 7.

West, James E., and Hillcourt, William: Scout Field Book, Pow-wow 16.

CAMPER'S STEW

'Case cookin' lak religion is—
Some's 'lected, an' some aint,
An' rules don't no mo' mak a cook
Den sermon's mek a saint.

HOWARD WEEDEN

# Chapter 31

# FOODS AND OUTDOOR COOKING

## PLANNING AND PACKING FOR TRIPS

### Planning the Menu

EVERY CAMPER wants to cook out occasionally; sometimes the excursion may be only a simple breakfast, lunch or supper trip involving no great problems of planning and packing since the short distance makes food transportation relatively simple. At other times it may be a *nosebag* or *poke* lunch consisting of sandwiches and other foods packed in a paper bag which you can burn as soon as the food is eaten. Overnight and longer trips pose difficult problems of selecting and packing food, for questions of bulk and weight then assume great importance.

Whatever type of outdoor meal you plan, you ought definitely to steer clear of the inevitable and indigestible picnic menu of weiners, buns, pickles and marshmallows which apparently constitutes the average American's idea of the only possible outdoor menu. It is important from the psychological as well as the health standpoint that meals in the out-of-doors be just as nutritious, well-cooked and attractively served as those indoors. The fact that vigorous exercise and the breathing of large quantities of fresh air produce ravenous appetites should not be used as an excuse for serving half-raw, half-burned "messes."

Let the campers help to plan their own menus, learning the elements of good nutrition as they do. This automatically leads them to greater appreciation of the importance of a well-balanced diet and often results in their eating and eventually learning to like foods previously spurned.

If they are to learn something of budgeting as well, give them a definite allowance for each meal, day or trip and a standard price list as furnished by the dietitian. Many books and pamphlets containing camp recipes are available, and you can use regular cook books by adapting cooking methods to out-of-door facilities. Working closely with one or more counselors, campers plan menus and figure out proportions of the footstuffs needed. Take into consideration (1) time needed for preparation (you seldom want to spend a long time in cooking on trips), (2) utensils needed (each item adds bulk and weight to the pack), (3) bulk, and (4) keeping qualities of the food. These criteria make *one-pot meals*, in which the various ingredients for the whole meal are cooked together in a single pot, popular in camp menus. Such romantic and unusual names as "blushing bunny" or "egg-in-a-nest" add glamour to a prosaic dish. Beginners in outdoor cooking should choose simple, easily prepared menus for their first ventures, saving the more challenging processes such as roasting chickens on a spit and baking beans in a hole for a later date. One new or difficult dish is enough at a meal.

When the campers have computed menus and proportions, make triplicate copies, one to be retained by the counselor in charge, the others to be turned over to the camp director and dietitian. Camps often supply forms for doing this which include the names of the personnel going, the date and time of leaving, destination, number of days and meals of the trip, menu and proportions of foodstuffs, and cooking vessels and other supplies needed. When the list has been approved, the representatives of the group who are to serve as *marketers* meet with the dietitian to measure out and pack the food and equipment. Many camps make it a custom to have all groups cook out on the cook's day off. Let your campers help with the cooking; they'll really enjoy the sense of accomplishment it brings.

If many campers are to participate, it is best to divide them into small groups of six to eight with one or two counselors, and let each group plan its own menu and cook it individually.

## Packing Food

Any kind of trip, but particularly one in which the group travels on foot, presents a challenge to plan menus which are not too bulky and cumbersome to carry.

Obviously, it is wise not to take most things in their original packages, which are usually crushable and too flimsy to stand the wear and tear of a journey. Instead, measure out just enough for the trip and place in sturdy containers kept on hand for just such a purpose. Mark all packages clearly as to contents on both the sides and tops so that you can quickly locate them en route. You may print labels for frequently used staples with indelible ink on metal-rimmed tags, or tag the containers themselves with gummed paper labels or adhesive tape protected and held secure with Scotch tape.

Avoid things which may spoil or become soft and those that may be mashed or broken by rough handling.

*Dry Materials.*    It is well to keep on hand a supply of bags in assorted sizes for packing dry materials. You can purchase them from an outing supply company, but it is easy and cheap to make them. The best are made of sail cloth, waterproofed with paraffin, double stitched at all seams, with a wide hem and drawstring at the top left long enough to tie with a half hitch and use as a handle. Some should consist of two thicknesses of cloth or of one bag placed inside another for carrying such fine materials as flour. Make them short and broad and with round bottoms (see pp. 304–305) so they'll stand upright with minimum danger of tipping over. Label the contents with wax crayon which will wash out or with India or indelible ink for permanence.

*Liquids.*    Because of the danger of breakage, never leave liquids in bottles or other glass containers, but empty them into tin cans with screw-on or press-in tops. Aluminum cans weigh less, but are so flimsy that they sometimes get dented and pressed out of shape when packed among heavier materials. You can purchase suitable containers from outfitting companies, but it is easy to acquire enough by saving cans from commercial products.

Carry water in canteens, thermos bottles, jugs, or in one- or two-gallon kerosene or gasoline cans kept for the purpose. Water bags keep the contents cool by evaporation, and five-gallon milk cans provide for large quantities.

Carry semiliquid materials, such as jam and peanut butter, in heavy, round cardboard cartons with tight-fitting lids (such as ice cream cartons).

*Other Packing Notes.*    It is best to carry eggs in heavy, cardboard egg panniers, although you can wash and bury them in such dry materials as flour or cornmeal.

Flavorings add much to the taste of food, and it is worth while to take small quantities of several varieties. You can pack a tight-fitting assortment of small metal or glass containers of individual flavorings in a metal can of appropriate size. Salt draws moisture and will eventually rust out a tin container. Make a rust-proof salt and pepper shaker by fitting corks into the

Bamboo Salt and Pepper Shaker.

ends of a section of bamboo with a division in the middle. Label each end of the container with its contents.

Use adhesive tape to seal opened evaporated milk cans and to secure doubtful corks or lids.

For a short, one-meal trip, you may simply pack and carry your food in a cooking kettle or no. 10 tin can stove. For longer trips it is best to pack all in waterproof knapsacks or duffel bags, each with a metal-rimmed tag stating its contents. Some like to collect all the crushables and breakables in one bag to give them especially careful handling. Pack the supplies for your next meal on top so that you need not unpack the whole lot to get what you want at each stop.

Use bread wrappers or waxed paper freely in packing, and newspapers make a good padding to prevent breakage.

## Lightening the Load

When going on a long trip, it may be possible to send a part of your food supplies and other equipment ahead by camp truck, parcel post or express. You may also replenish the larder at grocery stores and farm houses along the way.

Many varieties of dehydrated foods are now available, and their appearance and taste have been greatly improved since our experimentation with them during World War II. They are, of course, more expensive than regular foodstuffs, but make a great saving in space and weight since about 90 per cent of the water content of the foods has been removed. For instance, the nourishing portion of 100 pounds of potatoes weighs only 17 pounds, meaning that we will be burdening ourselves with excess baggage to the extent of 20 pounds of peelings and 63 pounds of water if we take them in their original form.

*Vegetables and Soups.* Such fresh vegetables as carrots, cabbage, beets and onions, keep pretty well on a trip, even as long as several weeks if you seal them in waxed paper and then a layer or two of other paper tightly wrapped over all. Clean them and remove such waste materials as tops and roots before starting.

Dried beans and peas are light and keep well, but must be soaked overnight and, consequently, require too long a cooking time to be practical on most trips. Rice is a light and versatile food, for you can use it as breakfast food, dessert, or the main dish of almost any meal. Coarse-grained cereals are "musts" in every day's menu.

Canned vegetables are bulky and heavy because of the large amounts of water canned with them. Canned soups are good, but most brands have the same drawback. Where they are used, buy small-sized cans especially made for trip camping.

Dehydrated soups and vegetables are light and take up little space, making them well worth their extra cost for a long trip. You can add extra noodles or some pre-cooked rice to give them more staying power. The following dehydrated vegetables are now available from the better supply houses: apple slices, okra, beans, sweet corn, cabbage, celery, onions, carrots, spinach, turnip and mustard greens, sweet and Irish potatoes, and mixed vegetables. Those dehydrated by modern methods require only about thirty minutes of soaking.

*Eggs and Dairy Products.*       Fresh eggs stay usable for some time.

*Powdered eggs* are fresh eggs with most of the water removed. A tablespoonful of powdered egg added to two tablespoonfuls of water give the equivalent of one fresh egg. They are highly perishable after being mixed with water and should be cooked immediately and eaten while still warm.

Butter and cheese, when packed in air-tight cans and cooled under primitive refrigeration methods, keep quite well, and butter is also available in $\frac{1}{2}$- and 1-pound tins which last indefinitely.

Fresh milk will not keep long, and it is not safe to buy from untested herds along the way. You can use evaporated or condensed milk for all cooking purposes, and most people even find it palatable to drink.

*Powdered milk* has the water removed and one cup of it added to $3\frac{1}{2}$ cups of water produces the equivalent of a quart of fresh milk. Beat it or shake it in a watertight can until no lumps remain. Powdered skim milk is better on long trips as it does not get rancid as whole milk powder may. Note that it supplies fewer calories since the fat has been removed. Rutstrum* recommends a chain mixing can consisting of a friction-top can with a well-plated chain inside for mixing dehydrated eggs and milk.

*Breadstuffs.*       Bread, particularly rye, remains fresh for some time if it is double-wrapped in waxed paper. Date, nut and brown breads are available in canned form.

You can bake cakes, fresh biscuits, muffins, flapjacks and shortcakes in a reflector oven along the way and they are a welcome addition to any meal. You can make them from prepared flour, but it is cheaper and just as satisfactory to mix your own dry ingredients before you leave camp. Whole wheat or graham flours are particularly healthful.

*Fruits and Desserts.*       Canned fruits contain large quantities of water and weigh too much and take too much space to be practical for long trips.

Dried apples, prunes, peaches, raisins, pears, black figs and mixtures of dried apples and apricots weigh little and need only the addition of water to transform them into delicious fruit dishes. You may mix them in breadstuffs, put them on cereals, or simply eat them as fruit as you wish. To prepare them, cover with cold water, bring to a boil, then simmer until done, adding more water if needed.

Puddings made from powders add variety to the diet. Tinned nuts are an exceptionally rich source of energy and may be munched along the way or used with desserts or in cooking.

* Rutstrum, Calvin: Way of the Wilderness, p. 135.

Supply quick-energy carbohydrates in ample quantity. Candy bars, jams, jellies, marmalades and occasional sweet desserts will serve. Saccharine has less bulk than sugar for sweetening purposes but does not supply any calories for energy needs.

Wild strawberries, blackberries, dewberries and blueberries ripen during camp season and add a new taste to muffins, flapjacks or shortcake.

*Meats.*    Do not take fresh meats for more than the first meal out unless you can take ice; bacon keeps a little better, particularly if bought in the chunk and sliced off as used. You will have to depend largely upon canned meats, supplemented with what you can procure en route. You may get fresh fish, clams, crabs, frog legs, turtles for soup, and the like, along the way according to the region you are in.

Bacon fryings furnish the fat you need for cooking, but you may prefer vegetable fats since they do not have as much tendency to soak into your food.

*Other Beverages.*    You can make good trip beverages from malted milk tablets or powders, hot chocolate powders, and such dehydrated juices as tomato, lemon, lime, orange and grape, or you can dehydrate your own juice by extracting fresh juice, mixing it with sugar, and then letting it dry.

Powdered coffee and tea bags are light weight and suitable for older campers and counselors.

## OUT-OF-DOOR COOKING

Only a few of the more woodsy recipes are included here. For further details about outdoor cooking and for additional recipes, consult the references at the end of the chapter.

### Some General Notes about Cooking

For general camp cooking, regular kettles with wire handles which can be hung over lug poles or on pot hooks are recommended.

Always coat the outside surfaces of kettles with a moistened bar of laundry soap until they are completely covered by a thick layer of soap paste before using them over an outdoor fire. The soap rinses off easily when the utensil is washed, taking the smoke and soot with it.

When preparing vegetables, do not leave them standing in water longer than necessary, for it removes some of their precious vitamins. Add them to rapidly boiling water and cook quickly, using as little water as possible. Avoid "cooking them to death," keeping them on just long enough to tenderize them without destroying all their original crispness. Add vegetables to water which is below the boiling point only if you want to extract their flavor as in making soups or stews.

You can skin tomatoes quickly by scalding them with boiling water or holding them over the flames until their skins crack.

When melting chocolate or measuring molasses, grease the vessel to prevent food waste by having it adhere to the sides.

Test eggs for freshness by dropping them into water. If they sink quickly, they are fresh; if slowly, proceed with caution, for they are doubtful; if they float, don't use them at all, for they are ancient.

When a recipe calls for sour milk, you can produce it immediately by adding two tablespoonsful of lemon juice or a few drops of vinegar for each cup of sweet milk.

You can improvise double boilers for cooking rice and other cereals by placing the vessel containing the food inside a larger vessel partly filled with water.

A little vinegar and water boiled inside the utensils in which fish has been cooked removes the fishy odor.

When cooking meat, use a low or moderate heat. This requires more time, but the meat will not shrink so much and will be much more palatable and tender. When you want to draw the juices and flavor out of meat, as in making soup or stew, start it in cold water and cook it with low heat. If you want to seal the juices and flavor in, drop it into boiling water or sear it on all sides over a hot fire, then cook it over low or moderate heat. Do not season until the meat is nearly done, for seasonings also tend to draw out the juices. Neither overcook or undercook fresh meat.

*Frying* is frequently overused in camp cookery and, when incorrectly done, results in an unappetizing and indigestible dish. The chief drawback to fried foods comes from letting them absorb too much fat as they cook. To avoid this, have the food as dry as possible when you put it into the skillet and get the grease hot (not smoking, for that means it is burning and will impart a disagreeable taste). The hot grease sears the food, sealing the juices in and the grease out. Drain fried foods on a paper napkin to remove excess grease. When frying in a skillet over an open fire, be careful not to cook over high flames lest they set fire to the grease in the pan.

*Pan broiling* is a form of frying, pouring off the excess grease as it forms and leaving just enough in the pan to keep the food from sticking. Turn the meat frequently. This form of frying is healthful and highly recommended.

*Broiling* is cooking food by direct exposure to the heat from glowing coals. Build a fire of hardwood well in advance of cooking time so that it will burn down to a good bed of coals. Place the meat over flame to sear it quickly on both sides and then place it over the coals and carefully watch it and vary the distance as needed. When cooking meat, remember to sear the juices in over direct heat first, then finish cooking with moderate or low heat. Dripping fat ignites, and you must move the meat about to avoid burning it in the flames. Avoid using resinous or strong-tasting woods lest they impart a disagreeable flavor to the food.

*Wilderness cookery* is cooking without utensils and includes cooking in ashes, in an imu or beanhole, or on a stick or spit. It is fun to plan a whole meal using only wilderness cookery, and it is surprising what a variety of tantalizing menus you can serve.

## Common Measures

3 teaspoons (tsp.) = 1 tablespoon (T)
16 T = 1 cup (C)
1 C = $\frac{1}{2}$ pint (pt.)
2 pts. = 1 quart (qt.)
4 qts. = 1 gallon (gal.)

#$\frac{1}{2}$ can = 1 cup
#1 can = 1$\frac{1}{2}$ cups
#2 can = 2$\frac{1}{2}$ cups
#2$\frac{1}{2}$ can = 3$\frac{1}{2}$ cups
#3 can = 4 cups
#5 can = 5 cups
#10 can = 1 gal. (12 cups)

2 T butter = 1 oz.
2 C butter or lard = 1 lb.
4 T flour = 1 oz.
4 C flour = 1 lb.
2 C granulated sugar = 1 lb.
3–3$\frac{1}{2}$ C brown sugar = 1 lb.
3–3$\frac{1}{2}$ C powdered sugar = 1 lb.
4 C cocoa = 1 lb.
3$\frac{1}{2}$–4 C cornmeal = 1 lb.
2 C rice = 1 lb.
2–2$\frac{1}{2}$ C dry navy beans = 1 lb.

## OUTDOOR RECIPES

### One Pot Meals

These are stews or mixtures which, as the name suggests, are cooked in one kettle and furnish a whole meal in themselves. They may be served hot on rice, toast or crackers.

#### Slumgullion (Serves 5)

6–10 slices of bacon
2 onions, diced
1 #2 can tomatoes

$\frac{1}{4}$–$\frac{1}{2}$ lb. cheese, diced
2 C meat, already cooked
$\frac{1}{2}$ tsp. salt

Cut the bacon into small pieces and fry the onion with it; drain off part of the fat, and add the tomatoes, meat, and salt. Cook for about 20 minutes; then add the cheese and continue cooking until it is melted.

#### Irish Stew (Serves 5)

5 onions, sliced
1 lb. meat, diced
5 potatoes

Other vegetables such as carrots, etc. as desired
Salt and pepper

Melt a little fat in a kettle and fry the onions and meat until brown. Cover them with cold water and bring to a boil. Cook slowly for 1$\frac{1}{2}$ hours, add the potatoes, and continue to cook slowly until they are tender. Season to taste.

#### Ring Tum Diddy (Serves 5)

6 slices bacon, diced
2 onions, sliced
$\frac{1}{4}$ lb. cheese, diced

1 #2 can tomatoes
1 #2 can corn
Salt and pepper

Fry the bacon and onions until brown, and pour off part of the fat. Add them to the tomatoes and corn and bring to a boil. Add the cheese and cook slowly until it is melted. Season to taste.

### Komac Stew (Serves 8)

| | |
|---|---|
| 1 small can tomatoes or 4 fresh tomatoes (diced) | 2 onions, diced |
| 1 green pepper | 3 eggs |
| | 4 T butter |
| | Salt and pepper |

Melt the butter and fry the onions until brown. Wash, seed, and dice the pepper and add to the tomatoes and onions and cook slowly for ½ hour, stirring frequently. Season to taste and add the eggs one at a time, stirring meanwhile. Avoid cooking over a fire which is too hot, for it will make the mixture curdle and look unappetizing even though not impairing the taste.

## Stick Cookery

For stick cookery, peel and sharpen a stick about 2 feet long. Resinous woods and willow impart an unpleasant taste, but sugar maple, sassafras, black birch or hickory are satisfactory. If in doubt about the suitability of the wood, peel the end and bite it. Remember that cooking should be done over coals, not flames.

Bread Twister or Doughboy.

1. *Bread Twister or Doughboy.* Mix regular biscuit dough, using just enough water to make it sticky, roll it out flat about ¼ to ½ inch thick and cut into long strips about 2 inches wide. Remove the bark from the end of a stick about twice the size of your thumb, heat the end and flour it and wind a strip of dough spirally around it, leaving a slight gap between the spirals. Bake for 10 to 15 minutes over coals, turning it so that all sides bake evenly. It will come off the stick in the form of a cylinder closed at one end. When filled with jam, jelly or cheese, it is known as *a cave woman cream puff*.

2. *Pig in a Blanket.* Cook a weiner or long sausage on a stick, then cover it with biscuit dough and bake.

3. *Bacon Twister.* Cook a piece of bacon thoroughly and cover it with dough and bake like a pig in a blanket. You can use sausage instead of the bacon.

### Pioneer Drumsticks (Serves 5)

| | |
|---|---|
| 1¼ lbs. beef, chopped fine | Onion (if desired) |
| ¾ C cornflakes, crumbled fine | Salt and pepper |
| 1 egg | |

Angel on Horseback.

Thoroughly mix the ingredients and wrap a thin portion tightly around the peeled end of the stick and squeeze firmly into place. Toast it slowly over coals, turning frequently, and serve in a roll. Some prefer to put the cornflakes on after the meat has been placed on the stick, so that they form a sort of crust over the outside.

5. *Angel on Horseback.* For each serving, thread one slice of bacon on the sharpened end of a stick, and partially cook. Then wrap the bacon tightly around a 1-inch square of cheese, and hold over the fire until the bacon is done and the cheese melted. Serve with lettuce in a bun.

6. *Kabobs*. Lace a slice of bacon in and out among alternate 1-inch squares of steak, slices of onion, oysters, small tomatoes, and so forth, as desired, impaled on a stick. The bacon will serve to baste them. Broil over gradual heat from coals. The kabob originated in Persia.

A Kabob.                    A Forked Stick Fork.

7. *Cooking on a Forked Stick*. A forked stick or a wire fork (I, p. 244) may be used for cooking steaks, oysters, weiners, sausages, bacon, toast, green corn, apples, parsnips or marshmallows. When cooking meats, toast, and like foods, run the tines in lengthwise of the food, so that it clings securely to the fork and can be turned to cook evenly on all sides.

8. *Date Dreams*. Make these by alternating pitted dates with halved marshmallows on a stick and toasting slowly over the fire.

## Cooking in Ashes or Coals

The secret of cooking in ashes or coals is to build a hardwood fire early and let it burn down to coals. If flames are needed for another part of the meal, the coals may be drawn over to one side and additional coals from the fire supplied as needed. Parsnips, fish (wrapped in clay), oysters (in the shell) and squash may be cooked in this way.

1. *Potatoes*. Scrub Irish, sweet potatoes or yams, of medium size and without blemishes, well and place on hot ashes in a single layer and with none touching; cover to a depth of about 1 inch with coals which are frequently replenished. They should be done in about 45 minutes, but it is best to bring one out and test it to be sure. As soon as they are ready, jab a small hole in each end to let the steam escape. Some like to coat them with a thick layer of wet mud or clay before roasting. Never, under any circumstances, toss them carelessly into the fire, for the only possible result will be a partly burned, partly raw potato, indigestion, and unhappy campers.

2. *Onions*. Cook them like potatoes.

3. *Eggs*. Prick a small hole through the egg shell (but not the membrane) on the large end of the egg and another through membrane and all at the small end (these holes are to let the steam escape and so keep the egg from bursting). Balance the egg carefully on its large end close to the fire where it will get moderate heat; avoid too much heat lest the egg

explode. The eggs should be ready to eat in five to twelve minutes, depending on whether you want them hard or soft. Some prefer to wrap the egg in wet leaves, wet mud or clay before baking.

4. *Little Pig Potatoes.* Slice the end off a potato and hollow out enough of the center to permit the insertion of a small, thin sausage (cheese, bacon or raw egg may be used instead). Replace the end of the potato and fasten it with slivers of wood and bake it as previously described.

5. *Roasting Ears.* Turn back the husks from young, tender roasting ears and clean the corn and remove the silks. Sprinkle lightly with salt, replace the husks, and bake like potatoes.

6. *Roasted Apples.* Core the apple and fill the cavity with raisins, brown sugar, nuts, and the like. Bake like a potato.

7. *Ash Bread.* Build a hardwood fire preferably on top of a large rock, at least a half hour before ready to bake. Rake the embers aside and place the loaf of bread, well floured and rolled out to a thickness of $\frac{1}{2}$ to $\frac{3}{4}$ inch, on the hot surface. Then cover it with ashes and a layer of coals, replenishing them as they cool. It is ready to eat when a sliver of wood inserted in it comes out without dough adhering.

You may use any bread dough, but baking powder biscuit dough is preferred because of the short baking time necessary. If desired, raisins, nuts, berries or fruit may be mixed with the dough. Unlikely as it seems, the loaf will emerge perfectly clean or so that it can be easily and quickly brushed off.

## Baking Potatoes in a No. 10 Tin Can

Scrub the potatoes well and wrap each in a layer of waxed paper, covered by damp newspaper. Then pack them in wet dirt or sand inside a no. 10 tin can so that none touch each other or the sides of the can. Place can among hot coals and leave about 45 minutes, adding additional glowing coals as needed. Keep the dirt in the can moist by adding more water if necessary.

## Baking in a Reflector Oven

Reflector ovens are most useful cooking utensils and should be a part of every outdoor cooking kit. Make them from tin cans (*L* and *M*, p. 244) or purchase them from outfitting companies. They fit into a canvas carrying case and are easy to carry if made with hinges which allow them to fold flat.

Set the reflector oven on the windward side of the fire so that the ashes and flames will be blown away from its contents; its efficiency is greatly increased by placing a reflector wall of rock or wood on the leeward side. Elevate the fire on green sticks so it is above the lower edge of the oven. Make the fire as high and as wide as the oven and add fuel to keep it the right size. Place the food to be baked directly on the oven shelf or in a baking pan set on the shelf. The sloping top and bottom catch and reflect the heat onto the food from both above and below, insuring thorough cooking and even browning, but the metal must be kept bright and shiny if it is to do its job well. Handles on the oven permit you to easily regulate its proper distance from the fire to insure just the right amount of heat. Prop it up so that the shelf is level. Get it hot enough to sizzle when you sprinkle a few drops of water on it before you place your food on it.

1. *General Baking*. Rolls, biscuits, pies, cakes, cookies, meat and small birds such as chickens can be baked to a turn in a reflector oven.

2. *Sweet Potato Soufflé* may be baked in hollowed-out orange peels (be sure to remove all the bitter lining) or in scooped out apple peels.

3. *Eggs Baked in Orange Shells*. Prepare the orange peel as above and break an egg into it; season, and set in the reflector oven to bake.

4. *Potatoes*. Scrub Irish potatoes, sweet potatoes or yams. Grease their jackets with butter or bacon fat to keep them tender. Bake them in a reflector oven for 45 minutes and test them to see when they are done.

5. *Some Mores*. Make a sandwich of a marshmallow and a piece of a chocolate candy bar between two graham crackers.

Baking in a Reflector Oven.

Press gently together and place in a reflector oven to bake.

6. *Banana Boats*. Peel back a narrow strip of peeling from the inside curve of a banana, scoop out part of the inside and fill with marshmallow, chocolate, nuts or raisins. Replace the strip of peeling and bake in a reflector oven.

## BAKING IN A SKILLET

Support the skillet on rocks or green sticks over coals, or prop it up in front of a fire.

1. *Bannock* is made by baking biscuit dough in a floured skillet in front of a fire. As with a reflector oven, place the skillet on the windward side of the fire away from the smoke and ashes; its efficiency is increased by a reflector wall. Turn the loaf over when done on one side, and both sides will be ready in about 15 minutes. Coals shoveled out and put behind the pan insure faster baking of the under side.

2. *Pancakes* (*Flapjacks*). Grease skillet lightly and brace as described. Use only moderate heat from a small fire or coals, and heat the skillet just under the smoking point before dropping the prepared or self-mixed batter from a spoon. Turn the flapjacks as soon as bubbles appear on top. Avoid too much heat for they are easily burned.

3. *Darn Goods*. Half fill a frying pan with fat and heat just short of the smoking stage (it is hot enough when a piece of bread dropped into it browns in 45 seconds). Pat biscuit dough with the shortening omitted into little biscuits about ¼ inch thick, and cut a few

Baking in a Skillet.

slashes in each to allow the grease to come up through. Place them in hot fat, turning them when the bottoms are brown, and cooking a total of approximately 10 minutes. Drop in a few at a time so as not to cool the grease enough to result in its absorption by the biscuit dough. Drain the excess grease from the darn goods by laying them on absorbent paper toweling or soft cloth.

4. *French Fries.* Dry potato strips by wrapping them in cloth or absorbent paper. Test the temperature of the fat as described for darn goods, and drop the potatoes in gradually so as not to cool the fat. When done, drain them on absorbent paper or soft cloth.

### Hush Puppies *(Serves 4)*

| | |
|---|---|
| 1 T flour | 1 tsp. baking powder |
| 1 C cornmeal | ½ C milk |
| 1 egg, well beaten | ¼ onion, diced fine |

Sift the cornmeal, flour, baking powder and salt together and add the onion. Stir the milk and egg with them into a batter stiff enough to form little balls. Drop them from a spoon into hot grease and cook like darn goods.

A Dutch Oven.

### Cooking in a Dutch Oven

The Dutch oven has been a favorite for everything from roasting to baking since the days of the early pioneers. It is made of heavy cast iron with a tight-fitting lid of the same material to keep all the heat and steam in and allow none of the succulent flavors to escape.

A Dutch oven intended for outdoor use has a flat cover with a turned-up flange around the edge so that hot coals can be placed on it. Its three sturdy legs raise it far enough off the ground to provide room for a few hot coals under it, but the coals must not actually touch it, or the food inside will burn.

Home-made Dutch Oven.

You can improvise a Dutch oven by inverting a *heavy* skillet tightly over a *heavy* kettle. Support this legless oven on green sticks or rocks to provide a little space for coals underneath.

1. *Pot Roast.* Put bit of fat meat or other fat in the bottom of the kettle. Sear all sides of the roast over an open fire, and put it in the kettle, with such vegetables as onions, parsnips, carrots, turnips, Irish or sweet potatoes added with the meat or about a half hour before it is ready to serve. This provides a delicious meal in itself, and you can make gravy from the stock left in the bottom if desired. A five-pound piece of meat requires about three hours to cook. This is a good way to cook tough meat, for it combines frying, baking and steaming, and the long exposure to even, moderate temperature tenderizes almost any cut. If the meat is quite lean, rub it with fat or lay a few stips of bacon across it to baste it as it cooks.

2. *Baking.* A Dutch oven is excellent for baking corn bread, biscuits, rolls, pies, cookies, potatoes in their skins, chicken; in fact, almost anything to be baked will come out cooked to a turn.

## The Imu or Pit Barbecue

This is another splendid method of cooking by steam using a moderate even heat. It is really a sort of fireless cookery, and justifies the long cooking time by the excellent results. About three hours are necessary to cook a chicken, about a half-day for a ten-pound roast, and as much as fifteen or sixteen hours for anything as big as a whole sheep.

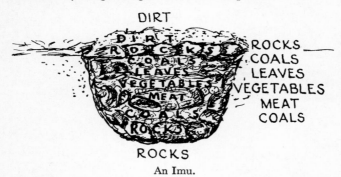

An Imu.

To begin the imu, dig a hole about two to three times as large as the food to be cooked and line the sides and bottom with nonpopping rocks; build a good hardwood fire in it and keep it going for an hour or two until the rocks are sizzling hot and there is a good bed of coals. Get all the food ready to place in the pit just as rapidly as possible so that no more heat than necessary will escape. Remove part of the coals and hot rocks, place the food in the pit, and pack the hot rocks and coals back in around and over it. Then shovel on about 6 inches of dirt to make a steamproof covering (if you see smoke or steam escaping, shovel more dirt over the leak). You can now forget the food until you dig it up ready to eat three to twenty hours later. You can cook green corn, parsnips, carrots, onions, ham, clams, potatoes with meat, and so forth, in this way.

A preheated Dutch oven makes the best container for the food, but if none is available you may wrap the meat and vegetables in damp butcher paper, damp paper towels, damp grass or seaweed, or damp nontasting leaves such as lettuce, cabbage, sassafras or sycamore. Bitter resinous leaves and burlap bags may be used if placed several layers away from the food.

### Bean Hole Beans

| | |
|---|---|
| ¾ lb. (2C) dry navy beans | ⅛ C sugar |
| ½ lb. salt pork or bacon, diced | ⅛ C molasses |
| 1½ tsp. salt | 2 onions, chopped fine |

These are excellent when cooked in a Dutch oven inside an imu or a bean hole made like an imu. Wash the beans and soak them overnight until their skins start to crack. Then mix all the ingredients and place them in a bean hole and let cook for six to eight hours.

## Cooking on a Stone Griddle

Prop a large, flat, nonpopping rock (slate is best) on green sticks or stones,

leaving plenty of room for draft. Build a fire both on and under the stone (which has been well scrubbed), and, when it is sizzling hot, clean off the top, grease it well with a swab and fry such food as bacon and eggs or flapjacks on it.

Stone Griddle.

## Barbecuing

There are several ways to barbecue meat; you can hold it directly over coals (never over flames) or place it a short distance away at the side of the fire. Barbecuing is a satisfactory method for cooking anything from a small chicken to large pieces of meat.

1. *Cooking on a Spit over the Fire.*    Dig a pit and build a good hardwood fire in it and let it burn down to coals. Place the meat on the *spit* and fasten it firmly in place so that it will turn as the stick does and be cooked evenly on all sides. The coals will cool off and need to be replaced frequently, so that it is best to keep a separate fire at one end or side of the pit so that fresh coals are constantly available.

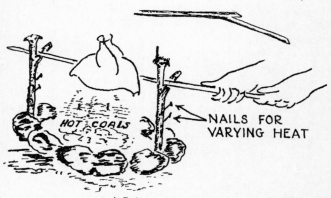

A Spit over the Fire.

When barbecuing a chicken, select a young, tender bird, commonly known as a springer or broiler. One weighing 2 pounds serves two people and you can cook several side by side on the same spit. Clean the chicken well and insert the spit firmly from tail to neck. Protect the wings and legs from burning by pinning them close to the body with wooden slivers inserted so they will not protrude. Rotate the spit slowly over the coals, and baste the bird every ten minutes with melted butter, bacon fat or other shortening applied with a swab made from cloth tied around the end of a stick.

Make the handle of the spit long so that you can stay well back from the fire and not roast yourself as well as the chicken. Place notches on the support for the spit at varying heights above the fire so that you can adjust the meat to the proper distance from the heat. You can use a peeled green stick for a spit, but a metal rod with a nonheating handle attached does a better job by conveying the heat into the meat to cook it from the inside as well as the outside.

Wire Grill Barbecuing.

Barbecuing at the Side of a Fire.

Cook roasts of beef or pork, ducks, turkeys and small game in this way.

2. *Cooking on a Wire Grill.* Select a wire grill or piece of gravel screening or other suitable mesh to fit on a framework of green wood or metal poles over a pit. Build a fire of hardwood and let it burn to coals, and place the food to be cooked (weiners, chickens, spare ribs, chops, steaks, and the like) on the grill over at one side of the pit out of the intense heat. Two persons, using garden forks or similar tools, fasten them in the food-laden grill and draw it into position over the coals. Use a long-handled spatula, further lengthened by tying a long stick to the end of it, to turn the meat. Do not use a fork for the holes made by pricking the meat with it will allow some of the juices to escape. Baste the meat with a cloth swab to keep it from drying out.

3. *Barbecuing at the Side of the Fire.* In this style of cookery, suspend the chicken or other piece of meat by a long string or wire from a lug pole between two forked sticks. Place it about a foot from the fire on the windward side and as close as possible to the ground where the heat is most intense. Prepare the chicken as described for cooking it over

the fire. The object of this type of barbecuing is to let the meat automatically turn itself as the cord suspending it winds and unwinds; the upper end of the string may be as much as 5 to 6 feet above the ground, for increasing the length of the cord causes it to turn better. Tie a flat piece of wood or tin (which may be obtained from a no. 10 tin can) about half-way down the string. The tin catches every bit of breeze and, even on a still day, will keep the meat rotating back and forth so that at least the side next the fire will be evenly cooked. Reverse the lug pole and meat to cook the other side. Set a pan under the meat to catch the drippings, and baste it every ten or fifteen minutes. A reflector fire on the leeward side speeds up the process.

### Cooking on a Rustic or Tennis Racket Broiler

Lace a broiler of green sweet-tasting branches securely together, and cook such foods as weiners, steaks, and some mores, on it. The branches must be fresh and green so that they won't burn through and let the food drop into the fire, and you may reinforce the two extremities where they lace together at the top with a piece of wire.

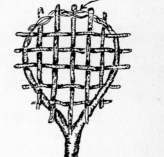

Tennis Racket Broiler.

### Aluminum Foil Cookery

Aluminum foil has proved to be a versatile and handy addition to the camper's equipment. One of its greatest uses is as a pressure cooker for food, which you can simply drop into the coals to cook to a turn with a minimum danger of burning. This eliminates the need for carrying bunglesome pots and pans and the onerous task of cleaning them after use. To cook in this fashion, take a piece of foil large enough to surround your food completely and leave enough edge to fold over three times. Crimp the edges into an air-tight covering which will seal in all the juices and flavors. Be careful not to punch any holes in your wrapping for keeping it air-and-steam-tight is the whole secret of its efficiency. Always add a bit of shortening, in the form of butter, fat, or bacon, or sprinkle a little water over your food.

As an example, if you wish to cook hamburger, place the patty on the foil with a pat of butter, a little bacon or a bit of shortening. Surround it with slices of onion and a slice of tomato, wrap as described and place in a bed of hot coals. The amount of cooking time varies with the heat of your coals, the size of the package, and similar factors, but fifteen to twenty minutes is ordinarily about right. Turn the package when about half the cooking time has elapsed. When the food is done, tear off the crimped ends and eat out of the foil.

Lamp or pork chops, steaks, fish, and chicken can be cooked in this way surrounding them with such vegetables as sliced carrots, turnips, potatoes, onions, or green beans. Wet a roasting ear thoroughly, leaving it in its husks, wrap a hot dog in biscuit dough, core an apple and fill the hole with brown or white sugar, cinnamon and raisins and cook in foil. You can wrap the ingredients for several meals before you start out, labeling them so that you can select the right one and toss it into the coals when ready to eat.

Foil makes a good reflector oven on a trip to bake biscuits, cookies or even small pies. Take a 24-inch piece of it and bend it at the center at a 45 degree angle. Place it on a flat stone 6 inches above ground level close to a hot fire and prop it up like a reflector oven, supporting the upper corners on forked sticks. Lightly grease the bottom of your oven and place on it 2-inch circles of biscuit dough. With this sort of reflector oven, you will have to turn your biscuits to cook the undersides as soon as the tops have browned. The whole thing takes about 10 minutes in front of a good fire.

You can also fashion pots and frying pans from foil, shaped around the forked ends of a stick, letting the ends of the stick protrude for a handle. A small piece of it can be shaped into a conical drinking cup or wrapped around your matches to waterproof them. Aluminum foil will not burn nor readily disintegrate if left in the open when you are through with it, so wad it up and bury it.

## ADDITIONAL READINGS

### BOOKS AND PAMPHLETS

Beard, James: Cook It Outdoors. Morrow, 1941.

Bourgaize, Eidola Jean: One-Pot Cookery. Ass'n Press, 1953, 126 pp.

Breland, J. H.: Chef's Guide to Quantity Cookery. Harper, 1947, 470 pp.

Brown, Cora; Brown, Rose; and Brown, Bob: Outdoor Cooking. Greystone, 1940.

Carhart, Arthur Hawthorne: The Outdoorsman's Cook Book. Macmillan, 1944, 211 pp.

Cooking. Boy Scouts (#3257), 1939.

Cooking Out-of-Doors. Girl Scouts (19–532), 1946.

Dana, Arthur W.: Kitchen Planning for Quantity Food Service. Harper, 1949, 229 pp.

Fernold, M. L., and Kinsey, A. C.: Edible Wild Plants of Eastern North America. Idlewild, 1943.

Hammett, Catherine T.: Campcraft A B C's, pp. 60–70.

Hammett, Catherine T.: Your Own Book of Campcraft, chap. 6.

Hammett, Catherine T., and Musselman, Virginia: The Camp Program, chap. 9.

Handel, Paul W.: The Outdoor Chef. Harper.

Hildebrand, Louise, and Hildebrand, Joel: Camp Catering, or How to Rustle Grub. Daye, 1941.

Jaeger, Ellsworth: Wildwood Wisdom, chaps. 10–12.

Joy, Barbara Ellen: Menus for Trip Breakfasts, Suppers and Lunches, and Wilderness and Crowd Cookery. Camp Publications, no. 53.

Joy, Barbara Ellen: Progressive Suppers. Camp Publications, no. 61.

Joy, Barbara Ellen: Tried and Tested Outdoor Recipes. Camp Publications, no. 65.

Kephart, Horace: Camping and Woodcraft, vol. 1, chaps. 12 and 15–23; vol. 2, chaps. 10, 21 and 22.

Mason, Bernard S.: Junior Book of Camping and Woodcraft, pp. 72–101.

Medsger, Oliver P.: Edible Wild Plants. Macmillan, 1939.

Outdoor Cooking with Reynolds Wrap. Reynolds Metals Company, Richmond 19, Virginia. 1950, 32 pp. (Aluminum foil cookery.)

Rutstrum, Calvin: Way of the Wilderness, chap. 11–13.

Some Common Edible and Poisonous Mushrooms. U.S. Dept. of Agriculture, no. 796.

Weaver, Robert W., and Merrill, Anthony F.: Camping Can Be Fun, chap. 7.

West, James E., and Hillcourt, William: Scout Field Book, Pow-wow 16.

Wilder, James Austin: Jack-Knife Cookery. Dutton, 1929.

Young America's Cook Book. Scribner, 1938.

## MAGAZINE ARTICLES

Bassett, Jeanne, and others: Setting up a Steak Barbecue. C.M., June, 1942. (Camp Publications, no. 52.)

Craig, Orval B.: All-Camp Outdoor Cooking Program. C.M., Dec., 1950.

Doermann, Marie C.: Menu Planning. C.M., April, 1952.

Hicks, Marjorie: Packet Foods Encourage More Camp Outings and Better Meals on the Trail. C.M., March, 1953.

Joy, Barbara Ellen: Miscellaneous Campcraft Hints. C.M., May, 1939. (Camp Publications, no. 54.)

Joy, Barbara Ellen: Outdoor Cookery for Crowds. Jr. H. and P.E., May, 1942. (Camp Publications, no. 58.)

Joy, Barbara Ellen: Packing Food for Trips. C.M., May, 1940. (Camp Publications, no. 59.)

Joy, Barbara Ellen: Special Foods for Trips. C.M., May, 1942. (Camp Publications, no. 67.)

Joy, Barbara Ellen: Try Different Ways of Cooking Out. C.M., June, 1953.

Joy, Barbara Ellen: Wilderness Cookery for Everybody. C. M., May, 1941. (Camp Publications, no. 67.)

King, Mary: The Mixers Are Made for Campers. C.M., May, 1952.

Kough, Blanchford: Successful Cook-Outs. C.M., Jan., 1953.

Walsh, Margaret M.: Good Nutrition, A Camp Obligation. C.M., Feb., 1954.

When there's a yellow sun on the hill
    And a wind is light as a feather
And the clouds frisk gaily, as young clouds
    will,
    Oh, then it is gypsy weather!
That's the weather to travel in,
    With the sun and wind against your skin,
No matter how glad to rest you've been,
    You must go when it's gypsy weather.
            MARY CAROLYN DAVIES,
              "Gypsy Weather"

## Chapter 32

## TRIP CAMPING

### TRIPS AND TRIP CAMPING

THERE SEEMS to be a wide diversity of sentiment and practice in regard to trip camping, for some camps scarcely engage in it at all, while others specialize in it, seemingly using the main camp for little more than a home base where the campers can return to get their mail and stock up on supplies to start out again on another trip. Undoubtedly there is an increasing emphasis on trip camping for girls as well as boys. This trend is all to the good, for teaching boys and girls to be at home in the out-of-doors should be one of the main objectives of camp, and none ought to leave camp without acquiring the campcraft and woodcraft knowledge and skills necessary to "rough it smoothly." Nearly every youngster who builds up to such expeditions gradually and under wise and skilled leadership will enjoy them, and, for most, they will prove the highlight of the summer's experience.

There are several reasons why some camps are still hesitant about including this type of activity in their programs. Trip camping on a widespread scale is fairly recent in organized camping and therefore many directors themselves have never experienced it and consequently are reluctant to promote it for their precious charges, the campers. They are strengthened in this feeling by the fact that some parents are unenthusiastic, if not actually averse to the idea. Even the campers, who have never known the thrill of sleeping out with only the stars for a roof, are somewhat backward about going, for who among them has not heard wild if completely unauthenticated tales of attacks by wild animals, snakes crawling in bed with unwary sleepers, and the like? If such things ever really happened, they have surely been repeated and exaggerated many thousands of times for each occurrence.

Some counselors are squeamish about trip camping, and many are completely untrained in it. Many colleges offering camp counselor training courses cannot or do not find the time and facilities to include such trips in their programs, thus leaving prospective counselors without the experience and confidence necessary to undertake them safely and enthusiastically in camp. The precamp training period is usually far too short for their inclusion. It is to be hoped that we will rapidly overcome this dearth of trained counselors and that every camp in the near future will include at least one trained staff member designated to supervise trips of appropriate length and ruggedness so that every physically able boy and girl in camp has the opportunity to go on at least one during the summer.

To be safe and comfortable, of course, campers must have the proper equipment for living in the open. In some camps, where they are financially able to do so, the campers furnish their own personal equipment, while the camp supplies such group equipment as tents, nested cooking outfits, and so forth. In others, where the children are less well-off, the camp owns the equipment and lends or rents it to the campers. Much personal and group trip equipment can be made at home, as has been described elsewhere.

## Values

When a trip has been well planned for and led up to, it usually becomes one of the most pleasant experiences of the summer. As a counselor, you must show just as much enthusiasm as your campers in planning and looking forward to it, for your attitude is indeed "catching." The whole trip should be cloaked in the blanket of romance and adventure which strongly appeal to the imagination and love of make-believe inherent in every child; it should be a truly thrilling expedition with definite objectives and a predetermined destination.

What better way can there be to learn to love nature and the great out-of-doors than spending all one's sleeping as well as waking hours in it? In addition to your planned experiences, only a person with closed eyes, ears and mind can fail to thrill to the unforeseen and unplanned-for events that are sure to crop up along the way.

Nowhere are people brought more closely together than when working, playing, and sleeping together on the trail, for the trip group is a little world unto itself where fast friendships quickly sprout and blossom. On the other hand, the camper who is selfish, lazy, or a rationalizer is quickly spotted by his camp mates and promptly subjected to one of the most effective treatments known—the disapproval or failure of acceptance by his own age group.

No counselor with open eyes and ears can fail to gain a clear insight into the true nature of his campers as he listens to their informal chatter. If alert, he can usually get much help in understanding what makes the problem child "tick" and fortify himself with real facts when trying to figure out how to tune his "tick" to ways more acceptable to society.

Campers on trips learn to be independent and self-reliant, yet the working and planning together bring about the true feeling of "we-ness" which is essential for good group living.

## What Kind of Trip Shall It Be?

By all means, adapt the length and ruggedness of the trip to the age, experience and stamina of the group. Give extremely young or inexperienced campers initial experience on simple breakfast or supper cook-outs. Their first experience in sleeping out might well be at a distance of only a few feet from their cabin, but they can most assuredly gain from it the techniques necessary for longer trips. Help them plan and pack their own food and equipment, using a check list to do so, thinking through the whole procedure carefully and pretending they are going too far from camp to return for anything they may have forgotten. Gradually, in succeeding summers, let them progress to short overnight trips away from camp and finally to long trips of several days' duration. These longer trips are not recommended for any but the older and more experienced campers.

Always remember that no trip is good camp practice when it degenerates into an endurance contest or a race against time. Allow plenty of time for seeing, exploring and just plain having fun, for it's not "how far" but "how much" that counts when evaluating a trip. On long excursions, it is wise to allow for a "lazy day" now and then when the group can stay at the previous night's campsite and have time to catch up on laundry and rest, with the day spent in playing games, fishing, singing, cheerful banter, or "just settin' " as the mood dictates. "Trippers" should return alert and rested, not mentally and physically fagged out so that they must spend the next few days in recuperating.

It is best, whenever possible, to have some of the counselors, and possibly a particularly able camper or two, go over a new trip before taking a group of campers on it. Most camps have a repertoire of such trips already planned and charted, varying from short, easy treks for beginners to longer and more rugged ones for seasoned campers. Provide enough to offer a new possibility for each trip even though there are several during the summer and plan a return trip over new territory.

At the end of each route, or at convenient spots along the way, it is a good idea to establish an *Outpost* or *Primitive Camp*, equipping it with rustic furniture and camp fixin's to make "trippers" more comfortable during their stay.

Make every trip a safe one, for danger is not at all essential to fun and adventure and has no place at all in the organized camp.

### Who Should Go on Trips?

The best size for a trip group is six to ten campers with two or three counselors—the ratio on long trips should not exceed five campers to each counselor. Have at least two counselors in every group—no matter how small—so that, in case of emergency, there will be one adult to stay with the campers while the other goes to use the telephone or secure help. The only safe exception might be with seasoned trippers who are sixteen years old or over. At least one counselor must be trained and experienced in trip camping, having learned how by practice as well as through training courses and extensive reading. At least one should have had training in first aid.

Campers should be of approximately the same age, strength and experience, lest the young and inexperienced ones wear themselves out or be unjustly called "lazy" or "sissy" while trying to keep up with the more experienced.

Every person going on a trip should have a physical check-up and "O.K." from the camp nurse or physician. The knowledge that they will have to pass such a test may serve as a stimulus to them to get plenty of rest and sleep and put themselves in tip-top physical condition beforehand.

It is wise to set up a progressive set of skills in campcraft and woodcraft which campers must pass before being allowed to go. The list should be short and easy for the first trips and become increasingly longer and more difficult for the more rugged ones. A chart on which a camper can check himself off as he passes a test keeps him aware of his status and shows him exactly what he must do to win the coveted right to go on a longer trip. As a preliminary to passing tests, include practice and instruction in campcraft and woodcraft as a regular part of the program, just as canoeing, arts and crafts, or swimming are. Set up an exhibit of such techniques as firebuilding, lashing, knot tying, outdoor fireplaces, and so forth at the campsite as a model for those attempting to perfect their own skills and pass tests. Bulletin board material and an ample supply of books and pamphlets should be available at all times.

A set of tests would include appropriate skills in such techniques as the following:

A demonstrated knowledge of good manners in the out-of-doors
Use and care of knife and hatchet
Selection of fuel and firebuilding; uses of various types of fires
Conservation and proper extinguishing of campfires
Outdoor cookery
Making a bedroll and experience in sleeping out-of-doors
Trip equipment and proper packing of duffel
Pitching a tent and ditching it properly
Camp sanitation and proper disposal of garbage
Knowledge of weather and weather prediction
Lashing and tying various useful knots
First aid
Experience in one-meal, then in all-day hiking and camping out
Paddling or horseback riding if the trip is to involve such methods of transportation

Requiring the passing of certain tests before going on trips gives real impetus to learning and perfecting camping skills. In addition, it insures that the participants will likely be safe, happy and comfortable on the trip.

## Preliminary Preparations

Spend the days preceding the trip in cooperative planning and preparation with every camper and counselor participating. You must definitely lay out the route and set up a tentative time schedule. Menus must be planned and proportions and food lists computed and turned in through the proper channels to allow ample time to measure out staple items and get any special ones called for. Each camp usually has its own individual procedure to follow, and you as a counselor should find out what it is and carefully adhere to it.

A list of personal equipment must be worked out and posted in each cabin for each "tripper" to check against as he packs, for leaving behind a single necessary item can be a minor or even major catastrophe for the person involved. Cut down the list to those things absolutely essential for comfort, health and safety.

Determine such group equipment as tents, cooking outfits, and the like and prepare a list in duplicate, keeping one copy to check against along the way and leaving the other in camp to check against on the return.

Turn in a detailed itinerary at the camp office so that your group can be quickly located in case of emergency.

Campers develop a proprietary interest in the trip when they have a hand in all the planning and preparations of the entire process, and much of the fun of a trip undoubtedly comes from this preliminary planning and dreaming about it. A wise counselor does not make a work horse of himself, but secures camper cooperation and participation by judiciously suggesting "let's" or "wouldn't it be fun to" or "how shall we?" The campers get much valuable experience from this logical planning and thinking through of the trip beforehand.

## General Suggestions for Trips

All the rules of health and sanitation are doubly important on a trip where the illness or incapacity of a single person is most annoying to all. A stimulating and refreshing bath every day is a "must." Wash well before each meal, using strong soap immediately after a possible exposure to poison ivy.

Never sleep in the clothes you have worn all day. A change to clean pajamas is restful and stimulating and permits you to wash out your soiled clothing and hang it up to dry over night. It is particularly important to wash out your socks each day.

Take care of minor ailments which clearly fall within the realm of first aid on the trail, but take anyone who shows signs of a serious ailment back to camp or to the nearest physician immediately. Counselors must be careful to avoid doing the wrong thing and should never try to play doctor or nurse.

Clothes Pole for Towels, Bathing Suits, etc.

If a camper shows symptoms of appendicitis (nausea and vomiting, abdominal pains which may be general at first but eventually become localized, inability to straighten the leg comfortably while lying down or to stand up straight) *do not apply heat or give a cathartic in any circumstance.*

You can make a good emergency hot water bottle by wrapping a heated s tone or canteen filled with hot water in a towel or flannel shirt.

Distribute trip equipment to be carried according to the strengths of the hikers, and do not hesitate to make changes during the trip if it seems advisable. Entrust important or perishable items only to responsible campers or counselors.

Make out a schedule of trip duties before leaving, rotating them so that no one will feel he has been unfairly burdened. Place different combinations of campers working together at various times to prevent the development of cliques and pet animosities. Outline duties clearly so that none can fail to do what he is supposed to because he misunderstood; this also makes it more difficult to get by with shirking.

Pool all money and divide it between two or three responsible persons. If your group passes through towns, it is best to set a limit (say ten or fifteen cents) for each to spend; this prevents stuffing on sweets and other indigestibles or "showing off" by those with greater allowances. A good trip menu will include all the sweets necessary or advisable for participants to have.

Make an earnest attempt to serve all meals on time, and maintain high standards for cooking, serving and eating them. The practice of subsisting on a diet of fried foods or on partially raw, overcooked, or poorly seasoned foods is pernicious and detrimental to the health and spirits of the group.

Strenuous days on the trail necessitate a maximum of rest and sleep. This means an early bedtime and *absolute quiet* soon after.

One or two campers may volunteer or be appointed to keep a trip diary, and alert persons with the ability to see unusual or funny events and put them into words will be much appreciated. Reading the diary furnishes good program around the campfire in the evening and may later be made into a little booklet, adorned in the arts and crafts department, and presented to each member of the trips soon after returning to camp. Such a diary is treasured, for it recalls many a funny happening and poignant memory long after the trip is over.

A counselor should give a good deal of thought to "program" on a trip, and should include in his duffel notes on carefully chosen ideas for games, songs, stunts, poems, and the like, for use at odd moments. A spelling bee, a nature quiz or a round-robin story may be just the thing for a rest period along the trail or to use around the campfire just before crawling into your downy soft bedrolls. A heart-to-heart discussion on a topic of interest to all or a spiritual program, at times, does much to improve group morale.

## Choosing a Campsite

It is well to begin looking for a good campsite an hour or two before sundown, for you will be tired and thankful to have supper over, the dishes washed, and everything made shipshape for the night well before dark, since camp lighting is usually quite inadequate for such chores.

When you wish to camp on other than camp property, it is only courteous to ask permission of the owner. An explanation of the nature of your group and what you are doing with an assurance that you will be careful about your campfire and leave a neat campsite usually secures willing permission. Remind your group that it represents *camp* and that the camp's continued good name depends on their observance of all the rules of consideration for others and out-of-door courtesy and good conservation practices. If others are sleeping near, you must be careful not to keep them awake or molest them in any way.

In choosing a campsite, consider a number of points. It will probably be impossible to find one combining all of the following good features, but you can at least look for one embodying as many as possible.

Privacy, a certain amount of isolation, and a beautiful view are much to be desired. Good drinking water is, of course, a big advantage, but you should take no chances, always sterilizing it in some way if there is any doubt. Good firewood and a safe place to build a fire are always essential.

An elevated gentle slope with fairly porous soil insures good drainage in case of storm. Avoid a place covered with a growth of lush grass, for it indicates that the ground is water-soaked and too damp for good sleeping or sitting. Sand is undesirable, for it permeates everything you eat and wear, and campers really can't work smoothly with "sand in their gears."

The Indians, always wise in matters of camping, usually pitched their tepees on open fields or plains where they were not endangered by falling trees and branches during a storm or by the attraction of lightning to the trees. A lone or unusually tall tree is, of course, particularly dangerous in

An Outdoor Shower.

this respect. Though trees may give some shelter during a deluge, they will continue to drip on the tent for hours after the rain is over. An open spot just at the edge of a woods is most desirable, for firewood is handy, yet you do not have to sleep under trees.

Dry streambeds and the banks of streams are risky, for a sudden storm may catch your camp in the midst of a flash flood; an island may be completely inundated during a storm. Look for high water marks before deciding to camp on such spots.

Rock piles may be the hang-outs for snakes. Ant hills or old, rotten trees which are infested with ants bring hordes of uninvited bedfellows to get into your food and all other possessions.

Mosquitoes also make mighty uncomfortable camp mates. A spot exposed to a good breeze is usually relatively free from them, but it is also a difficult and somewhat dangerous place on which to build a fire. Mosquitoes are so small that they rarely fly far against the breeze, and the windward side of a lake or stream is usually fairly safe. A fairly dense growth of trees between camp and their breeding places also serves as a pretty good protection.

## Making Camp

When a campsite has been chosen, everyone, after consultation with the work chart, should fall to and do his allotted share of the work as quickly as possible. The following procedure is suggested:

Take a short dip if you are not too hot or tired, you have a qualified waterfront person along, and you know the water is free from pollution. Examine the area for deep holes and hidden snags.

Put perishable supplies to cool.

Dig a latrine.

Get drinking water, taking steps to purify it if not sure of its source.

Make beds, clearing away all pebbles, sticks, lumps of grass, and so on, first. It is usually best to arrange the beds rather close together for general safety and companionship. Get out the personal equipment you will need. If you are going to unpack or rearrange large quantities of your duffel, it is best to spread it out on your poncho or other solid surface so small pieces can't lose themselves in the duff.

Pitch tents and dig trenches around them if there is any possibility of rain. It is best to pitch them facing north or northeast, since most violent summer storms come from the southwest (thus the sailor's name "Sou'wester," for his hat).

Take care of such general camping equipment as boats, canoes, lanterns, and so forth.

## Dividing Trip Duties

It is ordinarily best to divide the campers into committees for each meal, the duties of the committees running somewhat as follows:

1. *Cooks.*

Get the menu just after the previous meal and figure out methods and
approximate cooking time, type of fire and fireplace needed, and so
forth.

Tell the fire builders the kind of fire and fireplace you want and where and
when to build them.

At the proper time, get the food and measure out the proportions, covering
the remainder so that it will not be contaminated by insects and dirt.

*Soap the entire outsides* of the kettles and cook the food. Take pride in seeing
that everything is palatable and well seasoned.

Get out the eating utensils and set the table or arrange to have the food
served cafeteria style. Placecards and "woodsy" table decoration occasionally add much to the spirit of the meal and help to make a pleasant, attractive environment. Act as hosts or hostesses and serve the food.

As soon as everyone has finished eating, put left-over food away and replace
unused portions.

2. *Fire Builders.*

Equip yourselves with axe, knife, gloves and matches. Have handy a fire
poker, shovel and equipment to prevent fire spreading.

Consult the cooks and build the type of fire and fireplace wanted. Be sure
to build it early enough to let it burn down to coals by the time they
are ready for it.

Gather enough wood to last through the meal, chopping or breaking it up
into appropriate sizes and making a neat woodpile convenient to the
fire, but not where sparks might be blown into it.

Keep the fire going, at least one person standing by constantly to replenish fuel, rearrange coals, and so forth, at the direction of the cooks.
Don't forget to keep it hot long enough to heat dishwater.

Completely extinguish the fire as soon as all are through with it and leave
the fireplace neat, with enough fuel to start the next meal if it is to be
used again; if not, take down all equipment and leave the site as nearly
like it originally was as possible.

If the next meal is to be breakfast or if there are signs of rain, gather some
tinder, kindling and firewood and put them under a tent or extra tarpaulin.

3. *Clean up and Sanitation.*

Dig and line a grease pit.

Arrange a refrigerating or cooling system for perishable foods.

Put dishwater on to heat as soon as the cooks are through with the fire and
there are large containers available for it. Heat enough for sterilizing, too.

Rustic Wash Stand.

Latrine with Tin Can Shovel and Toilet
Paper Holder.

Wash all dishes and cooking utensils;
sterilize and put them away.

Wash out dishcloths and towels and hang
them out to dry. Scald them after the
evening meal.

Bury and cover all garbage.

Burn out, flatten and bury tin cans.

Be sure there is enough water properly
sterilized and on hand for drinking
purposes.

### Making a Latrine

Make some sort of latrine whenever two
or more campers are staying away from
camp. An easy one is the *straddle trench*,
which you dig from 2 to 3 feet deep, downhill from camp and at a distance of at
least 100 feet. Pile the dirt along the
sides where it can be kicked back into
the trench or shoveled in with a home-
made tin can shovel. Make the shovel
by pressing in the ends of a forked
stick and flattening a tin can over
them or by splitting a stick and inserting a flattened tin can in the slit,
nailing it fast and lashing the stick to
keep it from splitting further. If you
use the trench for several days, purify
it periodically by covering it with
chloride of lime, creosote or ashes, or by burning a fire over it.

Keep toilet paper nearby on a forked stick and cover it with a no. 10 tin
can as a shelter from wind and weather.
A 1-pound coffee can (X, p. 245) with
a detachable lid makes a better cover.
Cut a slot down one side to pull the
paper through. Make holes in each
end and support it by a stick run
through them and resting on forked
sticks driven into the ground.

Tin Can Shovel.

The latrine should be close enough
to the campsite for convenience, yet far enough away to provide privacy.
If no natural screen of bushes or underbrush is available, build one of brush
or canvas.

## Making Drinking Water Safe

The only way to be absolutely sure that untested water is safe is to chemically test it; if this has not been done, do not use it without sterilizing it, no matter how clear and sparkling it looks, for it may carry serious diseases such as typhoid fever. It is best to bring water from camp in clean canteens or thermos jugs or to fill them from *safe* sources along the way. When that is impossible, use one of the following methods to purify it:

1. Boil it for ten to twenty minutes (time it from when it actually starts to boil). This removes air, causing it to taste flat, but you can restore its good flavor by stirring it vigorously with a spoon or pouring it back and forth several times from one container to another.
2. Use 1 to 2 drops of iodine or 2 Helazone tablets to 1 quart of water and let stand thirty minutes. A few drops of lemon juice will make it taste better.
3. Use 10 drops of Zonite to a gallon of water, letting it stand for thirty to forty minutes before using it.
4. Use one part of chlorine to 100 parts of water. Let stand thirty minutes.
5. Use 1 to 2 drops of Clorox per gallon and aerate as in (1).

When there is water available at an outpost or frequently used campsite, it is worth while to send a sample to the State Board of Health for testing. Directions for doing this can be secured from your State or County Board of Health or the Camp Director.

During very hot weather you may want to add a little salt to your drinking water to prevent heat cramps and possible prostration. Consult the camp doctor or nurse about this.

## Garbage Disposal

Keep your campsite neat and clean, and dispose of all garbage immediately in an appropriate way, for slops and rubbish dumped about a campsite look unsightly, draw flies and other pests, and may even give off an offensive odor.

*Making a Grease Pit.* To make a grease pit for disposing of liquid wastes dig a hole on the downslope from camp and line it with small stones or gravel to act as a filter. Pour your dishwater and other liquid slops, waste fats, and the like into it. Burn it out periodically, using paper or kerosene to kindle a quick-burning fire.

*Disposing of Solid Wastes.* Carry bits of fruit and vegetables which

Drying Kiln for Solid Wastes.

would make good food for wild animals out some distance from camp and leave for them. Solid wastes are best dried out before burying, and you can do it in a semipermanent camp by building a fire in a hole and placing the food on a screen above it. On a trip, place it in the edge of the fire to dry out before burying. Such wastes as aluminum foil, banana, orange and apple

peelings will not burn; bury them instead. Remove both ends from tin cans and place them in the fire to burn out the inside contents and soften the solder so that you can mash them to minimum thickness with the side of a hatchet. The burning causes them to rust quickly to powder in the ground, and the flattening makes them require less space and keeps animals from getting claws, hoofs, or heads caught in them. Never leave tin cans lying around to catch rainwater and become mosquito breeding places.

Twist paper to be burned up tightly and burn it a little at a time, holding it down with a green stick poker so that the gases produced will not cause it to fly in the air and become a potential source of a forest fire. Tear cardboard boxes up into bits and feed a little at a time.

## Bedding Down for the Night

Cache all food safely (as illustrated in Chap. 29) against roving dogs and other animals. Turn pots and kettles upside down and stow everything neatly away for the night. See that your fire is completely out and safe from spreading.

Many animals like to chew on candles, soap, and the like; securely hide all such articles. Porcupines, in particular, crave salt and consequently may chew and completely ruin articles which have been perspiration-soaked, such as axe or paddle handles, oars, saddles, and so forth. Take them to bed with you to be sure.

Turn your shoes upside down as a protection against rain or heavy dew and place them close beside your bedroll where you can locate them quickly if you need them in the night. If you wear glasses, place them in their cases and inside your shoes or in a pack sack to avoid losing or breaking them.

Keep your flashlight close where you can instantly locate it in the dark.

### Breaking Camp

Pack your food with what you will want next on top, where it will be
readily available.

Cover your latrine and place sticks upright above it to warn others away.

Cover grease and garbage pits and mark in like manner.

Leave your campsite even neater than it was upon arrival. Remove all
traces of human habitation, restoring it to nature's beauty.

Take a last look around the outskirts of your campsite to see that you are
not leaving any personal or group equipment behind.

Your fire should be "dead as a mackerel."

### Upon Returning to the Main Camp

Each camper and counselor should have a physical check-up by the
physician or nurse within twenty-four hours after arriving back in camp. All
should return in the pink of condition, and cases of poison ivy, sunburn, indigestion, overfatigue, and the like, are intolerable for they indicate poor
planning and management of the trip.

Repair, air-out, and store all personal equipment and check in unused
food with the dietitian.

Check all group equipment against the inventory you made at the beginning of the trip, and care for any needing repairs. Air all thoroughly and
return it to its proper place.

"Trippers" should take it easy for a day or two after returning from a hard
journey, taking time for laundry and getting personal effects in order. You
may want to complete copies of your trip log, write up your adventures for
the camp newspaper, or describe it and dramatize episodes for yourselves or
your fellow campers at a subsequent campfire program.

Within a short time after returning, call a group meeting to evaluate the
trip, noting both the good and bad points of the preliminary planning and
preparations, the suitability of the food, morale of the group, and so on.
Carefully write down all suggestions and use to improve future trips. You
may want to relay your ideas on to the Director or others who work with
trip planning so that all may benefit from your experience.

## CANOE TRIPS

Trips by canoe are exciting and lots of fun for senior campers who
are already experienced in the skills of out-of-door living. Travel is relatively easy, and proportionately greater loads of food and equipment can
be taken than by any other mode of travel except wagon, automobile or
trucks.

Beginners should start with short trips, but those lasting from five days
to two weeks are feasible for seasoned paddlers. You can cover an average of

three to four miles an hour on a lake and even more when traveling with the current of a river and a total of ten to fifteen miles a day with comparative ease; even twenty miles may be attempted by experienced paddlers. When campers appear tired or disinterested, reduce the length of the daily coverage. On long trips, it is wise to plan an occasional layover of a day at the same campsite to allow for resting and exploring. Paddle after dark only in case of dire necessity.

Canoe trips may have the same purposes as other trips, and the smooth, effortless paddling through beautiful scenery has a charm all its own and affords rare studies in wildlife.

When only those who have passed the American Red Cross Intermediate Swimming Test and appropriate canoeing tests are permitted to go and proper safety precautions are taken, a canoe offers one of the safest possible modes of transportation. It does not capsize when properly used and, even if it should, the occupants should remember not to try to swim, but just hang onto the canoe for it will remain afloat and support even three or four persons indefinitely. Campers should always be instructed to hold onto their paddles in case of an upset if they can do so without endangering lives.

Another advantage of canoe travel is that, when rainy weather comes, you can invert your canoe and use it as a shelter, making an especially fine one when combined with a tarpaulin or ground cloth (*G*, p. 294).

Use a piece of mosquito net with small weights fastened along the edges as a protection when you wish to sleep in your canoe in fair weather.

### Preparation for the Trip

A good trip numbers four to six campers with two or three counselors at least one of whom is an experienced "tripper" who has already been over the proposed route. As previously mentioned, all should have hands sufficiently toughened not to blister with constant paddling.

When planning food and packing duffel, follow the same principles as for any other trip. In the canoe, it is advantageous to wear only your socks or light shoes, either light moccasins or light rubber sneakers, with an extra heavier pair for tramping about on shore. You will need your dark glasses.

Carefully choose your canoes for strength, stability in the water, and lightness if you will need to *portage*. Put them in first class repair and equip each with painter and proper thwarts. Flat-bottomed canoes are better for trips than the "barrel-bottom" type which, though easier to propel, are tippier in the water. Each camper should have a waterproof kneeling pad, preferably one which will float and so serve as a life preserver in case of an upset; such a pad also serves as a seat around camp and comes in handy as a pillow at night. Always include a well-equipped canoe-mending kit and a map of the route, if possible. Paddlers kneel on the bottom of the canoe, using thwarts and built-in seats to lean against, not sit upon.

Each camper should select a paddle and label it with his name in India or indelible ink on a piece of adhesive tape. Your paddle should reach between your chin and eye when standing erect (nearer the chin if you paddle bow). Place an extra paddle flat on the floor in each canoe in case one is lost or broken. Two or three persons usually travel in each boat depending on its size and the amount of gear to be taken.

Distribute personnel so that each canoe is manned by a crew of equal strength and stamina and keep the canoes abreast or not more than three canoe lengths apart for companionship and possible aid in case of trouble.

Always place an experienced paddler in the *stern* for his is the responsibility of steering. The bow paddler aids him by keeping a sharp lookout for half-hidden rocks or snags in the path, and should have the ability to "draw" or "pry" the canoe away from a sudden hazard.

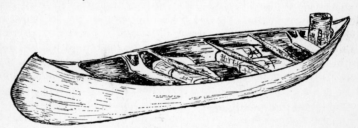

Packing the Canoe.

Have your canoe afloat as you pack duffel in it carefully. Stow one (two if not too bulky) bag under the bow seat or thwart, another just back of the middle thwart, and one (usually the heaviest) just back of the stern thwart. Anchor and lash all so they cannot slip and throw the canoe off balance, or will not be lost if the canoe should upset; distribute their weight so the canoe is steady and a bit heavier in the stern, which should ride about an inch lower than the bow. Keep the weight of the duffel low and toward the center line of the canoe with at least 4 inches of clear space (*freeboard*) above the gear. Load the canoe and take it out close to shore to test for balance; bring it back for rearranging if necessary.

Place raincoats and cameras on top where they are immediately available and make food and cooking utensils for lunch also readily accessible.

A good trip is a safe one, so never attempt to travel through dangerous white water or rapids. Stay close to shore on big lakes, for a sudden summer

The Long and the Short of It.

storm can capsize the best canoe-ists. Upsets can be serious, even though no harm is done the occupants for you may lose all your duffel unless it is lashed in securely. When you first notice a storm approaching, get *off* the lake, for it is particularly dangerous to remain on water during squalls or lightning. If necessary to continue paddling during a light sprinkle, raise your duffel a little off the floor, supported on poles or sticks. Pack it in waterproof bags and, if possible, cover it with a tarpaulin or ground cloth. If ever so unfortunate as to be caught in rough water, keep your weight low and well centered. Above all, keep the bow of your canoe pointed at an angle to the waves, never parallel, to minimize the danger of shipping water and capsizing. If you lose your paddle, kneel in the canoe and paddle with your hands.

Use special care when landing a canoe, making sure that all enter and leave it properly, and that it is secured by its painter or is placed where it is safe in the shade on shore.

On hot days it may be well to confine most of your strenuous paddling to the early morning and evening, with a long rest at lunchtime and a short pause for singing, guessing games and exploring every hour or so while paddling. Be ever alert to prevent sunburn and be sure all return rested and lively. Good food and plenty of sleep and rest are "musts" for this as for any trip.

## ADDITIONAL READINGS

### BOOKS AND PAMPHLETS

Brower, David R.: Going Light—With Backpack or Burro. Sierra.

Camp, Marjorie: All-Camp, All-Skill Contest—A Plan for an Afternoon of Team Competition in All-Camp Activities. Camp Publications, no. 13.

Campcraft Skills Charts (Primitive-Camp Sanitation). Girl Scouts.

Camping. Boy Scouts (#3256), 1946.

Camping and the Older Boy. Ass'n Press, pp. 9–12, 25–30.

Cooking Out-of-Doors. Girl Scouts, 1946, pp. 16–22.

Cycling. Boy Scouts (#3277), 1949.

Handel, Carle W.: Canoe Camping: A Guide to Wilderness Travel. Barnes, 1953, 288 pp.

Joy, Barbara Ellen: Organization of the Camp Craft Program in the Camp. Camp Publications, no. 55.

Joy, Barbara Ellen: Outline of Trip Duties. Camp Publications, no. 57.

Joy, Barbara Ellen: Overnight Trips—Yes and No. Camp Publications, no. 56.

Joy, Barbara Ellen: Progressive Scale of Skills for Trip Requirements. Camp Publications, no. 60.

Joy, Barbara Ellen: Progressive Suppers. Camp Publications, no. 61.

Outdoor Book, The—Camp Fire Girls, rev. ed., 1954 (#D 74).

Rutstrum, Calvin: Way of the Wilderness.

Trip Camp Book. Girl Scouts (#19–602), 1947.

Weaver, Robert W., and Merrill, Anthony F.: Camping Can Be Fun, chap. 2.

## MAGAZINE ARTICLES

Cumbee, Frances: Basic Campcraft Skills. Jr. H. and P.E., June, 1951.

Grimland, Tom C.: Small Wagon Camping. C.M., Nov., Dec., 1942.

Groder, Roland H.: Trip Programs Need Planning. C.M., April, 1949.

Hake, Margaret L.: 19 Campers and How They Grew. C.M., May, 1953. (Building outpost camp.)

Joy, Barbara Ellen: Campcraft on Display. C.M., June, 1949.

Joy, Barbara Ellen: Care of Food and Equipment on Trips. C.M., Jan., Feb., 1941 (Camp Publications, no. 51.)

Joy, Barbara Ellen: Consistent Careful Maintenance of Equipment Leads to Successful Campcraft Program. C.M., Nov., 1952.

Klee, Cecil H., and Epstein, Richard: Outpost Camping for All. C.M., May, 1949.

Paxson, C. G.: Po-Tiki On a Budget. C.M., May, 1952.

Thompson, Millicent: A Camp Dietitian Looks at Trips. C.M., April, 1952.

## CANOEING

### BOOKS AND PAMPHLETS

Bucher, Charles (Ed.): Methods and Material in Physical Education and Recreation, pp. 100–102.

Camp Safety Digest, pp. 18–20, 21–24, 31–35, 41–44.

Jaeger, Ellsworth: Wildwood Wisdom, chap. 14.

Rutstrum, Calvin: Way of the Wilderness, chap. 3.

### MAGAZINE ARTICLES

Christie, Roberts: Portaging with Ease. C.M., June, 1941.

Dennis, Edith C.: Canoe Trips for Women. Jr. H. and P.E., April, 1946.

DeWitt: Your Camp's Overnight Hikes. C.M., June, 1950.

Morrison, Flora M., and Northway, Mary L.: Adventuring by Canoe. C.M., Nov., Dec., 1942.

# FILMS AND SLIDES PERTAINING TO CAMPING

THE FIRM name given is that of the producer of the film who ordinarily sells but does not rent films. Consult the catalogues of your usual film suppliers to find out where they are available. The following abbreviations are used to show the age groupings of campers for whom the film will be most useful:

> pri (primary)—ages 6–8
> int (intermediate)—ages 9–12
> jh (junior high)—ages 13–15
> sh (senior high)—ages 16–18
> col (college)—college and adult

Combinations denote that the film can be employed for campers of the first-designated group through those of the last-mentioned category; for example, jh-col means that the film is usable for campers of the junior high through college group.

## THE CAMPING MOVEMENT

*Boy's Day Camp*—2 reels, color, YMCA. Day Camp program of Rochester, N. Y. Shows rich and varied program possible.

*Camping Education*—2 reels, sd., b&w, March of Time, col. The program at National Camp for training professional camp leaders. Life Camps, Inc.

*Camping for Girl Scouts*—18 min., sd., color, Girl Scouts, sh-col. Girl Scouts arrive at campsite and show troop camping, day camping, trip camping, and established camping. Standards, water safety, etc., shown.

*School Time in Camp*—18 min., sd., color, int-jh. School camping experience of 5th and 7th grades of New York City Schools at Life Camps.

*Youth in Camps*—2 reels, sd., March of Time, col. Decentralized, "Camptivity" plan of camping as used at Life Camps.

## UNDERSTANDING AND WORKING WITH CAMPERS

*Am I Trustworthy?*—11 min., sd., Coronet, pri-jh. Practice in being trustworthy in little things will carry over when more important issues are raised.

*The Bully*—11 min., sd., Young America, jh-col. Shows how Chick Allen, large for his age, bullies smaller boys into being on his side.

*Good Sportsmanship*—11 min., sd., Coronet, int-jh. Joe and Bill learn the rules for good sportsmanship.

*How We Cooperate*—11 min., sd., Coronet, int-jh. Necessity and techniques of co-operation shown.

*How to Say No*—11 min., sd., Coronet, sh-col. Discussion by a small group of high school students on how to say "no" without losing friends.

*Ways to Good Habits*—11 min., sd., Coronet, pri-int. Importance of good habits and how to substitute them for bad ones.

383

## PROGRAM

*Indian Dances*—11 min., sd., color, Enc. Brit. Films, (jh-col). Based on the keen powers of observation of the Indian as he portrays four dance patterns: the grouse, an eagle in flight, the buffalo, and the deer. Tom-tom accompaniment.

*Indian Pow-wow*—11 min., sd., color, Avalon-Daggett Productions. Tribes from Southwest arrive for pow-wow by various means of conveyance. Eagle Dancers from Laguna, Devil Dancers of the Apaches, Kiowa War Dancers from Oklahoma, the Yeibechi Dancers from the Navajo's. Indian rodeo at Cheyenne, Wyoming.

*Smoki Snake Dance*—11 min., sd., color, Avalon-Daggett Productions. Prayer dances of the Indians of the Southwest. Horsetail Dance of Taos, Feather Dance of Shawnees, and Clown Dance.

## DRAMATICS

*ABC's of Puppet Making*—20 min., sd., b&W, Bailey. Simple and more complicated puppets from cardboard, cotton, glue, papier mâché, etc. How to manipulate and stage puppet shows.

*How to Make a Puppet*—12 min., sd., b&w or color. Use of plasticine, papier mâché, etc. Several types of puppets shown and audience is challenged to find original ones to fit their own needs.

## ARTS AND CRAFTS

*ABC's of Pottery Making* (Coil Method)—11 min., sd., b&w, Bailey, jh-col. Making of bowl; use of templet pattern, hand tools, and potter's wheel; finishing; baking.

*Craftsmanship in Clay*—4 films, 11 min. each, sd., color, Indiana U. Techniques for using materials that come out of the camp environment.

*Let's Paint with Water Colors*—11 min., sd., pri-col. Shows methods used by class of young boys and girls in making covers for their scrapbooks.

*Loom Weaving*—6 min., sd., color, Internat'l Film Bureau, jh-col. Art teacher and manual training teacher cooperate to help students build loom out of old

broom and a few pieces of wood. Some techniques also shown.

*Making Indian Mocassins*—17 min., sd., color, Boy Scouts. From selection of hide to first fitting shown by Ben Hunt.

*Making A Pack Basket*—2 reels, sd., color, Boy Scouts. "Pop Williams" shows construction of a large pack basket from a green tree. Can be adapted to weaving of commercially prepared materials.

*Painting: Learning to Use Your Brush*—sd., b&w, Young America. Materials and basic brush strokes for the beginner.

*Portage*—20 min., sd., color, Nat'l Film Board of Canada. The making of a birch bark canoe.

*Pottery Making*—11 min., sd., Encyc. Britan. Films, int-col. Coil method of making Indian bowl from the preparation of the clay to the finished product.

## CREATIVE WRITING

*Describing an Incident*—11 min., sd., Coronet, int-col. Dramatizes the interesting and uninteresting ways of telling a story.

*How to Write Effectively*—11 min., sd., Coronet, int-col. The steps necessary for effective writing.

## STORY TELLING

*Paul Bunyan and the Blue Ox*—5 min., sd., Coronet, pri-int. Retells this famous story, using puppets as characters.

## NATURE AND CONSERVATION

*Animal Cunning*—1 reel, sd., b&w, Skibo. Shows instinctive cunning and alertness of many animals.

*Animal Land*—sd., b&w, Sterling. How animls fight to save their homes when faced with the ravages of nature.

*Ants*—11 min., sd., b&w, Encyc. Brit. Films, int-col. Life cycle carpenter ant. Also black ants and household ants.

*Arachnids—Spiders and Their Allies*—11 min., sd., b&w, United World, sh-col. Structures and habits of garden, water, and raft spiders.

*Beneath Our Feet* (Insects)—11 min., sd., Teaching Film Custodians, int-col. Ant drinking from dew drop, crickets fighting, cricket chirping, heads of wolf spiders, sand cricket struggling with trap-door spider and with centipede, aphids being eaten by ladybird larvae, bees taking honey from flowers.

*Butterfly Botanists*—11 min., sd., color, Coronet, int-col. Life history of monarch as a typical butterfly.

*City of Wax*—1 reel, sd., b&w, Skibo. The life of the bee.

*Conservation of Natural Resources*—11 min., sd., Encyc. Brit. Films, jh-col. Waste in water power, forests, farm lands, etc., with effective steps to control it.

*Heritage We Guard*—3 reels, sd., b&w, Institutional Cinema Service. Exploitation of land by trappers and settlers and the importance of wildlife and soil conservation.

*How Animals Defend Themselves*—10 min., sd., b&w, Young America, pri-int. Way animals are adapted to protect themselves against other animals and nature.

*How Nature Protects Animals*—1 reel, sd., b&w, Encyc. Brit. Films, int-col. Different types of protection as by fleetness of foot, mimicry, coloration, armor, secluded homes, keenness of vision, smell, and odorization. Tiger, giraffe, goat, rabbit, chameleon, woodpecker, grouse, measuring worm, and caterpillar demonstrate.

*Insects*—11 min., sd., color, Encyc. Brit. Films, jh-col. Uses a grasshopper to show the distinguishing features of insects as compared to other animals.

*Let's Catch Reptiles*—10 min., sd., color or b&w, Bailey, jh-col. Trip of three children to collect turtles, lizards, and snakes. Structure, care and habits shown.

*Life along the Waterways*—11 min., sd., color, Encyc. Brit. Films, jh-col. Many forms of plant and animal life shown throughout the changing seasons. Changes of waterway from brook to river.

*Life in a Pond*—11 min., sd., color or b&w, Coronet, int-col. Series of class field trips to pond. Shows underwater and microscopic scenes over several months.

*Monarch Butterfly*—11 min., sd., color or b&w, Simmel-Meservey, int-col. Complete cycle from caterpillar to adulthood.

*Monarch Butterfly Story*—11 min., sd., color, Encyc. Brit. Films, jh-col. Life cycle from egg to maturity. Geographic range and physical make-up shown.

*Pond Life*—11 min., sd., Encyc. Brit. Films, pri-jh. Activity and community life of many animals. Balance of plant and animal life.

*Snakes*—10 min., sd., color, Coronet, jh-col. How snakes differ from yet resemble other mammals and how they illustrate nature's principles of adaptation.

*Snakes Can Be Interesting*—11 min., sd., Young America, int. How bull snake is born, eats, sheds its skin, etc. Shows the usefulness of snakes to the farmer and how to distinguish poisonous from non-poisonous varieties.

*Snapping Turtle*—11 min., sd., Encyc. Brit. Films, int-col. Life cycle and its encounter with animals.

*Some Frogs and Toads*—14 min., sil., color, Rutgers, jh-col. Habitats, activities, and characteristics of bull frogs, green frogs, leopard frogs, cricket frogs, Fowler's toads, tree toads, and spade-foot toads.

*Songbirds of the North Woods*—11 min., sd., b&w, Teaching Film Custodians, int-col. Record of the songs and calls of the loon, white-throated sparrow, hermit thrush, magnolia warbler, scarlet tanager, goshawk, woodpecker, and chickadee. Some nesting habits shown.

*Spider and the Ant, The*—1 reel, sd., b&w, Sterling. The story of an ant trapped in a spider web and of his rescue by a snail.

*Spotty: Story of a Fawn*—10 min., sd., b&w or color, Coronet, pri. Story of how Spotty and other animals of the North Woods eat, drink, protect themselves, etc.

*This Vital Earth*—11 min., sd., color, Encyc. Brit. Films, jh-col. Interdependence of plant and animal life and dependence of land on past living forms.

*What Is Soil?*—12 min., sd., Films, Inc., int-col. Bobby learns by experimentation and exploration about the composition of soil, its effects upon plant life, and the various causes of soil erosion.

*Wonders in a Country Stream*—1 reel, sd., color, Churchill-Wexler, pri-jh. Newt, tadpoles, garter snake, and water insects and their life habits shown near a country brook.

*Wonders in Your Own Backyard*—1 reel, sd., color, Nat'l Bo. Review, pri-jh. Earthworm, millapede, sow bug, pill bug, house spider, and snail shown.

*Yours Is the Land*—20 min., sd., color, Encyc. Brit. Films, jh-col. Effects of wasting natural resources, balance of plant, animal, and insect life, and dependence of man upon the land. Shows methods of conservation.

## AQUATICS

*Advanced Swimming*—10 min., sd., Official, int-col. Perfecting the style and strokes of the average swimmer—body alignment, arm and leg action, breathing, etc. Supervised by Fred Cady.

*Aquatic Artistry*—9 min., sd., Teaching Film Custodians. Running front, cutaway somersault, full twist, forward one and one-half, backward one and one-half, forward two and one-half pike, half gainer, half gainer with twist, and front with half twist shown.

*Artificial Respiration*—6 min., sd., Seminar Films, jh-col. Back pressure arm lift method shown in detail.

*Boy Scout Methods of Waterfront Safety*—1 reel, sil., Boy Scouts. Do's and don'ts of waterfront safety in a humorous and everyday manner.

*Diving Fundamentals*—10 min., sd., Official, int-col. Fundamentals of doing many kinds of diving. Supervised by Fred Cady.

*Fundamentals of Swimming*—27 min., color, Castle Films. Especially designed for intermediate swimmers. American Red Cross.

*Heads Up*—24 min., American Red Cross. Designed especially for water safety classes and shows approaches, carries, and releases. Also valuable hints for other swimmers.

*Learning to Sail*—10 min., Hawley-Lord, jh-col. The technique of sailing expertly demonstrated for beginners. Ship's tackle and sailing maneuvers explained.

*Learning to Swim*—11 min., sd., Young America, int-jh. Six steps for beginners in learning the Australian crawl.

*Learning to Swim*—30 min., color, American Red Cross. Fundamentals of water adjustment, relaxation, and first strokes for beginning swimmers.

*Matt Mann's Swimming Techniques for Boys*—17 min., sd., Coronet, int-col. Elementary forms of swimming, crawl, breast, back, and butterfly strokes.

*Matt Mann's Swimming Techniques for Girls*—10 min., sd., color, Coronet, int-col. Crawl, breast, back, and butterfly strokes.

*Oars and Paddles*—24 min., sd., American Red Cross, int-col. Proper use of rowboats and canoes—launching and getting underway, handling oars, how to save self when boat overturns, boat rescue of swimmers, canoe paddling strokes, etc.

*Ornamental Swimming*—9 min., Ass'n Films. Team of girls show rhythmic patterns such as "submarine," "concertina," and "pinwheel."

*Skilled Swimming*—33 min., color, American Red Cross. For advanced swimmers.

*Springboard Techniques*—10 min., sd., color, Coronet, jh-col. Shows proper use of springboard with step by step analysis in slow motion at a sand pit with a diving belt. Lifts, tucks, somersaults, etc., shown.

*Swimming for Beginners*—8 min., sd., Official, int-col. Instructing a ten-year old child in conquest of fear, breathing, kicking, arm strokes, etc. Supervised by Fred Cady.

*Synchronized Swimming: Basic Skills*—20 min., sil., Consolidated Film Industries, jh-col. Strokes, stunts, and hybrids from beginning to advanced levels.

## ROPES AND KNOTCRAFT

*Useful Knots*—23 min., sd., U. S. Navy. How to tie and use such knots as the overhand, slip, square, sheet bend, two half-hitches, slippery hitch, clove, and rolling hitch.

## TENTS AND SHELTERS

*Making an Indian Tipi*—8 min., sd., color, Boy Scouts. Step by step process shown.

## MISCELLANEOUS ACTIVITIES

*Cameras Go to Camp*—16 min., sd., color, Eastman. Shows how campers and camp director can use cameras to best advantage.

*Tie Your Own Flies*—10 min., sd., Hawley-Lord, int-col. Shows proper technique.

## WEATHER

*Clouds Go to Work*—10 min., sd., b&w, Edited Pictures System. Cloud formations, making of streams, water-power, value, and purification of water.

*Clouds*—10 min., sd., U. S. Dept. of Agri. How movements of clouds cause weather changes and why rain falls. Various types of cloud formations and how layman can forecast weather.

*Clouds and Weather*—11 min., sd., U. S. Dept. of Agri. Typical weather cycle, types of clouds accompanying cyclone, factors of barometric pressure, movement of warm and cold air masses, etc.

*Clouds Above*—11 min., b&w or color, pri. Four main types of clouds and their significance. Absorption of water by air, formation of clouds, precipitation of rain, etc.

*Fair Weather Clouds*—14 min., sil., Films of Commerce. Each type of fair weather cloud, nature of fog, and effects of temperature on clouds.

*Foul Weather Clouds*—15 min., sil., Films of Commerce. Foul weather clouds, nature of fog-banks, "undecided" clouds, etc.

*One Rainy Day*—11 min., sd., Coronet, pri. Children listen to story which explains how storm begins with winds, clouds, thunder and lightning and how rain helps soil, plants, and people.

*Story of a Storm*—11 min., sd., Coronet, int-col. Shows how weather moves across country and affects the people who are in its path.

*What Makes Rain*—9 min., sd., Young America, int-jh. Explains how and why water moves from earth to sky and back again. Evaporation and condensation.

## GETTING ABOUT IN THE OUT-OF-DOORS

*How to Read a Map*—1 reel, sil. How to interpret symbols, such as mountains, roads, lakes, swamps, etc.

*Maps and Their Uses*—11 min., sd., Coronet, int-col. Use of symbols on maps and the use of special maps and their symbols.

*Maps Are Fun*—11 min., sd., color, Coronet, int-jh. Story of a boy who prepares a map of a paper route. Brings out how to read legends, scale, grid, color, the types of maps and how to read a map index.

*Sport of Orienteering*—20 min., sd., color, sh-col. Shows Scandinavians participating in this popular game and explains how they use a compass and map. Cross-country running.

## TIN CAN CRAFT

*Tin Can Craft*—11 min., sd., color, Boy Scouts. Ben Hunt bends tin cans into usable cooking equipment.

## KNIFEMANSHIP AND TOOLCRAFT

*How to Sharpen Your Knife and Use it Safely*—12 slides, Wards. Twelve slides illustrating correct techniques.

*Knifecraft*—11 min., sd., b&w, Boy Scouts. Ben Hunt show how to care for and use a pocket knife as he whittles a Katcina Doll lamp.

*Totems*—11 min., color, Nat'l Film Board of Canada. Explains history and meaning of totem poles of Pacific Coast Indians. Details of many fine specimens shown; background of Indian drums and chanting.

## AXEMANSHIP

*Axemanship*—9 min., sd., b&w, Boy Scouts. Peter McLarin demonstrates the use and care of various types of axes. How to chop down a tree, split logs, and cut firewood.

## FIRES

*Art of Building a Fire, The*—15 slides, Wards. Fifteen slides showing proper sequence of steps in building a fire.

*Fire Building and Cooking*—sd., b&w, Boy Scouts. Correct techniques shown.

*One Match Can Do It*—10 min., sd., Simmel-Meservey. Shows how one match can start a destructive forest fire, methods of fighting fire. Barren hillsides then result in floods, creating general havoc.

*The Frying Pan and the Fire*—18 min., color, U. S. Dept. Agri., int-col. Two girls leave their campfire to photograph a deer, the fire gets out of control and destroys their new camping gear and nearly starts a disastrous forest fire. Correct and incorrect ways of fighting forest fires shown.

*Then It Happened*—10 min., sd., color, U. S. Dept. Agri. Account of the 1947 Maine forest fire and its thirty million dollars worth of destruction.

## TRIP CAMPING

*Indian Canoeman*—10 min., sd., Hawley-Lord, int-col. Canoeing, portaging, camping and finding food in the wilds of Canada. Two Indians of the Tête de Boule tribe shown.

*Overnight*—2 reels, color or b&w, Girl Scouts, jh-col. Group and leader plan and enjoy overnight camping trip. All participate in group planning.

# SELECTED GENERAL BIBLIOGRAPHY

Benson, Reuel A., and Goldberg, Jacob A.: The Camp Counselor. McGraw-Hill, 1951, 337 pp.

Bucher, Charles A. (Ed.): Methods and Materials in Physical Education and Recreation. Mosby, 1954, 423 pp.

Burns, Gerald P.: The Program of the Modern Camp. Prentice-Hall, 1954, 320 pp.

Camp Director's Handbook and Buying Guide, The—C.M., ACA. (Issued annually.)

Camp Leadership Courses for College and Universities. ACA, 1949.

Camp Safety Digest, compiled and published by Center for Safety Education, Division of General Education, N.Y. Univ., 1952, 63 pp.

Camping and the Future: Report of Camp Seminar Held at George Williams College, March 28, 1947. Ass'n Press, 1948.

Camping and the Older Boy. Ass'n Press, 1940.

Chapman, Margaret, Gaudette, Marie E., and Hammett, Catherine: Program Helps for Camp Leaders. Rafter Crafters, 1947.

Des Grey, Arthur H.: Camping: A Guide to Outdoor Safety and Comfort. Ronald, 1950, 188 pp.

Dimock, Hedley S. (Ed.): Administration of the Modern Camp. Ass'n Press, 1948, 294 pp.

Dimock, Hedley S., and Statten, Taylor: Talks to Counselors. Ass'n Press, 1939.

Drought, R. Alice: A Camping Manual. Barnes, 1943, 167 pp.

Established Camp Book, The—A guide for Girl Scout Camp Directors and Camp Committees. Girl Scouts (#19–607), 1946.

Gardner, Ella: Handbook for Recreation Leaders. Superintendent of Documents, Children's Bureau of the U.S. Department of Labor, Publication No. 231, 1936.

Gottshall, Franklin H., and Hellum, Amanda Watkins: You Can Whittle and Carve. Bruce, 1942, 96 pp.

Graham, Abbie: The Girl's Camp: Program Making for Summer Leisure. Woman's Press, 1933.

Graham, Abbie: Working at Play in the Summer Camp. Woman's Press, 1941.

Geist, Roland C.: Hiking, Camping and Mountaineering. Harper, 1943.

Halstead, Homer: How to Live in the Woods, Little, 1948.

Hammett, Catherine T.: Campcraft ABC's. Girl Scouts (#19–609), 1944.

Hammett, Catherine T.: Your Own Book of Campcraft. Girl Scouts (#23–314).

Hammett, Catherine T., and Musselman, Virginia: The Camp Program Book. Ass'n Press, 1951, 380 pp.

Harbin, H. C.: The Fun Encyclopedia. Abingdon-Cokesbury, 1940.

Hartwig, Marie, and Petersen, Florence: Camp Counselor Training Workbook. Burgess, 1950, 104 pp.

Henderson, Luis M.: The Outdoor Guide. Stackpole and Heck, 350 pp.

Hunt, W. Ben: Ben Hunt's Whittling Book. Bruce, 1945, 127 pp.

Hunt, W. Ben: Indian and Camp Handicraft. Bruce, 1938, 180 pp.

Hunt, W. Ben: More Ben Hunt Whittlings. Bruce, 1947, 108 pp.

Ickis, Marguerite: Arts and Crafts, A Practical Handbook. Barnes, 1943, 309 pp.

Irwin, Frank L.: The Theory of Camping. Barnes, 1950, 192 pp.

Jaeger, Ellsworth: Wildwood Wisdom. Macmillan, 1948.

Jaeger, Ellsworth: Woodsmoke. Macmillan, 1953, 228 pp.

Kephart, Horace: Camping and Woodcraft. Macmillan, 1948, 894 pp.

Ledlie, John E., and Holbein, Francis W.: The Camp Counselor's Manual, rev. Ass'n Press, 1947.

Ledlie, John E., and Roehm, Ralph D.: Handbook of YMCA Camp Administration. Ass'n Press, 1949, 239 pp.

McBride, Robert E.: Camping at the Mid-Century. ACA, 1953, 41 pp.

Maine Camp Director's Ass'n (Publishers): The Art of Living Out of Doors in Maine. Maine Develop. Commission, 1950, 118 pp.

Mason, Bernard S.: The Junior Book of Camping and Woodcraft. Barnes, 1943, 120 pp.

Mason, Bernard S.: Woodcraft. Barnes, 1939, 580 pp.

Mason, Bernard S., and Mitchell, Elmer D.: Social Games for Recreation. Barnes, 1935, 444 pp.

Meinecke, Conrad E.: Cabin Craft and Outdoor Living. Foster and Stewart.

Morgan, Barbara: Summer's Children. Morgan & Morgan, 1951, 168 pp.

Mulac, Margaret E.: The Playleaders' Manual. Harper, 1941.

Osborne, Ernest G.: Camping and Guidance. Ass'n Press, 1937.

Ott, Elmer: So You Want to be a Camp Counselor? Ass'n Press, 1946.

Parkhill, Martha, and Spaeth, Dorothy: It's Fun to Make Things. Barnes, 1941, 176 pp.

Pashko, Stanley: Boy's Complete Book of Camping. Greenberg.

Price Betty: Adventuring in Nature. NRA, 1939.

Rubin, Robert: The Book of Camping. Ass'n Press, 1949, 152 pp.

Rutstrum, Calvin: Way of the Wilderness, rev. Burgess, 1952, 192 pp.

Safety-Wise. Girl Scouts (#19–502), 1950.

Slavson, S. R.: Recreation and the Total Personality. Ass'n Press, 1946.

Swanson, William E.: Camping for All It's Worth. Macmillan, 1952, 154 pp.

Ure, Roland W.: Fifty Cases for Camp Counselors, rev. Ass'n Press, 1946.

Weaver, Robert W., and Merrill, Anthony F.: Camping Can be Fun. Harper, 1948.

Webb, Kenneth B., and Susan H.: Summer Magic. Ass'n Press, 1953, 159 pp.

West, James E., and Hillcourt, William: The Scout Field Book. Boy Scouts (#3649), 1944, 540 pp.

Wittenberg, Rudolph M.: So You Want to Help People; a Mental Hygiene Primer for Group Leaders. Ass'n Press, 1947.

Zarchy, Harry: Let's Go Camping: A Guide to Outdoor Living. Knopf. 1951.

# DIRECTORY OF PUBLISHERS AND ORGANIZATIONS ASSOCIATED WITH CAMPING

*With abbreviations and contractions used throughout the book*

AAHPER—American Association for Health, Physical Education and Recreation, 1201 16th St., N.W., Washington 6, D.C.

Abingdon-Cokesbury — Abingdon-Cokesbury Press, 810 Broadway, Nashville 2, Tenn.

ACA—American Camping Association, 343 S. Dearborn St., Chicago 4, Ill.

Aladdin Books—Aladdin Books, 55 5th Ave., New York 3, N.Y.

Am. Ass'n of Sch. Administrators—American Association of School Administrators, 1201 16th St., N.W., Washington 6, D.C.

Am. Canoe Ass'n—American Canoe Association, 8224 S. Woodlawn Ave., Chicago, Ill.

Am. Forestry Ass'n—American Forestry Association, Washington, D.C.

Am. Handicrafts—American Handicrafts, 45–49 South Harrison St., East Orange, N.J.

Amer. Mus. of Nat. Hist.—American Museum of Natural History, Central Park West, 79th St., New York, N.Y.

Appleton—Appleton-Century-Crofts, Inc., 35 W. 32nd St., New York 1, N.Y.

ARC—American National Red Cross, 17th and D St., Washington 13, D.C.

Arts Coop.—Arts Cooperative Service, Inc., 340 Amsterdam Ave., New York 24, N.Y.

Ass'n for Childhood Ed.—Association for Childhood Education, 1201 16th St., N.W., Washington, D.C.

Ass'n Press—Association Press, 291 Broadway, New York 7, N.Y.

Association for Supervision and Curriculum Development, 1201 16th St., N.W., Washington 6, D.C.

Audubon—National Audubon Society, 1000 Fifth Avenue, New York 28, N.Y.

Bantam—Bantam Books, Inc., New York, N.Y.

Barnes—A. S. Barnes & Company, 232 Madison Ave., New York 16, N.Y.

Barnes & Noble—Barnes & Noble, Inc., 105 5th Ave., New York 3, N.Y.

Barrows—M. Barrows & Company, Inc., 114 East 3rd St., New York 16, N.Y.

Beach & Pool—Beach & Pool, 425 4th Ave., New York 16, N.Y.

Beacon—The Beacon Press, 25 Beacon St., Boston 8, Mass.

Bead—Bead Publishing Co., Brooklyn, N.Y.

Bemiss—Homer Bemiss, P.O. Box 796, Oakland, Calif.

Bennett—Charles A. Bennett Co., 237 N. Monroe St., Peoria 3, Ill.

Bicycle Institute—Bicycle Institute of America, New York, N.Y.

Birchard—C. C. Birchard & Company, 221 Columbus Ave., Boston, Mass.

Blue Ribbon—Blue Ribbon Books, Inc., 386 4th Ave., New York, N.Y.

Bobbs—Bobbs-Merrill Company, 724 N. Meridian St., Indianapolis, Ind.; 468 4th Ave., New York 16, N.Y.

Botanic Publishing Co.—Botanic Publishing Company, Cincinnati, Ohio.

Boy Scouts—Boy Scouts of America, 2 Park Ave., New York 16, N.Y.

Branford—Charles T. Branford Company, Boston, Mass.

Bruce—Bruce Publishing Company, 400 N. Broadway, Milwaukee 1, Wis.; 330 W. 42nd St., New York, N.Y.

Bruce Humphries—Bruce Humphries, Inc., 30 Winchester St., Boston 16, Mass.; 16 E. 43rd St., New York 17, N.Y.

Bureau of Educational Research and Service, The, Laramie, Wyoming.

Burgess—Burgess Publishing Company, 426–428 S. 6th St., Minneapolis 15, Minn.

Camp Fire Girls—Camp Fire Girls, Inc., 16 E. 48th St., New York, 17, N.Y.

Camp Publications—Camp Publications, 6 High St., Bar Harbor, Me.

Canadian Nature Magazine—Canadian Nature Magazine, 177 Jarvis St., Toronto 2, Canada.

Century—The Century Company, New York, N.Y. See Appleton-Century.

Character Craft Publications—Character Craft Publications, 1033–35 University Place, Evanston, Ill.

Child Study Ass'n of America—Child Study Association of America, 132 E. 74th St., New York, N.Y.

Children's Press—Children's Press, Chicago, Ill.

Children's Theatre Press—The Children's Theatre Press, Anchorage, Ky.

Clark-Sprague — Clark-Sprague Printing Co., 1901 Locust St., St. Louis, Mo.

Cleveland Crafts Co.—Cleveland Crafts Company, Cleveland, Ohio.

Clute—Willard N. Clute & Company, Butler University, Indianapolis, Ind.

C.M.—Camping Magazine, 181 Chestnut Ave., Metuchen, N.J.

Columbia U. Press—Columbia University Press, 2960 Broadway, New York 27, N.Y.

Comstock—Comstock Publishing Company, Inc., 126 Roberts Place, Cornell Heights, Ithaca, N.Y.

Conservation Yearbook—The Conservation Yearbook, 1740 K St., N.W., Washington 6, D.C.

Coop. Rec. Service—Cooperative Recreation Service, Rodnor Road, Delaware, Ohio.

Cornell Maritime—Cornell Maritime Press, Cambridge, Md.

Craft Service—Craft Service, 337 University Ave., Rochester 7, N.Y.

Crowell—Thomas Y. Crowell Company, 432 4th Ave., New York 16, N.Y.

Crown—Crown Publishers, 419 4th Ave., New York 16, N.Y.

Davis—Davis Press, Inc., 44 Portland St., Worchester, Mass.

Day—John Day Company, Inc., 210 Madison Ave., New York 16, N.Y.

Daye—Stephen Daye Press, 105 E. 24th St., New York 10, N.Y.

Devin-Adair—Devin-Adair Company, 23 E. 26th St., New York 10, N.Y.

Didier—Didier, Publishers, 660 Madison Ave., New York 21, N.Y.

Division of General Education, New York University, Washington Square, New York, N.Y.

Dodd, Mead—Dodd, Mead & Company, Inc., 432 4th Ave., New York 16, N.Y.

Donohue—M. A. Donohue & Company, 711 S. Dearborn St., Chicago, Ill.

Doubleday—Doubleday & Company, Inc., 575 Madison Ave., New York 22, N.Y.

Dover—Dover Publications, 1780 Broadway, New York, N.Y.

Drake—Frederick J. Drake & Company, Inc., 179 N. Michigan Ave., Chicago, Ill.

Dryad—Dryad Press, Leicester, England.

Dutton—E. P. Dutton & Company, Inc., 286–302 4th Ave., New York 10, N.Y.

Eastman Kodak—Eastman Kodak Co., 343 State St., Rochester, N.Y.; 356 Madison Ave., New York, N.Y.

Eisenberg—Larry Eisenberg, 2403 Branch St., Nashville, Tenn.

Enterprises—Enterprises, Inc., 35 E. Wacker Drive, Chicago 1, Ill.

Fawcett—Fawcett Publications, Greenwich, Conn.

Foster and Stewart—Foster and Stewart Publishing Corporation, 210 Ellicott St., Buffalo 3, N.Y.

Franklin Press—Franklin Press, Louisville, Ky.

Free Press—Free Press, Glencoe, Ill.

French—Samuel French, Inc., 25 W. 45th St., New York, N.Y.

Friendship—Friendship Press, New York, N.Y.

Fun With Felt—Fun With Felt Corporation, 390 Fourth Ave., New York 16, N.Y.

Funk & Wagnalls—Funk & Wagnalls Company, 153 E. 24th St., New York 10, N.Y.

Garden City Pub. Co.—Garden City Publishing Company, Inc., 75 Franklin Ave., Garden City, N.Y.

Girl Scouts—Girl Scouts of the U.S.A., 155 E. 44th St., New York 17, N.Y.

Greenberg—Greenberg, Publishers, Inc., 201 East 57th St., New York 22, N.Y.

Greystone—Greystone Press, 100 6th Ave., New York 13, N.Y.

Grosset and Dunlap—Grosset and Dunlap, 1107 Broadway, New York, N.Y.

Handcrafters—The Handcrafters, Waupun, Wisconsin.

Hanover House—Hanover House, New York, N.Y.

Harcourt, Brace—Harcourt, Brace and Company, Inc., 383 Madison Ave., New York 17, N.Y.; 1525 East 53rd St., Chicago, Ill.

Harper—Harper & Brothers, 49 East 33rd St., New York 16, N.Y.

Hart—Hart Publishing Company, New York, N.Y.

Harter — Harter Publishing Company, Cleveland, Ohio.

Harvard University Press—Harvard University Press, Cambridge 38, Mass.

Hazelton—Sidney Hazelton, 7 Dana Road, Hanover, N.H.

Heath—D. C. Heath & Company, 285 Columbus Ave., Boston 16, Mass.

Henley—Norman W. Henley Publishing Company, 254 W. 54th St., New York, N.Y.

Holden—Holden Publishing Company, Springfield, Mass.

Holt—Henry Holt & Company, Inc., 383 Madison Ave., New York 17, N.Y.

Houghton—Houghton Mifflin Company, 2 Park St., Boston 7, Mass.

International Textbook Co.—International Textbook Company, Scranton 9, Pa.

Interstate—Interstate Printers and Publishers, 19–27 North Jackson St., Danville, Ill.

Jacques—H. E. Jacques, Mt. Pleasant' Iowa.

John Wiley and Sons, Inc.—John Wiley and Sons, Inc., 440 4th Ave., New York 16, N.Y.

Jr. H. and P.E.—Journal of Health and Physical Education, published by The American Association for Health, Physical Education and Recreation, 1201 16th St., N.W., Washington 6, D.C.

Judd—Orange Judd Publishing Company, Inc., 15 E. 26th St., New York, N.Y.

Judson—The Judson Press, 1703 Chestnut St., Philadelphia 3, Pa.

Kalmback—Kalmback Publishing Company, Milwaukee, Wis.

Knopf—Alfred A. Knopf, Inc., 501 Madison Ave., New York 22, N.Y.

Lane—Lane Publishing Company, Menlo Park, Calif.

La Vee Studio—La Vee Studio, 22 E. 29th St., New York, N.Y.

Life Camps—Life Camps, Inc., 369 Lexington Ave., New York, N.Y.

Lippincott—J. B. Lippincott Company, 227–231 S. 6th St., Philadelphia 5, Pa.; 521 5th Ave., New York 17, N.Y.; 333 W. Lake St., Chicago 6, Ill.

Little—Little, Brown & Company, 34 Beacon St., Boston 6, Mass.

Longmans—Longmans, Green & Co., Inc., 55 5th Ave., New York 3, N.Y.

Lothrop—Lothrop, Lee & Shepard Company, Thomas Nelson & Sons, 381–385 4th Ave., New York, N.Y.

Macmillan—The Macmillan Company, 60 5th Ave., New York 11, N.Y.; 2459 Prairie Ave., Chicago 16, Ill.

Maine Development Commission—Maine Development Commission, Augusta, Me.

McGraw-Hill—McGraw-Hill Book Company, Inc., 330 West 42nd St., New York 36, N.Y.

McKnight—McKnight & McKnight, Market and Center Sts., Bloomington, Ill.

Morgan & Morgan—Morgan & Morgan, High Point Road, Scarsdale, New York.

Morrow—William Morrow & Company, Inc., 425 4th Ave., New York 16, N.Y.

Mosby— C. V. Mosby Company, 3207 Washington Blvd., St. Louis 3, Mo.

National Wildlife Federation—National Wildlife Federation, 232 Carroll St., N.W., Takoma Park, Washington 12, D.C.

Nat'l Ass'n Sec. Sch. Prin's—National Association of Secondary School Principals, 1201 16th St., N.W., Washington 6, D.C.

Nat'l Ed. Ass'n—National Education Association, 1201 16th St., Washington 6, D.C.

Nat'l Org. for Pub. Health Nursing—National Organization for Public Health Nursing, 2 Park Ave., New York 16, N.Y.

Nat'l Rifle Ass'n—National Rifle Association, 1600 Rhode Island Ave., N.W., Washington, D.C.

New England Section of ACA—New England Section of American Camping Association, 114 Beacon St., Boston 8, Mass.

Newman—F. Newman & Company, Los Angeles, Calif.

New Home Library—New Home Library, 14 W. 49th St., New York, N.Y.

NRA—National Recreation Association, 315 4th Ave., New York 10, N.Y.

N.Y. Public Library—New York Public Library, New York, N.Y.

Office of the County Superintendent of Schools, Los Angeles, Calif.

Open Road—Open Road Publishing Company, 729 Boylston St., Boston, Mass.

Oxford U.—Oxford University Press, 114 5th Ave., New York 11, N.Y.

Paine—Paine Publishing Company, Dayton, Ohio.

Peabody—George Peabody College for Teachers, Nashville, Tenn.

Penguin—Penguin Books, New York, N.Y.

Pitman Publishing Corporation, 2–6 W. 45th St., New York 36, N.Y.

Plays, Inc.—Plays, Inc., 8 Arlington St., Boston 6, Mass.

Plumb—Fayette R. Plumb, Inc., Philadelphia, Pa.

Popular Mechanics Press—Popular Mechanics Press, 200 E. Ontario St., Chicago 11, Ill.

Prentice-Hall—Prentice Hall, Inc., 70 5th Ave., New York 11, N.Y.

Progress—Progress Press, 19 S. Wells St., Chicago 6, Ill.

Putnam—G. P. Putnam's Sons, 210 Madison Ave., New York 16, N.Y.

Rafter Crafters—Rafter Crafters, P.O. Box 97, Pleasantville, N.Y.

Random—Random House, Inc., 457 Madison Ave., New York 22, N.Y.

Ronald—The Ronald Press Co., 15 E. 26th St., New York 10, N.Y.

Russell Sage Foundation—Russell Sage Foundation, 505 Park Ave., New York 22, N.Y.

Rutgers University Press—Rutgers University Press, New Brunswick, N.J.

Sargent—Portor Sargent, 11 Beacon St., Boston, Mass.

Saunders—W. B. Saunders Company, West Washington Square, Philadelphia 5, Pa.

Schirmer—G. Schirmer, Inc., 3 E. 43rd St., New York 17, N.Y.

Scott—William R. Scott, New York, N.Y.

Scribner—Charles Scribner's Sons, 597–599 5th Ave., New York 17, N.Y.

Sierra—The Sierra Club, San Francisco, Calif.

Silva, Inc.—Silva, Inc., Laporte, Indiana.

Silveus—W. A. Silveus, San Antonio, Texas.

Simon & Schuster—Simon & Schuster, Inc., 630 Fifth Ave., New York 20, N.Y.

Stackpole and Heck—Stackpole and Heck, Telegraph Press Bldg., Harrisburg, Pa.

Standard—Standard Publications, Inc., Huntington, W. Va.

Standard Education Society—Standard Education Society, Chicago, Ill.

Stanford U. Press—Stanford University Press, Stanford, Calif.

Studio—The Studio Publications, Inc., 381 4th Ave., New York 16, N.Y.

Superior—Superior Publishing Co., Seattle 1, Washington.

Supt. of Doc.—Superintendent of Documents, Government Printing Office, Washington, D.C.

U. Ill.—University of Illinois Press, Urbana, Ill.

Universal Handicrafts—Universal Handicrafts Service, New York, N.Y.

Van Nostrand—D. Van Nostrand Company, Inc., 250 4th Ave., New York 3, N.Y.

Viking—The Viking Press, Inc., 18 E. 48th St., New York 17, N.Y.

Vinal—William Vinal, Vinehall, R.F.D., Cohasset, Mass.

Watts—Franklin Watts, Inc., 119 W. 57th St., New York 19, N.Y.

Waverly—Waverly House, Boston, Mass.

Whittlesey—Whittlesey House, 330 W. 42nd St., New York 18, N.Y.

Wilde—W. A. Wilde Company, 131 Clarendon St., Boston, Mass.

Williams—C. Williams, 5454 Page Ave., St. Louis, Mo.

Wilson—H. W. Wilson Company, 950–972 University Ave., New York 52, N.Y.

Winston—John C. Winston Company, 1006–1016 Arch St., Philadelphia 7, Pa.

Wise—Wm. H. Wise & Company, Inc., 50 W. 47th St., New York 19, N.Y.

Woman's Press—Woman's Press, 600 Lexington Ave., New York 22, N.Y.

Yale U.—Yale University Press, 143 Elm St., New Haven, Conn.

Youth Service—Youth Service, Inc., Putnam Valley, New York, N.Y.

# Index